Judicial Policy Making, Empirical Data and Scientific Evidence

Judicial Policy Making, Empirical Data and Scientific Evidence

Can Courts Manage the Twenty-First Century?

Edited by

Rob van Gestel

Professor of Theory and Methods of Regulation, Department of Private, Business and Labour Law (PBLL), Tilburg University, the Netherlands

Jurgen de Poorter

Professor of Administrative Law, Department of Public Law and Governance, Tilburg University, the Netherlands

Edward L. Rubin

Distinguished University Professor of Law and Political Science, Vanderbilt University, USA

Edward Elgar PUBLISHING

Cheltenham, UK • Northampton, MA, USA

Cover image: Emma Podietz.

Published by

Edward Elgar Publishing Limited
The Lypiatts
15 Lansdown Road
Cheltenham
Glos GL50 2JA
UK

Edward Elgar Publishing, Inc.
William Pratt House
9 Dewey Court
Northampton
Massachusetts 01060
USA

Authorised representative in the EU for GPSR queries only: Easy Access System Europe – Mustamäe tee 50, 10621 Tallinn, Estonia, gpsr.requests@easproject.com

A catalogue record for this book is available from the British Library

Library of Congress Control Number: 2025951156

This book is available electronically in the **Elgar**online
Law subject collection
https://doi.org/10.4337/9781035367580

MIX
Paper | Supporting responsible forestry
FSC® C014540
FSC www.fsc.org

ISBN 978 1 0353 6757 3 (cased)
ISBN 978 1 0353 6758 0 (eBook)
ISBN 978 1 0353 9419 7 (ePub)

Printed and bound in the UK by Short Run Press Ltd, Exeter EX2 7LW

Contents

List of contributors

Sharngan Aravindakshan is a PhD student at Tilburg University, the Netherlands, on the comparative research project 'Courts in quest of legitimacy in public interest litigation cases'.

Juliana de Augustinis is a postdoc at Tilburg Law School in the Netherlands after finishing her PhD on Courts, Science, and Climate Justice.

Alysia Blackham is Professor at Melbourne Law School, The University of Melbourne, Australia.

Arthur Dyevre is Professor of legal theory and empirical jurisprudence at Leuven University, Belgium.

Rob van Gestel is Professor of theory and methods of regulation at Tilburg University, the Netherlands, and Professor of methodology of legal research at Leuven University in Belgium.

Elbert de Jong is Professor of private law at the Utrecht Centre for Accountability and Liability Law (UCALL) and the Molengraaff Institute for Private Law, at Utrecht University, the Netherlands.

Niels Petersen is Professor of public law, international law, and EU law at the University of Münster, Germany.

Dewy Pistora is a PhD student at Tilburg University, the Netherlands, on the comparative research project 'Courts in quest of legitimacy in public interest litigation cases'.

Jurgen de Poorter is Professor of administrative law at Tilburg University and judge in the Council of State (highest administrative court) in the Netherlands.

Jed S. Rakoff is a senior United States district judge of the US District Court for the Southern District of New York and Adjunct Professor at Columbia Law School and New York University School of Law, New York, USA.

Edward L. Rubin is Distinguished Professor of law and political science at Vanderbilt University, Nashville, Tennessee, USA.

J.B. Ruhl is Professor of environmental law at Vanderbilt University, Nashville, Tennessee, USA.

Wendy Wagner is Professor of administrative and environmental law at University of Texas, Austin, Texas, USA.

1. Introduction to *Judicial Policy Making, Empirical Data and Scientific Evidence*

Rob van Gestel, Jurgen de Poorter and Edward L. Rubin

COURTS AND POLICY MAKING

Throughout the world, knowledgeable and conscientious people understand that anthropogenic climate change is an onrushing catastrophe. Elected politicians have failed to respond. Whatever metaphor one chooses to describe their irresponsibility – whether they are fiddling while Rome burns, trying to stop the tides, or putting their heads in the sand – it seems clear that short-term thinking, lack of scientific literacy and political pressure from fossil fuel companies have combined to render legislators and executive leaders unwilling to adopt the necessary policies. With a sense of desperation, Urgenda Foundation, a Dutch organization committed to sustainable energy,[1] filed a lawsuit in its national courts to compel the Dutch government to set specific targets for greenhouse gas reduction. In 2015, to many people's astonishment, the trial court ruled in Urgenda's favor. Four years later, to still more people's astonishment, the Supreme Court of the Netherlands upheld the decision.[2] The Dutch government, it concluded, had violated its duty of care as prescribed by Articles 2 and 8 of the European Convention on Human Rights by failing to reduce the nation's greenhouse gas emissions in 2020 by at least 25% below its 1990 level.

1 Founded as a non-profit organization by Jan Rotmans and Marjan Minnesma. The name combines the English words "urgent" and "agenda".

2 Supreme Court of the Netherlands, 20 December 2019, ECLI:NL:HR:2019:2006; English translation ECLI:NL:HR:2019:2007 (affirming Appellate Court of The Hague, October 9, 2018, ECLI:NL:GHDHA:2018:2591; for the English translation: ECLI:NL:GHDHA:2018:2610).

Some observers regard the *Urgenda* decision as judicial imperialism, an unauthorized intrusion by the courts into policies that are supposed to be set by the legislature and the executive. Democratic nations like the Netherlands – and all other nations in the Western world – assign major political decisions to officials elected by the people. There is simply no basis, it is argued, on which to reject those decisions. For other observers, however, the Supreme Court was fulfilling an important and indeed essential role in the democratic system. It was compensating for defects and distortions that would otherwise produce results that the majority of the populace finds, or would find, undesirable.

The corrective role of the judiciary in policy decisions can be endorsed without invoking an independent set of moral principles such as natural law or historical necessity. One basis for doing so is the defective operation of the electoral process. This was classically identified by the United States Supreme Court in – oddly enough – a footnote to its decision in *United States v. Carolene Products*, where the Court stated: "[t]he possibility that legislation that undercuts democratic control and legislation directed at minorities who are cut out of the deal so that they cannot form effective pressure groups may deserve heightened judicial attention".[3] In other words, the judiciary should intervene if the rules that govern elections prevent the majority from prevailing as a result of practices such as voter suppression or gerrymandering, or if "prejudice against discrete and insular minorities" (e.g., racial or religious groups) prevents those minorities from forming the sorts of political alliances and coalitions that most other minority groups (e.g., doctors, insurance agents, small town residents, the elderly) can rely upon to protect their interests.

A second type of defect in democratic decision making is more controversial but at least equally widespread. It arises when the electoral process produces results that can be said to be contrary to the "better judgment" of the electorate. One reason why this might occur is the public choice observation that most decisions have differential impacts on members of the populace, which implies that sometimes minority groups will suffer a disproportionate burden from certain government policies that violate the principle of "*égalité devant les charges publiques*" (equality in bearing public charges is a French legal principle meaning everyone must contribute fairly to public expenses). Funeral costs, for example, are only a secondary and occasional concern for members of the general public – but they are of primary importance to funeral home owners and directors. By means of single-issue voting and campaign contributions, a small group with a special interest may sometimes prevail over the general desires of the electorate. Another reason why the democratic process may betray the true desires of the populace is that a wide range of

3 304 U.S. 144, 152 n.4 (1938).

voter concerns must sometimes be reduced to a single vote, often between only two viable options. Thus, policies that voters would prefer, but are of only secondary concern, can vanish below the surface of the political debate between the parties. Third, the dynamics of political campaigns may favor short-term over long-term considerations, since it is easier to mobilize and motivate voters about a matter of immediate concern. The result is that voters choose representatives who favor policies that the voters will subsequently regret. All these problems are prominently displayed by the policies modern democratic legislatures have enacted regarding the coming climate change disaster, and merit the characterization of those legislatures as akin to the policies of the Emperor Nero, King Canute or an ostrich.

THE ROLE OF EMPIRICAL DATA AND SCIENCE IN JUDICIAL POLICY MAKING

This book does not revisit the debate about judicial policy making. A great deal has been written about this issue, and a great deal more will be written in the future. Rather, the contributions in this book start from the premise that judiciaries in modern democratic nations often play a policy making role, and ask how this role should be carried out. Two fundamental, but also heavily intertwined, questions are crucial here: to what extent may courts engage in policy making without trespassing on the domain of other co-equal branches of government and how can they translate policy into law effectively? These questions are connected through the concept of legitimacy. After all, even if judicial policy making does not violate the separation of powers doctrine, it would nonetheless be illegitimate if it produced adverse effects because courts lack the knowledge or skills to frame effective alternatives.

The effectiveness of judicial policy making depends, among other things, on how courts deal with empirical data and scientific evidence to estimate the most likely consequences of their rulings. In particular, what sorts of empirical data should the judiciary rely on when reaching policy decisions, how should they access this information, and how should they evaluate it? Some of the urgency – and poignancy – of this question arises from institutional considerations. Courts were originally designed for a different purpose, specifically the resolution of disputes between private parties or between a private party and the government, and they evolved at a different time, specifically the Middle Ages. Their means of gathering and assessing information developed in that context and at that time. To achieve the fairness and independence deemed necessary for their role, the courts were insulated from outside pressures, an approach that greatly enhanced their institutional legitimacy. Unfortunately, that same design feature has also insulated courts from modern methods of information processing that have become standard practice in the executive and legislative branches. Because of the types of issues they confront, courts were also insulated from the pressures of military and economic competition that, according to Max Weber and Joseph Schumpeter,[4] have been the driving forces of modernization.

This is not to say that courts refuse to engage in information gathering and analysis, nor that they have failed to be both creative and critical in carrying out that task. But because of their institutional design and sense of their own legitimacy, judges have focused on information processing in the context of dispute resolution. In the United States, for example, the precedent most widely cited by courts in administrative cases is neither *Motor Vehicle Manufacturers Ass'n v. State Farm Ins Co.*,[5] or *Chevron USA, Inc. v. NRDC*,[6] the subject of so much controversy about the judiciary's role, but rather *Daubert v. Merrell Dow Pharmaceuticals*,[7] which delineates the conditions for admitting into evidence expert testimony about scientific knowledge. Along the same lines, courts have been notably open to accepting DNA testing as identification in criminal cases, and have often been so willing to accept results from fMRI and other medical tests that commentators have felt it necessary to caution them against their over-use.[8] This openness to modern scientific data, however, occurs within the context of the judiciary's traditional role of dispute resolution.

When courts engage in policy making, however, they have been less willing to make use of empirical data and less willing to rely on modern methodologies. Instead, they have relied more often on intuition, experience and practical wisdom. In part, this is because empirical data itself may be complex and its relevance to the questions that confront the court may be less obvious. Moreover, especially in an adversarial system, litigants may have an incentive to shop for empirical data and scientific evidence that serves the needs of the parties more than it serves the overarching purpose of seeking the truths needed to formulate effective public policy.

Apart from this, courts continue to be apologetic about their policy making role, and thus unwilling to be explicit, or perhaps even thoughtful, about the

---

4 See Hans Blokland, *Modernization and Its Political Consequences: Weber, Mannheim, and Schumpeter*, (New Haven, Conn: Yale University Press 2006).

5 463 U.S. 29 (1983) (holding that an agency's rescission of a regulation should be reviewed by the same statutory standard as adoption of a regulation, and clarifying the meaning of this standard).

6 467 U.S. 837 (1984) (holding that reviewing courts should defer to agency interpretations of law as well as findings of fact when the agency is interpreting a statute that Congress has assigned to that agency for implementation).

7 509 U.S. 597 (1993).

8 See, e.g., Stephen J. Morse, Brain Overclaim Syndrome and Criminal Responsibility: A Diagnostic Note, 3 Ohio St. J. Crim. L. 397 (2005).

methods and modes of information processing that this role requires. This counterfactual reluctance is perhaps most visible in United States Senate confirmation hearings for Supreme Court judges. In an effort to secure confirmation, judicial nominees go out of their way to proclaim that the only thing they will do once appointed is to interpret and apply the law "as written", leaving the creation of new law to the political branches of government. But everyone involved knows that the Supreme Court judges will be participating in the nation's policy making process, which is the reason that the hearings are so contentious and attract so much attention.

The judiciary's failure to pay serious attention to empirical data when issuing policy decisions, whether it results from ignorance about the way to gather and evaluate such data or from an unwillingness to acknowledge that judges are in fact making policy decisions, comes at a great cost. An obvious problem is that courts will seek the seeming comfort of doctrinal discourse. One of the reasons why textualism is still popular as a method of judicial interpretation in the US is that it can be seen as a way to avoid judicial politics and policy making. "We are all textualists now",[9] claimed Justice Elena Kagan in 2015, and although she later nuanced this position,[10] it is a sentiment that still has many adherents who condemn "legislating from the bench" and treating the Constitution as a "living instrument". In contrast, textualism is unpopular in most European Union (EU) member states because judges are willing to acknowledge their policy making role. In a speech for the Network of the Presidents of the Supreme Judicial Courts of the European Union, Maarten Feteris declared, based on a survey of supreme court judges, that:

> [I]t is generally recognised in many countries that law-making is not exclusively a task for the legislator, but also for the courts .... [T]he progressive development of the law through judicial interpretation is a well-entrenched and even a necessary part of legal tradition. Today we have moved far beyond the caricature drawn centuries ago by Montesquieu of the judge as a speaking puppet, an expressionless being who merely repeats the words of the statutes.[11]

A less obvious but equally serious problem is that judges recognize that they need information about the world beyond doctrine in order to reach a policy-based decision, but rely on unsubstantiated speculation in place of anything

---

9 Harvard Law School, The 2015 Scalia Lecture Series: A Dialogue with Justice Elena Kagan on the Reading of Statutes, YouTube, at 08:29 (November 25, 2015) See https://youtu.be/dpEtszFT0Tg.

10 *West Virginia v. EPA*, 142 S. Ct. 2587, 2641 (2022) (Kagan, J., dissenting) (quoting Kagan, 2015 Scalia Lecture Series, supra note 8).

11 Maarten Feteris, Development of the Law by Supreme Courts in Europe, 13(1) Utrecht L. Rev. 155, 156 (2017).

that a scientist or social scientist would recognize as data. In contrast to statements about statutory law or judicial precedent, which are backed up with elaborate and lengthy citations, replete with numbers and abbreviations, these declarations often appear without any documentation or reference to authority. Judicial decisions are often filled with declarations about what consumers believe, how institutions behave, what motivates crimes and what causes accidents. Judges regularly claim that consumers can obtain the information necessary to protect themselves, or that "the wheels of commerce will grind to a halt" if they impose legal restrictions on manufacturing firms without any substantiation of such bold assertions.

A variant of speculation about data is to pluck a single source out of the mass of academic literature on a particular subject and treat it as definitive evidence. Judges often cite one book or article that they happen to have read to support their position, ignoring the limitations on judicial notice (although they would be subject to discipline if they then made a telephone call to the author to ask for clarification). The most iconic example is the decision in *Brown v. Board of Education*,[12] the US Supreme Court's world-famous decision holding segregation in public schools unconstitutional. Aware that the decision rested on uncertain doctrinal grounds and that it would engender fierce opposition in the Southern states, the Court declared that separating Black children "from others of similar age and qualifications solely because of their race generates a feeling of inferiority as to their status in the community that may affect their hearts and minds in a way unlikely to ever be undone".[13]

It went on to assert that "this finding is amply supported by modern authority".[14] As we have learned since,[15] the "amply supported modern authority" referred to a single social psychology experiment[16] that proved to be far less authoritative than the Supreme Court's decision suggested.[17] Most leading

---

[12] 347 U.S. 483 (1954).

[13] Id. at 494.

[14] Id. at 494–95.

[15] Sanjay Mody, Note, *Brown* Footnote 11 in Historical Context: Social Science and the Supreme Court's Quest for Legitimacy, 54 Stan. L. Rev. 793, 803–14 (2002).

[16] Kenneth Clark, The Effect of Prejudice and Discrimination on Personality Development, in Midcentury White House Conference on Children and Youth (1950); Kenneth Clark & Mamie Clark, Racial Identification and Preference in Negro Children, in *Readings in Social Psychology*, E. Maccoley (ed.) (Theodore M. Newcomb and Eugene L. Hartley. 1947) pp. 169–178 (https://i2.cdn.turner.com/cnn/2010/images/05/13/doll.study.1947.pdf).

[17] See Lucas Powe Jr., *The Warren Court and American Politics* (Cambridge, Mass: Harvard University Press 2000), p. 43:

constitutional scholars in the US today, although supporting the outcome in *Brown*, are skeptical of the evidentiary approach that was taken by the Court.[18]

The courts' naïve and casual approach to data violates both their own rules and the discipline that they impose on other governmental bodies. Strict evidentiary rules govern the judges' introduction of specific facts; they are permitted to include information that can be verified by widely accepted sources, such as the distance from Paris to Berlin, but not allowed to determine how long it would take the defendant to get from one place to the other without submitting the issue to adversarial contestation. When supervising other institutions, notably legislatures and administrative agencies, many courts in Europe and the United States increasingly seek to determine whether policy choices are the result of a rational, evidence-based process. They tend to be quite skeptical about the sorts of unsubstantiated claims in which they themselves indulge when making policy-based decisions.

THE CHAPTERS IN THIS VOLUME

The goal of this volume is to explore the ways that courts currently use empirical science and social science data when they engage in policy making, and how they might expand and improve that usage in the future. If that seems like a useless inquiry, readers may throw the book into the proverbial fire (or return it to Amazon), but to do so, they must not only believe that courts should not

---

[Kenneth and Mamie Clark] had conducted a number of studies asking a sample of American school children to identify from an array of black and white dolls, which dolls looked 'nicer'. The outcome was that most black children generally found the white dolls to look nicer, which the researchers presented as evidence for the low self-esteem of black schoolchildren. Moreover, the Clarks believed that the state-sponsored school segregation was responsible for the fact that black children preferred the white dolls, associating them with the more privileged schoolchildren. However, this finding almost immediately raised scholarly criticism after the *Brown* decision. Not only would fellow social scientists criticize the sample-size of the study and the lack of a control group, they also objected to the causal link between school-segregation and low self-esteem of black children, among other things because black children from Northern states where there was no de jure school segregation, were even more likely to prefer the Clarks' white dolls than their Southern counterparts, which seemed illogical since segregation policies were much stronger and prevalent in the South.

18 Jack M. Balkin (ed.), *What Brown v. Board of Education Should Have Said* (New York: New York University Press 2002). Michael Heise, Brown v. Board of Education, Footnote 11, and Multidisciplinarity, 90 Cornell L. Rev. 279 (2005).

make policy, but must also believe that courts do not do so. We do not think we will lose very many readers on this basis.

Of course, policy making does not constitute the major portion of the judiciary's business in democratic nations – there are many more decisions that simply resolve disputes – but it is nonetheless an important component of that business and, one can plausibly argue, the most influential component. It is when courts intervene in the policy making process that they reverse executive decisions, fill in gaps in legislation and overrule regulatory choices. Everyone agrees that empirical information is central to the policy making process; it is simply unimaginable that the legislature or executive would proceed without it. But the means by which courts gather information remain bound by their traditional dispute resolution function. This book explores the ways in which this situation may be changed.

Our inquiry is divided into three main sections. Part I explores methods by which courts can use empirical science and social science to inform their decisions, reduce uncertainty, assist proportionality assessments and determine the probable effects of their own decisions. Part II discusses some of the most frequent problems that accompany the use of empirical data by courts, such as the difficulties that courts face when assessing the validity of the evidence or evaluating the way it is used by government actors such as regulatory agencies. In doing so, this part assesses the possible risks and disadvantages of different models for incorporating empirical evidence in judicial decision-making. Part III focuses on the current and future dilemmas that empirical data and scientific evidence pose for courts, given its essential role in judicial policy making as described in Part I, and the challenges that it presents for judges as described in Part II.

Part I: The Promise of Empirical Evidence in Judicial Policy Making

In Chapter 2, Edward L. Rubin argues that one reason American courts fail to make use of natural and social science data in policy is because they reject statistical evidence in cases where public policy issues are at stake. Two Supreme Court decisions are emblematic of this attitude. In *McCleskey v. Kemp*,[19] the Court refused to consider a study showing that defendants who murder white victims are 4.3 times as likely to receive the death penalty as defendants who murder Black people, on the ground that discrimination must be demonstrated in each individual case. In *City of Los Angeles v. Lyons*,[20] the Court denied standing to a plaintiff injured by a police chokehold based on the

---

19 481 U.S. 279 (1986).
20 461 U.S. 95 (1983).

unsubstantiated assertion that he was unlikely to be subject to another chokehold (in fact, the likelihood could be calculated from the facts to be about 1 in 20). Rubin argues that this aversion to statistical analysis is little more than abysmal ignorance. It reflects the Court's failure to understand the essentially statistical nature of empirical evidence. In fact, statistical analysis is the only way to demonstrate discrimination because discrimination often only emerges when patterns of behavior are considered.

Rubin goes on to argue that the Supreme Court's refusal to rely on statistical analysis not only leads to invalid results in discrimination cases but also reveals the Court's failure to understand both its own legal system and the basic character of natural and social science in the modern world. The method of proof that England developed during the Middle Ages, and of which it is justly proud, is essentially statistical. Unlike the approach that it replaced, which depended on revelation, and the approach that developed in mainland Europe, which depended on compelled confession, England relied on relative degrees of certainty, a probabilistic or statistical determination. The standard used in civil trials, which is a preponderance of evidence, asks whether the plaintiff's claims are more likely than not to be true; the criminal trial standard, which is beyond a reasonable doubt, asks whether the state has demonstrated its claims to a near certainty. This is the approach of the British colonies in North America which the United States inherited and continues to employ, and that since then has been adopted in many other democratic nations. In other words, even when making factual determinations about the behavior of a single individual or a single event, courts typically use a probabilistic method of proof that would often benefit from statistical analysis.

Rubin also points to a more comprehensive sense in which statistical thinking links legal decision making to natural and social science data. Over the course of the past century or so, physical science, specifically quantum theory, has demonstrated that the material world that we inhabit has an essentially statistical structure. It might be argued that this discovery is not relevant to law, which is a human creation that can establish, or legislate, its own internal structure and relationships. But quantum theory is the product of modernity's basic mode of thought, and we might be well advised to be guided by this approach, rather than approaches derived from earlier times such as revelation, mysticism or abstract speculation. The conclusions that this particular mode of thought has produced in its analysis of the physical world reveal basic principles about the nature of knowledge that apply to all fields of natural and social science. It teaches us that our intuitive sense of definitive causal relationships must be replaced by probabilistic determinations because of the irremediably indeterminate nature of that world, an inherent quality that compels us to redefine what we mean by "knowledge". The leading interpretation of this theory (Copenhagen) includes the observer as an essential feature of the phenomena being observed, and this can be combined with one of the leading versions of statistical analysis, Bayesian statistics, which asks "what information does the decision maker need in order to be convinced of a particular causal relationship". By ignoring or denying the essentially statistical nature of knowledge, and the essentially statistical nature of the Anglo-American legal system, the US Supreme Court has added additional layers of inaccuracy to its misunderstanding of discrimination law.

In a similar fashion, Juliana de Augustinis and Rob van Gestel (Chapter 3) point out that judges' typical lack of statistical training may lead to systematic difficulties when dealing with the highly complex combination of normative and empirical considerations involved in many discrimination cases. Such cases often require judges to distinguish between legitimate differential treatment of seemingly similar behavior and illegitimate but indirect discrimination. In the absence of statistical analysis, judges often rely too heavily on intuition, common sense and practical wisdom, thus failing to recognize the flawed empirical assumptions on which their argumentation rests. Building on the existing literature, de Augustinis and van Gestel distinguish three roles statistical data may play in replacing such assumptions with an accurate assessment of the situation: (i) to rationally explain a difference in treatment; (ii) to inform judicial proportionality assessments; and (iii) to indicate that a public policy or civil practice leads to disparate effects in a group of people, thus providing a presumption of discrimination.

With respect to rational explanation of (legitimate) differences versus indirect discrimination, de Augustinis and van Gestel offer the use of actuarial data to calculate insurance premiums as an example. The Court of Justice of the European Union (CJEU) has declared that using sex to differentiate insurance premiums or benefits violates Articles 21 and 23 of the Charter of Fundamental Rights. The intuition that such practices are prohibited because it results in discrimination between men and women is normatively appealing, but may not withstand statistical analysis. Abandoning sex as a relevant factor for calculating certain insurance premiums (e.g., car insurance) has been associated with increases in premiums for both men and women because insurance companies are no longer allowed to take relevant actuarial differences between the sexes into account (i.e., women on average cause fewer car accidents than men).

Regarding the proportionality issue, the "blood donation cases by gay and bisexual men" have also demonstrated that judges' laudable intuition, common sense and practical wisdom do not always produce desirable results. While excluding men who have sex with men (MSM) from blood donation appears troubling from an equality perspective, prohibiting such discrimination may create disproportionately serious health problems once statistical data is taken into account. The Belgian Constitutional Court used statistical data to carry out a proportionality assessment of a provisional exclusion of MSM from blood donation. The Court accepted up-to-date statistical data from Belgium indicating that male-to-male sexual contact, even by men in a stable monogamous relationship, would be associated with a higher risk of acquiring infectious diseases transmissible by blood. Recognizing that the quality of the donated blood and the safety of the transfusion chain is a legitimate public health objective, the Court concluded that the ban survived a proportionality analysis. In other cases, courts have concluded that normative considerations must prevail in these analyses, but statistical evidence is often essential in getting the proportionality assessment right.

To address the disparate effects of differential treatment, de Augustinis and van Gestel explore the complex issue of mandatory retirement rules. Across jurisdictions, courts are asked to decide whether such rules constitute direct age discrimination or whether they can be justified by the aims of "establishing a balanced age structure in order to encourage the recruitment and promotion of young people", and "to prevent disputes concerning employees' fitness to work beyond a certain age".[21] The usual approach for a court would be to reach its determination by speculating about the effects of these mandatory retirement rules, but the CJEU, in a 2011 case, rejected reliance on mere generalizations claiming that a measure is likely to contribute to social or employment policy objectives; requiring instead empirical evidence subject to statistical analysis.[22] Applying this approach, a German court invalidated a mandatory retirement program for civil servants by rejecting the claim that the program would create new vacancies, resulting in more opportunities for younger professionals and a balance between generations. This claim is based on a desirable goal and thus may seem adequately justified, but data showed that, in at least 43.3% of the cases, the vacant posts would not result in new hires. In addition, the percentage of employees retired upon achieving the age limit would be very small because at least 94% of the employees would have retired by the age that the employer wanted to impose anyway. All three sets of cases that de Augustinis and van Gestel discuss show how easily common intuition can lead to outwardly plausible but empirically unsupported conclusions, and how statistically analyzed data can remedy this problem and produce outcomes that more accurately give effect to the objectives of the governing legal framework.

While both of the previous chapters focus on the judiciary's use of empirical evidence in making policy by striking down legal violations, Arthur Dyevre addresses the use of empirical evidence in framing remedies (Chapter 4).

---

21 *Gerhard Fuchs* (C-159/10), *Peter Köhler* (C-160/10) *v. Land Hessen* ECLI:EU:C:2011:508 (Court of Justice of the European Union 2011) § 68.

22 Ibid. § 70.

According to Dyevre, if a policy is designed to achieve a goal, its ability to achieve that goal should be the main basis for its evaluation and justification. This is taken for granted with respect to policies enacted by the legislative and executive branches. Judicial policy making, however, is often concealed behind a cloak of legal formalism in which lawmaking is disguised as nothing more than statutory interpretation. In fact, there is no reason why goal attainment should not be an equally relevant measure in assessing policies enacted by judges, whether these take the form of doctrines, remedies or rules of procedure.

Any such assessment of judicial policy making occurs ex ante and tends to be a mixture of common wisdom, experience and professional judgment. Judges often have strong beliefs about what works and what does not, but this rarely seems to be based on systematically collected data or information. Instead, great weight is attributed to anecdotal or impressionistic evidence. It is not uncommon for a handful of instances where a judicial rule coincides with a positive outcome to be treated as sufficient evidence that the ruling is working. There is no effort to determine the actual effect of the judicially promulgated policy and whether any demonstrated effect is truly caused by the judicial decision.

These considerations lead Dyevre to examine the potential of field experimentation as an evaluation tool for courts. Field experiments have two basic features. First, they are experiments in the scientific sense of the term, in that they assign alternative treatments to their subjects (people, firms, localities) on a random basis. Second, they occur in the field; that is, with the entities that are the actual subjects of the treatments, rather than in a laboratory with simulated subjects. This approach is regularly used in medical research; it is the way the effects of a new drug are determined, for example. By assigning different treatments (drug versus no drug, or two different drugs) on a random basis to two groups, each of which contains a range of people of different genders, ages, socio-economic status and numerous other variables, the causal effects of the medicine or treatment can be validly assessed. It is thus a powerful means of obtaining essential empirical data about the effectiveness of a particular treatment or program.

Despite field experimentation's effectiveness and its widespread use in medical, natural science and social science research, it is extremely rare in judicial lawmaking. Dyevre argues that the reason lies in various ethical objections and cultural obstacles. A strong belief in the legal field is that like cases must be treated alike and that applying different treatments to similar subjects is antithetical to norms of fairness and justice. Another objection is that too much is at stake in judicial decision making to allow for experimentation. However, these and other ethical concerns have parallels in medical research, where being treated with a new medicine or receiving a placebo might be the difference between life and death. If there is genuine uncertainty about the effectiveness of the treatment, then providing it or withholding it stand on equivalent ethical grounds, and the real ethical violation is to proceed by guesswork rather than using established means of data gathering to guide the decision.

Dyevre sees three possible venues for field experiments in the context of judicial lawmaking: 1) to inform proportionality determinations, such as whether an administrative measure to protect fundamental rights will achieve its stated goal; 2) the introduction of AI and digital technologies – such as digital case management – that use algorithms in place of human decision-making; and 3) the development of new doctrines. Dyevre offers the example of *Sahara House v. Union of India*,[23] where India's Supreme Court oversaw access to second-line treatment for patients suffering from HIV/AIDS. The Court had to decide whether denial of treatment to patients violated the right to health, the right to life and the right to equality as laid down in the Indian Constitution. As the number of patients needing second-line treatment was unknown and there were concerns about capacity constraints, the Court held that second-line treatment should initially be made available at four centers in Mumbai, New Delhi and Kolkata. This pilot initiative was to be studied for three months, during which the number of people in need of second-line retroviral treatment could be determined and capacity could be adapted. Although not a genuine randomized controlled trial, this example still resembles a field experiment because the court used a number of pilot sites to determine the actual need for second-line retroviral treatment instead of deciding on the basis of government estimates, judicial speculation or false notions of equality.

Part II: The Problems of Empirical Evidence in Judicial Policy Making

The problems that courts face in making use of empirical evidence are implicit in its promise. Statistics and experimentation provide the judiciary with new ways to gather and deploy information, but that constitutes institutional innovation, a complex and ponderous process. The obvious problem is outright resistance, but even if that is overcome, other attitudes, ranging from ignorance to gullibility to excessive enthusiasm, impair the effective use of empirical data. Given the background and training of most members of the judiciary, scientific evidence presents further challenges. The second section of the book explores the difficulties that courts confront when dealing with empirical evidence in general and scientific evidence in particular. These difficulties do not

23 *Sahara House v. Union of India & Others*, Laws (SC) 20017-8-133.

refute the recommendations of the preceding section, but they counsel caution in its implementation.

In the first chapter of this Part, Chapter 5, Niels Petersen starts from the premise that legislatures usually act under uncertainty and that the way to deal with this situation is a political matter that should primarily be left to the legislature. At the same time, he argues, courts cannot give legislatures carte blanche if they want to exercise effective constitutional control. Therefore, the courts must find a balance between these two potentially conflicting approaches. The way they usually do so is by applying the doctrine of deference: the legislature has a decision-making prerogative, but that prerogative is limited and can be revised at the margins. Petersen then discusses three strategies that courts use to determine the boundaries of the doctrine of deference: 1) a substantive approach focusing on the decision itself and based on criteria imposed by the court; 2) a procedural approach in which courts basically assess the procedure through which legislatures or administrative agencies have reached their substantive conclusions; and 3) a generalized approach in which courts focus on the motives of the legislature or the agency.

The problem, according to Petersen's analysis, is that all these strategies have serious limitations, a problem that he demonstrates through a series of examples. Regarding the substantive approach, he discusses a decision by the German Federal Constitutional Court (GFCC) declaring a smoking ban in restaurants and bars partly unconstitutional.[24] The Court's conclusion was based on statistics demonstrating the negative impact of the ban on restaurant owners, but a closer analysis of the data showed that the connection between any such impact and the smoking ban was unlikely to be statistically significant. Thus, the Court refused to defer to the legislative decision on substantive grounds, but it did not possess the expertise that was needed to justify its conclusion.

Petersen illustrates the limits of the procedural approach by discussing the GFCC decision about whether the level of tax-financed social benefits was sufficient to provide a subsistence minimum for eligible individuals.[25] Although the Court granted the legislature a significant margin of discretion in identifying the minimum, it held that the procedure used to make this determination was deficient because it lacked sufficient empirical support. It thus found the level of benefits unconstitutional on this basis. But this approach, which is commonly employed by the CJEU, for example, is not necessarily any better than a substantive one. The fact that a court observes that some procedures were omitted during the preparation of a new statute does not automatically mean that the policy that the statute effectuates was flawed.

---

24 BVerfGE 121, 317.

25 Hartz IV, BVerfGE 125, 175.

Finally, Petersen discusses approaches to "smoke out illicit motives by the legislature". His example is a GFCC decision invalidating the State of Bavaria's legislated monopoly on sports betting. The State asserted that the purpose of the monopoly was to combat gambling addiction, but then assiduously advertised the state-controlled betting opportunities as an innocent leisure activity. Suspecting that the State's real motivation was to increase its own revenue, the Court held the monopoly to be an unconstitutional interference with private betting providers' freedom of profession. But the Court did not provide any direct evidence that the Bavarian legislature was being insincere, and instead relied on traditional legal criteria such as fit and consistency that do not necessarily demonstrate improper motivations. Given the limitations of all three approaches, Petersen argues that a combination of approaches is unavoidable. Ultimately, however, the preferable solution is a stronger focus on empirical methods in the training of judges or more comprehensive institutional reform, like the creation of specialized courts.

Alysia Blackham's contribution (Chapter 6) confronts a more specific problem with the use of empirical evidence by courts: how to deal with cases challenging government policy when the court believes that empirical evidence is essential to the decision but the government has failed to employ it. In such cases, courts are essentially being asked to make decisions on public interest questions in what Blackham describes as "an evidential vacuum". While the absence of empirical evidence can be attributed to defects in the government's policy making process, the legitimacy of the courts is affected by such decisions. The problem is not only an absence of empirical evidence that the court believes is relevant but also a lack of capacity to obtain such evidence. It is also the difficulty of dealing with the government's implicit assertion that empirical evidence is not needed for its decision when the court believes that such evidence is in fact required.

To illustrate this dilemma, Blackham discusses age discrimination cases where discrimination might be justified as a proportionate means of achieving a legitimate aim. This raises the question about the way courts should undertake such complex, fact-driven assessments. Blackham considers four aspects of this issue: 1) To what extent are courts candid about their policy choices? 2) How do courts take the potential macro-consequences of their decisions into account? 3) How do courts employ empirical data in their decision making? 4) In what way do these decisions affect the legitimacy of judicial decision making?

Blackham focuses on two related age discrimination cases from the United Kingdom – *Sargeant v. London Fire* and *McCloud v. The Lord Chancellor.* The cases, which concerned challenges to transitional pension provisions based on birth date, had significant and wide-ranging financial repercussions, for the UK government and for individual public sector workers. Under the

EU Equal Treatment Framework Directive, differences in treatment based on age are allowed if they are objectively and reasonably justified. Hence, less favorable treatment because of age is not considered direct age discrimination if it is a proportionate means of achieving a legitimate aim. In light of this, the employment tribunal in *McCloud* ruled that there was no proportionate means and no legitimate aim for the age discriminatory provisions, after which the government unsuccessfully appealed to the Employment Appeals Tribunal. In *Sargeant*, the employment tribunal held that the transitional provisions for the pension scheme were a proportionate means of achieving a legitimate aim but the Employment Appeals Tribunal, while agreeing that there was a legitimate aim, found the transitional provisions not proportionate, and thus invalid.

The government appealed both decisions, but the Court of Appeal held that the changes in the pension schemes were not objectively justified because the government had failed to show 1) that it had a legitimate aim; and 2) that it had acted proportionately in trying to achieve that aim. The aim that the government had asserted in both cases was to protect those closest to retirement from financial uncertainties. However, the Court of Appeal held that the government had shown no evidence in support of this aim, and the people closest to retirement were, in fact, the least affected by future financial events. The court also found that the Employment Appeals Tribunal was correct in ruling that the desire to protect older judges was irrational. Regarding the firefighters, the court specified that the government had not done enough to justify the discriminatory effect of the transitional provisions because a social policy aim is not automatically a legitimate one, and supporting evidence is required to substantiate such a claim.

The quandary that Blackham addresses is the lack of empirical evidence available to the courts. She argues that, while government officials understood "the need for cogent, evidence-based arguments" in support of the pension changes, and the need to gather as much evidence as possible, no such evidence was gathered or produced. Clearly, this lack of evidence rendered the legitimacy of government policy questionable and thus vulnerable to invalidation by the courts. But it also resulted in questions about the legitimacy of the courts' decisions because they were essentially being asked to make decisions in an "evidential vacuum". While an absence of empirical evidence might be the result of executive errors in advocacy and policy making, the legitimacy of the courts is also affected by such decisions because they have to "rule in the blind".

When empirical data is presented to courts, however, the courts may have trouble evaluating it. These problems often involve the reliability of the data and the judiciary's ability to evaluate it. Wendy Wagner and Jed Rakoff address different aspects of this dilemma (Chapter 7 and Chapter 8, respectively). Wagner argues that the institutional structures developed by US courts to evaluate the reliability of scientific evidence are faulty. In the heavily adversarial American system, litigants on both sides have a tendency to present biased information that advances their position and to filter out or suppress information that indicates the opposite. She observes that courts, in attempting to address this problem, tend to focus on the wrong questions and use tests that have little in common with the methods scientists themselves use to assess the trustworthiness of scientific information.

In Wagner's view, courts ideally should incorporate assessment methods similar to those that scientists employ. Specifically, courts should ask: 1) does the testimony or research suggest that it has been subjected to critical peer scrutiny of some sort and, if so, what did that scrutiny reveal; 2) what is known about the author's independence; and 3) what is known about the author's disinterestedness? Even if these questions yield only qualitative information, Wagner believes it will better inform courts about the reliability of scientific evidence. Research that is influenced by interested parties or financial incentives, that is written or conducted by others who are not identified, and that is not subjected to critical peer scrutiny by experts in the field is patently less trustworthy. Even research that might be substantively persuasive will be heavily discounted by fellow scientists and journal editors if it violates one or more of these essential process-oriented conventions.

Trying to find out what courts actually do, compared to how scientists review scientific evidence, Wagner discovered that courts generally assume scientific information is reliable as long as it is "empirical" in nature. More critical courts develop additional screening factors, but there is little overlap between the substance-based factors that the courts use for their assessment and the process-based conventions used by scientists to assess reliability. As a consequence, this limited oversight by the courts creates considerable room for manipulative, ends-oriented research and testimony. In fact, incomplete judicial oversight may even incentivize stakeholders to develop new ways to compromise scientific research that are designed to obtain judicial acceptance.

Wagner proposes two major changes. The first is to shift from the view of courts as adjudicators over the substance of each piece of challenged evidence toward a role as overseers who can demand documentation from the litigants about the integrity of the process underlying expert testimony and reports. Thus, courts should be conceived as supervisors with the power to insist on heightened transparency of the underlying processes used to produce the scientific evidence, rather than as toll-bridge styled gatekeepers deciding whether evidence is "in" or "out". Such a reconceptualization draws on the courts' strengths in overseeing process while recognizing their limitations in accurately judging the substantive accuracy of contested scientific information. To accomplish this new role, the courts should institute standardized, qualitative disclosures that require scientists to document the processes by which their expert analyses were produced. Specifically, the disclosures would require information on the independence and disinterestedness of the expert-author and require experts to provide details on how vigorously they sought out, and responded to, rigorous peer scrutiny. Some of this information is currently inaccessible to courts and litigants, either as a practical or a legal matter. The disclosures would thus provide a centralized dossier for judges and litigants to better understand the integrity of the processes by which an expert produced an analysis that informs a dispute. Wagner concedes that these disclosures will not eliminate all the challenges that courts face at the intersection of science and law, but argues that they would have the potential to achieve significant improvements over the status quo.

Jed Rakoff discusses a similar but more extreme version of the difficulty courts experience in evaluating scientific data. It occurs when courts are not evaluating data presented to them by litigants, and then deciding between the litigants on legal grounds, but rather using scientific or supposedly scientific instruments as the basis of their own decisions. Rakoff focuses on a particularly widespread and egregious example, which is the use of algorithms by American courts to aid in sentencing convicted felons. These algorithms purport to answer the crucial question that is on virtually every judge's mind when choosing a specific sentence for a felon within a prescribed, and often capacious statutory range: how likely is the felon to re-offend? Confronted by Yogi Berra's dilemma that "it's tough to make predictions, especially about the future", judges have been anxious for assistance. The algorithms promise to provide a solution. They are essentially computer programs that scrutinize vast quantities of data and then use artificial intelligence (AI) to generate predictions on the basis of the data. Supplied with data, much of it readily available, about the criminal history and demographic profiles of previous offenders, and with their post-release records, the algorithm claims it can inform the judge about the length of the sentence that is most likely to protect the public.

The problem that Rakoff recounts is that the most widely used sentencing algorithm in American courts, called COMPAS (Correctional Offender Management Profiling for Alternative Sanctions), is produced by a private, for-profit company. The company refuses to disclose the data that is used to produce the algorithm, the method that was used to generate it, or the algorithm itself. Thus, the courts are presented with a commercial product that claims to use a scientific methodology based on empirical data, but one that they cannot evaluate. In Wagner's terms, they cannot apply the accepted scientific criteria of peer review, independence and disinterestedness, or even the defective judicial methods of substantive review and adversarial challenge. They certainly cannot conduct their own field experiments on the validity and reliability of the AI algorithm, this being one of the applications that Dyevre specifically recommends. In some sense, the result is an "evidential vacuum" or the sort

Blackham describes; the evidence has supposedly been used to produce the decision protocol, but it is invisible to the court.

Perhaps this judicial abnegation of responsibility could be justified if the results produced by the algorithms were empirically confirmed and socially justified. After all, judges, like everyone else, access published sources and produce their written products on personal computers whose operation only experienced data scientists and engineers understand. But the COMPAS algorithm is neither confirmed nor justified. As Rakoff reports, "even the validation studies that COMPAS itself has chosen to disclose show an error rate of between 29% and 37% in predicting future violent behavior". The comparable error rate for the predictions of experienced judges is difficult to define and hard to measure, but preliminary studies suggest that it may not be any worse than the COMPAS algorithm. That algorithm, moreover, is socially unjustified because it seems to produce a higher error rate for Black defendants than for white defendants, perhaps the result of being based on racially biased data such as zip code or prior arrests.

Part III: Balancing the Promise and the Problems

How can courts benefit from the advantages that empirical data offers without succumbing to the dilemmas that threaten to undermine its value? The question has intrinsic, conceptual and institutional dimensions. The intrinsic issue involves the reliability of data. Even those scientists and social scientists who see their work as predominantly data-driven recognize that accurate data is often difficult to obtain and challenging to interpret. Conceptually, any use of data may seem discordant with the purposes of law, which might be viewed as structuring human relations on the basis of norms, rather than observing existing relations and crafting rules in response. The argument – to oversimplify – is that law is supposed to give orders to society, not take orders from its current practices. The institutional problem is that courts are structured as dispute resolution mechanisms, with the further problem, as stated earlier, that this structure was developed in the Middle Ages, when "R and D" was more likely to be understood as Revelation and Divinity. At present, judges simply do not possess the training, staff support and computational resources necessary to carry out effective data gathering and analysis.

In the first chapter of this Part (Chapter 9), Elbert de Jong focuses on the conceptual issue. In a traditional dispute resolution case, the direct effects of the decision are limited to the parties who are before the court and have participated in the adversarial process that has produced the decision. Perhaps the decision states a new principle of law that will influence decisions in other cases – most often, it does not – but even then, the effect is not immediate, and it is filtered through another dispute resolution case. When the courts address public policy issues, however, as in the case of climate change litigation, the court's decision is likely to impact the interests, behavior or policies of third parties who are not before the court. De Jong describes impacts of this sort as "macro effects".

The macro effects of a court's policy-based decision can be diverse. In climate change cases such as *Urgenda* or *Friends of the Earth Netherlands et al. v. Royal Dutch Shell*,[26] they might involve the availability and price of energy products, the relative competitiveness of different energy firms, the availability of jobs in the industry and a shift towards renewable energy sources. De Jong focuses on another set of macro effects, using the example of greenhouse gas emissions by third parties. One such effect is carbon leakage, where a judicial decision that reduces emissions in the subject nation induces increased emissions in another nation because the second nation obtains a trading advantage from its less restrictive policies. A second effect is substitution, where a decision that causes one company to limit production in order to reduce CO_2 emissions leads others to increase production. Still another results from consumer behavior, where a decision that restricts emissions by one company induces a price increase in its products and incentivizes customers to patronize a different company.

De Jong argues that it is important for courts to take potential macro consequences of their decisions into account, but he acknowledges that this creates dilemmas for the courts. It is notoriously difficult to identify links between litigation or the threat of litigation and corporate behavior, if only because the behavior of corporations is determined by a complex interplay of causal factors. Moreover, when courts attempt to assess macro effects, they usually lean heavily on the information provided by the litigating parties. As in the case of empirical information generally, the litigants will be motivated to misrepresent or misinterpret scientific data to support their position, and they will have no incentive to bring forward reliable information about macro effects that contravene that position. The result is that judges will often need to consult external experts or rely on amicus briefs. Doing so, however, poses further dilemmas, because judges with insufficient scientific knowledge then need to determine which source of information is reliable.

But the difficulties in assessing and accounting for the macro effects of policy-based decisions should not, in de Jong's view, lead courts to avoid such decisions when breakdowns in the political process render them desirable. The preferable approach is for courts to develop the capacity to gather relevant

---

[26] Supreme Court of the Netherlands, 20 December 2019, ECLI:NL:HR:2019:2006; English translation ECLI:NL:HR:2019:2007 (affirming Appellate Court of The Hague 9 October 2018, ECLI:NL:GHDHA:2018:2591; for the English translation: ECLI:NL:GHDHA:2018:2610).

data and make the necessary assessments. Legislators and regulators, after all, make such determinations regularly and have developed a range of methodologies for doing so. Courts will need to engage in a certain amount of reconceptualization to make use of these methodologies, but the delimited nature of judicial policy making means that the task is not as formidable as it might first appear. As Petersen points out, courts only decide policy-based questions involving macro effects when some breakdown or lapse in the political decision-making process has occurred. In such cases, even partial or preliminary data gathering and analysis may lead to better results.

J.B. Ruhl offers an institutional approach for viewing the role of courts when confronted with scientific uncertainties (Chapter 10). He begins by identifying the range of possible roles, from science avoider, which can be regarded as allied to Rubin's condemnation of the US Supreme Court refusal to consider statistical data, to producer of scientific evidence, which is allied to Dyevre's endorsement of field experimentation for alternative remedies. Ruhl focuses on two particular roles within this range that courts can adopt. The first casts the courts as science takers, factoring existing scientific certainty or uncertainty into existing legal doctrine and acting accordingly. In government failure litigation, this has not proved to be a difficult choice because the plaintiffs, in cases such as *Urgenda* or *Juliana v. United States*,[27] have been able to rely on definitively established evidence of climate change.

In harm liability litigation, however, the application of scientific data to assertions regarding particularized injuries induces defendants to contest the effects asserted by the plaintiffs, thus creating problems for the judiciary's science taking role. Instead, Ruhl suggests, courts should adopt the role of science maker, rather than science taker. This does not mean that courts would actually practice and produce science, a role usually seen as outside their legitimate domain, but rather that they would encourage the production of science by others – agencies, companies, advocacy organizations, cities – who are involved in science-driven litigation. Nor does science making presume choosing sides in the design decisions – plaintiffs versus defendants – but rather focuses on the benefit to courts in their role as adjudicators of science-laden litigation disputes.

Courts can carry out the role of science maker by translating scientific findings into evidence, by publishing relevant scientific data, and by determining what constitutes for example "the best available science". Doing so gives signals to others, such as the litigants, but also to amicus curiae, expert witnesses and other third parties, of what is expected from them. Ruhl argues that this could actually promote the advancement of science relevant to the judicial

[27] 947 F.3d 1159 (9th Cir., 2020).

challenges ahead, somewhat along the lines that Blackham recommends. In addition, science making of this sort provides a way in which courts can combat their own intuitive responses, which, as de Augustinis and van Gestel suggest, are often unreliable.

But Ruhl cautions courts to approach science making carefully, cognizant of concerns that may arise regarding the possible unintended consequences of overt science making and of the public perception that they are overstepping their judicial role. Yet, with so much litigation about science-related policy matters underway, and still more on the horizon – to return to the *Urgenda case* that inspired this volume – Ruhl believes it would be difficult to identify a more compelling case than climate change for courts to engage as science makers, where the basic facts regarding anthropogenic global warming are a certainty, but the resulting harms, and their causal connection to worldwide phenomena, are matters of serious uncertainty that require extensive and sustained research.

To conclude this section, and the volume, Dewy Pistora and Sharngan Aravindakshan (Chapter 11) discuss the interplay between the promise and problems involved in the judicial use of empirical evidence through a detailed institutional analysis. They focus on two more specialized courts, the National Green Tribunal of India (NGT) and the Council of State in the Netherlands. The NGT was established by statute on the recommendation of the Indian Supreme Court. Organized into five panels located in major cities throughout India, it consists of an equal number of judicial and scientific members. The judicial members must be current or retired judges of the high courts, while the expert members must have advanced degrees in a scientific or technical field and at least 15 years' experience in that field. The NGT has original jurisdiction in some environmental cases and appellate jurisdiction in others. It sets its own procedures, is authorized to conduct investigations and can consult external experts in addition to relying on the expertise of its members.

The Council of State relies heavily on the Stichting Advisering Bestuursrechtspraak (STAB) [Foundation for Advising Administrative Courts in Environmental Law and Spatial Planning Disputes], which is an independent body of experts that advises the Dutch Council of State's administrative court on environmental matters. In response to questions presented to it by the court, STAB conducts investigations that include interviews with the contesting parties, site visits and consultations with other experts, as well as deployment of its own members' expertise. The results are reported to the Court, generally within three months. The Court does not usually seek any expert assistance apart from STAB, which is free and readily accessible, and usually follows its advice. If the Court decides not to do so, it is obligated to explain the reason why.

While these are both promising judicial innovations, each suffers from problems that have emerged during the course of its operation. The government of India has tended to choose administrative officials with knowledge of only one delimited field as the scientific expert members of the NGT. Even if these expert members have more distinguished credentials, the fact that the NGT panels generally consist of only one judge and one expert means that the expert is likely to lack sufficient knowledge of the relevant subject matter, given the wide range of issues that come before the NGT. As a result, the NGT panels often resort to ad hoc committees whose membership and role are not readily available for public scrutiny. Pistora and Aravindakshan conclude that STAB has been more effective, in part because it functions as a collective body combining the expertise of all its members. But the decision to consult it lies entirely within the discretion of the Council of State, which has apparently referred a mere 3% of its environmental cases to STAB. Moreover, once STAB has issued its report to the Council, the parties have no opportunity to comment on it, even though it may be the decisive factor in the court's decision.

To sum up, it seems apparent that the challenges of the twenty-first century will place increased demands on all of our government institutions. Climate change confronts us with unexpected immediacy. Beyond it lie the possibilities that AI will cause massive unemployment or will escape from our control, that genetic engineering will transform the basic nature of our species, or that new levels of world conflict will emerge as outer space moves from an exotic frontier to an essential and exploitable resource. Legislative and administrative institutions will articulate our most basic responses, often because of their greater access to the scientific and technological information that is the essence of these challenges, and essential to our ability to deal with them. But the scope and complexity of the challenges is likely to overload or paralyze these institutions. The courts will thus serve as an important watchdog or safety valve, something we have already seen in the case of climate change. They will only be able to play this beneficial role, however, and assist our society in solving the formidable difficulties that await us, if they can access and understand this same scientific and technological data. They will need to fulfill the promise that this process offers, and meliorate the problems that it presents. That is the topic of the chapters in this volume.

PART I

The promise of empirical evidence in judicial policy making

2. Why courts can only tell the truth with statistics

Edward L. Rubin

There are three kinds of lies: lies, damned lies, and statements by the U.S. Supreme Court about general patterns of behavior.
Someone other than Mark Twain

In *McCleskey v. Kemp*,[1] decided by the US Supreme Court in 1987, the plaintiff, a black man sentenced to death in Georgia for murdering a white man during a robbery, challenged his sentence on the ground that Georgia courts systematically imposed the death penalty on defendants who killed white people 4.3 times as often as on defendants who killed black people. His evidence was a statistical study performed by Professor David Baldus and two colleagues. All three levels of the federal courts rejected the claim. The District (trial) Court held that the study "failed to contribute anything of value".[2] The Court of Appeals found that statistics were "insufficient to demonstrate … unconstitutional discrimination".[3] The Supreme Court, per Justice Lewis Powell, affirmed on the basis that an equal protection claim requires the claimant to prove "that the decisionmakers in *his* case acted with discriminatory purpose".[4]

In *City of Los Angeles v. Lyons*,[5] the plaintiff, a black man, claimed that he had been stopped by Los Angeles police officers for a traffic violation and, although he offered no resistance, was subjected to a "chokehold" that rendered him unconscious and damaged his larynx. He asked the District Court for an injunction that would forbid the City from using this means of control except in response to the threat of deadly force. The Court found his claims to be true and granted the injunction, and the Court of Appeals affirmed the deci-

1 481 U.S. 279 (1986).
2 Id. at 289 [brackets omitted].
3 Id.
4 Id. at 292 [emphasis in original].
5 461 U.S. 95 (1983).

sion. But the Supreme Court reversed. It held, per Justice Byron White, that the courts lacked jurisdiction to decide the case and issue an injunction because Lyons' claim did not satisfy the "case or controversy" requirement of the US Constitution. "[I]t is surely no more than speculation," Justice White wrote, "to assert either that Lyons himself will again be involved in one of those unfortunate instances or that he will be arrested in the future and provoke the use of a chokehold by resisting arrest, attempting escape, or threatening deadly force or serious bodily injury".[6]

These decisions, and many others, reveal that the US Supreme Court and the lower federal courts harbor an abiding hostility to statistics, that they simply do not believe that statistical analysis is reliable or worth learning.[7] Of course, the cases that reach the Supreme Court are generally controversial ones, and their resolution can be validly debated on interpretive, political or ethical grounds. But what would we say if the Court has decided *McCleskey* on the ground that there has never been discrimination against black people in the United States, or decided *Lyons* on the ground that police never violated constitutional standards? We would say that such decisions were simply invalid. Decisions that reject statistical analysis are similarly invalid. Statistical analysis is not a fancy, extra-legal argument like meta-ethics or literary theory. It is our society's basic methodology for making determinations about people's behavior in the collective or institutional settings to which law regularly applies. Decisions that reject this methodology for assessing claims about such behavior are not only invalid, but they are invalid as a result of purposeful, anti-intellectual ignorance.

The problem with the Supreme Court's rejection of statistics runs even deeper, however. The method of proof that England developed during the Middle Ages, and of which it is justly proud, is essentially statistical. Unlike

---

6 Id. at 108. Justice White added the caveats about an arrestee's behavior because of restrictions on chokeholds that the City had imposed while the case was pending. He acknowledged that these limits could be removed by the City at any time, as he needed to do in order to avoid a dismissal for mootness and reach the merits.

7 See, e.g., *Rucho v. Common Cause*, 588 U.S. 684 (2019). The Court, per Chief Justice Roberts, stated that partisan gerrymandering is incompatible with democratic principles, id. at 2506, but declared that the issue is non-justiciable. The Court had previously adjudicated a claim of unequal districting and imposed a one-person, one-vote rule; see *Reynolds v. Sims*, 337 U.S. 533 (1964), but a rule against partisan gerrymandering would involve more complex mathematics, specifically statistics, and thus the Court could not administer it (138 S. Ct. at 2501). For an elaboration of this argument, see Edward L. Rubin, 'Gerrymandering and Judicial Incapacity', Wisc. L. Rev. 257 (2000).

the approach that it replaced, which depended on revelation, and the approach that developed in Europe, which depended on confession, England relied on relative degrees of certainty, a probabilistic or statistical determination. This is the approach that the British colonies and then the United States inherited, that they continue to employ, and that has been adopted in other democratic nations. In other words, even when factual determinations are made about the behavior of a single individual, or a single event, a statistical method of proof is being used. What would we say if the Supreme Court held that the trials on the basis of testimony or documents were invalid and judicial decisions should return to the ordeal, trial by combat, or judicial torture? We would say that these determinations were definitively invalid and that the Court was not only ignorant of the contemporary methodology of social science, but also ignorant of the Anglo-American legal system, the one subject about which it is supposed to possess specific expertise. That is in fact the situation at the present time.

It is possible to go one step further. Over the course of the past century or so, physical science, specifically quantum theory, has demonstrated that the material world that we inhabit has an essentially statistical structure. It might be argued that this discovery is not relevant to law, which is a human creation that can establish, or legislate, its own internal structure and relationships. But quantum theory is the product of modernity's basic mode of thought, and we might be well advised to be guided by this approach, rather than by approaches derived from earlier times, such as revelation, mysticism or abstract speculation. Moreover, the conclusions that this particular mode of thought has produced in its analysis of the physical world reveal basic principles about the nature of knowledge that apply to any effort to understand the world that we experience. It teaches us that our intuitive sense of definitive causal relationships must be replaced by probabilistic determinations because of the irremediably indeterminate nature of that world, an inherent quality that compels us to redefine what we mean by knowledge. The leading interpretation of this theory (Copenhagen; see below) includes the observer as an essential feature of the phenomena being observed, and this can be combined with one of the leading versions of statistical analysis (Bayesian statistics) through an approach directly relevant to human decision making, and thus to law as a mode of such decision making.

The first section of this chapter argues that the essentially statistical nature of reality, as revealed by modern science, specifically quantum mechanics, is directly relevant to legal decision making in revealing problems of measurement and of generalization from particular cases. These problems indicate that the Court's rejection of statistical evidence in *McCleskey* denied the plaintiffs their only way to demonstrate discrimination, while the Court's failure to understand how statistical evidence can be used led it to deny relief in *Lyons* that should have been granted on legal grounds. The second section argues that the Anglo-American legal system is in fact grounded on statistical or probabilistic ideas of proof, and that current procedural rules can only be understood in these terms. Any sense that statistics is incompatible with law, it further argues, comes from ignorance of Bayesian analysis, a leading interpretation of statistics that focuses on the decision-making process. Finally, the third section surveys the way in which the statistical nature of quantum mechanics and the Bayesian interpretation of statistics emphasizes the role of the investigator and decision maker in any understanding of natural science and social science data. Based on these insights, it then recommends that judges engage in self-reflection about their prejudices, ideological commitments and anti-intellectual ignorance to avoid obviously invalid decisions of the sort that the Supreme Court reached in *McCleskey* and *Lyons.*

1. WHAT STATISTICS TELLS US ABOUT THE NATURE OF COLLECTIVE AND INSTITUTIONAL ACTION

Determinations of fact in our legal system are necessarily assessments of external conditions that can be roughly described as reality. What we have learned from modern physical and social science is that reality has an essential probabilistic structure; that is, a structure that can be best understood by means of statistical analysis. The Supreme Court's refusal to recognize the validity of this analysis leads it to make serious errors in assessing both factual findings and legal conclusions. Three quarters of a century after Jerome Frank threw down the challenge to our legal system that "facts are guesses",[8] the Court continues to declare that statistical analysis, the best method that we have for ascertaining the validity of data, is invalid because it is less than certain.

A. The Statistical Structure of Reality

To begin with the modern understanding of physical reality, consider a particle such as a photon moving through space. It can also be described as moving through time since it has a velocity, which is its distance traveled per unit of time. We tend to picture the particle, on the basis of our ordinary experience, as a tiny round ball. But when we pass a beam of photons through a double slit, and then place a detector, such as a photographic plate, behind the slits, what we see is an interference pattern. This suggests that the beam is something

---

[8] Jerome Frank, *Courts on Trial: Myth and Reality in American Justice* (Princeton, N.J.: Princeton University Press, 1949), p. 14.

that we describe with the still familiar (albeit slightly less so) image of a wave. Quantum theory, the most accurate body of knowledge that human beings have ever developed, holds that the photon can be more accurately characterized as an array of probabilities; that is, the likelihood that it will impact a detector, whether a photographic plate or a human retina, at a given place. Some places are highly likely, others less so, still others extremely unlikely, and it is this array of probabilities that forms the interference pattern. The array, or wave function, although difficult to grasp intuitively, is the most complete description available to us of the particle in motion.[9]

When the particle hits the detector, these probabilities resolve to a single point, a process that is called the collapse of the wave function. At that point, the exact position of the particle is known, but its prior velocity has been changed and can be pictured as having been reduced to zero. Once the particle has been detected, it is possible to know, from the identity of the particle, the wave function that generated the impact on the photographic plate, but we cannot know the position and velocity of the particle as it traveled through space and time. This is because it truly existed as a wave function; that is, a set of possibilities that existed simultaneously. Such simultaneous possibilities are described as superposition. If we try to measure the particle while it is moving, we have, of course, detected it, and this means that we have altered its velocity in a similar way to its detection by the photographic plate. This result, generally called the Heisenberg Uncertainty Principle, is sometimes described as the problem that the process of measurement alters what we are trying to measure.[10] Stated thus, it seems equivalent to the Hawthorne Effect

---

9 See, e.g., B. Bohm & B.J. Hiley, *The Undivided Universe: An Ontological Interpretation of Quantum Theory* (London: Routledge, 1993); David J. Griffiths & Darrell F. Schroeter, *Introduction to Quantum Mechanics*, 3rd ed. (New York: Cambridge University Press, 2018); J.J. Sakurai & Jim Napolitano, *Modern Quantum Mechanics*, 3rd ed. (New York: Cambridge University Press, 2021). There are many summaries of quantum theory accessible to the general public. See, e.g., Timothy Ferris, *The Whole Shebang: A State-of-the-Universe(s) Report* (New York: Touchstone,

1997); Brian Greene, *The Fabric of the Cosmos: Space, Time, and the Texture of Reality* (New York: Vintage, 2004); John Gribbin, *In Search of Schrodinger's Cat: Quantum Physics and Reality* (New York: Bantam, 1984); Heinz R. Pagels, *The Cosmic Code: Quantum Physics as the Language of Nature*, 3rd ed. (Toronto: Bantam, 1984); Gary Zukav, *The Dancing Wu Li Masters: An Overview of the New Physics* (Toronto: Bantam, 1980).

10 Ferris, supra note 9, pp. 257–89; Greene, supra note 9, pp. 95–100; Sakurai & Napolitano, supra note 9, pp. 75–82; Pagels, supra note 9, pp. 67–112. See David Lindley, *Uncertainty: Einstein, Heisenberg and the Struggle for the Soul of Science* (New York: Anchor 2008).

in sociology.[11] In fact, it must be understood as more than a problem of measurement because it is theoretically irremediable. It is a limit on measurement that results from superposition; that is, the essential character of the moving particle as an array of probabilities.

Proceeding to the sort of human interactions to which legal rules apply, suppose we want to find out whether the hiring practices of a large corporation discriminate against a minority group. We might ask the human resources (HR) officer who makes hiring decisions for the corporation whether he or she feels prejudice against the minority group in question. There are two problems with this mode of inquiry. The first, which can be described as the problem of measurement, is readily analogized to problems with the accuracy of the detector. Most obviously, the HR officer might lie if there is a social norm that condemns prejudice against minorities. We might think that this problem can be ameliorated by asking a less direct but revelatory question, such as whether the members of the minority group commit more crimes than members of other groups in the society. But this strategy presents difficulties of its own. The officer, particularly if he or she is an HR professional, might be aware that the revelatory questions are intended to reveal the prohibited attitudes and might lie again. In other words, the HR officer might be as smart as the investigators. Alternatively, the revelatory question might not uncover the attitudes it is intended to determine. For example, the officer might agree that the members of the minority group commit more crimes, but that belief may stem from a favorable attitude toward that group; perhaps the HR officer thinks that people in power have criminalized harmless behaviors characteristic of that group, or that members of the group commit crimes only because they suffer from disadvantages that should be remediated. In other words, the investigators may not be as smart as they think they are. Still another possibility is that the investigators might harbor their own prejudices against the minority group and frame their questions in a way that elicits attitudes that did not previously

---

11 So named after experiments conducted with factory workers at the Hawthorne Western Electric plant. See Richard Gillespie, *Manufacturing Knowledge: A History of the Hawthorne Experiments* (Cambridge, UK: Cambridge University Press, 1991); Henry A. Landsberger, *Hawthorne Revisited* (Ithaca, N.Y.: Cornell University Press, 1958); Elton Mayo, *Hawthorne and the Western Electric Company: The Social Problems of an Industrial Civilization* (London: Routledge, 1949). In the original experiment, university professors observed a group of young women workers to see if changes in their working environment would lead to increased productivity. It turned out that their productivity increased dramatically no matter what the conditions were, leading to the hypothesis that they were working harder because of the special treatment they received or the attention being given to them by high-status observers.

exist; perhaps the officer did not think of the minority group members as committing more crimes but realized, when confronted with the question, that they seemed to do so.[12] In other words, the investigators may not be as unbiased as they think they are.

The only way to remedy these difficulties with the problem of measurement is through statistical analysis. Each individual's response may be inaccurate; that is, it may not reveal the person's underlying attitudes about the issue that is being investigated, but if we are concerned with collective or institutional behavior, we can hope that inaccuracies resulting from dishonesty, idiosyncrasy and elicited attitudes will disappear when we aggregate a large number of responses. More specifically, we can hope that the statistical analysis will even out the inaccuracies of individual responses and reveal underlying attitudes. When the attitudes are judgments about a desirable course of action, rather than something negative like racial prejudice, this is described as "the wisdom of crowds".[13] It is St. Thomas Aquinas' reason for favoring customary law over legislation by individual rulers.[14]

The second problem with asking the HR officer whether he or she feels prejudice is not related to the accuracy of the detector, but with the phenomenon of detection itself. The officer is one specific person. If we want to know if racial prejudice is operating in some particular institutional setting, asking a specific person or observing his or her behavior will not give us the answer. The individuals who compose an institution present an array of probabilities

---

[12] In case this example sounds unrealistic, in the sense that an HR professional would have been aware that prejudiced people accuse black people of excessive criminality, consider the Minnesota Multiphase Personality Instrument, a standard device used by these professionals to make hiring decisions. The instrument supposedly tests for conditions such as depression, paranoia, schizophrenia, and hypochondria. See, e.g., John R. Graham, *MMPI-2: Assessing Personality and Psychopathology*, 5th ed. (New York: Oxford University Press, 2011); David S. Nichols, *Essentials of MMPI-2 Assessment* (New York: John Wiley & Sons, 2011); Richard Rogers, Kenneth W. Sewell, Mary A. Martin & Michael J. Vitacco, 'Detection of Feigned Mental Disorders: A Meta-Analysis of MMPI-2 and Malingering', 10 Mental Health Awareness 160 (2003). Among the MMPI's true/false questions that test for serious mental illness are: "67. I like poetry. 137. I used to keep a diary. 163. I do not have a great fear of snakes. 207. I would like to belong to several clubs. 344. I enjoy gambling for small stakes. 467. I like to read about science". MMPI-2 Test Questions, https://psychtest.net/mmpi-test-questions/

[13] See James Surowiecki, *The Wisdom of Crowds* (New York: Doubleday, 2005). See David M. Estlund, *Democratic Authority: A Philosophical Framework* (Princeton, N.J.: Princeton University Press, 2008).

[14] St. Thomas Aquinas, *Summa Theologica* (Fathers of the English Dominican Province, trans.) 1022–25 (New York: Benziger Bros. 1948), I-II Q. 97.

with respect to any particular attitude or behavior. They will react one way in one situation, and another way in another. Perhaps a minority group member will be treated fairly one day and unfairly the next, whereas members of the racial majority are always treated fairly. Perhaps both are sometimes treated unfairly, but minority group members are treated unfairly more often. Perhaps the minority group is generally treated unfairly but particular minority group members are treated well because they are physically attractive by majority group standards or behave in accordance with majority group preferences. Perhaps particular members of the minority group are treated harshly when they elicit the personal hostility of someone in a position to make decisive determinations.

The overall behavior of a collectivity or an institution thus comprises a social function, that is, a probability array. When we ask particular members of the institution about their views, we are, in effect, interposing a detector at a particular point. The social function then collapses, as the wave function does, into individualized observations. The probability array of the institution as a whole is no longer observable.[15] This will be true for each individual we ask; each one represents a collapse of the social function. The only way to determine the behavior or operation of the collectivity or institution as a whole is, here again, to ask a sufficient number of individuals so that we can discern a pattern of individual attitudes, akin to the interference pattern on the photon detector. Then, using statistics, we can construct the institution's probability array, the way it treats all the people with whom it interacts.

This second problem – the fact that each individual is a collapse of the social function – is separate from the problem of measurement. The problem of measurement involves the way that we discern each individual's own motivations. The analogy with particle physics partially breaks down at this point because we cannot determine an interference pattern from a single entity's behavior. Perhaps, if we investigate an individual's attitudes at great depth, we could discern the range of attitudes that most people in the institution possess. But the analogy to particle physics breaks down more completely because we have no mathematical theory (and – Isaac Asimov notwithstanding – we never will)[16] that enables us to calculate the social function from a single individual. The statistical analysis of many different individual observations is necessary

[15] This process resembles the so-called macro-micro transition discussed in sociology. See Jeffrey C. Alexander, Bernhard Giesen, Richard Munch & Neil Smelser, eds., *The Macro-Micro Link* (Berkeley, Cal.: University of California Press, 1987).

[16] See Isaac Asimov, *Foundation* (New York: Bantam, 1991). Asimov imagines the science of psychohistory, which enables a small group of specialists to predict the future on the basis of scientific principles. In fact, their predictions

to describe the phenomenon in motion, that is, the way the collectivity or institution treats people during the time of its operation.

There is a further way in which the analogy to particle physics does not apply to social phenomena, but far from reducing the necessity of statistical analysis, it provides an additional reason for this necessity. Human beings, unlike photons, are conscious actors who respond to their surrounding environment. The result is often emergent phenomena that simply cannot be captured by any measurement of individual attitudes. This is most apparent with respect to institutions, which generate behavior patterns specific to the institutional setting, patterns that cannot be reduced to any individual action.[17] While economically oriented organization theorists tend to be somewhat skeptical of the process, due to their commitment to methodological individualism, even they concede its reality in certain situations. Herbert Simon discusses means-ends displacement,[18] Simon and James March discuss uncertainty absorption,[19] and Chris Argyris discusses social learning[20] as distinctly institutional behaviors. More sociologically oriented theorists discern a range of irrational behaviors that are generated by the institution as a totality. There is more controversy about emergent phenomena in a social collectivity, but many sociologists recognize patterns such as herd behavior that cannot be reduced

---

are thrown into disarray by the unexpected appearance of a human mutation. See Isaac Asimov, *Foundation and Empire* (New York: Bantam, 1991).

[17] See generally Walter W. Powell & Paul J. Dimaggio, *The New Institutionalism in Organizational Analysis* (Chicago: University of Chicago Press, 1991).

[18] Herbert Simon, *Administrative Behavior: A Study of Decision-Making Process in Administrative Institutions* (New York: Free Press, 1997). Means-ends displacement occurs when a subordinate (person or unit) in an administrative structure is assigned a task intended to further the ends of the structure but treats that task as an end in itself. Id., pp. 72–91. For example, police who are supposed to find thieves in order to reduce crime offer a person who has committed one theft lenient treatment if he will confess to other thefts as well.

[19] James March & Herbert Simon, *Organizations*, 2nd ed. (Cambridge, Mass.: Blackwell, 1993), pp. 182–89. Uncertainty absorption occurs when simplified or interpreted versions of data are communicated by successive subordinates to their superiors. For an extended discussion, see Niklas Luhmann & Rhodes Barrett, *Organization and Decision* (Cambridge, UK: Cambridge University Press, 2018), pp. 147–80.

[20] Chris Argyris, *Reasoning, Learning and Action: Individual and Organizational* (San Francisco: Jossey-Bass 1982); Chris Argyris & Donald A. Schon, *Organizational Learning II: Theory, Method, and Practice* (Reading, Mass: Addison-Wesley, 1996). Institutional learning occurs when decisions become embedded in organizational practices that serve as a basis for action.

to individual action,[21] and economists often concede the latter's existence in financial markets.[22]

In other words, the basic reality of collective or institutional behavior, as we understand it, is a phenomenon that is only accessible to statistical analysis. We are not really interested in the way individuals respond when asked questions about their behavior. What we care about is the way they act and interact over time, in the actual settings where prejudice might occur. Detection or measurement is performed at a separate time, and inevitably results in the collapse of the probability array that determines the operation of those settings. The performance of people in collective or institutional settings is simply a different phenomenon from the measurement of their performance, and there is simply no reason to assume that a measurement process carried out on an individual basis, no matter how accurate, will capture the actual experience of people when dealing with collective or institutional action.

B. The Assessment of Reality by the Legal System

In the *McCleskey* case, there were two patterns of behavior relevant to McCleskey's equal protection claim.[23] First was the collective behavior of the jurors in all the cases that were subjects of Baldus's statistical study. Second was the institutional behavior of the public prosecutors in those cases. To begin with the measurement problem, Justice Powell, writing for the Court, stated: "because discretion is essential to the criminal justice process, we would demand exceptionally clear proof before we would infer that the discretion has been abused".[24] The required proof is "that the decisionmakers in *his* case

---

21 See Mark Earls, *Herd: How to Change Mass Behavior by Harnessing Our True Nature* (Chichester, UK: Wiley, 2009); William N. McPhee, *Formal Theories of Mass Behavior* (New York: Free Press, 1963).

22 Christopher Avery & Peter Zemsky, 'Multidimensional Uncertainty and Herd Behavior in Financial Markets', 88 Am. Econ. Rev. 724 (1998); Abhijit Banerjee, 'A Simple Model of Herd Behavior', 107 Quarterly J. Econ. 797 (1992).

23 For purposes of this chapter, it will be assumed that the death penalty itself is a valid punishment, which is obviously a necessary premise of the majority opinion. Justice Brennan challenged this in his dissent, see 481 U.S. at 320 ("Adhering to my view that the death penalty is in all circumstances cruel and unusual punishment forbidden by the Eighth and Fourteenth Amendments, I would vacate the decision below insofar as it left undisturbed the death sentence imposed in this case"). He then went on to analyze the majority opinion on the assumption that the death penalty could be constitutionally imposed. That is what will be done here as well.

24 481 U.S. at 297.

acted with discriminatory purpose".[25] How could such a demanding standard be satisfied for members of a jury that met only once and considered only a single case? Any juror whose prejudice was obvious enough to satisfy this standard would likely have been challenged by the defense attorney. Perhaps a sustained and comprehensive investigation of each juror's correspondence and personal interactions (and, at present, social media postings) would reveal such prejudice, but there was no evidence that any investigation of this was undertaken and such investigations are generally prohibited, as the Court itself noted.[26] Only statistical evidence could possibly reveal more subtle but nonetheless real prejudices on the part of Georgia jurors considered as a group.[27]

---

25 Id. at 292 (emphasis in original).

26 Id. at 296. See *McDonald v. Pless*, 238 U.S. 264 (1915) (cited by the Court). Powell used this legal principle as an argument for denying McCleskey's claim. He pointed out that it meant that "the State has no practical opportunity to rebut the Baldus study". Apparently, Powell didn't think that a critique of the statistical analysis, on the basis of data or method, was "practical". Even more egregiously, he failed to notice that, by his own argument, rejecting the statistical argument gave McCloskey no chance to prove his constitutional claim. In other words, he made the implicit assumption that Georgia's ability to defend against a constitutional claim was more important than a citizen's ability to make such a claim. It is hard to find any explanation for this other than racial prejudice against McCleskey, an ideological commitment to assert that American criminal law is just, and an abiding anti-intellectual hostility to statistics. See section 3B infra.

27 Powell conceded that the "Court had accepted statistics as proof of intent to discriminate in certain limited contexts". Id. at 293. His examples were "as proof of an equal protection violation in the selection of the jury venire in a particular district" id., and "multiple-regression analysis to prove statutory violations under Title VII of the Civil Rights Act of 1964"; id. at 294. But imposition of the death penalty is different, he argued, because "[e]ach jury is unique in its composition, and the Constitution requires that its decision rest on consideration of innumerable factors that vary according to the characteristics of the individual defendant and the facts of the particular capital offense"; id. His position, in other words, is that the existence of several different variables renders statistical analysis impossible, or, more accurately (to give Powell credit he probably doesn't deserve), unreliable. It is difficult to understand this argument, since he had before him a statistical analysis that controlled for all the relevant variables. Powell went on to say: "Thus, the application of an inference drawn from the general statistics to a specific decision in a trial and sentencing simply is not comparable to the application of an inference drawn from general statistics to a specific venire-selection or Title VII case". Id. at 294–95. It would appear that he did not understand that the Baldus study, although its results were being applied to a particular case, was in fact based on data from multiple cases. But at the very least, he should have realized that he was confused and had someone explain this to him. More likely, here again, his

Conceivably, a single prosecutor could be shown to harbor explicit bias that would meet the standard. As an institutional actor, a prosecutor is a repeat player whose pattern of behavior can be observed. But prosecutors are also educated public officials who are unlikely to provide "exceptionally clear proof" that they are violating established legal rules or social norms. Only statistical analysis is likely to reveal a pattern of biased behavior, either for a single prosecutor or for some defined group such as the prosecutors' office in a city or state. As in the case of the jurors, it is theoretically possible to imagine evidence that would solve the problem of measurement in accordance with the Court's standards. The prosecutor might be revealed to be a secret member of the Ku Klux Klan, or a personal communication from him may be found where he declares that he singles out black people for prosecution. But without the use of statistical evidence and analysis, it is virtually impossible to do so as a practical matter. In short, it is difficult to read the majority opinion as anything other than a thinly veiled effort to permit unconstitutional discrimination in the administration of the death penalty.

The problem generated by the collapse of the social function reveals the jurisprudential as well as the evidentiary defects that result from the Court's refusal to accept statistical analysis. Contrary to the Court, discrimination in "his" particular case is not the only interpretation of McCleskey's claim. An alternative formulation is that the operation of the Georgia criminal justice system in cases where the defendant is subject to the death penalty is also discriminatory. That is, the discrimination occurs as the system operates in time, prior to the collapse of the social function resulting in the detection of a particular sentence. In his dissent, Justice Brennan highlighted this issue by pointing out that "the Court has been concerned with the *risk* of the imposition of an arbitrary sentence, rather than the proven fact of one".[28] Brennan puts the issue in subjective terms with the observation that "counsel would feel bound to tell McCleskey that defendants charged with killing white victims in Georgia are 4.3 times as likely to be sentenced to death as defendants charged with killing blacks".[29] That makes sense, but a better formulation is that the greater likelihood of receiving the death penalty for killing a white person is a feature of the probability array that precedes the collapse of the social function.

This greater probability is reality itself, the conditions to which Georgians subject to capital sentences confront. The fact that this social function will collapse at some time in the future does not alter its reality prior to its collapse. It is, in its own right, racially discriminatory, and thus a direct violation of the

---

decision-making process was addled by various emotional and ideological reactions. See section 3B infra.

28 481 U.S. at 322.

29 Id. at 321.

Equal Protection Clause, which forbids such discrimination. As a reality, people in Georgia know, or suspect, that they are more likely to be executed if they kill a white person than a black person.[30] But this is a reality that is inherently statistical and can only be understood in statistical terms. Just as the wave function is our best description of physical reality, that is, our best description of a moving particle, the greater probability of receiving a death sentence for murdering a white person is the best description of the discriminatory nature of Georgia's death penalty administration. The Court's refusal to consider a statistical analysis of this situation is simply a refusal to respond to an outright violation of the law.

City of Los Angeles v. Lyons[31] provides another example of the Supreme Court's failure to understand the operation and relevance of statistics. It also provides a tragic example of the way that this failure led the Court to betray its essential purposes, and thereby cause misery and disruption that it was in a uniquely good position to prevent. In one sense, there is no problem of measurement in the case, and no need for statistical analysis, because Lyons was trying to impose a legal rule on the City of Los Angeles, a constitutional prohibition against the use of chokeholds by its police officers. The Supreme Court could have declared chokeholds to be a violation of the Constitution regardless of how many or how few were being used.[32] But the Court converted the case into a statistical one by requiring Lyons to demonstrate the probability that he would suffer another chokehold in the future.[33] Having raised the issue, the

---

30 This is, of course, another way in which the analogy between quantum mechanics and social behavior is inaccurate. In both cases, we cannot measure the probability array without collapsing the probabilistic function. But people, unlike photons, have feelings, and we can take those feelings into account, either by asking them about those feelings at the point of measurement, or assuming their existence on the basis of how we know, from our own experience, how humans react to such situations.

31 461 U.S. 95 (1983).

32 Had it done so, by means of an injunction, a future case might have arisen where a plaintiff claimed that the police were using chokeholds in violation of the law. That claim would have required measurement, such as questioning police officers or riding with them on patrol, but the *Lyons* case itself did not.

33 It is difficult to see why this would run afoul of the case or controversy requirement, apart from the Court's desire to achieve a particular result. Suppose the defendant had been subjected, by a police officer who was both cruel and antiquarian, to a heretic's fork that he had obtained from a museum. (This device, used during the Inquisition, is a double-sided set of sharp prongs, one side of which would be placed under the chin and the other side against the chest). Why would there be any procedural problem in deciding that this violated the Constitution and telling the city not to do it again, whatever the likelihood of its doing so?

Court then got the facts wrong and the law wrong by misunderstanding both the measurement problem and the social collapse problem.

The measurement problem in this case does not arise from any difficulty gathering or assessing data, but rather from the Court's inability to perform the simplest calculations on the data that appeared in the trial court record, or that could be obtained by judicial notice. The population of the City of Los Angeles in 1976, when Lyons was subjected to the chokehold, was a little less than three million people.[34] Assuming that – even in Los Angeles at that time – the police were not using chokeholds on women, children, the elderly or the disabled, we can estimate that the number of people at risk of being subjected to a police chokehold was about one million.[35] Lyons, a 24-year-old male,[36] obviously belonged to this at-risk population. In the trial court, the officer-in-charge of the Physical Training and Self-Defense Unit of the LAPD testified that the police had applied at least 975 chokeholds during a five-and-a-half-year period between 1975 and 1980, or about 175 chokeholds per year, and also conceded that this tally was incomplete.[37] Thus, an adult male resident would have at least a 1 in 5,700 chance of being subject to a chokehold in a given year.[38] Given his age when he was subjected to the chokehold, he would remain in the at-risk population for about 40 years. Thus, his odds of being subjected to another chokehold over the course of his adult life were about one in 140.[39]

---

[34] See Los Angeles Almanac, General Population by City, Los Angeles County: 1960–2000 Census, http://www.laalmanac.com/population/po27.php. The city population was 2,811,601 in the 1970 Census, and 2,968,579 in the 1980 Census.

[35] The assumption, for these purposes, is that children are people below 16, and the elderly are people above 65. That adds up to an exclusion of 30 years from an 80-year lifespan, leaving five-eighths of the male population at risk of chokeholds.

[36] 461 U.S. at 114 (Marshall, J., dissenting).

[37] Id. at 116 & 116 nn. 5 & 6.

[38] This is not meant to minimize the mistreatment of women, and particularly women of color, by American police departments. See Peter B. Kraska & Victor E. Kappeler, 'To Serve and Pursue: Exploring Police Sexual Violence Against Women', 12 Justice Q. 85 (2006); Philip Matthew Stinson Sr., Steven L. Brewer Jr., Brooke E. Mathna, John Liederbach & Christine M. Englebrecht, 'Police Sexual Misconduct: Arrested Officers and Their Victims', 10 Victims & Offenders 117 (2015). In the case of women, as these articles demonstrate, much of the violence tends to be sexual. Anecdotal evidence suggests that chokeholds are primarily used against men.

[39] The population of Los Angeles increased to 3,792,621 in the 2010 census, and to 3,898,747 in 2020. See Los Angeles Almanac, General Population, Cities and Unincorporated Communities, Los Angeles County, 1990 through 2020 Census, http://www.laalmanac.com/population/po03.php. But the number of police officers has been increasing as well. There were 7,146 uniformed officers

But Lyons was a black man, and as Justice Marshall pointed out in dissent, 12 of the 16 people who died from police chokeholds in the seven years between 1976 and 1983, when the decision was issued, were black men,[40] a proportion that seems consistent with anecdotal evidence from news reports. The black population of Los Angeles was about 9% at the time of the case, and continues at roughly that same level until the present. There have thus been about 90,000 to 120,000 black men in Los Angeles during the years of Lyons' adulthood. If the proportion of chokeholds suffered by them is the same as their proportion of chokehold deaths, that means that about 130 of the roughly 175 annual chokeholds were administered to black men. Over the 40 years of Lyons' adulthood, he would thus have about a one in 20 chance of being subject to a chokehold by the police.[41]

Obviously, these computations are approximate, although the largest inaccuracy is probably that the number of chokeholds administered by the police was significantly under-reported.[42] But the odds for Lyons can be raised to one in 40 by assuming that the police would have become more cautious after facing litigation, or to one in 140 by ignoring the racial issue, without changing the conclusion that dismissing the risk of another chokehold as excessively

---

in 1980, see Los Angeles Police Department, Annual Report, 1980 https://www.ojp.gov/pdffiles1/Digitization/81878NCJRS.pdf and 10,002 in 2019, Los Angeles Almanac, Municipal Police Departments, Los Angeles County, http://www.laalmanac.com/crime/cr69.php. Thus, the number of officers who can administer chokeholds seems to be increasing in approximate proportion to the increase in population.

40 Id. at 415–16 & 16 n. 3.

41 Assuming that the number of chokeholds increased in proportion to the number of officers, which increased roughly in proportion to the general population of the city, see note 39, supra.

42 The Court qualified Lyons' risk on the basis of a caveat that the police only used chokeholds for those "resisting arrest, attempting escape, or threatening deadly force or serious bodily injury". But those restrictions had been added by the Board of Police Commissioners on the eve of litigation, as part of a temporary moratorium on chokeholds, 461 U.S. at 101 & n. 4. Lyons then argued that the case was moot, apparently preferring the precedent established by the lower courts to the risk that the Supreme Court would reverse. The City argued that "the case is not moot, because the moratorium is not permanent, and may be lifted at any time" and the Court agreed. Having proceeded to decide rather than dismiss the case on the basis of the City's assertion that it might lift the moratorium, the Court could not rely on the restrictions in the moratorium when assessing Lyons' risk over time. For an argument that the Court erred in this part of its decision as well, see Richard H. Fallon, Jr., 'Of Justiciability, Remedies, and Public Law Litigation: Notes on the Jurisprudence of Lyons', 59 N.Y.U. L. Rev. 1, 24 (1984).

remote was incorrect. We know, and the Court could have determined by judicial notice, that the odds that one's home will be struck by lightning are about one in 200,[43] yet most people take this possibility seriously enough to spend several hundred dollars on a lightning rod. The odds that a non-smoker will contract fatal lung cancer from a home radon level of 4 picocuries per liter are about one in 150,[44] yet most people subject to this level of risk spend around one thousand dollars to reduce this level.[45] In other words, we have the economists' best evidence, the willingness to spend money, to indicate that people are seriously concerned about risks of this magnitude. Lyons chance of being subjected to another chokehold was substantially higher.

Beyond the Court's inability to perform even the most rudimentary statistical measurements on the available data is its basic misunderstanding of statistical relationships. Although willing to recognize that Lyons had the right to bring suit for damages resulting from the chokehold that he actually experienced, and presumably willing to grant him an injunction if the police had declared that they would inflict a chokehold on him the next time they saw him, the Court held that his concern about being subjected to a chokehold in the future was too speculative to grant relief. But the chokehold Lyons experienced was a collapse of the social function, that function being Los Angeles police practices. The danger of being detained by the police and subjected to a painful and possibly damaging procedure, either for no reason or because the police interpreted one's response to the detention as aggressive, was a real, palpable concern. It was less than a certainty, but it was a concern nonetheless. It was a particular concern for black men, most obviously because the danger was so much greater, but also because it signaled a general attitude of hostility

---

43 https://www.quora.com/Whats-the-chance-of-your-house-being-hit-by-lightning

44 Environmental Protection Agency, 'A Citizen's Guide to Radon: The Guide to Protecting Yourself and Your Family From Radon 12' (2012), https://www.epa.gov/sites/default/files/2016-12/documents/2016_a_citizens_guide_to_radon.pdf

45 HomeGuide, 'How Much Does Radon Mitigation Cost?', https://homeguide.com/costs/radon-mitigation-cost (accessed May 4, 2022) (national average is $1,112, but costs range "from $500 to $4,700 with most homeowners spending between $700 and $1,500"); Devon Thorsby, 'How Much Does a Radon Mitigation System Cost?', US News, Apr. 29, 2021, https://realestate.usnews.com/real-estate/articles/how-much-does-a-radon-mitigation-system-cost ("between $771 and $1,179, but the cost can reach as much as $3,000 for a large home or property with multiple foundations").

toward them on the part of the public officials who are supposed to provide them with protection.[46]

Commentators have noted the cruel irony and grotesque insincerity of an opinion that precludes people from obtaining an injunction against police brutality that they experienced in the past because they could not definitively prove that they would be brutalized again.[47] Given that the case could have readily been dismissed as moot, leaving the lower court injunction intact, it seems clear that the Supreme Court was making a concerted effort to achieve its result. Perhaps, if we give its conservative majority the benefit of the doubt, they saw the case as an opportunity to maintain order and combat crime. But subsequent events have demonstrated how mistaken their judgment was. The practice that the Court sought to protect as a means of strengthening the police forces has become the emblem of their brutality and racism, and it has gone far to undermine their legitimacy.[48] The image of Derek Chauvin methodically killing George Floyd with a variant of the chokehold will remain with us for decades to come. While a number of major city police forces, like Los Angeles, have banned or restricted chokeholds, there is considerable evidence that these

---

46 See generally Michele Alexander, *The New Jim Crow: Mass Incarceration in the Age of Colorblindness* (New York: New Press, 2010), 97–139; Paul Butler, *Chokehold: Policing Black Men* (New York: New Press, 2017); Joshua Correll, Bernadette Park, Charles M. Judd, Bernd Wittenbrink, Melody S. Sadler & Tracie Keesee, 'Across the Thin Blue Line: Police Officers and Racial Bias in the Decision to Shoot', 92 Personality & Soc. Psych. 106 (2007); Renee McDonald Hutchins, 'Racial Profiling: The Law, the Policy and the Practice', in *Policing the Black Man: Arrest, Prosecution and Imprisonment*, ed. Angela J. Davis (New York: Pantheon Books, 2017), 95; E. Ashby Plant & B. Michelle Peruse, 'The Consequences of Race for Police Officers' Responses to Criminal Suspects', 16 Psych. Sci. 180 (2005).

47 See, e.g., Vicki C. Jackson, 'Standing and the Role of the Federal Courts: Triple Error Decisions in *Clapper v. Amnesty International USA* and *City of Los Angeles v. Lyons*', 23 Wm. & Mary Civ. Rights J. 127, 169 (2014) ("the Court's assertion that Lyons had no more reason to fear such police assaults in the future than any other person seems willfully blind to the facts of American life"); Gene R. Nichol, Jr., 'Standing for Privilege: The Failure of Injury Analysis', 82 B.U. L. Rev. 301, 329 (2002) ("The Justices simply could not empathize with Lyons' apparent worry that he would have another encounter with the Los Angeles police. 'All our friends keep their noses clean,' the opinion seems to say").

48 For a detailed discussion of this practice and its impact on black communities, see Butler, supra note 46. See also J.J. Fyfe, 'Enforcement Workshop: The Los Angeles Chokehold Controversy', 19 Crim. L. Bull. 61 (1983) (chokeholds should be treated as a form of lethal force).

policies have not been effective.[49] A definitive decision by the Supreme Court, a declaration that chokeholds were an unconstitutional violation of people's rights, would have buttressed these policies. It might have avoided some of the misery that citizens experienced in the intervening decades, and some of the disgrace that police departments have brought upon themselves.[50]

There are more powerful, and less admirable factors underlying the Court's opinion than its ignorance of statistical arguments. Insincerity, lack of empathy and institutional racism are obvious candidates. Nonetheless, the ignorance of the Justices regarding statistical analysis contributed to their ability to reach such an indefensible and deleterious result in at least two ways. First, deciding that a claim does not satisfy the case or controversy requirement because it is "conjectural" or "speculative" misunderstands the probabilistic nature of any statement about collective or institutional behavior. Such behavior is generally complex, arises from multiple sources, and is difficult to discern. We must conjecture or speculate about it in order to reach working conclusions, and we must proceed on the basis of likelihoods or probabilities. What might be called conjectures and speculations can be more favorably described as theories or hypotheses; no matter what one calls them, they should be evaluated for their plausibility, not dismissed out of hand for their unavoidable uncertainty.

Second, probabilities not only form a real and definite component of human experience, as noted above, but the fact that they are less than certain may exaggerate, rather than restrict, their impact on people. It requires only the most minimal amount of human empathy to perceive the sense of threat and danger that a black man in Los Angeles would experience once police practices regarding chokeholds became known. The one in 20, or one in 40 or one in 140 odds that can be calculated for Mr Lyons as a matter of rational analysis do not provide reassurance that one is more likely than not to avoid a chokehold. Rather, it creates a general sense of uncertainty about one's safety. This sense can be amplified by a person's particular personality characteristics, and is amplified in a consistent manner for most people as a result of what psychologists call the salience bias – the process by which people overestimate the probability of events on the basis of their notoriety.[51] In other words, statistical

---

49 See Trevor George Gardner & Esam Al-Shareffi, 'Regulating Police Chokeholds', 112 J. L. & Criminology 111 (2022).

50 See Ben Jones, 'Police-Generated Killings: The Gap Between Ethics and Law', Pol. Res. Q., May, 2021.

51 Shelley E. Taylor, 'The Availability Bias in Social Perception and Interaction', in *Judgment Under Uncertainty: Heuristics and Biases*, ed. Daniel Kahneman, Paul Slovic & Amos Tversky (Cambridge, UK: Cambridge University Press, 1982), 190; Amos Tversky & Daniel Kahneman, 'Availability: A Heuristic for Judging Frequency and Probability', in *Judgment Under Uncertainty: Heuristics*

probabilities correctly communicate a sense of uncertainty about one's ultimate experience, that is, one's experience when the social function collapses, and this will be processed by individuals in complex ways. If called upon to explain their result in policy terms, the Justices would certainly have invoked people's fear of crime and possibly – if they were being honest – their own.[52] But no one would argue that unless people can prove that they are more likely than not to be victims of a crime, their fear of it is not worthy of consideration.

2. WHAT STATISTICS TELLS US ABOUT THE NATURE OF ANGLO-AMERICAN LEGAL PROCEDURE

The failure of modern courts to recognize the statistical nature of the truths that they are being asked to find not only represents a failure to employ basic elements of current social science, but also represents a failure to understand the basic concepts of the Anglo-American system. This can be seen by considering the origins of the system's current methods of proof in civil and criminal law, which involved a shift from the certainty of divine revelation to probabilistic assessments of fact by human decision makers. Any sense that these assessments are not truly statistical, or that statistical analysis is incongruent with ordinary legal fact-finding, can be dispelled by considering one of the leading interpretations of statistical analysis.

A. The Evolution of Probabilistic Determinations of Fact in Anglo-American Law

In Anglo-Saxon and early Norman England, the standard method of resolving disputes between common people was the ordeal of fire or water.[53] The ordeal of water involved binding a litigant hand and foot and lowering him into a pool

---

and Biases, ed. Daniel Kahneman, Paul Slovic & Amos Tversky (Cambridge, UK: Cambridge University Press, 1982), 163. This phenomenon can be observed in social relations regarding group membership. See Lacey J. Hilliard & Lynn S. Liben, 'Differing Levels of Gender Salience in Preschool Classrooms: Effects on Children's Gender Attitudes and Intergroup Bias', 81 Child Development 1787 (2010) (salience of gender differences affected preschool children's behavior); Brian Mullen, Rupert Brown & Colleen Smith, 'Ingroup Bias as a Function of Salience, Relevance, and Status: An Integration', 22 Eur. J. Soc. Psych. 103 (1992) (meta-analysis concluding that salience of ingroup bias amplifies its effects).

52 See section 3B infra.

53 See generally Robert Bartlett, *Trial by Fire and Water: The Medieval Judicial Ordeal*, 2nd ed. (Brattleboro, Vt.: Echo Point, 2014), 13–33.

of water to see if he would float or sink. After the Norman Conquest, land disputes between nobles were determined by combat.[54] The rationale behind these practices was to create a situation where God would reveal the truth of the litigants' claims.[55] When Henry II became king in the mid-twelfth century, he found these procedures inadequate to resolve the conflicting land grants resulting from the civil war that brought him to the throne. Any such dispute could be decided in the king's court (that is, the king's court before the king himself)[56] but this was impractical for all but the most important cases. Each baron administered his own court to resolve disputes among his followers, but these courts were worse than impractical for resolving the barons' disputes against each other.

Henry's solution was to promulgate a statute, the Assize of Clarendon, that created a group of royal justices who would travel to the shires and hold trials in the shire courts, which were thus transformed into royal courts when the justice was present.[57] Henry did not prescribe the rules for resolving these disputes, but left that question to the justices themselves. What he cared about was that the disputes got settled, and settled by a set of rules that were uniform or common for his entire realm. This is the reason why the judge-made legal rules of England came to be called the common law.

The procedure for resolving disputes in accordance with the evolving common law was adopted from the royal inquest, the information gathering process that had led to the compilation of the famous Domesday Book in 1086.[58] It consisted of a jury of recognition, local knights who would give evidence about the rightful ownership of the property based on their personal knowledge of

---

[54] See generally George Neilson, *Trial by Combat* (Glasgow: William Hodge & Co., 1890). Combat was not used in Anglo-Saxon England.

[55] Prior to the Conquest, and continuing thereafter, men who were regarded as reliable, most often nobles, could also prove their case by oath-swearing, the idea being that a person (or at least a person of honor) would not endanger his immortal soul by lying after swearing an oath before God.

[56] *Curia regis coram rege.* See Richard Mortimer, *Angevin England, 1154–1258* (Oxford, UK: Blackwell, 1994), 51–76; W.L. Warren, *Henry II* (Berkeley, Cal.: University of California Press, 1973), at 301–16.

[57] Arthur R. Hogue, *Origins of the Common Law* (Bloomington: Indiana University Press, 1966), 145–60; Richard Mortimer, *Angevin England, 1154–1258* (Oxford, UK: Blackwell, 1994), pp. 51–63; Austin Lane Poole, *From Domesday Book to Magna Carta, 1087–1216*, 2nd ed. (Oxford, UK: Oxford Univ. 1993), 398–411; Warren, supra note 56, 317–61.

[58] Robin Fleming, *The Domesday Book and the Law* (Cambridge, UK: Cambridge University Press 1998).

the locality and an inspection of the property at issue.[59] Originally, the purpose of this procedure was only to determine who was entitled to hold the property until a final resolution was reached by the established means of trial by combat. It was generally known as the petty assize because of its preliminary status. In the increasingly settled and commercial era of the Angevin kings, however, the procedure became popular, not only because it forestalled violence regarding current possession of the property, but also because it seemed a less violent and more reasonable means of resolving the ultimate dispute. In response, Henry offered litigants a similar procedure as a final resolution of the issue, and thus an alternative to combat. Known as the grand assize, it involved a jury of 12 knights who carried out their investigation and determined who possessed the "greater right" (*maius ius*).[60] Ultimately, jury trial became so well regarded that the leading barons demanded that it be made available for all their disputes with the king when they compelled Henry's second successor, King John, to sign the Magna Carta in 1215. It was this procedure that the famous Chapter 39 of the document was referencing when it provided that the king should not "go or send against" any free man "except by … the law of the land".[61]

Criminal law in England followed a similar trajectory, not surprisingly since any clear distinction between the two had yet to be established. Chapter 39 offers an alternative to its law of the land restriction, which is "by the lawful judgment of his peers". While this sounds like a jury trial, it was not, as juries were not used in criminal matters at this time. It probably refers to the special council of 25 barons established by Chapter 61. Later in the year 1215, however, the Lateran IV Council prohibited priests from officiating at

---

59 The change should not be overdrawn. The ordeal, in England and elsewhere, was not used in every contested case, but only where ordinary evidence, such as witnesses or oath, was deemed unreliable. See Bartlett, supra note 53, 24–33. The ordeal was thus embedded in a more general and varied system of justice, but it responded to the desire for certainty – if people felt that they could not be sure of the relevant facts, they would resort to God rather than doing their best under the uncertain conditions.

60 See Warren, supra note 56, 317–61.

61 J.C. Holt, *Magna Carta* (Cambridge, UK: Cambridge University Press, 1992), 123–87. The juries of recognition were typically invoked by freemen of modest means, often for properties of a few acres or services worth a few pennies a year. What was particularly extraordinary about the barons' demand is that they were, in this highly status-oriented society, requesting that they be granted the treatment provided to those who ranked below them. This indicates the desirability that common law procedure had acquired by this time, only a few decades after its creation.

the ordeal.[62] The pragmatic reason for this canon was that the priests were regularly being bribed, while the theological reason was that it is improper to demand a miracle from God.[63] King John needed to comply with this sudden and discomforting change in legal procedure immediately, as he had made himself a vassal of the Pope (Innocent III) in order to obtain Church support in his dispute with the barons.[64] Again, juries provided the solution. Initially, as in the case of property disputes, and revealing its derivation from the royal inquest, the jury in a criminal case consisted of local knights who could inform the judges about the facts of the dispute. Over time, it evolved into its current form where the jurors are initially uninformed about the case and reach their decision on the basis of evidence provided by witnesses.

This account of the origins of civil and criminal trials reveals a basic conceptual shift in the approach to legal evidence, a shift that determined the distinctive features of the English legal system and ultimately the American system as well. Prior to Henry II's momentous reforms, methods of proof were based on a demand for certainty. Trial by ordeal and combat seem bizarre to us today, but that is because modern people, even if they are devout, do not share the religious sensibility of the Early Middle Ages. At that time, supernatural forces were seen as interwoven with the material world in an intense and visceral mélange. The air between the earth and sky was filled with demons, the land was studded with sacred prominences and accursed hollows, churches were places of refuge while the forests harbored monsters and the mountains seethed with spirits. Misfortunes that had no other explanation, such as drought, disease, famine, floods and fires, were attributed to Satan's malevolence or God's displeasure. These forces could be invoked with spells and incantations, placated with personal sacrifices and enlisted by prayer and ritual.[65] It was only natural, in this setting, to think that divine judgment could be obtained by practices like lowering a person into water or staging physical combat between opposing parties.

---

62 Twelfth Ecumenical Council, Lateran IV 1215, Canon 18, available at: http://www.intratext.com/IXT/ENG0431/_PI.HTM ("Neither shall any [cleric] in judicial tests or ordeals by hot or cold water or hot iron bestow any blessing"). See Bartlett, supra note 53, at 34–42, 70–101.

63 See Finbarr McAuley, 'Canon Law and the End of the Ordeal', 26 Oxford J. Legal Stud. 473 (2006).

64 W.L. Warren, *King John* (London: Eyre Methuen, 1961), 206–17.

65 See Heinrich Fichtenau, *Living in the Tenth Century: Mentalities and Social Orders* (Patrick J. Geary, trans.) (Chicago: University of Chicago, 1991), 303–32; Jacques Le Goff, *The Medieval Imagination* (Arthur Goldhammer, trans.) (Chicago: University of Chicago, 1985), 27–59.

During the course of the twelfth century, there seems to have been a growth of pragmatism and rationality akin to the growth of secularism in the eighteenth century.[66] While there was no loss of faith in God's ability to intervene in human affairs, people began to realize that the demand for a miracle would not generate the legal principles or factual precedents that would lead to predictable rules for future decisions.[67] The juries of recognition, established to provide a temporary resolution pending final determination of the issue by combat, became popular because they decided on the basis of relevant facts, such as the current condition of the property and the recollections of the people in the neighborhood. After a relatively brief time, grand juries were made available to provide permanent resolutions, again on the basis of facts. Lateran IV's prohibition of the ordeal, although based on theological arguments, was the product of a similarly rationalized approach, in this case resulting from the Church's revival of Roman law.

The effect of this rationalizing process was to replace certainty with probability. What the juries were determining was not a divine and thus a certain truth, but rather the greater right of one party or another. People were concluding that such determinations, while they could not achieve the certainty of divine judgment, were preferable. Because they were based on evidence accessible to human observers, they were consistent with ordinary experience. This experience was inevitably afflicted with uncertainty, but was the best that could be achieved by human beings. Storm clouds would probably mean rain, warm days would probably produce a good harvest, larger and better-armed

---

66 See Norman F. Cantor, *The Civilization of the Middle Ages* (New York: HarperPerennial, 1993), 305–56; Charles Homer Haskins, *The Renaissance of the 12th Century* (Cleveland: World Publishing, 1957); R.W. Southern, *The Making of the Middle Ages* (New Haven, Conn.: Yale University Press, 1953) (somewhat wider temporal span). For the eighteenth century, see Peter Gay, *The Enlightenment, vol. 1: The Rise of Modern Paganism* (New York: W.W. Norton, 1966); Anthony Pagden, *The Enlightenment: And Why It Still Matters* (New York: Random House, 2013).

67 See Peter Brown, 'Society and the Supernatural: A Medieval Change', in *Society and the Holy in Late Antiquity*, ed. Peter Brown (Berkeley, Cal.: Univ. of California 1982), 302; Paul Hyams, 'Trial by Ordeal: The Key to Proof in the Early Common Law', in *On the Laws and Customs of England: Essays in Honor of Samuel E. Thorne*, ed. Morris S. Arnold (Chapel Hill, N.C.: University of North Carolina Press, 1981), 90. Bartlett expresses skepticism about this argument, noting that the ordeal remained widely used and well regarded until Lateran IV. Bartlett, supra note 53, 34–69. But it does seem to be undermined, at least in England, by the growth of common law writs, and the Church's dramatic and definitive prohibition in 1215 must have originated in some sort of conceptual shift.

troops would probably win the battle. The rationalized, secular procedures of the grand jury and the jury of recognition made legal judgment continuous with this experience, a process that could be managed by the regime and improved or adapted over time.

Because cases were no longer being decided by God's definitive judgment, but rather by fallible humans, questions naturally arose about standards that jurors were supposed to use to determine whether the evidence was sufficient to support their conclusion. The original formulation that the party with the "greater right" (*maius ius*) would prevail developed into the current rule that the party who presented the "preponderance" of the evidence would win in civil trials. The basis for this rule is that there is no reason to favor one party over the other when a buyer is suing a seller, or two people involved in an accident are suing each other. By the late eighteenth century, evolving notions of due process and personal liberty led to the principle that the government, when prosecuting a person for a crime, must satisfy the higher standard of "proof beyond a reasonable doubt".[68] This somewhat opaque formulation can be seen, according to Barbara Shapiro, as a seventeenth and eighteenth century rationalization of the older idea that the juror must have a satisfied conscience in order to convict.[69] In various areas of modern law, the intermediate standard of "clear and convincing evidence" is sometimes used, while its mirror image, "clear error", is generally the standard that a judge must satisfy when reversing the decision of a jury.

We have become so familiar with this approach to legal process that we tend to overlook its innovative character at the time it was adopted and dismiss

---

68 See John H. Langbein, *The Origins of Adversary Criminal Trial* (Oxford, UK: Oxford University Press, 2003), 33, 261–63. Somewhat surprisingly, the first definitive use of this standard came in the late eighteenth century and in the American colonies, specifically the Boston Massacre Trials. See L. Kinvin Wroth and Hiller B. Zobel, eds. *Legal Papers of John Adams* (Cambridge, Mass.: The Belknap Press of Harvard University Press, 1965), vol. 3, 243.

69 Barbara J. Shapiro, *Beyond a Reasonable Doubt and Probable Cause: Historical Perspectives on the Anglo-American Law of Evidence* (Berkeley, Cal.: Univ. of California, 1991). See also Barbara J. Shapiro, 'To a Moral Certainty: Theories of Knowledge and Anglo-American Juries 1600–1850', 8 Hastings L.J. 153, 172 (1986). While it is clear that the standard has medieval origins, the idea that it was instituted to save the souls of the jurors from improperly punishing the defendant, see James Q. Whitman, *The Origins of "Reasonable Doubt"* (New Haven, Conn.: Yale University Press) is unconvincing, given that its first definitive application occurred in the late eighteenth century, when religiously based thought was being so extensively displaced by Enlightenment rationalism and the liberty of the individual was being so forcefully advanced. See Lynn Hunt, *Inventing Human Rights: A History* (New York: W.W. Norton, 2007).

the now-abandoned alternative approaches. It is thus worth recalling that the response to Lateran IV on the European Continent was not jury trials but the inquisitorial system. Foucault provides an illuminating explanation of its rationale as it was used in criminal cases. Like the English trial, the inquisitorial process depended on evidence accessible to human observers. But the goal of gathering this evidence was not to decide which party had the greater right, but rather to achieve the certainty that the ordeal had previously been provided by eliciting divine intervention. Having identified and detained a suspect, the state prosecutors proceeded on two parallel tracks. First, they gathered evidence, without revealing to the suspects what the evidence was, or even what charges were being brought against them. The quality of the evidence was carefully assessed, and determinations of guilt were based on complex calculations of its cumulative effect. Two irreproachable witnesses who observed the crime constituted a "full" proof. One witness or a documented death threat by the accused counted as an approximate or "semi-full" proof, and two such "semi-full" proofs added up to one full proof.[70]

The second track was judicial torture, the application of pain, using all the inventiveness that human beings exhibit when engaged in this activity, to obtain a confession from the accused. Such confessions served two purposes. First, of course, they were convincing evidence of guilt, although not quite foolproof without supporting evidence because people were aware that the accused might confess to avoid further pain. Second, however, confessions made the accused "accept responsibility for his own crime" and thus provided the only way that "the truth might exert all its power".[71] Governmental authorities recognized judicial torture as a form of punishment, and in fact acknowledged its severity. The rationale for using it, Foucault convincingly suggests, is that arrest or accusation by the government was taken to be a partial indication of guilt, and that each further piece of evidence constituted a further stage along the path toward definitive conviction.[72] Thus partial evidence simultaneously merited partial punishment and justified the infliction of further pain as a means of moving toward the final determination of guilt.

The motivation behind this system was the quest for certainty. In his truly revolutionary condemnation of it, Beccaria declares: "This shameful crucible of the truth is a standing monument law of ancient and savage times when ordeal by fire, by boiling water and the lottery of armed combat were called

---

70 Michel Foucault, *Discipline and Punish: The Birth of the Prison* (Alan Sheridan, trans.) (New York: Vintage, 1979), 35–37.

71 Id., p. 38.

72 Id., p. 42 ("Guilt did not begin when all the evidence was gathered together; piece by piece, it was constituted by each of the elements that made it possible to recognize a guilty person").

the *judgments* of God …".[73] In other words, the inquisitorial practice that developed in Europe after Lateran IV reflected a refusal to accept the probabilistic character of factual determinations made by human beings, and sought instead the false certainty of mathematical calculation or abject confession.

To the English, and therefore the Americans, the whole approach seemed horrifically unjust, and with the help of Montesquieu and Beccaria, they taught the rest of the Western world to reject the secret collection of evidence as inaccurate and the use of torture as barbaric. As it turned out, this did not require a shift from the inquisitorial system that had developed on the Continent to the adversarial system of the English-speaking, common law nations. It only required the substitution of quest for certainty with the same willingness to accept the reality that evidence would often only indicate which party was more likely to be right. To go beyond that is to substitute ritual for reality, to assert that one has achieved a definitive result by fiat.

B. The Essentially Statistical Nature of Legal Fact-Finding

As this brief historical account makes clear, Anglo-American legal procedure is based essentially and explicitly on probabilistic determinations. From the very beginning of the common law, it was clear that human decision makers necessarily possess less than perfect knowledge and need to make judgments by weighing the amount and reliability of the evidence available to them. If one wants to be tendentiously disparaging, one can describe this process as speculative, as the Court did in *Lyons*, but the most rudimentary understanding of our legal system indicates that statistical evidence is no different, in kind, from testimonial evidence. We desire certainty, of course, and in the movies, where the scriptwriter exercises God-like control over the depicted circumstances, such certainty can be supplied to satisfy the audience.[74] But in the world that we inhabit, it is simply not available.

Asserting a distinction between probabilistic determination of a single person's behavior and the behavior of a group or institution confuses methods of proof with their underlying function. When we are dealing with the behavior of an institution, we need to gather data about a series of events and aggregate that data in some fashion. To determine whether a particular business firm is

---

73 Césare Beccaria, 'On Crimes and Punishments', in *On Crime and Punishments and Other Writings*, ed. Becarria (Richard Bellamy, ed., Richard Davies, trans.) (Cambridge, UK: Cambridge University Press, 1995), 1, 41 (emphasis in original).

74 Although not in the masterpiece of trial movies, *Twelve Angry Men* (Sidney Lumet, dir.: Orion-Nova, 1957), which depicts the jury deliberations in a first-degree murder case where the truth is, and remains, uncertain.

discriminating against members of a minority group when making employment decisions, for example, we would need to look at a significant number of its decisions. It would obviously be an error to exonerate the firm because it hired one particular member of the group, or to condemn it for deciding not to hire that person. But determining whether a single incident of discrimination occurred would involve a similar process of aggregation. We would need to ask how often an observed behavior indicates discrimination, as opposed to a different, legally acceptable basis for its action.

To continue with this example, we might decide that asking a black person whether any members of his family have served time in prison, or asking a woman whether she plans on getting pregnant in the next few years, represents forbidden discriminatory behavior. But that is because we are aggregating a large number of incidents where such behavior reveals a pattern of discrimination. It is entirely possible that the interviewer asks everyone the question about prison out of genuine and non-judgmental curiosity, or asks a woman about getting pregnant because he and his wife are planning to do so and the subject is simply on his mind. But in assessing these single incidents, we make the probabilistic determination that such innocent motivations are unlikely, and that the question indicates negative attitudes about hiring black people or women. We make the opposite determination if the interviewer asks about the applicant's educational background, but that might be inaccurate as well. In both situations, we are speculating.

The murder trial that serves as an iconic image of our legal system is no different. According to the coroner, the victim was stabbed to death between six and ten o'clock on Saturday night. Two witnesses saw the accused at nine o'clock running from the place where the victim's body was found, holding a blood-covered knife in his hand. If the victim was in fact not stabbed until midnight, however, the witness's testimony is not evidence of guilt. How often do coroners make errors of this sort? How often are they bribed by police who want to obtain a conviction? Suppose the suspect claims that he was nowhere near the scene of the crime on Saturday night. How often do people make mistakes in identifying a person? Quite often, as it turns out.[75] How often do

---

[75] See, e.g., Jed S. Rakoff, *Why the Innocent Plead Guilty and the Guilty Go Free: And Other Paradoxes of Our Broken Legal System* (New York: Farrar, Strauss & Giroux, 2021). The observed unreliability of eyewitness identification is confirmed by experimental studies. Studies also demonstrate that juries give excessive weight to eyewitness identification, particularly when delivered in a confident manner. See S. Penrod & B. Cutler, 'Witness Confidence and Witness Accuracy: Assessing Their Forensic Relation', 1 Psychology, Pub. Pol. & L. 817 (1995).

two people make the same mistake?[76] Does the error rate increase at night, or when the person is running? Suppose the suspect admits that he was correctly identified by the witnesses, but claims that he always carries a blood-covered knife to discourage assaults. How often do people do that? Not so often – but suppose there has been an increase in the number of assaults in the neighborhood, and that behavior has been observed on occasion.

Every step in the process involves a determination of probabilities. More specifically, we are necessarily making judgments about patterns of group behavior, even when we are adjudicating a specific incident such as this murder. How could it not be relevant that systematic data collection reveals that eye witnesses have a 14% error rate identifying a suspect, or that the error rate increases to 28% at night? How could it not be relevant that there is only a .001% frequency rate of innocent people running around the streets with a blood-covered knife? Absent divine intervention, all we can do, whether we are judging the actions of a group of people or a single person, is to make estimates based on patterns of behavior, whether we have quantitative data or rely on intuitive judgment. As Henry Fonda says in *Twelve Angry Men*, the classic Hollywood depiction of a jury deliberation, "Gambling on probabilities, we may be wrong. We may be trying to let a guilty man go free. I don't know. Nobody really can".[77] It is distressing that a motion picture script writer understands our legal system better than a majority of the Supreme Court Justices.

Perhaps the sort of evidence presented in a typical trial involving individual behavior does not sound "statistical" to the Justices because it does not involve numerical measurements or percentages. But that impression may be derived from another form of ignorance, in this case a lack of knowledge about the alternative interpretations of statistical analysis. At the most basic level, the two leading interpretations are frequentist and Bayesian. The frequentist approach, sometimes described as classical statistics, is data-oriented or objectivist.[78] It uses information to assign probabilities to a set of hypotheses, and

---

76 See, e.g., C.A. Elizabeth Luus & Gary L. Wells, 'The Malleability of Eyewitness Confidence: Co-Witness and Perseverance Effects', 79 J. Applied Psych. 714 (1994) (witness confidence strongly affected by testimony of co-witness).

77 *Twelve Angry Men* (Sidney Lumet, dir.: Orion-Nova, 1957).

78 See Ronald A. Fisher, *Statistical Methods and Scientific Inference*, 3rd ed. (New York: Hafner, 1973); Jerzy Neyman & Egon S. Pearson, *Joint Statistical Papers* (Berkeley, Cal., University of California Press, 1967); Abraham Wald, *Statistical Decision Functions* (New York: John Wiley & Sons, 1950). For presentations of the underlying theory or interpretation, see Ludwig von Mises, *Probability, Statistics and Truth*, 2nd ed. (New York: Dover, 1981); Hans Reichenbach, *The Theory of Probability* (Berkeley, Cal.: University of California Press, 1949).

these can be regarded as frequencies from which the hypothesis that best fits the data can be chosen. These frequencies are regarded as an intrinsic part of the physical world that the statistician discovers by means of logical analysis. Bayesian statistics, in contrast, is belief-oriented or subjectivist. It begins from a decision maker's commitment to a particular hypothesis prior to the collection of data (her priors), and proceeds to revise or alter that belief through analysis of the data.[79] It thus expresses probabilities as degrees of persuasion, and uses statistical calculation for the process of revision.[80] Bayesian statistics locates its results in the behavior of a decision maker and, in effect, defines probability as the decision maker's willingness to bet against a set of odds determined by that discovered probability.

If the Justices have in fact rejected the relevance of statistics because they have an incomplete understanding of its underlying interpretations, then their decisions on the matter become less surprising. The frequentist interpretation roughly corresponds to the Anglo-American approach to epistemological questions, which assumes a mind-independent reality and accepts the intuitions embodied in ordinary language as a valid guide to philosophical inquiry. It is most dramatically embodied in G.E. Moore's declaration, "here is one hand", which declares our understanding of the world to be a matter of readily perceived common sense that is more reliable than skepticism.[81]

---

79 See Andrew Gelman, John Carlin, Hal Stern, Donald Rubin, David Dunson & Aki Vehtari, *Bayesian Data Analysis*, 3rd ed. (Boca Raton, Fla.: CRC Press, 2013); Thomas Leonard & John S.J. Hsu, *Bayesian Methods: An Analysis for Statisticians and Interdisciplinary Researchers* (Cambridge, UK: Cambridge University Press, 1999). For presentations of the underlying theory, see Bruno de Finetti, *Theory of Probability: A Critical Introductory Treatment* (Antonio Machi & Adrian Smith, trans.) (New York: John Wiley & Sons, 2017); Irving John Good, *The Estimation of Probabilities: An Essay on Modern Bayesian Methods* (Cambridge, Mass.: MIT Press, 1965); Joseph B. Kadane, *Principles of Uncertainty* (London: Chapman & Hall, 2011); Leonard Savage, *The Foundations of Statistics* (Garden City, N.Y.: Dover, 1972).

80 In more technical terms, it calculates one conditional probability in terms of another conditional probability, using the basic formula $P(A \mid B) = P(B \mid A) \times P(A) / P(B)$.

81 George Edward Moore, 'Proof of an External World, A Defense of Common Sense', in *Philosophic Papers*, ed. George Edward Moore (London: George Allen & Unwin, 1959), 127. See also George Edward Moore, 'A Defense of Common Sense', in id. at 32. More fully, Moore's argument is: here is one hand, and here is another. Therefore, there are two objects in the world, and the world exists. This is a meaningful argument, he argues, because it states a premise that is different from the conclusion, the premise can be demonstrated by sensory information, the most reliable information available to us, and the conclusion follows. For

In contrast, the Bayesian interpretation is essentially phenomenological, allied to the radical subjectivism of Continental philosophy that problematizes our own sense of self. In response to Descartes' famous proof of his existence[82] – "I think, therefore I am" – phenomenology asks: "What is the "I" in that formulation? Can it be unproblematically taken as self-evident, or is it rather a complex social construction, formed by the individual's interaction with the surrounding society?"[83] People immersed in the Anglo-American tradition tend to find this phenomenological approach disconcerting, but – and this is a partial response to Moore – phenomenology is not a solipsistic rejection of reality. Rather, it rests on an insistence that the observers be factored into the process of observation, that the way they process their experience is relevant to their assessment of that experience. From the phenomenological perspective, the adverse reaction of Anglo-American thinkers to a phenomenological approach is evidence that this approach is valid.

To clarify the distinction, consider the hypothesis that has just been advanced, which is that the Supreme Court Justices fail to perceive the relevance of statistical analysis because they think of statistical analysis only in frequentist terms and are unaware of the Bayesian alternative. A frequentist approach would begin by cataloging the number of times that the Court's majority opinions that referred to statistics spoke in frequentist terms and compared this to the total number of references to statistics. Because the Court decides only a small number of cases, it would be relatively easy to do this through a census, that is, to take account of every time the Court discussed statistics over some relevant period (since 1937, for example). This ratio could then be compared to the ratio between the two approaches found in a sample of social science articles that rely on statistical analysis, with the comparison being evaluated for statistical significance. A Bayesian approach might begin with the hypothesis that the Court thinks of statistics in frequentist terms. The

---

one of many responses, see Ludwig Wittgenstein, *On Certainty*, 4th ed. (G.E.M. Anscombe & G.H. Wright, eds) (New York: Harper & Row, 1969): "It needs to be *shown* that no mistake is possible. Giving the assurance 'I know' doesn't suffice. For it is after all only an assurance that I can't be making a mistake, and it needs to be *objectively* established that I am not making a mistake about *that*" (emphases in original).

[82] Rene Descartes, 'Meditations', in *Discourse on Method and the Meditations*, ed. Descartes (F.E. Sutcliffe, trans.) (New York: Penguin (1970), 93.

[83] See Edmund Husserl, *Cartesian Meditations: An Introduction to Phenomenology* (Dorion Cairns, trans.) (Dordrecht, Neth.: Kluwer Academic 1993). See also Edmund Husserl, *Experience and Judgment: Investigations in a Genealogy of Logic* (James S. Churchill & Karl Ameriks, trans.) (Evanston, Ill.: Northwestern University Press, 1993).

first test would take a sample of the Court's opinions and then a sample of journal articles, perhaps smaller than in the frequentist study but more specifically focused on judicial decision making. The results might be sufficient to convince us, using the same standard of statistical significance, that the hypothesis is true. On the other hand, they might be insufficient, in which case we would choose to abandon the hypothesis or repeat the analysis with larger samples. The mathematical tools used for the statistical analysis would be essentially the same in either case. But the differing approaches might affect the coding process; that is, the way we decide whether a particular decision or journal article was employing a frequentist or Bayesian approach.

The point here is not to argue for the superiority of the Bayesian approach to statistics, but rather to combat the impression, which apparently has the Supreme Court in its grip, that statistical analysis is antithetical to legal decision making. There is at least one theory of statistics – an increasingly prevalent one, it might be added – that is congruent with the mode of discourse found in legal opinions. Bayesian statistics focuses on the decision process, telling the investigator what to look for and what will be deemed sufficient to answer the relevant questions. It evaluates the results of the investigation on the basis of their power to convince, and points toward further inquiry that might be needed if the results are deemed to be inconclusive. In other words, rather than presenting statistical relationships as fixed features of the external world, which might be seen as irrelevant from a legal perspective, Bayesian analysis regards these relationships as a guide for the decision maker.

The standards of proof that we have evolved for deciding cases in our legal system translate readily into Bayesian terms. "Beyond a reasonable doubt" means that the decision maker feels certain that the defendant is guilty and would be astonished if that turned out not to be true. No further evidence is needed to achieve that level of certainty. "Preponderance of the evidence" means that the decision maker feels, on balance, that the evidence supports the plaintiff's case. It would not be surprising if the actual facts turned out to point in the reverse direction, but the evidence is sufficient for the purpose. Further evidence might provide a higher level of certainty, but we have decided that we do not need it because there is no reason to favor one party over another. "Clear and convincing", the intermediate standard, means that the decision maker is fairly certain, and would be surprised, but not astonished, if the actual facts turned out to be different. We use it in situations where we want to favor one of the parties, but not as strongly as we favor a person whose liberty is at stake in a criminal trial. All these standards are subjective determinations of probability, even though they are determinations about particular people and particular incidents.

Even more basically, the existence of the evidence on which these judgments are based corresponds to the Bayesian concept of data. In the Anglo-American legal system, facts are not objective, mind-independent features of reality. If they were, then we would attempt to ascertain them by any means at our disposal. Even if we factored in consideration of human rights to prohibit such practices as judicial torture, we would still be left with a wide range of methods for determining the supposedly objective facts. But that is not what we do. Instead, we begin with a procedure, a commitment to a certain decision-making protocol. That protocol, to be sure, is designed to achieve a certain level of correspondence with reality – it developed as an alternative to the ordeal, after all – but it is the protocol, the decision-making process that serves as the starting point. The facts on which decision must be based are those that appear "on the record". This means that they must be put in issue by the plaintiff's complaint or the government's indictment, and that they must be presented in court and subject to challenge by the opposing party.[84] If an assertion does not go through this process, it is simply not a fact for purposes of the decision, whatever its status in the world external to the trial might be. Thus, if it has been omitted from the notice or indictment, it may not be subsequently introduced and relied upon. If the only evidence is hearsay, even hearsay by the proverbial Anglican bishop, it is not a fact because hearsay cannot be effectively cross-examined. In short, Anglo-American fact-finding, like Bayesian analysis, begins with a hypothesis by the decision-making body – the plaintiff's complaint or the government indictment.[85] It then uses a decision protocol to

---

[84] There are exceptions, as might be expected. An indicative one is judicial notice, the discretionary authority of the judge to rely on facts that have not been subject to the adversary process. According to The Uniform Rules of Evidence (National Conference of Commissioners on Uniform State Laws, 1974, as amended), Rule 201(b): "A judicially noticed fact must be one not subject to reasonable dispute in that it is either (1) generally known within the territorial jurisdiction of the trial court or (2) capable of accurate and ready determination by resort to sources whose accuracy cannot reasonably be questioned". The provision in the Federal Rules of Evidence (United States House of Representatives, Committee on the Judiciary, 2014), Rule 201(b) is virtually identical. Note that neither rule provides that a court can take judicial notice of a fact because it is "true". Rather, the basis for this exception to the adversary process for determining facts is that certain facts cannot be reasonably contested; that is, the adversary process could not be expected to produce a contrary result. This is emphasized by the caveat in both sets of Rules that "[a] party is entitled upon timely request to an opportunity to be heard as to the propriety of taking judicial notice"; Uniform Rules, supra, Rule 201(e). Thus the limit on judicial notice is not that the noticed fact is false, but that it can be contested.

[85] To be clear, the indictment must be distinguished from the presumption of innocence. All citizens are presumed innocent. But the government begins a criminal case (typically) by presenting the hypothesis to a grand jury that the defendant

revise the hypothesis on the basis of data gathered according to specified rules. It makes no claim; that is, it gives no consideration, to any reality that exists outside the process; that is what we mean when we say that the decision must be based "on the record".

The Supreme Court's position in *McCleskey* and *Lyons* can now be recharacterized. Although virtually all judicial decisions that turn on factual evidence are essentially statistical in nature, the Court believes that this reality should not be acknowledged in judicial decision-making. The probabilities that we must assess in order to satisfy our standards of proof must not be demonstrated by our best scientific and mathematical models, but rather must be based on guesswork. But the fact that the decision is based on guesswork should never be acknowledged. Instead, we should condemn our best scientific and mathematical models as guesswork and ignore their findings on that basis. When a claim can only be understood and demonstrated by statistical data, such as the behavior of an institution or an individual's risk of future mistreatment, relief should be denied without considering that data. All these lacunae should be filled by declarations that the United States possesses the most just judicial system in the world, one that serves as an essential basis of our democratic system.

3. WHAT STATISTICS TELLS US ABOUT THE ROLE OF THE JUDGE

To summarize thus far, modern physics teaches us that the structure of the material world is, according to our best description, essentially statistical, and that this same structure is the best description of the legally relevant behavior of institutions such as corporate HR departments, police departments, or the criminal justice system of a particular state. The Anglo-American legal system incorporates this statistical approach to fact finding as its original and most distinctive feature. It began with the shift from determinations of fact by divine revelation to probabilistic assessment by human decision makers that relies on assumptions or estimations that are essentially statistical in nature, and that are readily described in terms of Bayesian statistical analysis. But recognizing the relevance of statistics provides further insights. Specifically, it

---

is guilty. If the grand jury indicts the defendant, it is, in effect, endorsing that hypothesis. In order for the hypothesis to be confirmed, however, the government must meet a high standard, which is to convince the jurors (or the judge in a bench trial) "beyond a reasonable doubt"; that is, to a matter of certainty. The Bayesian analyst might make precisely the same demand if the decision involved serious risk, such as betting all one's savings as opposed to betting an amount equal to one's weekly income.

highlights the role of the decision maker in our legal systems and offers important recommendations about the judicial decision-making process.

A. Copenhagen Physics and Bayesian Statistics

There are a number of interpretations for the superposition of a moving particle; that is, its apparent existence as a simultaneous array of possibilities. Perhaps the leading one at present, and the one that will be most useful for the discussion that follows, is the Copenhagen interpretation championed by Niels Bohr. It holds that the interposition of the measuring instrument that results in the collapse of the wave function is not simply an unavoidable intrusion into an independently occurring process, but rather part of the process itself. In other words, it is not only true that we cannot perceive the particle until we measure it, but also that our act of perception is part of what we are measuring. According to Bohr, the measuring instrument and the object being measured cannot be separated from each other but form an interacting or dynamic totality.[86]

Bohr's position is illustrated, or perhaps dramatized, by Erwin Schrödinger's famous thought experiment. A cat is placed in an enclosed box with a radioactive substance whose half-life and quantity are such that there is an even chance that a single atom will decay within a specified period. If the atom decays, a Geiger counter produces a signal that triggers a hammer, smashing a flask of poison that kills the cat. Because the decay of a single atom cannot be predicted by quantum theory, it is impossible to know whether the cat will be alive or dead when one opens the box after the specified period. Schrödinger asked whether the cat itself was therefore in superposition; that is, either alive or dead until the box is opened.[87] One common answer is that the collapse of the probability function (the radioactive decay being a quantum event like the wave function of a moving particle) occurs the first time the quantum-level world – that is, the atom – interacts with the macroscopic world, in this case the Geiger counter. There is, according to this response, no possibility that the cat is in two states, and thus no contradiction in the macroscopic world. But this answer only solves the thought experiment; it does not alter the Copenhagen interpretation that the detection device (which can be conceived here as the

---

86 See Jan Faye, *Niels Bohr: His Heritage and Legacy: An Anti-Realistic View of Quantum Mechanics* (Dordrecht, Neth.: Kluwer Academic 1991), 113–56; Henry J. Folse, 'Bohr's Framework of Complementarity and the Realism Debate', in *Niels Bohr and Contemporary Philosophy*, ed. Jan Faye & Henry J. Folse (Dordrecht, Neth.: Kluwer Academic 1994), 119.

87 See Gribbin, supra note 9, 177–213.

Geiger counter; or the Geiger counter, hammer, flask, cat and observer who opens the box) is an intrinsic part of the event.

Bayesian statistics involves a similar integration of the observer into the matter that is being observed. It begins from a decision maker's commitment to a particular hypothesis, guides the decision maker regarding the data that needs to be collected, leads the decision maker to revise or alter her or his belief on the basis of the data, and continues the process until satisfied that she or he has a rational basis for action (e.g., is willing to bet on the chosen decision). The decision maker is an integral part of this process, and the statistical calculations cannot be described in isolation from that person. The Bayesian critique of frequentist statistics focuses on this subjective element. If statistical relationships are viewed as intrinsic components of an external reality, how does one know which relationships to investigate? How does one know how much data to gather? How does one decide whether the resulting level of correlation is sufficient for the purpose it is intended to serve?[88]

Schrödinger's thought experiment can be used to illustrate this feature of Bayesian statistics. The experiment is set up to present us with a conundrum, not to inform us about the world. We know in advance that there is an equal chance that the cat is alive or dead, but that is because the behavior of the radioactive substance in the box has been previously determined. We measure this behavior as the substance's half-life; that is, the time in which half the total substance will decay into a different substance. Knowing this figure for the chosen substance, we can set the time period of the experiment to produce an equal chance that the cat will be alive or dead. But suppose we did not know the half-life of the substance and we wanted to use the device to test a hypothesis (assuming it would be possible to get IRB approval for this). We could do so by running the experiment repeatedly and recording the number of times that the cat was found dead. Note first that our decision to use this mode of determining the half-life of a substance depends on our prior hypothesis about the substance. If we think the half-life is measured in nanoseconds, the experiment would be useless because the cat would always be dead by the time we opened the box; if it is measured in billions of years, the experiment would also be useless because the cat would almost always be alive for any sample of manageable size.

For the hypothesis that a substance has a moderate half-life – a few days, perhaps – Schrödinger's imaginary apparatus could generate relevant data. Bayes' Theorem can then be used to determine the probability that the cat would be found dead given a fixed amount of the substance and a specified time. We would keep running the experiment until we had achieved our desired level of

---

88 See, e.g., Savage supra note 79, 27–30.

certainty, which might be thought of as the number of decimal places in the result that we can confirm with repetition. We would thus have achieved an acceptably reliable prediction for the odds that a single atom of the substance will decay within a given time, a quantum event that is inherently unpredictable. As this example indicates, the experimental method – that is, the intervention – is deeply interconnected with the phenomenon being observed. Any statement about the "real" half-life of the substance in question requires dubious metaphysical assumptions that cannot be derived from the experiment. It purchases the psychological comfort that our cultural intuitions about the nature of reality are true at the cost of reliance upon assertions that we cannot justify according to those same intuitions.

A number of theorists have noted the connection between the Copenhagen interpretation and Bayesian statistics. This has led to the development of Quantum Bayesianism, sometimes called QBism. Its central tenet is that a Bayesian analysis of the wave function generates the Copenhagen interpretation because it incorporates the unification of the event and the instrument into the analysis in the manner that the Copenhagen interpretation asserts.[89] Thus, the collapse of the wave function as a result of measurement is, in effect, the same thing as the Bayesian analyst's revision of a previous hypothesis on the basis of new data. In both approaches, the observer is an essential element in the object of the investigation and there is thus a radical subjectivity in our understanding of the world that we inhabit.

The connection between Bayesian statistics and the Copenhagen interpretation might appear to present a problem in terms of cultural history. The Copenhagen interpretation is a product of the early to mid-twentieth century, and thus contemporaneous with the development of phenomenological philosophy by Edmund Husserl. But Bayes lived in the early to mid-eighteenth century; his theorem was published posthumously in 1763. The close relationship of Bayes' approach to phenomenology was noted above, but this would seem to raise a problem of anachronism, or at least discordance, from a historical perspective.

One answer is that Bayes' thinking was a product of British Empiricism. The seminal work of this epistemological approach is probably John Locke's

---

[89] Christopher A. Fuchs, 'On Participatory Realism', in *Information and Interaction: Eddington, Wheeler and the Limits of Knowledge*, ed. Ian T. Durham & Dean Rickles (New York: Springer, 2017), 113; Christopher A. Fuchs, 'QBism: The Perimeter of Quantum Bayesianism', arXiv:1003:5209; Christopher Fuchs, N. David Mermin & Rudiger Schack, 'An Introduction to QBism with an Application to the Locality of Quantum Mechanics', 82 Am. J. Physics 749 (2014); N. David Mermin, 'Physics: QBism Puts the Scientist Back in Science', 507 Nature 421 (2014).

Essay Concerning Human Understanding, published in 1689, and its apotheosis is David Hume's *Enquiry Concerning Human Understanding*, published in 1748. What they argued was that the human mind begins as a blank slate (*tabula rasa*), and that our ideas are products of experience.[90] Much of Western philosophy took a different turn with Immanuel Kant, who asserted that Hume had awakened him from his "dogmatic slumber" and framed much of his own theory in response. Kant's answer to empiricism is the synthetic a priori; our minds are not blank slates, but structured in advance of any empirical knowledge by primordial conceptions of space, time and causation.[91] Kant may have been right about the structure of our minds, but twentieth-century physics revealed that our synthetic a priori conceptions are not confirmed by empirical data. At that point, the pure empiricism that prevailed in British philosophy during Bayes' lifetime was in effect reasserted. Our only means of understanding the world is through our own experience, and what we have learned does not correspond to our native intuitions.

B. The Role of the Judge

The statistical nature of physical reality, as amplified by the Copenhagen interpretation, and the essentially statistical nature of factual knowledge, as amplified by the Bayesian approach, both point to a profound insight about our decision-making processes. They indicate that the observer is part of that reality and that knowledge. All we can know are the results of our own investigations, and as these are in fact our own investigations, this is a process from which we cannot separate ourselves. We can, if we like, make declarations about what is really "out there". We can assert that "here is one hand" tells us something definitive and irrefutable. We can insist that all truth comes from God. But these are all statements of faith, personal declarations that in an important sense deconstruct themselves by revealing the central role of the observer's commitments and beliefs. It is preferable to deal with that role directly, rather than trying to deny it by making assertions that only demonstrate its validity.

Recall the basic measurement problem regarding discrimination by the HR department of a large corporation. Simply asking the HR officer about discrimination is unlikely to produce a reliable result because the officer might

90 See generally Stephen Priest, *The British Empiricists* (London: Routledge, 2007); Marco Sgarbi, *The Aristotelian Tradition and the Rise of British Empiricism: Logic and Epistemology in the British Isles (1570–1689)* (Dordrecht: Springer, 2013).

91 Immanuel Kant, *Critique of Pure Reason* (Paul Guyer & Allen W. Wood, trans.) (Cambridge, UK: Cambridge University Press 1998 [1781]).

not tell the truth. An investigator can try to design a revelatory question to avoid this problem, but the question might be subject to the same objection, or to the misconceptions of the investigator, or to the investigator's own discriminatory attitudes. The investigator can never be eliminated from the inquiry into the behavior of the corporation. All that we can possibly do is increase the likelihood that we will achieve an answer that we find sufficiently persuasive by using statistical analysis. This analysis is our best instrument for obtaining reliable data about a given situation, but it simultaneously reveals to us the limits of our ability to do so.

Note the way that the use of statistics has been formulated: it is the best method for achieving an answer that is convincing to the decision maker and it simultaneously reveals the limits of the decision maker's ability to obtain reliable information. Thus, it not only tells us that we cannot eliminate the investigator from consideration, but also that we cannot eliminate the decision maker from the decision. It has long been recognized that legal fact finders, both jurors and judges, harbor personal feelings that can affect their decisions. Our legal system identifies certain feelings as biases that interfere with what we call objective judgment, and legal procedure has evolved over the centuries to control or eliminate them. Thus, jurors, originally local people who decided on the basis of their personal knowledge, are now expected to have no knowledge about the case outside the evidence presented at the trial. Both parties in an adversarial trial are granted peremptory challenges that they can use to eliminate prospective jurors who they think are prejudiced against them. The judge cautions the jurors against discussing the case with outsiders and can sequester the jury in exceptional circumstances to implement this restriction. Similarly, judges are expected to recuse themselves if they have prior knowledge of the case or a personal connection to one of the parties.

These controls are widely recognized as insufficient. Juries, traditionally praised as embodying the views and spirit of the citizenry, embody its prejudices as well. From the end of Reconstruction until the start of World War II, juries in Southern states, composed entirely of white members,[92] systemati-

[92] Reconstruction legislation, the Civil Rights Act of 1975, ch. 114, § 4, 18 Stat. 335, prohibited exclusion from juries on the basis of race. But the Supreme Court allowed Southerners to circumvent the law in *Strauder v. West Virginia*, 100 U.S. 303 (1880) (exclusion from juries is permissible on the basis of various criteria, including educational qualifications; see Albert W. Alschuler & Andrew G. Deiss, 'A Brief History of the Criminal Jury in the United States', 61 U. Chi. L. Rev. 867, 892–95 (1994)); James Forman, Jr., 'Juries and Race in the Nineteenth Century', 113 Yale L.J. 895, 930–34 (2003). For other cases denying relief to black people on the basis of the Civil War Amendments and their enforcing legislation, see, e.g., *Plessy v. Ferguson*, 163 U.S. 537 (1896) (segregated facilities do not deny black

cally convicted black people when they were accused of crimes against white people and exonerated white people accused of killing black people, even though white people engaged in systematic lethal terror against black people,[93] and occasionally in wholesale slaughter.[94] Judicial attitude studies reveal that a judge's decisions are generally predictable on the basis of biographical data such as party affiliation or membership in organizations prior to appointment to the bench.[95] Jerome Frank identified this issue three quarters of a century ago. In *Courts on Trial*, he declared that "there is no objective measure of the

---

people equal protection of the law); *Reese v. United States*, 92 U.S. 214 (1876) (the Enforcement Act of 1870, prohibiting racial discrimination in voter registration, is unconstitutional); *United States v. Cruikshank*, 92 U.S. 542 (1876) (the Fourteenth Amendment does not apply to action by private parties).

93 Most dramatically by lynching, see National Assoc. for the Advancement of Colored People, *30 Years of Lynching in the United States, 1889–1918* (NAACP, 1919); Amy Louise Wood, *Lynching and Spectacle: Witnessing Racial Violence in America, 1890–1940* (Chapel Hill, N.C.: University of North Carolina Press, 2009). The legal system perpetrated other injustices as well. In the South, it permitted, and indeed implemented, the system of convict leasing by convicting black people of minor or non-existent crimes and sentencing them to work, essentially as slaves, in white farms, factories and mines. See Douglas A. Blackmon, *Slavery by Another Name: The Re-Enslavement of Black Americans from the Civil War to World War II* (New York: Anchor 2008).

94 In 1921, a white mob destroyed a prosperous black neighborhood in Tulsa, Oklahoma, killing somewhere between 30 and 300 residents. No one was punished for this outrage. See James S. Hirsch, *Riot and Remembrance: The Tulsa Race Massacre and Its Legacy* (Boston: Houghton Mifflin, 2002); Tim Madigan, *The Burning: The Tulsa Race Massacre of 1921* (New York: St. Martin's, 2021). This was certainly a notorious incident, but it was not unique. Two years earlier, after police and railroad detectives initiated a shootout at a meeting of black sharecroppers in Elaine, Arkansas, white people from surrounding areas descended upon Elaine, shooting dozens – perhaps hundreds – of black people on sight. The only legal response was to try 12 black men for killing white people (who had probably been accidentally shot by each other) and sentence all 12 of them to death. See Richard C. Cortner, *A Mob Intent on Death: The NAACP and the Arkansas Riot Cases* (Middletown, Conn.: Wesleyan University Press, 1988); Grif Stockley, *Blood in Their Eyes: The Elaine Race Massacres of 1919* (Fayetteville, Ark.: University of Arkansas, 2001); Robert Whitaker, *On the Laps of the Gods* (New York: Three Rivers, 2008), 159–308.

95 See, e.g., Jeffrey A. Segal & Harold J. Spaeth, *The Supreme Court and the Attitudinal Model Revisited* (Cambridge, UK: Cambridge University Press, 2002); James L. Gibson, 'Judges' Role Orientation, Attitudes and Decisions: An Interactive Model', 72 Am. Pol. Sci. Rev. 911 (1978); Theodore W. Ruger, Pauline T. Kim, Andrew D. Martin & Kevin M. Quinn, 'The Supreme Court Forecasting

accuracy of a judge's finding of the facts. There exists no yardstick for that purpose". In a review of his book, Julius Cohen[96] challenged this view, arguing that "if this be true, there would be no valid basis for judge Frank ever asserting that the 'facts' in any such case were ever 'wrong' or 'mistaken'". But acknowledging the absence of an objective measure or yardstick is the only valid basis on which to assert that facts are wrong or mistaken, because it leads to a methodology that recognizes the inevitable role of the investigator and decision maker in assessing the facts and reaching the result.

The Copenhagen and Bayesian approach to statistical data indicates that beliefs and commitments of the decision maker are not defects in the system that we can eliminate. They are part of the system that must be confronted and taken into account, part of the human decision-making process that is central to our system of law. We disparage the Middle Ages as "Gothic", but the English government at that time was willing to confront an even more disconcerting challenge, which was the withdrawal of divine authority from legal determinations. It took this problem into account by establishing juries that decided cases on the basis of humanly accessible facts, a solution that we now celebrate as the essence of our legal system and that has been accepted by every democratic nation. Why should we not be able to achieve the smaller amount of creativity and flexibility that is needed to refine this system on the basis of the statistical nature of our knowledge?

These approaches also endorse another point that Frank advanced in *Courts on Trial*. He suggested that all judges should be psychoanalyzed so that they can recognize and counteract their unconscious prejudices.[97] While psychoanalysis is not as fashionable now as it was in Frank's day, the challenge on which his recommendation is based is that legal decision makers simply cannot assume that they are capable of neutral or objective judgment. Like the investigator or the jury, they are part of the decision-making process and bring with them into that process the totality of their beliefs and attitudes. This suggests that, at a minimum, judges should acknowledge in their opinion that they have personal views about the subject at issue and make some effort to identify those views and to explain their decision in light of their recognition. To move from the language of psychology to that of law, judges should interrogate themselves the way an attorney might interrogate a juror and acknowledge the results.

It is possible that such acknowledgments might change the results in some opinions, that judges would become aware of previously unrecognized biases

Project: Legal and Political Science Approaches to Predicting Supreme Court Decision Making', 104 Colum. L. Rev 1140 (2004).

96 Julius Cohen, 'Review', 17 Univ. of Chicago L. Rev. 557 (1950).

97 Frank, supra note 8, 247–53.

that they would not regard as proper, or find that the attempt to justify their beliefs led them to disown those beliefs instead. More likely, they might modify their reasoning, altering the arguments that they employ to support their conclusion or stating the conclusion in somewhat different terms. At the very least, they might write more reflective and – not to be overly ironic – more judicious opinions. Many appellate majority opinions, notably by the Supreme Court, read more like advocacy briefs. They are assertive, even intemperate efforts to support a particular position. Often, they pile one argument upon the other, thereby muddling legal doctrine by failing to identify the determinative argument and to distinguish between holding and dictum. A modicum of self-reflection might enable judges to write more thoughtful opinions that give credit to countervailing arguments and identify the precise basis for their decisions.

One common concern among legal scholars is that the legitimacy of the courts will be undermined if judges admit to their personal views. This became something close to an obsession in the Legal Process School's discussions of Supreme Court decision making.[98] The simple answer is that the Supreme Court has never succeeded in convincing anyone of its political neutrality. John Marshall was widely regarded as a loyal (and pretty much the last) Federalist, and a strong proponent of national power against the Jeffersonian Republicans and then the Jacksonian Democrats. Roger Taney was excoriated as a tool of Southern slave owners. During the Second Industrial Revolution of the late nineteenth century, the Court was perceived as having joined the capitalists' effort to suppress labor unions, and during the Progressive Era which followed, it was widely seen as having allied itself with property owners in their political struggle against pro-regulatory Progressives.[99] Everyone recognized that the Warren Court was a strong proponent of human rights, and that the Burger, Rehnquist and Roberts Courts that followed were pro-police and pro-business.

---

[98] See, e.g., Alexander Bickel, *The Least Dangerous Branch: The Supreme Court at the Bar of Politics* (New Haven, Conn.: Yale University Press, 1962) (Supreme Court should use procedural devices to avoid deciding controversial cases that would impair its legitimacy); Herbert Wechsler, 'Toward Neutral Principles of Constitutional Law', 73 Harv. L. Rev. 1 (1959) (Court decision in *Brown v. Board of Educ.* endangered the Court's legitimacy because it failed to view the rights of Southerners to avoid integration as equal to the rights of blacks who wanted to implement it).

[99] See Erwin Chemerinsky, *The Case Against the Supreme Court* (New York: Penguin 2015); Gerald N. Rosenberg, *The Hollow Hope: Can Courts Bring About Social Change?*, 2nd ed. (Chicago: University of Chicago Press, 2008); Jeffrey A. Segal, Harold J. Speath & Sara C. Benesh, *The Supreme Court in the American Legal System* (Cambridge, UK: Cambridge University Press, 2005), 41–70.

It is impossible to see the Court's decision in *Bush v. Gore*[100] as doing anything other than delivering the Presidency to the Republican Party. In short, if the Court's legitimacy rests on the perception that it is non-partisan, it has nothing to lose. Far better to ground that claim on the Justices' honesty about their commitments, and their willingness to acknowledge those commitments, think seriously about them, and at least give credence to opposing arguments.

The two decisions noted at the outset, *McCleskey* and *Lyons*, illustrate this point. Both cases centered on the criminal justice system's treatment of black citizens, and specifically black men: *McCleskey* involved jury trials and *Lyons* involved police practices. Both decisions were written by middle-aged white men, *McCleskey* by Lewis Powell and *Lyons* by Byron White, who had reached adulthood in the era of segregation. Powell was 79 at the time he wrote *McCleskey*; he had grown up in Virginia and received his undergraduate and law degrees from Washington and Lee University (named for George Washington and Robert E. Lee). He was Chair of the Richmond, Virginia School Board at the time when it was subject to, and then defying, the Supreme Court's decision in *Brown v. Board*.[101] White was 65–66 when he wrote the opinion in *Lyons*. He had grown up in rural Colorado, attended the University of Colorado and then Yale Law School. In 1938 and 1940, he starred as a running back in the National Football League, which had effectively banned black players in 1934.[102] It is simply inconceivable that either of the Justices, or any of the other Justices on the Court (all of whom were white with the exception of Thurgood Marshall) did not have ambivalent and complex feelings about black people, perhaps particularly about black men. Moreover, both cases centered on the issue that had served as the most visceral and widespread basis of discrimination against black men, which is the image of them as dangerous criminals. For Powell and White to write opinions without at least some effort

---

[100] 532 U.S. 98 (2000). Legal scholars are virtually unanimous in condemning this decision as unprincipled and cynical. See, e.g., Jack Balkin, '*Bush v. Gore* and the Boundary Between Law and Politic's, 110 Yale L.J. 1407 (2001); Erwin Chemerinsky, '*Bush v. Gore* Was Not Justiciable', 76 Notre Dame L. Rev. 1093 (2001). Predictably, Republicans became more favorably disposed to the Court as a result of the decision, and Democrats became less favorable. But few people seem to have been truly surprised, or expected anything else. See Herbert M. Kritzer, 'The Impact of Bush v. Gore on Public Perceptions and Knowledge of the Supreme Court', 85 Judicature 32 (2001).

[101] John C. Jeffries, *Justice Lewis F. Powell* (New York: Scribner, 1994). This massive book, written by a former law clerk of Powell's, is predictably hagiographic, but nonetheless reveals Powell's basically racist attitudes quite clearly.

[102] See Dennis Hutchinson, *The Man Who Once Was Whizzer White: A Portrait of Justice Byron R. White* (New York: Free Press, 1998).

to recognize their own subjective reactions to the issue presented by the case was simply dishonest. The absence of any such effort justifies viewing the cases in the way many observers perceived them, namely, as outright racism.

Beyond this obvious point lies a further concern. The treatment of black Americans by what we call the American criminal justice system for the entire lifetimes of the Justices was a direct refutation of our nation's basic claims about its commitment to justice. Juries in Southern states – composed entirely of white people in direct violation of applicable legal rules – served as means of authorizing white people to commit any offense against black people that they wished, and a means of enforcing any accusation that white people chose to level against black people. Police in black communities often functioned as an occupying force, regularly brutalizing or killing residents without justification. Thus, in addition to their failure to take account of their own inevitably complicated attitudes toward black men, the authors of *McCleskey* and *Lyons* failed to take account of the social and cultural practices that generated the two cases. As such, they were engaged in a campaign to justify a legal system that consistently violated its own constitutional principles. Their personal commitment to the prevailing myth that this system is a paragon of justice blinded them to its realities. This does not, by itself, prove that such injustice occurred in the two cases that were under consideration. What it does show is that the Justices who decided those cases had failed to interrogate their own beliefs, beliefs that were contradicted by a mass of readily available evidence. As such, they were unqualified to reach fair, impartial judgments in those cases.

There is one final failure by the Justices in *McCleskey* and *Lyons* that the Copenhagen interpretation of reality and the Bayesian interpretations of statistics reveal. It is the failure of the Justices to acknowledge their hostility to statistics. The majority opinion in *McCleskey* in effect dismisses statistics as an invalid methodology for understanding the world. The majority opinion in *Lyons* makes entirely unsubstantiated and invalid statistical assumptions without any effort to learn or apply a valid statistical methodology. These opinions exhibit an ignorant, dismissive, anti-intellectual attitude toward the methodology that currently dominates natural and social science research. While every undergraduate who studies any of these fields learns statistical analysis, and while nearly every serious scholar in these fields uses it on a regular basis, the American Supreme Court is content to dismiss it the way people in an earlier era dismissed the rotation of the Earth and its orbit of the Sun. On this basis alone, the Court is an embarrassment to our legal system and to our nation.

CONCLUSION

It is time for American judges to understand the statistical nature of the data that we can obtain about the world, and the inherently statistical way in which facts are determined in the Anglo-American legal system. It is time for them to examine their own ignorance, and their willingness to wallow in that ignorance. Until they do so, they will be reaching decisions on the basis of the unexamined assumptions and inherent biases that modern statistical theory reveals as inherent in human decision making. The only antidote, that theory tells us, is successive assessment and revision of one's conclusions on the basis of evidence gathered by statistical methods. In short, it is time for the American judiciary to learn statistics.

3. Discrimination by generalisation: about judicial use and abuse of statistics in anti-discrimination cases

Juliana de Augustinis and Rob van Gestel

If men happen to have, on average, more accidents than women when driving, should insurance companies be allowed to charge men higher insurance premiums? In systems where judges are required to retire by law at the age of 70, but some of them feel really fit and enjoy their profession, should they be able to challenge their official retirement age because there is no valid reason for them not to continue their judicial role in a responsible manner and the statutory age is somewhat arbitrary from a physical and mental health perspective?[1] Does the fact that over half of the children belonging to a minority group of Roma in a Czech town are placed in "special schools", and that these children are 27 times more likely to be placed in these schools, result in indirect discrimination?[2]

These and many similar questions can be raised regarding situations in which certain general distinctions are being made that are often claimed to result in unlawful discrimination. What we are interested in is how courts decide these cases. More specifically, what role may statistical data play in establishing whether a certain (seemingly) general distinction is discriminatory? In this chapter, we will show that courts in anti-discrimination cases are faced with a highly complex combination of normative and empirical considerations that can easily go wrong, especially since judges are not usually trained to deal with statistics. They may therefore rely too heavily on intuition, common sense, and practical wisdom, while ignoring the flawed empirical assumptions on which their argumentation rests. This may result in judicial decisions – with sometimes far-reaching adverse effects for the public interest – that lack transparency as to the methodology of law-making. We believe

1 Centrale Raad van Beroep 12 August 2021; ECLI:NL:CRVB:2021:1803.
2 *D.H. and Others v. the Czech Republic*, ECtHR 13 November 2007, App. No. 57325/00.

that in an era where attention to evidence-based decision-making is increasing in different policy spheres,[3] it is crucial to make judges more familiar with statistical evidence in order for them to avoid all too obvious errors.

Hereafter, we first provide an overview of the different roles that empirical data and statistics can play in anti-discrimination court cases. We will show that statistics are, among other things, used to (i) rationally explain a difference in treatment between groups of individuals (sometimes referred to as "statistical discrimination") because they, for example, pose different risks; (ii) provide input for the proportionality assessments that courts have to perform when unequal treatment may infringe upon fundamental rights; and finally (iii) demonstrate the disparate effects of seemingly neutral measures relative to a group (indirect discrimination) and invert the burden of proof.

To illustrate the problems empirical data and statistics pose to courts, we will conduct an in-depth comparative case law analysis of "typical" anti-discrimination cases[4] in the fields of a) insurance law, by studying to what extent sex may or may not play a role in the calculation of insurance premiums due to allegedly relevant differences between men and women when it comes to insurance risks; b) public health law, by studying a well-known dilemma that courts are faced with when it comes to disputes about the rights of gay and bisexual men to function as blood donors, where opponents argue there might be an increased risk of spreading, for example, HIV infection; and c) labour law: in this broad field where one could find all sorts of practices resulting in discrimination, we focus on the role that statistics play in justifying different treatment of workers based on age. We will therefore explore court cases concerning mandatory retirement policies.

After the in-depth analysis of typical cases in the different fields of law, we look for patterns and hypotheses that may explain the different outcomes of the cases across jurisdictions. We conclude with a discussion of the results of the overall case law analysis and present a brief agenda for future research.

---

3 Antokolskaia, M. V. (2013). Van politiek gestuurde wetgeving naar evidence based wetgeving: Nog een lange weg te gaan. In W. van Boom, I. Giesen, & A. Verheij (Eds.), *Capita Civilologie. Handboek empirie en privaatrecht*, Den Haag: Boom Juridische uitgevers, pp. 173–207.

4 Typical anti-discrimination cases refer to legal or workplace disputes where someone alleges they were treated unfairly or unlawfully because of a protected characteristic. These cases usually arise under civil rights, employment, housing, education, or public-accommodation laws.

DATA, STATISTICS, AND DISCRIMINATION

Academic legal publications on different topics[5] in various knowledge domains[6] address how courts engage with statistical data in anti-discrimination cases. Building on the existing literature, we distinguish three roles statistical data may play in anti-discrimination cases. Namely: (i) to rationally explain a difference in treatment; (ii) to inform judicial proportionality assessments; and (iii) to indicate that a public policy or civil practice leads to disparate effects in a group of people, providing a presumption of discrimination. In this section, we explore each of these uses separately.

Statistics are a valuable tool for investigating relationships between features of a sample of individuals, such as age or sex and their ability to drive a car, and for predicting the likely behaviour of an entire population (e.g. how likely are accidents among younger drivers?).[7] Hence, statistics can also play a role in justifying differential treatment, for instance in calculating insurance premiums for members of a certain group (e.g. young motorists).[8]

---

5 Discussing statistics in civil rights cases see, for instance, Kiefer, D., Sacks, J., & Ylvisaker, D. (2016). Statistics, civil rights and the US Supreme Court: A cautionary tale. *Significance*, *13*, 30–33. https://doi.org/https://doi.org/10.1111/j.1740-9713.2016.00898.x. On statistics in indirect discrimination cases in employment, Blackham, A. (2016). Legitimacy and empirical evidence in the UK courts. *Griffith Law Review*, *25*(3), 414–440. https://doi.org/10.1080/10383441.2016.1259975. In civil cases more generally, Gastwirth, J. L. (2020). The role of statistical evidence in civil cases. *Annual Review of Statistics and Its Application*, *7*, 39–60. https://doi.org/https://doi.org/10.1146/annurev-statistics-031219-041238. On the assessment of empirical evidence in judicial proportionality reviews of legislation, van Gestel, R., & de Poorter, J. (2016). Putting evidence-based law making to the test: judicial review of legislative rationality. *The Theory and Practice of Legislation*, *4*(2), 155–185. https://doi.org/10.1080/20508840.2016.1259899. On discrimination in insurance, Avraham, R. (2017). Discrimination and Insurance. In K. Lippert-Rasmussen (Ed.), *The Routledge Handbook to Discrimination* (pp. 335–347). Routledge; Rego, M. L. (2014). Statistics as a basis for discrimination in the insurance business. *Law, Probability and Risk*, *14*(2), 119–134. https://doi.org/10.1093/lpr/mgu017.

6 In political philosophy and ethics of discrimination, see, for instance, Lippert-Rasmussen, K. (2011). "We are all Different": Statistical discrimination and the right to be treated as an individual. *The Journal of Ethics*, *15*(1), 47–59. https://doi.org/10.1007/s10892-010-9095-6.

7 Faigman, D. L. (2008). *Constitutional fictions: A unified theory of constitutional facts*. Oxford University Press.

8 The practice of treating a group of people (X) worse than another group (Y), supported by statistical analysis, is sometimes mentioned in literature as

Statistical discrimination can easily become controversial, though, when related to sensitive attributes like age, sex, gender, ethnicity, or sexual orientation. To what extent may individuals' age, sexual orientation, weight, or lifestyle be used to allow for different treatment in terms of premiums for health insurance or pension schemes? There might be a statistical relationship between these features and the likelihood of certain diseases and, hence, future medical costs; or on the life expectancy of individuals and the likely duration of someone's pension. Insurance companies or pension funds may, for instance, argue that they are simply relying on statistical correlations.

People belonging to a minority seen as "higher risk" may, however, claim that such a generalization results in unequal treatment on the basis of characteristics they should not be held accountable for – e.g. they may argue that being gay is not a "choice" but a human right – or they perhaps claim that correlation is not to be mistaken for causation and hence argue that the chance that a risk unfolds can be the result of a variety of reasons. Moreover, the minority member could argue that the extent to which certain risk indicators should be taken into account is context dependent. For example, wearing masks in the vicinity of a bank might be a legitimate reason for police officers to strip-search someone, but perhaps not on Halloween or during the annual Carnival parade.

Little is known, though, about how courts in different circumstances respond to the use of statistical data as a legal justification for differential treatment of members supposedly belonging to a certain group. On what grounds do courts regard policies involving statistical discrimination as being permissible? What role do fundamental rights play in this respect, and to what extent may the social or economic costs of highly individualized risk analysis be considered?

Statistics can serve as input in proportionality assessments. Statistics and other types of empirical evidence can provide courts with relevant information when balancing the fundamental right to equal treatment against public interests. In the US, data was provided in court cases, for instance, to show that

---

"statistical discrimination". Lippert-Rasmussen presents the following definition: "statistical discrimination occurs when there is statistical evidence which suggests that a certain group of people differs from other groups in a certain dimension, and its members are being treated disadvantageously on the basis of this information". Lippert-Rasmussen, K. (2013). Discrimination. In H. LaFollette (Ed.), *The International Encyclopedia of Ethics*. Oxford: Wiley-Blackwell. Also see Schouten, G. (2017). Discrimination and gender. In K. Lippert-Rasmussen (Ed.), *The Routledge Handbook of the Ethics of Discrimination* (1st ed.). Routledge. https://doi.org/10.4324/9781315681634 and Lippert-Rasmussen, K. (2007). Nothing personal: On statistical discrimination. *The Journal of Political Philosophy*, *15*(4), 385–403.

adoption by same-sex couples caused no harm to the healthy development of adopted children, which debunked the assumption that the prohibition would attend to the public interest of protecting children.[9] Statistical data can also inform structured proportionality analysis used by courts in different jurisdictions when balancing fundamental rights and interests. During the Covid-19 pandemic, the *Bundesverfassungsgericht* in Germany applied this framework, for instance, to evaluate whether the temporary legal measures that restricted religious gatherings (to control the spread of the virus) resulted in discrimination against religious activities compared to secular activities deemed essential by the government and not subject to these measures.[10] The proportionality analytical framework traditionally consists of four distinct steps or subtests: namely, the worthy purpose, the suitability, the necessity, and the balancing of costs and benefits (proportionality *stricto sensu*).[11] Empirical evidence can play a meaningful role in two steps of the analysis.

The first step of the test includes a normative judgment concerning whether the contested measure has a *legitimate purpose* (e.g. in the aforementioned Covid-19 cases, the protection of public health). When the legislative aim is regarded as legitimate, the court analyses whether the examined policy is *suitable* to promote this goal. Here, statistical evidence can play a relevant role to show, for instance, the effectiveness of the contested measure (e.g. is limiting the number of people in religious gatherings an effective way to control the transmission of the virus?).

The next step of the analysis concerns the *necessity* of the legislative measure to achieve the legitimate purpose. The court considers potentially more lenient alternatives for achieving that purpose, which result in fewer restrictions on

---

9 Despite the lack of empirical support for the assumption that the prohibition of adoption by same-sex couples would be suitable and necessary to achieve the legitimate aim of protecting the best interests of children, some decisions relied on this unfounded assumption. Elovitz, M. E. (1995). Adoption by lesbian and gay people: The use and mis-use of social science research. *Duke Journal of Gender Law & Policy*, *2*, 207–226. https://scholarship.law.duke.edu/djglp/vol2/iss1/13

10 See, for instance, Martínez-Torrón, J. (2021). COVID-19 and religious freedom: Some comparative perspectives. *Laws*, *10*(2), 1–16. https://EconPapers.repec.org/RePEc:gam:jlawss:v:10:y:2021:i:2:p:39-:d:557215. Bappenheim, S. T. (2020). State of emergency and religious freedom: constitutional stress in German law (art. 4 of the Basic Law for the Federal Republic of Germany). *Diresom*. https://diresom.net/2020/06/01/state-of-emergency-and-religious-free-dom-constitutional-stress-in-german-law-art-4-of-the-basic-law-for-the-federal-republic-of-germany/

11 M. Kremnitzer, T. Steiner, & A. Lang, (Eds.) (2020). *Proportionality in Action: Comparative and Empirical Perspectives on the Judicial Practice*. Cambridge University Press. https://doi.org/DOI:10.1017/9781108596268

human rights and freedoms.[12] At this stage, empirical evidence can inform the decision about the availability of less restrictive alternative measures to reach the same goal. For instance, are there options other than limiting the number of people in religious gatherings that could ensure the same level of public health protection?

The last step consists of analysing the *strict proportionality* of the public policy or civil practice that results in unequal treatment. The court then engages in a balancing exercise between the disadvantages of imposing a difference in treatment (e.g. limiting religious freedom) and the advantages of achieving a legitimate goal (e.g. limiting the spread of infectious diseases and promoting public health). In this decisive step of the analysis, a court may conclude that, despite empirical evidence that the policy is suitable and necessary to achieve a legitimate goal, the disadvantages caused by the difference in treatment outweigh the benefits. Thus, this last step shows that although empirical evidence can play a relevant role in determining whether a difference in treatment is suitable and necessary to achieve a legitimate aim, it is not the only factor in deciding whether a policy is discriminatory or not.

Second, statistics are used as evidence of disparate effects and differential treatment. They are used in anti-discrimination cases by potential victims to demonstrate in court what the disparate effects of seemingly neutral measures are for them and thereby serve as potential evidence for indirect discrimination. Suppose that a young high school graduate wants to work in retail but is refused time and again for certain jobs because she has not already spent at least ten years working in retail. Could statistics showing that a certain employer automatically refuses every applicant with less than ten years' experience in retail serve as evidence to prove in the case of rejection of an applicant that this results in age discrimination, especially since the employer has shown no interest in whether this applicant might have the skills and qualifications required for the job? And does it make a difference here whether the job advertisement explicitly mentioned the required ten years of experience?

This simple example may already show that relevant statistical data might be used to prove indirect discrimination because employers will often mention multiple reasons for refusing applicants of a certain age, sex, or ethnic background. Furthermore, employers may try to hide a particular prejudice. In the case of the example just mentioned, the employer, instead of requiring ten years of experience, might demand that applicants have a certain specific experience or skill that would be hard to acquire for younger applicants, even

12 As put by Nilsson, "this is sometimes referred to as the 'least restrictive means' rule". Nilsson, A. (2020). Same, same but different: Proportionality assessments and equality norms. *Oslo Law Review*, 7(3), 126–144. https://doi.org/10.18261/ISSN.2387-3299-2020-03-01

though this skill or experience does not seem strictly necessary if one compares this vacancy to similar vacancies in the same industry. Again, statistical employment data could potentially serve as more convincing evidence than the story of one individual job applicant. While statistical evidence does not prove whether a difference in treatment is unjustified and discriminatory, it can raise a *presumption* of discrimination. Thus, if statistics are reliable, this presumption can be enough to shift the burden of proof to the defendant (the employer in our example), who would need to reject the basis for the *prima facie* case or provide a justification for it.

Courts like the European Court of Human Rights (ECtHR) and the Court of Justice of the European Union (CJEU) acknowledge that statistical differences in treatment do not automatically prove indirect discrimination.[13] Even when it induces a presumption of discrimination and is used to shift the burden of proof, these differences may still be objectively justified by other reasons. In addition, controversies can easily arise concerning, for instance, whether the presented statistical evidence is reliable to prove disparate impacts on a group. Here again, it is interesting to learn more about how courts deal with claims that the evidence is flawed.

STATISTICAL DISCRIMINATION IN INSURANCE LAW

Most forms of discrimination are "non-instrumental" in the sense that they stem from prejudice and bigoted beliefs rather than from an attempt to achieve a specific policy objective. This differs from what is commonly called statistical discrimination, where decision-makers typically pursue a legitimate (policy) goal and rely on statistically relevant correlations between that goal and certain general features of a group. To give an example: insurance companies

---

[13] See, for instance, the ECtHR judgment of *D.H. and Others v. the Czech Republic*: "Recently, the Court had indicated in its decision in Hoogendijk (cited above) that, while statistics alone were not sufficient to prove discrimination, they could – particularly where they were undisputed – amount to *prima facie* evidence requiring the Government to provide an objective explanation of the differential treatment". *D.H. and Others v. the Czech Republic* [GC] (European Court of Human Rights 2007). On the differences that might raise a presumption of discrimination, see the Advocate General opinion in the CJEU case *Nolte v. Landesversicherungsanstalt Hannover*: "Secondly, in order to be presumed discriminatory, the measure must affect 'a far greater number of women than men' (44) or 'a considerably lower percentage of men than of women' (45) or 'far more women than men' (46)". Opinion of Advocate General Léger of 31 May 1995, paras 57–58 in ECJ, *Nolte v. Landesversicherungsanstalt Hannover* (C-317/93) ECLI:EU:C:1995:154, 14 December 1995.

frequently charge younger motorists higher insurance premiums than they do older and more experienced drivers. The reason is that insurers believe age to be a good predictor of the chances of getting into car accidents, although there will always be individual, responsible and skilful younger drivers.[14] Such practices are often regarded as acceptable in principle, but statistical generalization may sometimes result in direct or indirect discrimination.

Whether statistical generalization results in discrimination between women and men was the underlying legal question in the *Test Achats* case heard by the CJEU,[15] which revolved around Article 5 of the Directive 2004/113/EC (on equal treatment between women and men in the access to and supply of goods and services).[16] Article 5(1) prohibits the use of sex as a factor in the calculation of insurance premiums and benefits in insurance contracts entered into after December 21, 2007. By way of derogation, however, Article 5(2) determined that Member States, after this date, would still be allowed to permit exemptions from the rule of unisex premiums and benefits so long as they could ensure that the underlying actuarial and statistical data on which the calculations were based were reliable, regularly updated, and available to the public.

In 2008, a Belgian consumer organisation (abbreviated as "Test-Achats") and two individuals asked the Constitutional Court to annul the law of December 21, 2007 which made use of the exemption provided in Article 5(2) of the Directive because they believed the law was incompatible with the principle of equal treatment for men and women as enshrined in the Belgian constitution and with, among other things, Article 13 of Directive 2004/113/EC and Articles 20, 21, and 23 of the Charter of Fundamental Rights. The Constitutional Court decided to ask preliminary questions to the CJEU.

A lengthy Opinion by Advocate General (AG) Kokott laid the foundation for invalidating Article 5(2) of the Directive. According to the AG, the Council had made a conscious decision in Article 5 to adopt anti-discrimination legislation in the field of insurance, which is why she believes that Article 5(2) should be seen as an infringement of the general prohibition on discrimination

---

14 Schauer, F. (2017). Statistical (and non-statistical) discrimination. In K. Lippert-Rasmussen (Ed.), *The Routledge handbook of the ethics of discrimination*. New York: Routledge, p. 42 ff.

15 *Association des Consommateurs Test-Achats ABSL, Yann van Vugt, Charles Basseler v. Conseil des Ministres* (C-236/09) ECLI:EU:C:2011:100 (Court of Justice of the European Union 2011). See: https://eur-lex.europa.eu/legal-content/EN/TXT/?uri=CELEX%3A62009CJ0236.

16 In full: Council Directive 2004/113, Implementing the principle of equal treatment between men and women in the access to and supply of goods and services, [2004] OJ L373/37 (EC).

on the grounds of sex as laid down in, among other things, the Charter. What is interesting, though, is that the AG sometimes seems to contradict herself in the Opinion.

On the one hand, she claims there is no reason to assume that the prohibition of discrimination on grounds of sex under European Union law provides less protection than the prohibition of discrimination on the basis of race or ethnic origin, because sex would be a characteristic inseparably linked to the insured person as an individual and over which he has no influence.[17] On the other hand, she argues that discrimination on grounds of sex – with the exception of affirmative action – would only be permissible if it can be established with certainty that there are relevant differences between men and women which necessitate such discrimination.[18] This raises questions like: How is it possible that discrimination based on sex is, in principle, possible in case of "relevant differences" if sex is inseparably linked to the person as an individual? But most of all, one wonders what are to be considered "relevant differences" if these cannot be statistical differences?[19]

Of course, one may readily agree with the AG that traditional role models have changed, and life expectancy can no longer be linked to sex as much as in the past because both men and women nowadays engage in demanding and sometimes extremely stressful professional activities, and other previous differences have also changed. Nevertheless, this does not rule out that when it comes to something like life expectancy, sex may still be one of the most reliable indicators. This is especially true since *despite* all the changes in role modelling, lifestyle, and habits, the average (hence statistical) difference in life expectancy between men and women is still undeniably present. One could even have serious doubts whether there is another more precise and reliable indicator. The AG even admits that economic and social conditions and habits of insured persons are much more complicated to use as risk-indicators, but practical difficulties would not justify the use of sex as a distinguishing criterion. But again: why not? With respect to the answer to this question, Kokott appears to rely on an older opinion by AG Van Gerven in the *Ten Oever* case.[20] There he argues that while women as a group live longer than men, it is equally true that not all individual men and women exhibit the average characteristics of their sex. The question whether discrimination exists should,

---

17 Paragraph 50.

18 Paragraph 60.

19 Paragraph 52 (it is confusing that the terms sex and gender seem to be used interchangeably).

20 Joined Opinions of Advocate General Van Gerven, *Ten Oever*, ECLI:EU:C:1993:158.

according to Van Gerven, be dealt with by treating women not as a group but as individuals.[21]

Van Gerven relied for this, among other things, on the American Supreme Court's case law where actuarial factors based on sex for the calculation of contributions to pension schemes have been invalidated as an infringement of the Civil Rights Act of 1964.[22] AG Kokott follows Van Gerven and proposes that the Court should declare Article 5(2) of Directive 2004/113 to be invalid due to infringement of the prohibition of discrimination on grounds of sex more than 30 years after the Supreme Court of the United States of America held something similar with regard to pension insurance funds. Although this may sound convincing, one may still have doubts here. After all, EU legislation regulating the right to maternity leave, for instance, also treats women as a group, although not all women want to have children,[23] while some male couples might also want to have children and to be granted time to prepare for this.[24] Does the EU legislature not also treat men and women as a group here?

---

[21] Ibid para. 35. What is confusing is that AG Kokott admits, on para. 46 of her Opinion, that it is perfectly legitimate with regard to risk evaluation that group examinations are used rather than individual examinations. This looks inconsistent with the argument of injustice by generalization or, as Van Gerven puts it: not being able to treat men or women as a group instead of as purely individuals.

[22] *Los Angeles Department of Water and Power v. Manhart*, 435 U.S. 702, 98 S. Ct. 1370 (1978). See also: *Arizona Governing Committee for Tax Deferred Annuity and Deferred Compensation Plans v. Norris*, 463 U.S. 1073, 103 S. Ct. 3492 (1983).

[23] AG Kokott justifies in a footnote (38) to her Opinion the fact that male insured persons are enlisted to finance the costs related to pregnancy and maternity of women by "the principle of causation", because women can only become pregnant by involving a man. But what she seems to forget here is not only that some individuals deliberately choose not to have children, but that some same-sex couples may have children with the help of sperm donors, who agreed to help them under the condition of remaining anonymous and not having to be involved in the family life of the recipient parents and their future children. Why would these individuals need to bear the costs of other people's wish to have children from this perspective? We argue, instead, that although potentially causing "injustice by generalization" against people who decide not to have children or do so without personally involving a man, the distribution of costs of maternity leave among society is admitted for promoting common good aims; for instance, the well-being of children and fair employment conditions for women who have children.

[24] If we apply the logic of individualization of rights to maternity leave systems, these rules can create "injustice by generalization" virtually against every parent that does not give birth to a child (unless the legislation extends the same rights to them).

Regarding the latter, is it not unavoidable that when we try to make *general* rules for consumers, workers, refugees etc. we almost always treat them as a group – because that is what legal rules do? They work with general classifications, such as: "the reasonable consumer" or "a good housekeeper". These generalizations do not treat people as individuals, just as actuarial indicators do not, but turn them into "ideal types" that represent certain normatively desired general features. Normally, we do not consider such classifications to be discriminatory. So why would we suddenly find considering average life expectancy differences between men and women in insurance premiums discriminatory? What is the normative basis for the legally required solidarity here? Moreover, some of the differences between men and women surely have to do with culture, social pressure, and lifestyle but why would this, for example, justify that female drivers should pay for higher insurance premiums because men cause more traffic accidents due to stereotypical behaviour?

Because of these kinds of controversies, it is perhaps no surprise that the Court of Justice is far more succinct in its reasoning than the AG. The Court simply states that the Article 5(2) exemption from the rule of unisex premiums and benefits, without temporal limitation, works against the objective of equal treatment between men and women, which is the purpose of Directive 2004/113. That would be incompatible with Articles 21 and 23 of the Charter. Therefore, the derogation by Article 5(2) must, according to the Court, be considered invalid from December 21, 2012 onwards, upon the expiration of an appropriate transitional period.

Even after the CJEU ruled in the *Test-Achats* case, whether sex is a relevant risk-rating factor in (life) insurance remains a contentious issue. Avraham, for example, has shown that some US courts find that automobile insurance rates based upon sex are fair unless those sex-based rating factors are actuarially unsound, while others do not allow this.[25] What is more striking, though, is that while the CJEU drew inspiration from the US Supreme Court in *City of Los Angeles v. Manhart* and *Arizona Governing Comm. v. Norris*, which prohibited sex as a relevant factor to discriminate between men and women in pension insurance (ruling out the use of sex in life insurance schemes), the European Commission has argued that this does not apply to pensions. Article 9[1][h] of Directive 2006/54/EC still allows for the setting of different levels of contributions between men and women for certain defined pension contribution schemes when these can be justified by actuarial factors.

It is difficult to see why premiums for life insurance and contributions to pension benefit schemes should be treated differently when it comes to the

---

25 Avraham, R. (2017). Discrimination and Insurance. In K. Lippert-Rasmussen (Ed.), *The Routledge Handbook to Discrimination* (pp. 335–347). Routledge.

use of actuarial differences in life expectancy between men and women. Apart from that, there is a debate on actuarial fairness versus socio-economic fairness. Adherents to the first perspective want to avoid the situation where the unlucky sex with shorter lives needs to subsidize the lucky group with better life expectancy. Therefore, it relies on statistical differences between the sexes when it comes to life expectancy. Conversely, those who believe that differences in socio-economic conditions ultimately determine life expectancy reject this idea. According to this group, the idea is that as women increasingly get more full-time jobs in more demanding working environments, the existing life-expectancy differences will sooner or later level out.[26]

STATISTICAL DISCRIMINATION IN PUBLIC HEALTH: BLOOD DONATION BY GAY AND BISEXUAL MEN

A few years following the *Test-Achats* judgment, a case involving statistical discrimination by public health agencies reached the CJEU. *Geoffrey Léger v Ministre des Affaires Sociales, de la Santé et des Droits des femmes, Établissement français du sang* (C-528/13)[27] (hereafter *Léger*) concerns the compatibility of permanent limitations of blood donation to men who had sexual relations with other men (MSM) with EU legislation and the right to non-discrimination.[28]

Geoffrey Léger, a French citizen, brought an action before the Administrative Court of Strasbourg seeking the annulment of a decision by the French Blood Agency in Metz refusing his blood donation on the grounds that he had had sexual relations with another man. The doctor in charge of blood donations based this decision on a French Decree of January 2009 which prescribed a permanent deferral to blood donation for MSM. This act relied on the empirical assumption that sex between men was considered to put the group of MSM at a high risk of contracting severe infectious diseases that can be transmitted by blood. Therefore, allowing blood donations by this demographic would lead to an increased risk for blood recipients of being exposed to these diseases.

---

26 De Baere, G. & Goessens, E. (2012). Gender differentiation in insurance contracts after the judgment in case C-236/09, Association Belge des Consommateurs Test-Achats ASBL v. Conseil des Ministres. *Columbia Journal of European Law, 18*(339), 350–351.

27 *Geoffrey Léger v. Ministre des Affaires sociales, de la Santé et des Droits des femmes and Etablissement français du sang* (C-528/13) ECLI:EU:C:2015:288 (Court of Justice of the European Union 2015).

28 Despite not directly differentiating men for their sexual orientation, the Decree in France affected virtually all gay or bisexual men who had been sexually active.

The Administrative Court referred a preliminary question to the CJEU as to whether the existence of a permanent deferral to donate blood for MSM by a Member State was consistent with point 2.1 of Annex III of EU Directive 2004/33/EC. This EU norm provides a blood donation deferral to persons whose sexual behaviour puts them at high risk of acquiring severe infectious diseases.

In 2015 the CJEU ruled that the Directive would allow a Member State to justify a permanent deferral under three cumulative conditions. As the first step in this analysis, a State must establish whether sex between men puts the group of MSM at a high risk of acquiring severe infectious diseases based on reliable and up to date medical, scientific, and epidemiological data and knowledge. In case of actual high risk, the State must evaluate the proportionality of a permanent deferral in light of other effective methods for detecting those infectious diseases. In the absence of such methods, the State should still consider the availability of any other less onerous method capable of ensuring a high level of health protection of the recipients. Thus, only a scenario of high epidemiological risk, no effective detection techniques, and no alternative measures apt to promote safe blood donations would justify a permanent deferral.

Despite criticism of the cautious approach against discrimination and stigmatization of gay and bisexual men,[29] the decision in *Léger* resonated with French public policy, which progressively eased restrictions on MSM blood donation. In the wake of the judgment, French officials announced a policy change to lift the decade-old permanent deferral that had been in force in the country since the outbreak of HIV. As of 2016, the legislator limited the deferral period to 12 months since the last sexual contact,[30] adding that the effects of the policy would be periodically monitored. Assuming the new policy

---

[29] On a Case Note about *Léger*, Belavusau commented that "The cautious approach adopted by the Court seems even more problematic considering that specifically targeting the MSM population relies on cultural demeaning representations of gay and bisexual sexualities connected to promiscuity. This reinforces the division between 'virtuous straights' and 'contagious gays' and supports the perception of gays as 'dangerous' or as social outcasts. Overall, the EU Court seems to have missed a timely occasion to explain why – both legally and politically – such health policies are discriminatory and humiliating". Belavusau, U. (2016). Towards EU sexual risk regulation: Restrictions on blood donation as infringement of active citizenship. *European Journal of Risk Regulation*, *7*(4), 801–809. https://doi.org/10.1017/S1867299X00010230

[30] Nordstrom, L. (2016). After 30-year ban, gay men in France allowed to donate blood. *France 24*. https://www.france24.com/en/20160711-france-gay-men-30-year-ban-donate-blood-lgbt-rights-equality

would not increase health risks, the deferral period should gradually align with the one for heterosexual donors.[31] In this context, in April 2020, a new blood donation selection criterion was introduced, reducing the deferral to four months.[32] In June 2020, 100 members of the French National Assembly voted for an amendment to allow MSM to donate blood under the same conditions as heterosexual men, later approved as part of the 2021 bioethics law, removing the specific abstinence requirement for MSM.[33] The reform was later implemented in 2022 via administrative regulations introducing a uniform, behavior-based blood-donation screening system applicable to all donors.[34] In 2025, the *Établissement français du sang* announced the deletion of records containing sexual-orientation data, aligning its administrative practices with the post-2022 non-discriminatory blood-donation framework.[35]

The *Léger* case also had implications for other EU Member States applying a similar policy of permanently excluding homosexuals from blood donation.[36] In 2017, Belgium amended its legislation to adapt to the CJEU ruling. The Law of August 11, 2017 inserted parameters for a temporary exclusion of prospective blood donors in the Annex to the existing Law of July 5, 1994. In a

---

31 Breeden, A. (2015). France to lift ban on gay men donating blood. *The New York Times*. https://www.nytimes.com/2015/11/05/world/europe/france-gay-blood-donation.html

32 See: https://www.lexpress.fr/actualite/societe/sante/don-du-sang-la-periode-d-abstinence-imposee-aux-homosexuels-reduite-d-un-an-a-4-mois_2090073.html

33 Pollet, M. (2020). French MPs debate ending restrictions on gay blood donors. *Euronews*. https://www.euronews.com/2020/07/29/french-mps-debate-ending-restrictions-on-gay-blood-donorshttps://www.info.gouv.fr/actualite/don-du-sang-suppression-du-critere-d-orientation-sexuellehttps://www.info.gouv.fr/actualite/don-du-sang-suppression-du-critere-d-orientation-sexuellehttps://www.info.gouv.fr/actualite/don-du-sang-suppression-du-critere-d-orientation-sexuelle

34 Gouvernement français. (2022, January 12). Don du sang: suppression du critère d'orientation sexuelle. *info.gouv.fr*. https://www.info.gouv.fr/actualite/don-du-sang-suppression-du-critere-d-orientation-sexuellehttps://www.info.gouv.fr/actualite/don-du-sang-suppression-du-critere-d-orientation-sexuelle

35 L'Établissement français du sang. (2025, September 30). *L'Établissement français du sang a effacé les anciennes données de contre indications au don de sang relatives à des relations sexuelles entre hommes* [Press release]. https://presse.efs.sante.fr/actualites/letablissement-francais-du-sang-a-efface-les-anciennes-donnees-de-contre-indications-au-don-de-sang-relatives-a-des-relations-sexuelles-entre-hommes-a01c2-08a0a.html

36 It is also worth noting the global feature of the legal issue, with cases brought to the judiciary across jurisdictions. See, for instance: *Thangjam Santa Singh v. Union Of India* (Supreme Court of India Pending).

nutshell, the Belgian parliament determined a transition from a permanent to a temporary exclusion policy by setting up a 12-month deferral period to MSM and any person having an MSM as a sexual partner. Despite the mitigation of the prohibition, the question remained whether a temporary deferral would still violate the principle of equal treatment. Against this backdrop, two non-profit LGBTQI+ organizations in 2018 challenged this rule before the Belgian Constitutional Court for being discriminatory by treating all MSM differently from other blood donors without differentiating between MSM with or without risky sexual behaviour.[37] Relying on scientific reports presented by the legislator, the Belgian Constitutional Court held the 12-month deferral to be justified, only annulling the challenged legal provision for plasma donations.

It is interesting to compare the Belgian decision to a case decided by the Brazilian Supreme Court in 2020,[38] where a provision with a similar content was challenged: namely, a 12-month blood donation deferral since the last sexual contact directed to MSM and to any person who had an MSM as a sexual partner. This case resulted in a different outcome. Unlike the Belgian Constitutional Court, the Brazilian Supreme Court ultimately concluded that the temporary deferral resulted in unjustifiable discrimination against MSM, invalidating its legal basis. One of the things that could explain the difference in outcome is the approach to scientific and normative issues by the two courts.

In Belgium, the Constitutional Court carried out a proportionality assessment of the challenged policy. In the review of the legislative purpose, the court acknowledged as legitimate the objective of ensuring the quality of the donated blood and the safety of the transfusion chain in the interest of public health. The court considered that the 12-month ban was based on up-to-date scientific knowledge and reliable statistical data from Belgium indicating that male-to-male sexual contact, even by men in a stable monogamous relationship, would be associated with a high risk of acquiring infectious diseases transmissible by blood, such as HIV I and II, hepatitis B and C, and syphilis.

Next, it assessed the availability of detection techniques and other mechanisms that might serve as an alternative for a donation ban. Regarding the first, the court pointed to the "window period" before infectious diseases can be noticed. This poses a residual risk non-detectable by the available technology. This circumstance would make a temporary deferral for groups with a high risk of acquiring infectious diseases (incidence rate) and higher rates of these diseases (prevalence rate) a necessary additional safety measure.

---

37 Arrest nr. 122/2019 van 26 September 2019, (Het Grondwettelijk Hof 2019). https://www.ejustice.just.fgov.be/cgi/article_body.pl?language=nl&caller=summary&pub_date=19-11-12&numac=2019204488

38 ADI 5.543/DF (Supremo Tribunal Federal 2020). http://portal.stf.jus.br/processos/detalhe.asp?incidente=4996495.

Finally, the court noted that existing scientific research was unclear as to whether a shorter ban or other alternative measures alone[39] could provide the same (high) level of health protection/safety as the ban by *not increasing the residual risk of transmission of infectious diseases by transfusion*. This fact should be reassessed every two years, according to the Belgian legislation. The court also considered the fact that in countries performing individual risk assessments, such as Italy and Spain, HIV seroconversions among known donors were ten times higher than in Belgium. Therefore the court decided that the legislature could, for the time being, reasonably assume that the scientific evidence was insufficient to allow a ban for less than 12 months deferral. Concerning the strict proportionality test, the court balanced, on the one hand, the interest of MSM in donating blood and, on the other hand, the interest of blood recipients in obtaining donor blood free of severe infectious diseases. It noted that the State:

> may reasonably consider, without infringing the principle of equality and non-discrimination, that the protection of the health, and indeed the life, of the recipients of blood is of such fundamental importance that it requires the elimination of all options which do not afford the recipients a sufficiently high level of health protection.[40]

Accordingly, the court found the 12-month deferral to blood donations by MSM proportional. The only exception being made concerned the donation of fresh frozen plasma collected by apheresis and secured by quarantine. For this case, given the presented evidence that scientific techniques could reduce the residual risk related to the window period to an acceptable level or even eliminate this risk, the judges concluded that there was no justification for the exclusion period in this situation.[41]

---

39 For instance, the combination of testing with pre-donation questionnaires and interviews.

40 See item B.14.5 of the ruling for the original version in Dutch.

41 The court noted in section B.18.4 that the Superior Health Council analyzed numerous technical and practical options, quoting a Parliamentary Document that stated: "With regards to the scientifically established options (such as a retention period for inactivated plasma, the viro-inactivation using a validated method, the temporary exclusion for 12 months, and the securisation of plasma for fractionation), it would be possible to invoke one or more measures less restrictive than the permanent deferral (Parl. St., Room, 2016-2017, DOC 54-2599/001, p. 11)". However, it is not clear from the parliamentary preparations for what reasons that technique was not taken into account, even though that technique entails less burden to ensure a high level of safety of the transfusion chain than the exclusion of MSM for a period of 12 months since the last sexual contact between men.

In a different direction, the Brazilian Supreme Court invalidated regulations that provided a 12-month blood donation deferral for MSM and their sexual partners. The prevailing votes highlighted that by considering risky groups rather than risky behaviour, the rules presumed that gay and bisexual men would be possible vectors of transmission of various diseases because of their sexual orientation. That assumption is seen as incompatible with the right to equality and human dignity. By adopting this perspective, the regulations would (unintentionally) prohibit the free exercise of sexuality to this group for the empathetic practice of donating blood, impacting its members disproportionately. Additionally, the norms would unlawfully hinder the self-determination of this group.[42]

The judges barely mentioned the scientific inputs presented during the trial. One of the judges remarked that a 12-month restriction would be disproportionate considering technological advances allowing for the detection of new infectious diseases in 15 days. The same judge also noted that the transmission rate of HIV by blood transfusion in countries that had lifted the restriction would be very similar to the numbers in Brazil. Unlike the Belgian court,

---

42 It is also worth noting that the Covid-19 pandemic reignited this debate across the globe, bringing to light an additional factor in governments' evaluation of blood donation criteria: namely, the decrease of blood donations caused by the time-based deferrals to MSM against the urgent need for blood donations. These circumstances were considered, for instance, in the decision of the US Food and Drug Administration (FDA) to reduce the deferral period for MSM from its previous duration of one year to three months. Likewise, during the pandemic in Ireland, the importation of blood donation from the UK, which has less stringent requirements relative to the blood donation by MSM, caught the public and media attention. The question was also argued in a recent case before the Indian Supreme Court, where a member of the transgender community challenged the national blood donation guidelines banning transgender persons, members of the gay community, and sex workers from donating blood. In the context of the Covid-19 pandemic, the plaintiff argued that the guidelines perpetuated a stigma and harmed many members of the community who were unable to get blood donations from their trans relatives. See: Park, C., Gellman, C., O'Brien, M., Eidelberg, A., Subudhi, I., Gorodetsky, E. F., Asriel, B., Furlow, A., Mullen, M., Nadkarni, G., Somani, S., Sigel, K., & Reich, D. L. (2021). Blood donation and COVID-19: Reconsidering the 3-month deferral policy for gay, bisexual, transgender, and other men who have sex with men. *American Journal of Public Health*, *111*(2), 247–252. https://doi.org/10.2105/ajph.2020.305974, *Thangjam Santa Singh v. Union Of India* (Supreme Court of India Pending); Thompson, S. (2021). Is it time to lift restrictions on sexually active gay men giving blood? *The Irish Times*. https://www.irishtimes.com/life-and-style/health-family/is-it-time-to-lift-restrictions-on-sexually-active-gay-men-giving-blood-1.4636352

some of the votes by the Brazilian Supreme Court stated that the lack of conclusive evidence on the efficacy of alternative measures (e.g., serological tests) to promote a high safety level could not serve as a justification for a 12-month deferral. One of the votes suggested that even in a scenario of more scientific uncertainty, the deferral could not be permitted, given that it was disproportionate. To amplify the argument, one of the judges mentioned that, according to the 2018 HIV epidemiological report, the male population in Brazil had an HIV contamination rate more than two times higher than that of women. Nevertheless, the legislation does not prohibit – and should rightfully not do so – men as a group from donating blood. Similarly, statistics concerning the increase of incidence of HIV among the elderly population would not justify a ban for this group. Another argument the court accepted referred to injustice by generalization, as the law would not differentiate between MSM who had not engaged in risky sexual behaviour (e.g. unprotected sex or sex with multiple partners) and those who did engage in unsafe sex. The norm would also impermissibly distinguish between different types of sexual relationships (same-sex versus non-same sex). While the first group would be unsuitable for blood donation even when using protective measures, the second group would in principle qualify as donors despite potentially engaging in risky sexual behaviour.

The exploratory case study of blood donation cases reveals that scientific evidence may provide relevant inputs for proportionality assessments of potentially discriminatory policies. The Belgian case illustrates how the evidence on safe alternatives to a 12-month deferral played a role in invalidating the contested measure, having influenced the outcome of the judgment concerning plasma donations. The analysis shows, moreover, that proffering scientific knowledge by the parties, based on reliable sources and a high level of certainty, can put an argumentative burden on the courts, which need to justify more extensively when they deviate from the scientific findings presented. In the Belgian case, once scientific evidence indicated that a temporary ban would be unnecessary to promote the safety of blood donations, the empirical justification for a prohibition dissolved. To keep the deferral for plasma donations, the court would need to put forward other arguments to justify why that measure would still be necessary.

The comparison also reveals that in cases where there is no clear scientific evidence, courts seem inclined to solve the issue through a strict proportionality test. Judges balanced, on the one side, the risk of increasing transmission of infectious diseases and, on the other hand, the risk of unjustly restricting individual self-determination, causing stigmatization of a historically disadvantaged group in society, and limiting the number of blood donors. Interestingly, the courts' decisions show how this balancing act can result in diverging conclusions depending on the approach adopted. By adopting a more risk-averse position and applying the precautionary principle, the Belgian court concluded that the lack of scientific evidence did not allow lifting the deferral and required more evidence. Conversely, by assuming a principle-oriented line of reasoning, the Brazilian Court judged that statistical data did not justify a discriminatory treatment. Together, the cases show that even the presence of clear and trustworthy evidence will not automatically determine the outcome of a proportionality assessment. Even in a scenario of more scientific certainty on the necessity of the 12-month restriction to promote the safety of blood donation banks, judges could still invalidate the regulation by relying on a human rights-based approach. Through a justified strict proportionality balance, a court could conclude, for instance, that the disadvantages of causing injustice by generalization would outweigh the (possible) public health benefits sought by the norm of reducing the risks of transmitting infectious diseases.

This poses a dilemma. Pierik and Verweij argue that, while "refraining from donor selection is clearly preferable from the perspective of equal treatment", such a choice "will inevitably result in a higher risk of transfusion-transmitted HIV-infections".[43] For the authors, it would be up to society at large to decide between minimizing risks for blood recipients or treating all citizens as equals. The latter – leaving it "to society at large" – might be a solution in an ideal world. In the real world, such complex cases will inevitably reach courts, which requires, at a minimum, transparency about the balancing of interests via a proportionality assessment. Whereas the existence of reliable scientific evidence on the suitability and necessity of a governmental decision is not a one-way street leading to an inevitable judicial verdict, it has, nonetheless, the potential to place an argumentative burden on the parties and the courts. In this light, while maintaining judicial autonomy, scientific evidence can contribute to better-motivated decisions where judges justify why they have reached a certain decision.

STATISTICAL DISCRIMINATION IN LABOUR LAW: COMPULSORY RETIREMENT

Labour law is a prolific field for anti-discrimination disputes based on grounds such as age, origin, gender, religion or belief, and sexual orientation. This can take place in different circumstances – e.g. biased recruitment processes, disparate treatment in promotions and career opportunities, or prejudiced dismissals. A typical case that emerges in this context concerns compulsory

43 Pierik, R. H. M., & Verweij, M. F. (2022). Facing difficult but unavoidable choices: Blood safety, donor selection, and MSM deferral. *Bioethics*, *36*(8), 840–848. https://doi.org/10.1111/bioe.13063

retirement for employees. Across jurisdictions, courts are asked to decide whether such rules result in direct age discrimination against civil servants or private-sector workers.

Article 6(1) of the Council Directive 2000/78/EC[44] allows EU Member States to provide that a policy imposing a difference of treatment based on age may be justified as long as it has a legitimate aim of public interest and is proportional to meet these goals. On diverse occasions, the CJEU clarified whether the objective of certain mandatory retirement policies, such as promoting career opportunities to younger workers, more diversity in the workplace, or saving costs for the employer, were considered legitimate within the meaning of the Directive.[45]

For the purposes of this chapter, the ruling in *Fuchs and Peter Köhler v. Land Hessen*[46] stands out in the European Court's case law for addressing evidentiary aspects of proportionality assessments. To identify the roles that statistical data can play in this type of case, we start the analysis with this CJEU judgment in *Fuchs & Köhler.* Next, we investigate several decisions by domestic courts and tribunals in the UK that applied the guidelines set by the CJEU in *Fuchs & Köhler* in order to see to what extent this happens in a consistent manner.

The preliminary ruling in *Fuchs & Köhler* concerns the justification for a rule of the German state of Hessen that provided for the compulsory retirement of permanent civil servants at the age of 65, while simultaneously allowing the postponement of retirement for an extra year in the interests of the service. Affected by this policy, two State prosecutors alleged discrimination on the grounds of age before the Administrative Court of Frankfurt am Main. In the course of the main proceedings, the German court refers multiple questions to the CJEU regarding (i) whether particular legislative aims (e.g. creating a favourable age structure and planned staff departure) meet with the standards of EU law; (ii) what information Member States must produce to demonstrate the appropriateness and necessity of the retirement policy and whether they should provide "statistics or precise data with figures"; and (iii) whether the

---

44 Council Directive 2000/78/EC of 27 November 2000 establishing a general framework for equal treatment in employment and occupation (2000).

45 See, for instance, *Domnica Petersen v. Berufungsausschuss für Zahnärzte für den Bezirk Westfalen-Lippe* (C-341/08) ECLI:EU:C:2010:4 (Court of Justice of the European Union 2010), *Vasil Ivanov Georgiev v. Tehnicheski universitet – Sofia, filial Plovdiv* (C-250/09C-250/09 & C-268/09) ECLI:EU:C:2010:699 (Court of Justice of the European Union 2010).

46 *Gerhard Fuchs* (C-159/10), *Peter Köhler* (C-160/10) *v. Land Hessen* ECLI:EU:C:2011:508 (Court of Justice of the European Union 2011).

law was systematically coherent with other legal provisions – for instance, allowing elected civil servants to remain in their posts beyond the age of 65.

In 2011, the European Court of Justice ruled that the challenged law could be justified by the aims of "establishing a balanced age structure in order to encourage the recruitment and promotion of young people, to improve personnel management and thereby to prevent disputes concerning employees' fitness to work beyond a certain age".[47] Nonetheless, what makes *Fuchs & Köhler* particularly interesting is not the specification of legitimate goals for mandatory retirement policies, which had already been done by the court in prior cases, but the conclusions on the role of statistical evidence in such disputes. By referring to its jurisprudence in *Age Concern England*,[48] the court first rejects as evidence mere generalizations claiming that a measure is likely to contribute to social or employment policy objectives in the public interest. The burden to prove the legitimacy of the aim relied on as a justification would fall on Member States. In the court's words: "Article 6(1) of Directive 2000/78 imposes on Member States the burden of establishing to a high standard of proof the legitimacy of the aim relied on as a justification".[49]

In this vein, the court elucidates that besides not appearing unreasonable in light of the aim pursued, the appropriateness and necessity of a mandatory retirement policy to pursue a legitimate goal must be supported by evidence. It also follows from the judgment that national courts would keep a "broad discretion" to assess the evidence and establish its probative value according to the rules of national law. The evidence adduced would not need to comprise statistical data, but might include it.[50]

Following the CJEU preliminary ruling, the Frankfurt am Main Administrative Court decided that the general age limit for automatic retirement of civil servants was not justified under EU Directive 2000/78, because it resulted in discrimination against the applicant. One of the central aims alleged by the defendant consisted of promoting a favourable age stratification in the justice system. As the policy would create new vacancies, this would result in more opportunities for younger professionals and a balance between generations. The simultaneous presence of employees at the beginning of their careers and a more advanced stage would enable the exchange

---

[47] Ibid. § 68.

[48] *The Queen on the application of: The Incorporated Trustees of the National Council on Ageing (Age Concern England) v. Secretary of State for Business, Enterprise and Regulatory Reform* (C-388/07) ECLI:EU:C:2009:128 (Court of Justice of the European Union 2009).

[49] *Fuchs & Köhler v. Land Hessen* (Court of Justice of the European Union 2011), § 70.

[50] Ibid. § 82.

of experience and introduction of fresh perspectives and knowledge between older and younger employees, ultimately resulting in the provision of a high-quality public justice service. By relying on figures provided by the defendant regarding, for instance, the rate of vacancy creation by the retirement policy and the number of hirings relative to the retirements due to the age limit, the court concluded that the regulation would not achieve the objective in a sufficiently systematic and coherent manner. Data showed that the vacant posts would not result in new hires in at least 43.3% of the cases. According to the court, this low recruitment rate (in contrast to the retirements) would not have been adequately explained by the state. The domestic court pointed out that the numbers would indicate that the retirement age limit scheme achieved the indicated aims only to a limited extent while allowing for budgetary savings. It notes, in this regard, that according to the CJEU case law, a fiscal objective could not alone justify the measure but only do so when associated with other social policy objectives.

Besides not resulting in new hirings to a certain extent, the percentage of employees retired by reaching the age limit would be very small (3% in 2006, 4.6% in 2009, and 4.8% in 2010). Of these employees, only a reduced number would request an extension of employment (5.7%). The fact that at least 94% of the employees would retire anyway at 65 years would suggest a limited impact on new vacancies and consequently on recruits. As the chances of promotion in the career lost because of employment above the age limit would be small compared to the total number of vacancies, the policy would also not sufficiently achieve intergenerational justice related to the promotion opportunities for younger employees.

The judgment reveals that empirical evidence can also play a role in proportionality assessments showing to what extent a policy is adequate to achieve a legitimate aim. Such information can influence the court's assessment of strict proportionality when it concludes, for instance, that a limited policy effect would not outweigh the discriminatory effect. The determination of the yardstick for this final balancing exercise remains, nevertheless, at the court's discretion.

In the UK, the Employment Equality (Age) Regulations 2006[51] set the measure by which the UK transposed Council Directive 2000/78/EC, establishing a general framework for equal treatment in employment and occupation. The Regulations allowed employers to force employees to retire at the age of 65. However, the Regulations were replaced by the Equality Act 2010, which provides that mandatory retirement ages are only lawful if the decision

---

51 Employment Equality (Age) Regulations 2006 (SI 2006/1031).

by the employer can be "objectively justified" as proportionate to achieving a legitimate aim.

In *Seldon v. Clarkson Wright & Jakes*,[52] the UK Supreme Court determined what may count as a legitimate aim. Seldon was a partner at Clarkson Wright & Jakes solicitors, where a partnership deed determined that the retirement age for all partners was set at 65. He asked the firm if he could stay after his 65th birthday, but his request was declined, although the firm did offer him £30,000 as a goodwill gesture to reflect his long-time service to the firm. Seldon argued that the decline of his request would result in direct age discrimination. His employer, however, claimed there would be legitimate aims to stick to the retirement age of 65.

The Employment Tribunal (ET) accepted three of the aims of the retirement policy of Clarkson Wright & Jakes, namely: 1) ensuring that associates are given the opportunity of partnership after a reasonable period, thereby ensuring that they stay with the firm; 2) facilitating the planning of the partnership and workforce by having a realistic long-term expectation as to when vacancies will arise; and 3) limiting the need to expel partners by way of performance management, thus contributing to a congenial and supportive corporate culture.[53]

The ET decided that the use of a compulsory retirement clause was a proportionate means of achieving these aims. Seldon appealed to the Employment Appeal Tribunal (EAT) and the Court of Appeal,[54] but was largely unsuccessful in both instances, although the EAT decided that the employment tribunal ought to further consider whether 65 was the right age to choose to meet the legitimate aims in a proportionate way. The Court of Appeal dismissed the case, concluding that the aim to justify discriminatory action related only to the government and legislation enacted by it, but not to a private employer. It was therefore held sufficient for the employer's aims to be consistent with the government's social and labour policy.

Seldon then appealed to the UK Supreme Court, which had to decide three issues: (1) whether any or all of the three aims of the retirement clause identified by the ET were legitimate for justifying direct age discrimination; (2) whether the firm had not only to justify the retirement clause generally but also its application in the individual case; and (3) whether the ET was right to conclude that relying on the retirement clause in this case was a proportionate means of achieving any or all of the identified aims.

---

52 *Seldon v. Clarkson Wright & Jakes* [2012] UKSC 16; [2012] I.C.R. 716.

53 *Seldon* [2012] UKSC 16; [2012] I.C.R. 716 § 11.

54 Employment Appeal Tribunal [2009] I.R.L.R. 267 and Court of Appeal [2010] EWCA Civ 899; [2011] I.C.R. 60.

Regarding the first question, Lady Hale noticed that employers and partnerships can establish a legitimate aim. However, this aim must pursue an objective of a public interest nature, it must conform to UK social policy aims, and it must also be proportionate and necessary. She then argued that inter-generational fairness and preserving the dignity of older workers can be legitimate aims. Inter-generational fairness concerns creating opportunities for younger people to join the workforce, as well as ensuring a balanced workforce. Dignity concerns protecting older people who may underperform and avoiding their potential humiliation in this regard. With respect to the second question, the Court decided that the partnership only needed to demonstrate that the mandatory age requirement can be justified as a general rule:

> I would accept that where it is justified to have a general rule, then the existence of that rule will usually justify the treatment which results from it. In the particular context of inter-generational fairness, it must be relevant that at an earlier stage in his life, a partner or employee may well have benefited from a rule which obliged his seniors to retire at a particular age. Nor can it be entirely irrelevant that the rule in question was re-negotiated comparatively recently between the partners.[55]

Overall, the court found that the aims of the partnership were legitimate, as staff retention and workforce planning were social policy aims that fell within the realm of inter-generational fairness, while limiting the need to expel partners due to poor performance was compatible with employee/partner dignity. Concerning the third question, the Supreme Court decided that this would have to be decided by the ET, as it had not been demonstrated that the mandatory retirement age of 65 was an appropriate means of achieving the third aim, thereby indicating that inter-generational fairness and employee dignity could, in principle, justify almost any retirement age, but this would not automatically mean that the age of 65 would be proportionate in this situation.

Since the UK Supreme Court requires that employers opting for a mandatory retirement policy support this policy with a "legitimate aim", and need to prove that the application of the policy in individual circumstances is a "proportionate measure" to serve this aim, most employers abandoned mandatory retirement ages. Oxford University, however, has continued a mandatory retirement age for its faculty. Oxford introduced an Employer's Justified Retirement Age ("the EJRA") policy requiring employees to retire at the age of 67 and adopted procedures allowing for employees to make an application to work beyond the EJRA of 67. The EAT handed down judgment in two conjoined appeals concerning age discrimination and unfair dismissal arising out of the EJRA at Oxford University and its constituent Colleges in the cases of

---

55 *Seldon* § 65.

Pitcher and *Ewart*.[56] Interestingly, this policy has led to two judgments with opposite outcomes by the ETs.

Pitcher was an associate professor of English Literature, employed jointly by the university and St John's College. Both employers refused his application for an extension to work beyond the EJRA age of 67 years. Although the university and St John's College acknowledged that the mandatory retirement rule was less favourable treatment on the basis of age, they argued that the EJRA was a proportionate means of pursuing the legitimate aims of ensuring there were opportunities for: 1) progression for younger academics; 2) facilitating succession planning; and 3) promoting equality and diversity (providing opportunities for women, younger academic staff, those of a different race, and those with disabilities). The EJRA was said to facilitate these aims by ensuring vacancy creation was not delayed and recruitment could take place from a younger and more diverse cohort of applicants.

Although the ET acknowledged there was limited evidence to demonstrate the impact of the mandatory retirement on the three social policy aims because the EJRA was relatively new,[57] it gave weight to survey evidence regarding those who would have continued in employment if the EJRA had not been there. The survey showed that 24% of the retired employees would have worked a further three years. That would mean that the number of those retiring would be much lower if there had been no EJRA.[58] On the issue of proportionality, the ET further considered that the mandatory retirement age of 67 had been decided after careful consultation of staff, unions, and other interest groups, whereas negotiated and (voluntary) financial induced departures were considered too expensive. Moreover, the claimant was given the opportunity to persuade the EJRA Panel that he should be retained, and his application was considered in a fair manner, but the panel found he did not meet the requirements for an extension. Finally, the forced retirement would not have to divorce Professor Pitcher from academic life, as he could continue to use the facilities and even obtain research funding. Hence, the application of the mandatory retirement policy was considered proportionate.

Ewart worked as an associate professor in the Department of (atomic and laser) Physics at Oxford. He was initially due to retire in September 2015 but was given a two-year extension of his contract. The revised EJRA of 2015 stated that second extensions would only be granted exceptionally

---

56 *Pitcher v. (1) The Chancellor, Masters and Scholars of the University of Oxford (2) The President and Scholars of the College of St John the Baptist in the University of Oxford* EA-2019-000638-RN and *Ewart v. The Chancellor, Masters and Scholars of the University of Oxford* EA-2020-000128-RN.

57 Referring to: *Air Products Plc v. Cockram* [2018] I.R.L.R. 755.

58 § 369.

in case of unforeseeable circumstances frustrating the purpose of the original extension. Nevertheless, Ewart applied for a second extension because five of his eight research projects would be delayed for unforeseeable reasons. However, his second extension was denied and he therefore appealed to a different ET than Pitcher, where the university invoked highly similar policy aims for mandatory retirement as in Pitcher's case, of which the ET accepted four as legitimate, namely: safeguarding high academic standards, inter-generational fairness, facilitation of succession planning, and promoting equality and diversity.

This time, the ET found the refusal of the contract extension disproportionate. The university was unable to show sufficient evidence that the EJRA was effective in achieving the aims of the retirement policy since it was in this case not "so obvious" that it would not require evidence. A statistical analysis provided by Ewart showed that the vacancies rate created by the EJRA would be rather trivial (2–4%). The ET thus found that there was insufficient proof that the EJRA effectively contributed to the realisation of the legitimate aims of Oxford's retirement policy. It further found that since the discriminatory impact against Ewart was severe, and not significantly mitigated by the extension provisions, the EJRA was not shown to be proportionate. The ET concluded that: "The increase in the number of vacancies in support of the legitimate aim is trivial in comparison with the discriminatory effect".[59]

An appeal was filed in both *Pitcher* and *Ewart*, but the EAT in both cases decided to leave the decisions of the ET on the proportionality of the mandatory retirement intact, even though the employment tribunals came to opposite conclusions concerning the same employer (Oxford University) in quite similar cases. The EAT seemed to find several factors relevant, such as the absence of statistical evidence in the *Pitcher* case, which was heard when the EJRA was still relatively new, thus making it difficult for the employer to prove the effects of its policy other than via a survey. Secondly, some of the facts seemed to show slight differences regarding the mitigation of the detrimental effects of forced retirement. For instance, the fact that the impact on Professor Ewart, as a physicist depending on a larger project team and facilities, was greater than the impact on Professor Pitcher, who conducted his research more on an individual basis and could more easily continue to do so after retirement by being granted access to certain facilities without his contract being extended.

How can we explain the difference in outcome of the *Pitcher* and *Ewart* cases? Of course, there were minor differences in the facts of the cases, such as the type of research conducted. More interesting, however, seems to be the way in which the evidence in both cases played a role in the proportionality

59 § 279

assessment. In Pitcher's case, it was acknowledged by the ET that there was no statistical evidence available to demonstrate the impact of the policy because the EJRA was still relatively new. The EAT therefore agreed that the ET had been entitled to take the results of a survey into account, which demonstrated that "[o]f 69 people surveyed, 29 responded. Of those, 7 (24%) indicated that they would have continue [sic] working if there had been no EJRA. The typical figure given for how long they would have wanted to continue working was three years". According to the EAT, this resulted in improved intergenerational fairness, diversity, and staff morale, while the discriminatory impact of the policy would be sufficiently mitigated by the extension provisions. In *Ewart*, the ET had the benefit of statistical evidence when assessing the impact of EJRA. The statistics demonstrated that vacancies were being created at a rate of between 2–4%. This increase was considered to be "trivial" in comparison to the discriminatory impact of the policy. The EAT also agreed that the discriminatory impact was not mitigated by the extension provisions, but one wonders: why not? After all, the prior extension had already given Ewart additional time to work past the regular retirement age, while in Pitcher's case there had been no extension of his contract at all.

Apart from this, it is surprising that the EAT did not seem to look at the quality of the evidence provided. After all, of a survey to which only 29 people took the effort to respond, only seven indicated they might want to continue work, which seems to be a very meagre result. It might even be a distorted outcome because people in these kinds of surveys may easily be inclined to give socially desirable answers to the question, which does not necessarily mean that the seven respondents would have actually continued working for another three years if given the opportunity in a real-life situation. In Ewart's case, the statistical data were provided by the claimant himself, while the university had no counter-evidence available in the form of statistical data, but one may wonder whether Pitcher's survey data would not also apply here since it concerns the same university with the same retirement policy. Finally, what is the yardstick for calling certain percentages "trivial"? How many newly created vacancies would suffice? Why was it from a perspective of relational instead of distributive fairness irrelevant that Oxford's retirement in Pitcher's case failed to acknowledge the extent of the detrimental impact of the policy on older academics?[60]

60 Goosey, S. (2020, April 16). Oxford University's mandatory retirement age: A justified experiment to promote equality or unlawful age discrimination? *UK Labour Law Blog*, available at https://wordpress.com/view/uklabourlawblog.com).

CONCLUSION

When people are asked about discrimination, their first inclination is usually to think in terms of different treatment between individuals. For example, a business is looking to hire a secretary. On the job application form, there is a question asking whether the applicant suffers from disabilities that will make doing the job difficult, which is forbidden because this is a legally protected characteristic. Far more difficult, however, are forms of indirect discrimination between certain groups where the rules or practices in question are neutral on the surface, but the effects of the rules or practices are disproportionately unfavourable to specific groups by comparison to others in a similar situation. To stay in the same sphere, a business may require a certain standard clothing style for employees that people from a certain religion just "happen" to be unable to fulfil, while the employer argues that he merely wants his staff to look representative. In such a case, the clothing requirements as such do not result in a legally prohibited practice, but they can raise suspicion, in particular when they disadvantage a certain group. The challenge in many of these cases is to prove a discriminatory practice. Statistical data in combination with, for example, a shift in the burden of proof may in these cases suffice to establish a discriminatory practice that violates certain fundamental rights. The ECtHR made this clear in the case of *Hoogendijk v. the Netherlands*:

> [T]he Court considers that where an applicant is able to show, on the basis of undisputed official statistics, the existence of a prima facie indication that a specific rule – although formulated in a neutral manner – in fact affects a clearly higher percentage of women than men, it is for the respondent Government to show that this is the result of objective factors unrelated to any discrimination on grounds of sex.[61]

The examples we have discussed in this chapter, however, reveal that reality is unfortunately more complex than this. For instance, the *Test-Achats* case we discussed shows that there may be a fine line between what counts as a legitimate aim justifying different treatment and unlawful discrimination. In that case, the Court prohibit the use of statistical data relating to the sex of the insured person, such as (natural) differences in life expectancy or behaviour, in the calculation of insurance premiums, even where evidence suggested that such data represented actuarial fairness. One argument against the use of statistical data to justify differential treatment between men and women is that men and women should be treated as individuals rather than as groups, but this reasoning appears to have difficulties as well. After all, why would one then

[61] ECtHR, *Hoogendijk v. the Netherlands* (dec.), No. 58641/00, 6 January 2005.

allow the legislature to organize a system of maternity leave for women when there are also women who prefer not to have children and male couples who choose to have children and want to prepare for parenthood? In other words, how far should this individualization be taken? To take the logic further, if brighter coloured cars were statistically less often involved in traffic accidents than darker cars because of better visibility, and women, on average, would tend to prefer brighter coloured cars, would the charge of lower prices to drivers of more brightly coloured cars then result in indirect discrimination, or would it instead reflect actuarial fairness?

In the blood donation cases, the CJEU held that a permanent deferral from blood donation for MSM may be possible under three cumulative conditions, namely: where there is a high risk of acquiring serious infectious diseases based on reliable and up to date medical, scientific, and epidemiological data; where there is the absence of methods for detecting the relevant infectious diseases; and where there are no less intrusive means to promote safe blood donation methods. Interestingly, though, the comparison between the case law of the Belgian Constitutional Court and the Brazilian Federal Supreme Court on a similar 12-month blood donation deferral for MSM after the latest sexual contact reveals that courts may come to divergent conclusions regarding the proportionality of such a deferral. While the Belgian court relied on statistical data to take a nuanced position that a deferral can be proportionate with regard to limiting the exercise of fundamental rights, holding that this was not the case for plasma donations because alternative methods exist to detect the risk of infections, the Brazilian Supreme Court relied much more heavily on normative considerations. That court ruled that a temporary deferral results in "injustice by generalization" – MSM having safe sex and unsafe sex would be treated the same way – and therefore decided that the negative effects, such as stigmatization of MSM, outweigh the potential benefits of reducing the risks of transmitting infectious diseases. Hence the blood donation cases not only reveal that scientific evidence and statistical data can be used to debunk certain alleged risks, but they also show that such evidence does not preclude the possibility that a court may decide that normative arguments concerning fairness outweigh empirical arguments regarding the effectiveness of measures to achieve a legitimate aim.

The age discrimination cases reveal that statistics play an important role when it comes to delivering evidence. Member States carry the evidentiary burden of proving not only the legality of the objective pursued but also the appropriateness and necessity of the measure to achieve it, which implies that mere generalizations of alleged effects that could serve a legitimate aim to discriminate on the basis of age do not suffice. Statistics can deliver valuable information, especially in cases of discrimination where certain groups are faced with disproportionate effects of, for example, retirement policies.

However, statistics usually do not show how much impact a retirement policy must have to outweigh the negative effects of different treatment – e.g. how many new vacancies a policy should create in order to be justified. The cases of *Pitcher* and *Ewart* show again how easily courts may come to opposite conclusions here in rather similar circumstances simply because they seem to apply a different yardstick to evaluate the weight of the consequences of early retirement of academics. However, these cases also reveal the importance of looking at the quality of the statistical data that is being used to assess the effects on policy. In this respect, it is surprising that the EAT seems to have paid no attention to the fact that in *Pitcher* the ET relied on data from a small-scale survey concerning how existing employees might respond to future retirement, which is rather speculative, versus statistical data concerning how many new hirings were actually created due to Oxford's retirement policy. This begs the question: is it legitimate to put statistical data from ex ante and ex post evaluations on the same footing?

To conclude, scientific evidence can put an argumentative burden on courts. If the statistical data prove that a policy is not suitable or not necessary for achieving a legitimate aim, a court can no longer justify that policy on the basis of empirical argument regarding effectiveness and efficiency as we have, for example, seen in the blood donation cases when it comes to plasma donation. When statistical data prove that a policy contributes to achieving a legitimate aim that may allow a difference in treatment, courts should at least consider this information in the decision. Disregarding an argument backed by evidence (just like relying on empirical assumptions not supported by evidence) will otherwise compromise the transparency and thereby the legitimacy of judicial decisions, as we have witnessed in the insurance cases where in the end both men and women were worse off in terms of the payment in insurance premiums. Last but not least, the more intensely a policy helps to achieve a legitimate aim, the higher the bar is going to be to invalidate this policy – as we have found in the age discrimination cases.

Given the exploratory nature of the current research, which relies on a rather limited number of cases, one route for fruitful research could be to conduct a more systematic analysis of a larger and probabilistic sample of case law. In this respect, a structured content analysis would allow identifying whether the findings noticed in a small-scale doctrinal analysis of the use of statistics in insurance, health, and labour law may be generalized to these fields of law as a whole and perhaps also offer interesting challenges for research in other areas of the law. A second recommendation for future research might be to conduct a more qualitative study focused on explaining the differences found in the case law analysis. Interviewing judges and confronting them with the outcomes could perhaps provide insights into what determines the sometimes different approaches chosen by courts from different jurisdictions in dealing with statistical data, especially while conducting proportionality tests. This could provide a better idea of why courts act in the ways observed and what lies behind the differences. Here, one can imagine explanations related to, for instance, differences in the substantive and procedural legal frameworks that apply to judicial decision-making, but perhaps also to the influence of legal culture, training programmes for judges, and perceptions of judges themselves on their role and capabilities in the judicial process. The third and final proposal for further research could be to study the macro-consequences of the different courts' approaches to scientific evidence in anti-discrimination cases. For example, in the insurance domain, it would be useful to investigate whether unisex premiums have resulted in higher premiums overall, because insurance companies are risk-averse.

4. Adopting the gold standard: field experimentation for evidence-based judicial lawmaking

Arthur Dyevre

INTRODUCTION

In all legal systems, some courts, at least some of the time, make law. The inevitability of judicial lawmaking is in large part a consequence of the inherent under-determinacy of legal rules. Disputes are bound to emerge for which the law does not provide a single right answer. This is equally true in Common Law and in Civil Law jurisdictions. In fact, it holds for courts in any legal tradition.

In hierarchical court systems, lower courts typically focus on fact-finding and individual dispute resolution, while law-finding and law-creation are functions primarily performed by appellate and supreme courts.[1] As with politically salient domestic courts like the UK Supreme Court and the German Constitutional Court, international courts such as the Court of Justice of the European Union or the Inter-American Court of Human Rights also regularly engage in policy making.

That judges sometimes make policy is an inescapable fact, although its significance and frequency seem to have grown, variously driven by the diffusion of judicially enforceable human rights catalogues and treaties, the expanding power of regulatory agencies and, in Europe, by integration dynamics that have led to the formation of a supranational legal system.[2]

Judges effectively make policy decisions when they spell out rules of procedure; when they decide about the internal organisation (e.g. panel/chamber composition, case management system) of their own court; when they review

[1] L.A. Kornhauser, "Adjudication by a Resource-Constrained Team: Hierarchy and Precedent in a Judicial System". S. Cal. L. Rev. 1994 68: 1605.

[2] F. Vibert, *The Rise of the Unelected: Democracy and the New Separation of Powers*. Cambridge University Press 2007.

the rules promulgated by the legislative and executive branch; and, of course, when they articulate legal doctrines.

When a policy is made, it is made in order to achieve a goal. That the policy's ability to achieve this goal should form the main basis for its evaluation and justification is also beyond dispute. At any rate, this is taken for granted when it comes to policies passed by legislatures in the shape of statutes. Legal discourse often hides the true extent of judicial policy making behind a cloak of formalism. Yet there is no reason why goal attainment should not be an equally relevant measure in assessing policies enacted by judges, whether these take the form of doctrines, remedies or rules of procedure.

How is judicial rule-making evaluated in practice? The default approach to policy evaluation is mostly a mixture of common wisdom, experience and professional judgment.[3] Practitioners can have strong beliefs about what works and what doesn't – whether it is the impact of cookie banners (to protect privacy rights), pre-trial mediation or legal aid. "We already know" is the response of many practitioners when questioned about the validity of their empirical assumptions.[4] Great weight is often attributed to anecdotal or impressionistic evidence. It is not uncommon for a handful of instances where a rule coincides with a positive outcome to be treated as sufficient evidence that the rule works – with blithe disregard for sample representativeness and principles of causal inference.

Occasionally, experts are called in to help the magistrates in coming to a more informed decision, or a brief may elaborate on the findings of an empirical study, as with Louis D. Brandeis's famous brief in *Muller v. Oregon*. But recourse to this type of evidence is less than systematic on matters pertaining to the effectiveness and efficacy of legal rules and doctrines, especially in Europe.

Legal academics differ little in how they go about evaluating legal rules. Law journals are replete with evaluative statements and prescriptions for judges and judicial lawmaking. But, despite the emergence of a burgeoning empirical legal literature, causal assumptions ordinarily appeal to the same combination of visceral beliefs and received wisdom.[5] Comparative legal analysis is

---

3 H. Lynch, D. Fernandez, J. Greiner and I.G. Cohen, "Overcoming Obstacles to Experiments in Legal Practice". *Science* 2020 367(6482): 1078–80.

4 D. Greiner, J. Matthews and A. Matthews, "Randomized Control Trials in the United States Legal Profession". *Annual Review of Law and Social Science* 2016 12(1): 295–312. https://doi.org/10.1146/annurev-lawsocsci-110413–030732. Lynch, Fernandez, Greiner and Cohen, "Overcoming Obstacles to Experiments in Legal Practice". *Science* 2020 367(6482): 1078–80.

5 L. Epstein and G. King, "The Rules of Inference". *The University of Chicago Law Review* 2002 69(1): 1–133. https://doi.org/10.2307/1600349.

frequently called into service to establish what works and what doesn't but suffers from similar flaws, including selection biases.[6]

This stands in sharp contrast with the situation in other domains such as medicine, technology, education and development economics, where randomised controlled methods are widely used and regarded as the gold standard for policy evaluation.[7] Many lawyers may have a vague notion of what a randomised controlled trial (RCT) looks like from research evaluating the efficacy of vaccines and drugs – which rose to public prominence during the Covid pandemic. But why and how such a methodology could and should be applied to the legal field may not be readily apparent.

The present contribution examines the potential for using field experimentation – RCT and its tech-sector equivalent, A/B testing – as an evaluation tool in the judicial domain. I argue that field experimentation holds great promise for legal impact assessment. While legal field RCTs may sometimes raise delicate ethical issues that need to be properly addressed, they have the potential to improve the quality and efficiency of judge-made rules and practices.

The chapter proceeds as follows. I first explain the basics of field experimentation before setting out the advantages of field experimentation as a causal identification method. I compare field RCTs and A/B testing to lab experiments and other approaches to causal inferences employed in quantitative observational studies. I then survey some field RCTs conducted in the legal field. Next, I discuss the resistance to the diffusion of field experimentation in the legal community, including common ethical objections and cultural factors. Finally, I highlight some of the most promising avenues for the application of randomised controlled approaches. I contend, more controversially, that RCTs may help evaluate new doctrines and A/B testing to optimise the introduction of artificial intelligence and decision support systems in the judiciary.

WHAT IS FIELD EXPERIMENTATION?

Field experiments have two fundamental characteristics. The first is that they are experiments in the scientific sense of the term. They involve comparison

---

6 R. Hirschl, "Question of Case Selection in Comparative Constitutional Law, The". *American Journal of Comparative Law* 2005 53: 125.

7 E. Duflo and A. Banerjee, *Handbook of Field Experiments*. Elsevier 2017. B. Styles and C. Torgerson, "Randomized Controlled Trials (RCTs) in Education Research–Methodological Debates, Questions, Challenges". In *Educational Research*. Taylor & Francis 2018. Greiner, Matthews and Matthews, "Randomized Control Trials in the United States Legal Profession". *Annual Review of Law and Social Science* 2016 12(1): 295–312. https://doi.org/10.1146/annurev-lawsocsci-110413-030732.

between units – human subjects, firms, villages, public bodies – exposed to different treatments with the distinctive feature that unit assignment to treatment is random. In a clinical study, participants are randomly assigned to treatment and control groups (where participants are often given a placebo). The number of groups can be larger than two, as in multi-arm experiments. But assignment invariably involves randomisation.

The second characteristic is that field experiments take place in the field, with real patients, real end users, real firms, real villages or real public bodies. This is the difference from a lab experiment, where human volunteers are presented with a hypothetical scenario.[8] Field RCTs assessing the impact of legal aid, for example, involve real clients fighting in real disputes.[9]

A/B testing is used in the tech sector to optimise the structure and layout of internet applications and platforms. Users are randomly presented with one of several versions of a portal or website. Behaviours – e.g. bounce rate, average time on page, conversion rate, etc. – can then be compared across versions to determine the optimal one according to the owner's preferred metric. But the underlying principle, randomised assignment to treatment, remains the same.

WHY FIELD EXPERIMENTATION HAS BECOME THE GOLD STANDARD FOR CAUSAL INFERENCE

Does pre-trial mediation encourage parties to settle? Does the use of data-driven risk assessment scoring improve the quality of bail decisions? Do rehabilitation programmes, which judges have the option of imposing, decrease the probability of recidivism? Do arbitration clauses in employment contracts make employees more likely to lose legal disputes? Such questions essentially ask what difference the rule, practice, or remedy makes. Would the world look different without the rule or the practice at issue?

Without randomising a rule's application, demonstrating that it actually makes a difference (or doesn't) and, more specifically, that it causally

---

8 A. Dyevre and M. Ovádek, "Experimental Legal Methods in the Classroom". *Utrecht Law Review* 2020 16(1), 1–12.

9 D.J. Greiner, "The New Legal Empiricism & Its Application to Access-to-Justice Inquiries", *Daedalus* 2019 148(1): 64–74. https://doi.org/10.1162/daed_a_00536. D.J. Greiner, E.L. Degnan, T. Ferriss and R. Sommers, "Using Random Assignment to Measure Court Accessibility for Low-Income Divorce Seekers". *Proceedings of the National Academy of Sciences* 2021 118(14); A. Aberra and M. Chemin, "Does Legal Representation Increase Investment? Evidence from a Field Experiment in Kenya". *Journal of Development Economics* 2021 150(May): 102612. https://doi.org/10.1016/j.jdeveco.2020.102612.

influences the conduct of its addressees is difficult.[10] There are two reasons for this. First, multiple causal explanations – not just the rule under consideration – may plausibly account for the same pattern of behaviour. Worse, we may not even be sure we know all of the factors affecting the behaviour in question. Second, the addressees of a rule may differ in many unknown (and unobservable) as well as known (and observable) ways. These differences may affect individual responses to the rule. But the researcher is, by definition, unable to track the influence of unobserved variables. Because of what we don't know – all the possible causal pathways – and/or cannot observe, linking cause (rule, practice) and effect (patterns of behaviour) is always a tricky exercise when conducted on the sole basis of observation, even with a large data set.

Statistical techniques exist to control for and mitigate the effects of confounding factors. But these techniques require that researchers make assumptions about the imperfectly known data-generating process. The causal claims they support, therefore, are only as good as these assumptions.

While qualitative methods – interviews and case studies – can be useful, they are an absolute non-starter for establishing causation. Any attempt to ascribe causality with a single data point is bound to produce explanations overfitting this single observation.

The great advantage of field experimentation over observational analysis stems from randomisation. Random assignment entails that every unit faces the same probability of being assigned to one group or the other. The effect of randomisation is to equalise the groups in terms of both observable and non-observable covariates. Patients who volunteer for a clinical study may differ in gender, age, socio-economic status or unknown intolerance, but randomisation will ensure that the distribution of these characteristics is comparable in the control and treatment group.

Similarly, in a legal aid study, randomisation will ensure that the litigants who receive legal assistance are comparable to the litigants in the control group. Without randomisation, the risk of selection bias would preclude a valid causal inference. For example, if legal aid is offered on a first-come-first-served basis, litigants in the treatment group may differ systematically in unobserved ways from participants in the control group because those who invest more time and energy in their case are both more likely to spot an opportunity for free legal assistance and more likely to win their case in the first place. The group receiving legal aid may show a higher success rate than the control group. But this may reflect the diverging distribution of individual characteristics in the two groups rather than the impact of legal aid. When the experiment is well

---

[10] M. Abramowicz, I. Ayres and Y. Listokin, "Randomizing Law". *University of Pennsylvania Law Review* 2010 159: 929.

designed, randomisation produces strong internal validity. Any statistically significant difference in behaviour or outcome between the groups can be confidently ascribed to the difference in treatment.

RCTs further have the advantage over their laboratory cousin in that they are conducted in real conditions. In a lab setting, participants, by definition, are aware of the artificial character of the trial, which may affect their conduct. In a field experiment, by contrast, the stakes are real from the vantage point of the units involved. Subjects may be aware that they have been randomly assigned to a treatment as part of a research experiment, but everything else doesn't merely look real; it is real.

Randomisation and lab-in-the-field implementation are what make field experimentation the gold standard for the evaluation of policy interventions as well as for testing drugs and vaccines.[11] Likewise, the rigour and reliability of A/B testing have made it a ubiquitous tool for the deployment and improvement of online applications. Google and Facebook run thousands of A/B tests every year. As Mark Zuckerberg put it:

> At any given point in time, there isn't just one version of Facebook running, there are probably 10,000. Any engineer at the company can basically decide that they want to test something. There are some rules on sensitive things, but in general, an engineer can test something, and they can launch a version of Facebook not to the whole community, but maybe to 10,000 people or 50,000 people—whatever is necessary to get a good test of an experience.

Additionally, the practice of pre-registering experimental protocols, which has become the rule in most scientific fields, offers a precious guarantee of transparency. Because data typically predate the analysis, observational methods are susceptible to p-hacking and other forms of manipulation. By explicating ex ante how the data generated by the experiment will be analysed, the pre-registered protocol ensures that the choice of statistical test cannot be retrofitted to the data or manipulated to produce results researchers or policymakers deem, for one reason or another, more desirable. Pre-registration significantly reduces the risk of ideologically motivated distortions of research results by politicians and interest groups.

---

11 D.B. Rubin, "The Design versus the Analysis of Observational Studies for Causal Effects: Parallels with the Design of Randomized Trials". *Statistics in Medicine* 2007 26(1): 20–36; J.D. Angrist and J.S. Pischke, "The Credibility Revolution in Empirical Economics: How Better Research Design Is Taking the Con out of Econometrics". *Journal of Economic Perspectives* 2010 24(2): 3–30; E. Duflo and A. Banerjee, *Handbook of Field Experiments*. Elsevier 2017.

RCTs: A SHORT SURVEY

Field RCTs in the judicial domain are relatively rare. Surveying field RCTs in the US legal profession over a period spanning six decades, Jim Greiner and Andrea Matthews found only 50 studies.[12] There is no comparable survey in the European context, but, if anything, the number of field experiments in Europe's judiciaries is likely to be considerably smaller.

The subject areas covered by randomised trials encompass legal aid and access to justice;[13] mediation and alternative dispute resolution;[14] and mandatory counseling programmes for drug and domestic abuse offenders.[15] Whereas several authors have advocated the use of experimental methods to test and evaluate laws and regulations passed by legislatures and regulatory bodies;[16] it seems that no field experiment has ever been conducted with the explicit purpose of evaluating the impact of substantive judicially enacted doctrines. Some authors are sceptical that courts may randomise the application of their *ratio decidendi*.[17]

---

12 J.D. Greiner and A. Matthews, "Randomized Control Trials in the United States Legal Profession". *Annual Review of Law and Social Science* 2016 12(1): 295–312. https://doi.org/10.1146/annurev-lawsocsci-110413-030732.

13 Aberra and Chemin. "Does Legal Representation Increase Investment? Evidence from a Field Experiment in Kenya". *Journal of Development Economics* 2021 150(May): 102612. https://doi.org/10.1016/j.jdeveco.2020.102612; Greiner, Degnan, Ferriss and Sommers, "Using Random Assignment to Measure Court Accessibility for Low-Income Divorce Seekers". *Proceedings of the National Academy of Sciences* 2021 118(14).

14 J. Goldman, "The Civil Appeals Management Plan: An Experiment in Appellate Procedural Reform". *Columbia Law Review* 1978 78(6): 1209–40. J. Zuberbuhler, "Early Intervention Mediation: The Use of Court-Ordered Mediation in the Initial Stages of Divorce Litigation to Resolve Parenting Issues". *Family Court Review* 2001 39(2): 203–6.

15 D.C. Gottfredson, B.W. Kearley, S. Najaka and C.M. Rocha, "The Baltimore City Drug Treatment Court: 3-Year Self-Report Outcome Study". *Evaluation Review* 2005 29(1): 42–64; M. Labriola, M. Rempel and R.C. Davis, "Do Batterer Programs Reduce Recidivism? Results from a Randomized Trial in the Bronx". *Justice Quarterly* 2008 25(2): 252–82.

16 M. Abramowicz, I. Ayres and Y. Listokin, "Randomizing Law". *University of Pennsylvania Law Review* 2010 159: 929; M. Abramowicz, "Randomized Legal Experimentation". GWU Legal Studies Research Paper, 2008, no. 447.

17 M. Abramowicz, "Randomized Legal Experimentation". GWU Legal Studies Research Paper, 2008, no. 447.

RESISTANCE TO EXPERIMENTATION IN THE LEGAL COMMUNITY

Evidence-based judicial rule-making remains a foreign concept in the legal community. In the United States, proposals advocating the more systematic use of RCTs to assess judicial policy interventions have met with resistance.[18]

The resistance to empirical evaluation in the legal realm comes into sharper relief when contrasted with the near-universal embrace of RCTs in medicine. Law and medicine are both practice-oriented disciplines. Like law, medicine started as an individualised craft. The first documented medical RCT only preceded its first legal counterpart by two years.[19] But from then on, the two disciplines followed distinct trajectories. Medicine turned clinical research into a science. Thousands of clinical RCTs are conducted every year in nearly all aspects of medical practice, from hospital admission protocols to pharmaceuticals. Legal practice, on the other hand, remained a professional craft and failed to develop an evidence-based culture. Resistance to empiricism appears to stem from both ethical objections and cultural obstacles.[20]

Field experimentation may seem at odds with the ethical intuitions of lawyers. The rule of law mandates that like cases be treated alike, and flipping a coin to decide which rule or remedy should be applied to a given person seems antithetical to the traditional understanding of judging. Another objection is that too much is at stake (e.g. freedom vs. incarceration) in judicial decision-making to allow experimentation.

However, these and other ethical concerns associated with randomised legal experimentation have parallels in medical research, where they have been convincingly resolved. For example, randomly granting judges access to risk assessment scores in order to assess their impact on the quality of bail decisions may seem shocking because of the difference in treatment it involves in

---

[18] Fernandez, Greiner and Cohen, "Overcoming Obstacles to Experiments in Legal Practice". *Science* 2020 367(6482): 1078–80; D.J. Greiner and A. Matthews, "Randomized Control Trials in the United States Legal Profession". *Annual Review of Law and Social Science* 2016 12(1): 295–312. https://doi.org/10.1146/annurev-lawsocsci-110413-030732.

[19] D.J. Greiner, "The New Legal Empiricism & Its Application to Access-to-Justice Inquiries". *Daedalus* 2019 148(1): 64–74 (at 73). https://doi.org/10.1162/daed_a_00536.

[20] Fernandez, Greiner and Cohen, "Overcoming Obstacles to Experiments in Legal Practice". *Science* 2020 367(6482): 1078–80; Abramowicz, Ayres and Listokin, "Randomizing Law". *University of Pennsylvania Law Review* 2010 159: 929; Greiner, "The New Legal Empiricism & Its Application to Access-to-Justice Inquiries". *Daedalus* 2019 148(1): 64–74. https://doi.org/10.1162/daed_a_00536.

what is indubitably a high-stakes criminal context. This problem has a parallel in clinical research, when there is concern that participants in the control group may be harmed by treatment denial. Yet an RCT is considered ethical, or even ethically mandated, if there is professional uncertainty over the safety and efficacy of the treatment compared to the standard of care applied to participants in the control group. This reflects the principle of "clinical equipoise".[21] Equipoise would allow a legal RCT if there is uncertainty over the impact of risk assessment scores on bail decisions. Using randomisation to test the effectiveness of a parole programme may similarly clash with lawyers' ethical intuition. However, if prisoners are not entitled to parole, randomly assigning them to (default) incarceration or parole does not take away a right.

To be sure, ethics does place constraints on the scope of experimentation. But clinical research demonstrates, again, that high stakes (life vs death) do not preclude experimentation. On the contrary, the dominant view in the medical community is that high stakes make the case for randomised experimentation stronger, not weaker.

Jim Greiner and Andrea Matthews speculate that the cultivation of certainty creates a strong cultural barrier to the adoption of empirical evidence in law:

> Without a deep sense of uncertainty about how the world works, there is little reason to seek methodologies for producing knowledge external to one's own experiences and those of elites within one's profession. [...] [M]edicine's adoption of the RCT stemmed in part from a desire among elite physicians to establish an irrefutable methodology to distinguish effective therapies from commercially promoted snake oil. Such a project had to depend on the elite physicians' ability to persuade their contemporaries to view the claims of commercial interests, and the knowledge gained by their own experiences, with skepticism.[22]

Judges and attorneys prefer to appear certain even when there is scant basis for certainty. Rarely does judicial rhetoric acknowledge uncertainty, whether it is about the facts or about the law. Professional incentives also favour thought processes that are instrumental to advocacy, rather than being analytical.[23]

---

21 Fernandez, Greiner and Cohen, "Overcoming Obstacles to Experiments in Legal Practice". *Science* 2020 367(6482): 1078–80.

22 Greiner and Matthews, "Randomized Control Trials in the United States Legal Profession". *Annual Review of Law and Social Science* 2016 12(1): 295–312. https://doi.org/10.1146/annurev-lawsocsci-110413-030732.

23 Greiner, "The New Legal Empiricism & Its Application to Access-to-Justice Inquiries". *Daedalus* 2019 148(1): 64–74 (at 73). https://doi.org/10.1162/daed_a_00536; D.J. Greiner and A. Matthews, "Randomized Control Trials in the United States Legal Profession." Annual Review of Law and Social Science 2016 12(1): 295–312. https://doi.org/10.1146/annurev-lawsocsci-110413–030732.

These cultural obstacles are not insurmountable. But we lack a playbook on how to persuade the key stakeholders – judges, attorneys and legal scholars – to embrace this form of policy evaluation. Fostering an empirical, evidence-based culture will take a great deal of persuasion, and the task ahead is, no doubt, immense.

SOME AVENUES FOR APPLYING FIELD EXPERIMENTATION IN THE JUDICIAL REALM

Besides the subject areas listed above which have already seen some RCTs, I see strong potential for field experimentation in three domains.

The first is administrative review. The means-end tests courts apply when reviewing legislative and executive policies can be viewed as requiring some form of empirical evaluation. The proportionality test, widely used in Europe, requires that administrative measures be 1) suitable; and 2) necessary to attain their stated goal. RCT-generated evidence offers a firm basis for establishing whether a measure meets these conditions. As some scholars have argued, this also implies that judges should exert greater deference towards the executive and legislative branches when the contemplated measure is supported by the results of an RCT.[24] We could also imagine that, where no RCT has been conducted, judges might require that one be completed before coming to a final decision.

A second area pertains to the introduction of AI and digital technologies – such as digital case management, document assembly and decision support systems – in adjudication. There is evidence that judicial decision-making in high-frequency litigation is far from being consistent.[25] On clear and well-defined quality metrics (e.g. recidivism and re-arrest rates in bail cases), algorithms can vastly outperform professional judges.[26] On the other hand, there are concerns that algorithms might be biased and that digital tools may negatively impact the conduct of human decision makers (e.g. by inducing cognitive

[24] Abramowicz, Ayres and Listokin, "Randomizing Law". *University of Pennsylvania Law Review* 2010 159: 929.

[25] J. Kleinberg, H. Lakkaraju, J. Leskovec, J. Ludwig and S. Mullainathan, "Human Decisions and Machine Predictions". *The Quarterly Journal of Economics* 2018 133(1): 237–93. D.L. Chen, "Judicial Analytics and the Great Transformation of American Law". *Artificial Intelligence and Law* 2019 27(1): 15–42.

[26] Kleinberg, Lakkaraju, Leskovec, Ludwig and Mullainathan, "Human Decisions and Machine Predictions". *The Quarterly Journal of Economics* 2018 133(1): 237–93.

laziness).[27] Failure to tailor the user-facing interface of AI applications to the needs of judges and litigants risks nullifying the benefits of digitalisation.

There is a need to rigorously evaluate the impact of AI decision support systems and to find the optimal human-machine combination.[28] Intensive A/B testing is also needed to develop and fine-tune the human-machine interface to determine the pace and success of e-justice programmes.

The third area is arguably the most controversial: legal doctrines. Using RCTs in this area presupposes that courts explicitly acknowledge their policy-making function – which they remain reluctant to do. Practically, in order to test a new doctrine, a supreme court would need to randomly instruct lower courts or administrative units to either follow the new doctrine or retain the old one.

Designing effective doctrinal field RCTs would raise some challenges. First, clear metrics would have to be identified to assess results across the treatment and control groups. Second, precautions would need to be taken to prevent forum shopping in instances where some classes of litigants may inherently prefer one doctrine over the other. Third, the temporal window of the experiment would have to be clearly delineated and publicised. Fairness should normally preclude enrolling litigants whose case was initiated before the announcement of the experiment.

While technically uncontrolled and thus not a proper RCT, the *Sahara House v. Union of India* case, in which the Supreme Court of India oversaw access to second-line treatment for patients suffering from HIV/AIDS, helps illustrate how a doctrinal RCT might look. The Court was petitioned that denial of treatment to patients suffering from HIV/AIDS violated the right to health, the right to life, and the right to equality enshrined in the Constitution of India. As the number of patients needing second-line treatment was unknown and there were concerns about capacity constraints, the Court held that second-line treatment should initially be made available at four centres in Mumbai, New Delhi and Kolkata. This pilot initiative was to be studied for three months, during which the number of people in need of second-line retroviral treatment could be determined and capacity could be adapted. A report was submitted at the end of this phase and the Court ruled that second-line treatment should be made universally available. The pilot initiative was effectively a field experiment, albeit not a randomised controlled one. While the Court allowed for

[27] J. Ludwig and S. Mullainathan, "Fragile Algorithms and Fallible Decision-Makers: Lessons from the Justice System". *Journal of Economic Perspectives* 2021 35(4): 71–96.

[28] I. Kosuke, Z. Jiang, J. Greiner, R. Halen and S. Shin, "Experimental Evaluation of Algorithm-Assisted Human Decision-Making: Application to Pretrial Public Safety Assessment". ArXiv Preprint 2020, ArXiv:2012.02845.

patients across India to be referred to the four centres, it ignored the selection effects that might distort the evaluation of the pilot initiative. In a proper RCT, the centres offering treatment would have had to be randomly selected. Yet, for the rest, the process – determining the policy problem, specifying the design and duration of the experimental phase, reporting of the results, and final decision – would have been virtually identical.

One problem with RCTs in the judicial context is that in some instances there might not be enough courts, judges or administrative units (e.g. hospitals with access to treatment) to run the experiment. A court with ten panels and 30 judges may look like a large court. But an RCT would lack statistical power to detect even a relatively large difference between treated panels or judges. Concerns about statistical power may sometimes be addressed by selecting the right design. Imagine, for example, that we wanted to assess the creation of a constitutional remedy against the decision of a court of last instance. Such a decision might involve the submission of a reference for a preliminary ruling in a dispute where EU law is material,[29] and the question was whether the constitutional remedy has a positive impact on the referral activity of last instance courts. Under EU law, only courts of last instance have a duty to submit a reference when EU law is material to the case. However, no Member State has both a constitutional court with the power to review ordinary court decisions and a sufficiently large number of last instance courts to run a conventional RCT with one treatment group and one control group. However, a novel design, known as "stepped-wedge RCT",[30] in which units are sequentially treated, may help achieve the desired level of statistical power in such a setting.

CONCLUSION

Field experimentation has revolutionised decision making in many areas, from healthcare to development aid and internet platforms. Esther Duflo, Abhijit Banerjee and Michael Kremer earned the Nobel Prize for their efforts to advance the use of field RCTs in economics.

RCTs have become the gold standard for the assessment of medical practices and policy interventions but remain rare in the legal realm. I have tried to show the potential for field experimentation by the judiciary. I have explained

29 C. Lacchi, "Review by Constitutional Courts of the Obligation of National Courts of Last Instance to Refer a Preliminary Question to the Court of Justice of the EU". *German Law Journal* 2015 16(6): 1663–1700.

30 K. Hemming, T.P. Haines, P.J. Chilton, A.J. Girling, and R.J. Lilford, "The Stepped Wedge Cluster Randomised Trial: Rationale, Design, Analysis, and Reporting". BMJ 2015 350(February): h391. https://doi.org/10.1136/bmj.h391.

why randomised experiments provide the most solid evidence for policy evaluation and addressed some obstacles to their broader adoption.

Where experimentation is ethical and feasible, the case for evidence-based doctrine-making is as strong as the case for evidence-based policy making in other areas.

PART II

The problems of empirical evidence in judicial policy making

5. The design of judicial deference and the use of scientific evidence in constitutional public interest litigation

Niels Petersen

The use of scientific evidence in constitutional jurisprudence is a controversial topic. It has gained renewed prominence with the recent rise of public interest litigation. In many cases, public interest litigation rests on the evaluation of scientific data. This is particularly obvious for constitutional obligations of nations to mitigate climate change. However, there is significant uncertainty surrounding the causal mechanisms of climate change and the effectiveness of different mitigation strategies. The core question regarding the use of scientific evidence is the extent to which courts can second-guess the empirical assessment of the legislature. In this context, courts are facing a particular tension. On the one hand, the question of how to deal with uncertainty is a political matter that should primarily be answered by the legislature and not by courts. On the other hand, courts cannot give legislatures carte blanche if they want to exercise effective constitutional control over them.

This chapter takes a closer look at how courts can deal with this tension. The argument will proceed in two steps. The first section analyzes the theoretical conundrum that courts face in more detail. The second section then proposes a typology of different approaches that courts have adopted to construct judicial deference and to delineate the margins of this deference. First-order approaches focus on the decision itself. Here courts often grant deference to the legislature if the latter acted under uncertainty. By contrast, second-order approaches focus on the decision-making process. Such a process-based approach can come in two forms. On the one hand, courts can look at the legislature's decision-making procedure. On the other hand, they can try to identify the legislative motivation. I will argue that none of these approaches presents us with the holy grail – all have their deficiencies. Thus, it is not surprising that courts are often driven by pragmatism, combining elements of various approaches in determining the degree of judicial deference.

THE NORMATIVE DEBATE ON THE USE OF SCIENTIFIC EVIDENCE IN CONSTITUTIONAL JURISPRUDENCE

The central theoretical issue behind the use of scientific evidence by apex courts when reviewing legislation is the distribution of power between the legislature and the judiciary. In principle, the legislature is in a better position to evaluate scientific evidence.[1] It has more resources than the judiciary to draw on scientific evidence and also the political mandate to draw policy conclusions from its evaluations of that evidence.[2] Even if we are certain, for example, about the human influence on climate change and the catastrophic effects that climate change has already caused to the ecosystems and the living conditions on our planet,[3] the conclusions to be drawn from this evidence imply political choices:[4] Which social costs are we ready to bear today in order to avert

---

1 Jeffrie G. Murphy, & Jules L. Coleman, *Philosophy of Law. An Introduction to Jurisprudence* (Westview Press 1990); Horst Eidenmüller, *Effizienz als Rechtspinzip* (J.C.B. Mohr 1995), 428; Robert E. Charney, 'Evidence in Charter Cases: Expert Evidence and Proving Purpose', (2004) 16 *National Journal of Constitutional Law* 1, 5; Robert E. Charney, & S. Zachary Green, 'Prophets of Doom, Seers of Fortune: 20 Years of Experience under the Oakes Test', (2006) 34 *Supreme Court Law Review* 479, 481.

2 Murphy & Coleman (n 1); Charney & Green (n 1), 481. But see also some earlier contributions to the discussion, arguing that the courts are in a better position than the legislature to evaluate social science facts: Fritz Ossenbühl, 'Die Kontrolle von Tatsachenfeststellungen durch das Bundesverfassungsgericht' in Christian Starck (ed.), *Bundesverfassungsgericht und Grundgesetz. Erster Band: Verfassungsgerichtsbarkeit* (J.C.B. Mohr 1976), 458, 472; Christoph Gusy, *Parlamentarischer Gesetzgeber und Bundesverfassungsgericht* (Duncker & Humblot 1985), 165. See, finally, Klaus Jürgen Philippi, *Tatsachenfeststellungen des Bundesverfassungsgerichts* (Carl Heymanns Verlag 1971) (studying the practice of the German Federal Constitutional Court and arguing that the prognoses of the court are often more evidence-based than those of the legislature).

3 The evidence in this respect is quite overwhelming, see Thomas F. Stocker, D. Qin, G.-K. Plattner, M. Tignor, S.K. Allen, J. Boschung, A. Nauels, Y. Xia, V. Bex, & P.M. Midgley (eds.), *Climate Change 2023: The Physical Science Basis. Working Group I: Contribution to the Fifth Assessment of the Intergovernmental Panel on Climate Change* (IPCC 2013). See also Jody Freeman, & Andrew T. Guzman, 'Climate Change and US Interests', (2009) 109 *Columbia Journal of Transnational Law* 1531, 1544–45 (with further references).

4 On the interplay between empirical evidence and normative choices to be drawn from this evidence, see Julia de Augustinis & Rob van Gestel, 'Discrimination by Generalization: About Use and Abuse of Statistics in Anti-Discrimination Cases', Chapter 3 in this volume.

catastrophe tomorrow? How should these costs be distributed across social groups and nation states? Furthermore, if we add uncertainty into the equation, decisions about how to mitigate specific dangers become questions of societal risk preferences.[5] Some societies might prefer a rather cautious approach, while others tolerate more risk. Again, this is not a decision to be made by courts, but one that should be negotiated in the political process.[6] Therefore, courts cannot impose a strict burden of proof on legislatures.[7] Justice La Forest argued in his dissenting opinion in *RJR-MacDonald* that to do so "could have the effect of virtually paralyzing the operation of government".[8]

For these reasons, courts usually exercise deference towards the legislature or executive. That means that they grant latitude to the political branches to make empirical determinations.[9] Yet, this deference cannot be unlimited.[10] While the legislature may have more resources to obtain scientific facts and while it may have the political prerogative to determine the consequences of scientific findings, it cannot be assumed that the legislature always acts in the public interest.[11] First, legislative and executive actors may have been captured by powerful interest groups.[12] In the case of climate change, there is a

---

5 Niels Petersen, 'Avoiding the Common Wisdom Fallacy: The Role of Social Sciences in Constitutional Adjudication', (2013) 11 *International Journal of Constitutional Law* 294, 311.

6 See Joseph H.H. Weiler, 'Epilogue: Towards a Common Law of International Trade' in Joseph H.H. Weiler (ed.), *The EU, the WTO, and the NAFTA. Towards a Common Law of International Trade?* (Oxford University Press 2000), 201, 222–23.

7 Sujit Choudhry, 'So what is the real legacy of *Oakes*? Two Decades of Proportionality Analysis under the Canadian Charter's section I', (2006) 34 *Supreme Court Law Review* 501, 524–25; Anne Carter, *Proportionality and Facts in Constitutional Adjudication* (Hart 2021), 171.

8 *RJR-MacDonald Inc. v. Canada (Attorney General)*, [1995] 3 S.C.R. 199, at para. 67 (La Forest J. dissenting).

9 Cora Chan, 'A preliminary framework for measuring deference in rights reasoning', (2016) 14 *International Journal of Constitutional Law* 851, 854.

10 See Choudhry (n 7), 525.

11 Joseph H.H. Weiler, 'Comment: Brazil – Measures Affecting Imports of Retreaded Tires (DS32)', (2009) 8 *World Trade Review* 137, 144.

12 On the concept of capture, see, seminally, Mancur Olson, *The Logic of Collective Action: Public Goods and the Theory of Groups* (Harvard University Press 1965). See also Anthony J. Nownes, & Grant Neeley, 'Public Interest Group Entrepreneurship and Theories of Group Mobilization', (1996) 49 *Political Research Quarterly* 119, 121–25; Andrew McFarland, 'Interest Group Theory' in L. Sandy Maisel, & Jeffrey M. Berry (eds.), *Oxford Handbook of American Political Parties and Interest Groups* (Oxford University Press 2010), 37.

long history of the oil and coal industry financing disinformation campaigns and influencing political decision-making.[13] The agricultural lobby has been a powerful player with regard to food security standards,[14] the tobacco industry has spent billions to block anti-smoking legislation, and the construction industry has tried to downplay the harmful effect of asbestos. As Wendy Wagner's chapter in this volume shows, interest groups influence the fact-finding that underlies legislative projects.[15] There is a long history of interested groups financing research that is not intended to generate knowledge, but rather to obscure it and to sow uncertainty.[16]

Second, political actors have incentives to apply a disproportionately large discount rate when it comes to future benefits. If a decision promises to have positive effects in twenty or thirty years, but imposes immediate costs, it will likely be unpopular with the majority of the electorate. While the causal mechanisms of measures protecting the climate are often latent and uncertain, the costs of environmental regulation are usually immediately salient. A fuel tax increases the gas prices at the pump instantaneously, while the benefits of this tax will not be felt for years or even decades.

---

13 James Hoggan, & Richard Littlemore, *Climate cover-up: The crusade to deny global warming* (Greystone Books 2009); Riley E. Dunlap, & Aaron M. McCright, 'Climate change denial: sources, actors and strategies' in Constance Lever-Tracy (ed.), *Routledge Handbook of Climate Change and Society* (Routledge 2010), 240; William Carroll, Nicolas Graham, Michael K. Lang, Zoë Yunker, & Kevin D. McCartney, 'The corporate elite and the architecture of climate change denial: a network analysis of carbon capital's reach into civil society', (2018) 55 *Canadian Review of Sociology* 425.

14 See Kirk Semple, Adam Westbrook, & Jonah M. Kessel, 'Meet the People Getting Paid to Kill Our Planet', *New York Times*, https://www.nytimes.com/2022/02/01/opinion/climate-sustainability-agriculture-lobby.html.

15 Wendy Wagner, 'Unreliable Science in the Courtroom: Shifting the Court's Focus from Assessing the Substance of an Expert's Analysis to the Process by Which it is Produced', Chapter 7 in this volume.

16 For an overview, see Tess Legg, Jenny Hatchard, & Anna B. Gilmore, 'The Science for Profit Model – How and why corporations influence science and the use of science in policy and practice', (2021) 16 PLoS ONE. See further Thomas O. McGarity, & Wendy E. Wagner, *Bending Science: How Special Interests Corrupt Public Health Research* (Harvard University Press 2008); David Michaels, *Doubt is their product: How industry's assault on science threatens your health* (Oxford University Press 2008); Naomi Oreskes, & Erik M. Conway, *Merchants of doubt: How a handful of scientists obscured the truth on issues from tobacco smoke to global warming* (Bloomsbury Publishing 2011).

Third, climate change is a public good or common pool resource problem.[17] States usually reap the full benefits of policies that are detrimental to the climate, while the costs are imposed on the commons.[18] Thus, the mitigation action of most individual states will only have a minor impact on climate change as such, lessening the political incentives to take action in the first place.[19] Accordingly, many policy areas which are subject to public interest litigation are prone to political market failures.

Such political market failure, in principle, justifies judicial intervention.[20] Nevertheless, it does not mean that any judicial intervention is justified. Instead, courts must find the right balance between respecting the legislative choice and exercising effective control of this choice. The most common doctrinal tool for finding this balance is the doctrine of deference.[21] The core of the concept is that the legislature has a certain decision-making prerogative, which is nevertheless limited and can be reviewed at the margins.[22] The decisive question is where these margins should be drawn. The following section will

---

17 On common pool resources, see seminally Garrett Hardin, 'The Tragedy of the Commons', (1968) 162 *Science* 1243. On public goods and related concepts, see generally Richard Cornes, & Todd Sandler, *The Theory of Externalities, public goods, and club goods* (Cambridge University Press, 2nd edn. 1996); Katharina Holzinger, 'Common Goods, Matrix Games and Institutional Responses', (2003) 9 *European Journal of International Relations* 173.

18 This is often called the commonize costs-privatize profits (CC-PP) game, see Garrett Hardin, *Filters against Folly: How to Survive Despite Economists, Ecologists, and the Merely Eloquent* (Viking Penguin 1985).

19 External effects do not necessarily lead to market inefficiencies. Ronald Coase has shown in a seminal article that trade can resolve the matter effectively if there are no transaction costs, see Ronald H. Coase, 'The Problem of Social Cost', (1960) 3 *Journal of Law & Economics* 1. However, contracting about public goods and common pool resources often entails significant transaction costs because of the number of affected people, so that a Coasean bargaining solution seems unrealistic, see Alexander Morell, 'Demand, Supply, and Markets' in Emanuel Towfigh, & Niels Petersen (eds.), *Economic Methods for Lawyers* (Edward Elgar 2015), 32.

20 Seminally John Hart Ely, *Democracy and Distrust. A Theory of Judicial Review* (Harvard University Press 1980). See also Niels Petersen, *Proportionality and Judicial Activism: Fundamental Rights Adjudication in Canada, Germany and South Africa* (Cambridge University Press 2017), 13–37.

21 This doctrine comes in different terminological variations and might in some jurisdictions also be called margin of discretion or margin of appreciation.

22 See David M. Beatty, 'Law and Politics', (1996) 44 *American Journal of Comparative Law* 131, 134.

discuss this issue in more detail, propose a typology of different approaches to construct judicial deference, and discuss the merits of the different approaches.

JUDICIAL DEFERENCE CONCERNING THE USE OF SCIENTIFIC FACTS: A TYPOLOGY

Determining the limits of judicial deference is far from straightforward.[23] Some voices in the legal literature even doubt that it is possible to draw limits to judicial deference in the abstract.[24] This section proposes a typology of different approaches to constructing judicial deference that can be observed in judicial practice. First, it will discuss a substantive approach, which focuses on the decision itself. It tries to identify situations in which the legislature should be granted deference through the use of substantive criteria. Concerning the assessment of scientific facts, courts often focus on uncertainty, giving legislatures discretion in situations where such uncertainty prevails. Second, courts often take a procedural approach. Instead of trying to identify situations in which legislatures should have a margin of discretion, they analyze the legislature's decision-making procedure and vary the level of deference depending on the quality of that procedure. The third approach focuses on legislative motivation. As we have seen in the previous section, the legislature does not always have incentives to follow scientific advice. This approach tries to analyze the motivation underlying the challenged decision. The three approaches are not exclusive, however. Instead, there may be cross-connections: judicial decision making may combine elements of these models.

A. Substantive Criteria for Delimiting Deference

Prima facie, the most intuitive approach is a substantive, first-order approach that focuses on the legislative decision itself.[25] It tries to identify substantive criteria for why the legislature should be granted deference by the judiciary

---

23 For a conceptual framework measuring the level of deference that courts apply, see Chan (n 9).

24 See Julian Rivers, 'Proportionality and Variable Intensity of Review', (2006) 65 *Cambridge Law Journal* 174, 202–06; Mark Elliott, 'Proportionality and Deference: The Importance of a Structured Approach' in Christopher Forsyth, Mark Elliott, Swati Jhaveri, Michael Ramsden, & Anne Scully Hill (eds.), *Effective Judicial Review: A Cornerstone of Good Governance* (Oxford University Press 2010), 264, 272–76. See also Niels Petersen, *Verhältnismäßigkeit als Rationalitätskontrolle* (Mohr Siebeck 2015), 107–08.

25 See, e.g., Rüdiger Breuer, 'Legislative and administrative Prognoseentscheidungen', (1977) 16 *Der Staat* 21, 39 (arguing that the legislature

and how extensive this deference should be.[26] An important consideration in determining the extent of a legislative margin of appreciation is the degree of scientific uncertainty.[27] Both the German Federal Constitutional Court (GFCC) and the Supreme Court of Canada (SCC) have at times applied such an approach.[28]

The Federal Constitutional Court developed its approach in its co-determination decision of 1979. The case concerned a legal reform that granted workers co-determination rights for certain corporate decisions of their employers. Several German corporations had asked the Court to declare the reform unconstitutional because it violated the property guarantee of the German Basic Law. The Court argued that the effects of the legislative reform were uncertain and then set out the basic dilemma:

> Uncertainty about the effects of a law in an uncertain future cannot preclude the legislature's authority to enact a law, even one of momentous importance. Conversely, uncertainty cannot in itself suffice to justify a margin of appreciation of the legislature that is not subject to judicial review. Legislative prognoses always contain a probability judgment, the basis of which can and must be demonstrated; this is not exempt from assessment.[29]

The Court then developed different tiers of scrutiny depending on several factors, such as "the subject area in question, the possibility to make a sufficiently certain assessment, and the significance of the legal interests at stake".[30] Therefore, the degree of indissoluble uncertainty is one factor that determines the amount of deference that is granted to the legislature.

The Supreme Court of Canada had to decide in *Irwin Toy* whether the prohibition of commercial advertising targeting children under 13 years of age violated the guarantee of freedom of expression under the Canadian Charter of Rights and Freedoms. Concerning the question of whether commercial advertising has a manipulative effect on young children, the Court referred to a report of the US Federal Trade Commission.[31] According to this report,

---

should only enjoy deference if there is uncertainty that cannot be dissolved through empirical data).

26 See Chan (n 9), 858.

27 This approach has certain similarities with the consensus rule proposed by Ed Cheng, 'The Consensus Rule: A New Approach to Scientific Evidence', (2022) 75 *Vanderbilt Law Review* 407.

28 See *Irwin Toy Ltd. v. Quebec (Attorney General)*, [1989] 1 S.C.R. 927 (for Canada) and BVerfGE 50, 290, at 332 (for Germany).

29 BVerfGE 50, 290, at 332 (translation by the author).

30 *Id.*, at 332–33.

31 *Irwin Toy* (n 28), at 988.

children under six years of age were specifically vulnerable to manipulation. This vulnerability decreased for older children who had become aware of the strategic intention of advertising.[32] The Court was asked to decide whether the choice of 13 years as the threshold age was arbitrary. It argued that "the government was afforded a margin of appreciation to form legitimate objectives based on *somewhat inconclusive social science evidence*".[33]

However, the Court did not give the government unlimited discretion. Instead, it turned to a procedural argument and reasoned that:

> [i]f the legislature has made a reasonable assessment as to where the line is most properly drawn, especially if the assessment involves weighing conflicting scientific evidence and allocating scarce resources on this basis, it is not for the Court to second-guess. That would only substitute one estimate for another.[34]

Yet the concept of inconclusive scientific evidence is less straightforward than it might seem prima facie. Uncertainty is not a binary concept.[35] Instead, we will never have a situation without uncertainty because we cannot deduce from past observations that the observed patterns will continue in the future. Karl Popper's famous example of the black swan illustrates this idea: Just because we have never seen a black swan does not mean that there are no black swans and that there will never be any black swans.[36] Courts, therefore, would have to measure the extent of the uncertainty, which is impossible in the abstract.[37]

If courts use the scientific discourse as an indication of uncertainty, they must determine how much scientific dissent is necessary to come to the conclusion of inconclusiveness. Is the existence of climate change deniers sufficient to argue that the evidence on the human causation of climate change is uncertain? Certainly, courts are unlikely to give much credit to the denial of climate change today. However, a comparable problem came up in the *Perinçek*

---

32 *Id.*, at 989.
33 *Id.*, at 990 (emphasis added).
34 *Id.*, at 990.
35 Klaus Ferdinand Gärditz, 'Gerichtliche Feststellung genereller Tatsachen (legislative facts) im Öffentlichen Recht' in Hans-Ullrich Paeffgen, Martin Böse, Urs Kindhäuser, Stephan Stübinger, Torsten Verrel, & Rainer Zaczyk (eds.), *Strafrechtswissenschaft als Analyse und Konstruktion. Festschrift für Ingeborg Puppe zum 70. Geburtstag* (Duncker & Humblot 2011), 1557, 1571.
36 Karl Raimund Popper, *Logik der Forschung* (J.C.B. Mohr, 10th edn. 1994), 438–44.
37 Karsten Schneider, *Normativität und Risikoentscheidung* (Duncker & Humblot 2008), 149.

judgment of the European Court of Human Rights (ECtHR).[38] The applicant, Dogu Perinçek, a Turkish politician, had been convicted in Switzerland for denying the Armenian genocide during World War I. There is indeed controversy about whether the death of up to 1.5 million Armenians during death marches and in concentration camps qualifies as genocide. However, most of the voices denying the qualification as genocide come from Turkey – with very few independent observers taking the same position. Nonetheless, the European Court of Human Rights held that there was too much historical uncertainty for Switzerland to convict Mr Perinçek of a crime.[39] In this case, the Court turned uncertainty against the legislature that had enacted the criminal norm and required more historical evidence as a basis for the Swiss legislation. Yet, the problem of this approach is obvious, both here and in the climate change context: Are deviant positions from scientists who might have a clear interest in advocating their position sufficient to qualify scientific evidence as inconclusive?

A further problem involves the sources on which courts rely in order to assess the scientific state of the art. How can judges determine that academic studies are methodologically sound and correctly describe the state of the art?[40] Here, we find some indications in judicial practice. First, courts may rely on scientific reports with some formal authority.[41] For example, the SCC relied in *Irwin Toy* on a report of the US Federal Trade Commission.[42] In its recent decision on German climate change regulation, the German Federal Constitutional Court resorted, inter alia, to reports of the Intergovernmental Panel on Climate Change (IPCC) and the German Advisory Council on the Environment, a panel of independent experts advising the German government.[43]

Second, courts may call on expert witnesses. For example, in its decision regarding the Public Sector Purchase Program (PSPP) of the European Central Bank, the GFCC relied heavily on the expertise of the German Central Bank as well as on the expertise of certain German professors of economics.[44] Finally, courts may interpret empirical data themselves. For example, the GFCC relied

---

[38] *Perinçek v. Switzerland* [GC], 15 October 2015, app. no. 27510/08, ECHR 2015-VI, p. 181.

[39] *Perinçek v. Switzerland*, 17 December 2013, app. no. 27510/08.

[40] See Schneider (n 37), 82–83; Gärditz (n 35), 1570–71.

[41] Rupert F. Stuart-Smith, Friederike E.L. Otto, Aisha I. Saad, Gaia Lisi, Petra Minnerop, Kristian Cedervall Lauta, Kristin van Zwieten, & Thom Wetzer, 'Filling the Evidentiary Gap in Climate Change Legislation', (2021) 11 *Nature Climate Change* 651.

[42] Irwin Toy (n 28), at 988–89.

[43] BVerfG, 24 March 2021, 1 BVR 2656/18, NJW 2021, 1723, at para. 32.

[44] BVerfGE 154,17, para. 82.

on statistics from the German Federal Office of Statistics in its smoking ban decision, in which it had to decide about the constitutionality of a smoking ban in restaurants and bars.[45]

However, all of these approaches face considerable difficulties. If courts rely on scientific reports or expert witnesses, the conclusions depend heavily on the choice of reports and experts. The PSPP litigation is particularly illuminating in this respect.[46] The question of the effects of quantitative easing is highly controversial among economists.[47] Many of the experts consulted by the Court were known to be critical of the ECB's policy even before their testimony before the Court. Had the Court chosen different experts, it would probably have received a different assessment of the situation. Furthermore, the evidence that the Court relies on may not reflect the state of the art. A recent study observed that courts in climate change litigation often did not apply the most recent methodology available for attributing responsibility for climate change events.[48]

One solution to these difficulties might be that judges acquire the expertise to assess empirical evidence themselves.[49] However, this is a process that will take time. Currently, judges in continental Europe do not seem to have the necessary skills for the assessment of empirical evidence. For example, in the smoking ban case, the German Federal Constitutional Court unwittingly revealed that relying on statistics without proper expertise may lead to problematic conclusions.[50] In that case, the Court declared a smoking ban in restaurants and bars to be partly unconstitutional.[51] In order to identify the severity of the restriction on the freedom of profession that the smoking ban imposed on restaurant and bar owners, the Court relied on data on the industry turnover from the Federal Office for Statistics.[52] The data showed that the turnover had been reduced more significantly in regions that had enacted a smoking ban than in regions that had not enacted such a ban. However, a closer analysis shows that there was a significant variance between regions in both categories

45 BVerfGE 121, 317, 355 and 364.

46 See BVerfGE 154, 17.

47 See Christopher Martin, & Costas Milas, 'Quantitative easing: a sceptical survey', (2012) 28 *Oxford Review of Economic Policy* 750; Peter Karadi, & Anton Nakov, 'Effectiveness and addictiveness of quantitative easing', (2021) 117 *Journal of Monetary Economics* 1096. See also the discussion in 'Should egalitarians fear low interest rates?', *The Economist*, July 13, 2019.

48 Stuart-Smith *et al.* (n 41).

49 Petersen (n 5), 318.

50 See Petersen (n 5), 307–9.

51 BVerfGE 121, 317.

52 BVerfGE 121, 317, 355 and 364.

so that the difference identified in the press release was unlikely to be statistically significant.[53] Finally, judges sometimes rely on experience and common sense to make empirical evaluations.[54] However, the experiences of judges may not always be representative and thus may be misleading.

Overall, the discussion illustrates that judges are not currently in a good position to assess empirical evidence in complex public interest cases. They have difficulty in determining the degree of deference that they should afford to the legislature and executive because they do not have proper standards for such a determination. Consequently, it is difficult to find pure substantive approaches in the case law of courts. Both the *co-determination* decision of the GFCC and *Irwin Toy* of the SCC stem from the courts' early fundamental rights jurisprudence. While the co-determination decision is still often cited as an authority, the GFCC has rarely used the approach in its later jurisprudence. Furthermore, even the early decisions contain a mix of different elements. For example, *Irwin Toy* used procedural considerations in order to determine whether the government acted reasonably in the face of uncertainty. Consequently, the substantive, first-order approach – as an exclusive approach – is not able to resolve the problems that courts are facing when dealing with empirical uncertainty. Instead, courts might occasionally use elements of it in combination with other approaches.

B. Focusing on the Decision-Making Procedure

The alternative to substantive criteria for deference is procedural approaches. These approaches rely on second-order criteria: They do not consider the decision itself, but rather focus on the legislative or administrative procedure by which the decision was made. If the decision-making procedure followed certain standards, courts will grant the legislature more deference. For example, courts will require the legislature to justify its choices,[55] to consider scientific

---

53 Niels Petersen, 'Braucht die Rechtswissenschaft eine empirische Wende?', (2010) 49 *Der Staat* 435, 449–50. See also the warning of Christoph Engel, 'Verhaltenswissenschaftliche Analyse: eine Gebrauchsanweisung für Juristen' in Christoph Engel, Markus Englerth, Jörn Lüdemann, & Indra Spiecker gen. Döhmann (eds.), *Recht und Verhalten* (Mohr Siebeck 2007), 363, 367 (arguing that lawyers should not trust the comparison of data without any reference to the statistical significance of the difference).

54 See Oliver Lepsius, 'Sozialwissenschaften im Verfassungsrecht – Amerika als Vorbild?', (2005) 60 *Juristenzeitung* 1, 2; Choudhry (n 7), 527.

55 See Konrad Redeker, & Ulrich Karpenstein, 'Über Nutzen und Notwendigkeit, Gesetze zu begründen', (2001) 54 *Neue Juristische Wochenschrift* 2825; Vesco Paskalev, *Taking Reasoning Seriously: The Role of Courts in*

evidence, to consult experts, to establish the empirical basis for its decisions,[56] and to take into account all relevant factors.[57] Even if the legislature fails to follow these standards, this does not automatically lead to the unconstitutionality of the measure in question. But it indicates that the challenged measure was not based on proper scientific evidence and shifts the burden of justification to the legislature.[58]

In academic discussions, such procedural approaches have been advocated for quite some time.[59] In recent years, we have also seen more and more

---

Enforcing Argumentative Rationality (EUI Working Paper Law 2012/16); Indra Spiecker gen. Döhmann, *Staatliche Entscheidungen unter Unsicherheit* (Mohr Siebeck 2025), part IV, ch. 2, B III.

56 See Rivers (n 24), 204; Julian Rivers, 'Proportionality, Discretion and the Second Law of Balancing' in George Pavlakos (ed.), *Law, Rights and Discourse. The Legal Philosophy of Robert Alexy* (Hart 2007), 167, 183; Alberto Alemanno, 'The Emergence of the Evidence-Based Judicial Reflex: A Response to Bar-Siman-Tov's Semiprocedural Review', (2013) 1 *The Theory and Practice of Legislation* 327; Patricia Popelier, 'The Court as a Regulatory Watchdog: The procedural approach in the case law of the European Court of Human Rights' in Patricia Popelier, Armen Mazmanyan, & Werner Vandenbruwaene (eds.), *The Role of Constitutional Courts in Multilevel Governance* (Intersentia 2013), 249, 258–62.

57 See Gunther Schwerdtfeger, 'Optimale Methodik der Gesetzgebung als Verfassungspflicht' in Rolf Stödter, & Werner Thieme (eds.), *Hamburg – Deutschland – Europa. Beiträge zum deutschen und europäischen Verfassungs-, Verwaltungs- und Wirtschaftsrecht. Festschrift für Hans Peter Ipsen zum siebzigsten Geburtstag* (J.C.B. Mohr 1977), 173, 182; Olivier De Schutter, & Françoise Tulkens, 'Rights in Conflict: The European Court of Human Rights as a Pragmatic Institution' in Eva Brems (ed.), *Conflicts between Fundamental Rights* (Intersentia 2008), 169, 208.

58 On the shifting of the argumentative burden in the context of the proportionality analysis, see Francisca Pou-Giménez, 'Unilateralism, Dialogue and False Necessity' in Francisca Pou-Giménez, Laura Clérico, & Restrepo-Saldarriaga (eds.), *Proportionality and Transformation: Theory and Practice from Latin America* (Cambridge University Press 2022), 289.

59 See Ossenbühl (n 2), 513; Ernst Benda, 'Bundesverfassungsgericht und Gesetzgeber im dritten Jahrzehnt des Grundgesetzes', (1979) 32 *Die öffentliche Verwaltung* 465, 467–68; Brun-Otto Bryde, *Verfassungsentwicklung* (Nomos 1982), 326–30; Martha Jackman, 'Protecting Rights and Promoting Democracy: Judicial Review under Section 1 of the Charter', (1996) 34 *Osgoode Hall Law Journal* 661, 679; Ernst Gottfried Mahrenholz, 'Verfassungsgerichtsbarkeit und Gesetzgebung' in Peter Badura, & Rupert Scholz (eds.), *Verfassungsgerichtsbarkeit und Gesetzgebung* (C.H. Beck 1998), 23, 32–34; Klaus Meßerschmidt, *Gesetzgebungsermessen* (Berlin Verlag 2000), 875–77; Rivers (n 24), 203–04; Rivers (n 56), 182–83; Joseph Corkin, 'Science, legitimacy and the law: Regulating

evidence that a procedural interpretation of deference is taking hold in judicial practice. One of the pioneers adopting a procedural interpretation of judicial deference is the Court of Justice of the European Union (CJEU). The CJEU examines whether the decision-making procedure that led to the challenged measure took into account all relevant factors. In particular, the Court analyzes whether the decision followed the recommendations of the legislative impact assessment[60] or was at least based on scientific data.[61] This does not mean that the European legislature has an obligation to follow the recommendations of the scientific impact assessment. However, if it chooses to deviate, these deviations have to be properly justified.[62] Furthermore, the CJEU analyzes whether the viewpoints of all relevant stakeholders were heard[63] and all relevant interests taken into account.[64] Finally, the Court assesses whether the EU institutions gave proper reasons for their decision.[65]

---

risk regulation judiciously in the European Community', (2008) 33 *European Law Review* 359; De Schutter, & Tulkens (n 57), 208–10; Janneke Gerards, 'Pluralism, Deference and the Margin of Appreciation Doctrine', (2011) 17 *European Law Journal* 80, 118–20; Ittai Bar-Siman-Tov, 'Semiprocedural Judicial Review', (2012) 6 *Legisprudence* 271; Kai Möller, *The Global Model of Constitutional Rights* (Oxford University Press 2012), 132; Patricia Popelier, 'Preliminary Comments on the Role of Courts as Regulatory Watchdogs', (2012) 6 *Legisprudence* 257; Popelier (n 56); Spiecker gen. Döhmann (n 55), part IV, ch. 3, D.

60 See, e.g., Case 58/08, *Vodafone*, [2010] ECR I-4999, at para. 55; Case C-176/09, *Luxembourg v. Parliament and Council*, [2011] ECR I-3727, at para. 65; Case C-358/14, *Poland v. Parliament and Council*, 4 May 2016, EU:C:2016:232, at para. 101; Case C-128/17; *Philip Morris*, 4 May 2016, EU:C:2016:325, at para. 189; *Poland v. Parliament and Council*, 13 March 2019, EU:C:2019:194, at paras. 109–112; Case C-547/14.

61 See, e.g., Case 78/16, *Pesce*, 9 June 2016, EU:C:2016:428, at paras. 71–73; Case C-547/14, *Philip Morris*, supra note 60, at paras. 207–208; Joined Cases C-643/15 and C-647/15, *Slovak Republic and Hungary v. Council*, 6 Sept. 2017, EU:C:2017:631, at paras. 222, 242, 272.

62 See Case C-477/14, *Pillbox 38*, 4 May 2016, EU:C:2016:324, at paras. 65–66.

63 See, e.g., Case C-15/10, *Etimine*, [2011] ECR I-6681, at para. 127; Case C-477/14, *Pillbox 38*, *supra* note 62, at para. 66.

64 See, e.g., Case C-127/07, *Arcelor Atlantique et Lorraine*, [2008] ECR I-9895, at para. 59; Case C-343/09, *Afton Chemical*, [2010] ECR I-7027, at paras. 60–64; Case C-358/14, *Poland v. Parliament and Council*, *supra* note 60, at para. 102; Case 78/16, Pesce, *supra* note 61, at para. 74; Case C-59/11, *Association Kokopelli*, 12 July 2012, EU:C:2012:447, at para. 40; Case C-547/14, Philip Morris, *supra* note 60, at paras. 185–187.

65 See, e.g., Case C-62/14, *Gauweiler*, 16 June 2015, EU:C:2015:400, at paras. 69–70.

One case that well illustrates the approach of the CJEU is *Spain v. Council*.[66] Spain challenged a Council regulation establishing a new subsidy scheme for cotton which reduced the level of subsidies awarded to the cotton industry to 35% of the level of the previous scheme. In its proportionality assessment of the challenged regulation, the Court of Justice noted that the regulation had not been based on a legislative impact assessment.[67] This approach deviated from the previous practice regarding agricultural subsidy schemes.[68] However, the lack of an impact assessment did not per se lead to the determination that the regulation was disproportionate. But the Court found that the EU institutions had not calculated the margins of the cotton farmers correctly and thus failed to include all relevant factors in their assessment.[69] It was because of this deficient decision-making procedure that the Court found the measure to be disproportionate.[70] If we evaluate the judgment, we see that the Court of Justice did not assess the appropriateness of the subsidy as such. Instead, it mostly focused on the procedure by which the regulation was established. The lack of a legislative impact assessment and the objective mistake in calculating the farmers' margins led the Court to the conclusion that the EU legislature had transgressed the limits of its discretion.

Further evidence of a procedural approach appears in the case law of the German Federal Constitutional Court. The Court gave some early pointers in the already discussed co-determination judgment.[71] It established certain procedural requirements: In particular, the legislature had to exhaust all accessible sources of knowledge and to assess the probable effects of its legislation as reliably as possible.[72] The Court then argued: "If these procedural requirements are met, the decision can generally be considered to be justifiable; they establish the margin of discretion of the legislature, which has to be respected by the Federal Constitutional Court".[73]

The most prominent application of this procedural approach can be found in the *Hartz IV* judgment of the GFCC.[74] In *Hartz IV*, the Court had to decide whether the level of tax-financed social benefits was sufficient to provide a subsistence minimum for individuals who received these benefits. The Court acknowledged that the legislature had a significant margin of discretion for

66 Case C-310/04, *Spain v. Council*, [2006] ECR I-7318.
67 *Id.*, at para. 103.
68 *Id.*
69 *Id.*, at paras. 110–33.
70 *Id.*, at para. 135.
71 BVerfGE 50, 290, at 334.
72 *Id.*
73 *Id* (translation by the author).
74 BVerfGE 125, 175.

identifying the subsistence minimum.[75] However, it required the legislature to determine all expenditures necessary for subsistence through a transparent and reasonable procedure that would assess the actual need.[76] Based on this standard, the Court argued that the legislative procedure was deficient.

On the one hand, the Court used consistency considerations: while the legislature had relied on a statistical model for its calculation of the subsistence level, it had made reductions without justifying how it determined the extent of these reductions. The Court argued that these reductions did not have a sufficient empirical basis.[77] On the other hand, the Court criticized the lack of any discernible empirical evidence as a basis for other determinations. In particular, the Court held that the calculation of the social benefits for children made assumptions "without any empirical or methodological foundation".[78] Because of these procedural deficiencies, the Court held that the challenged provisions were unconstitutional.[79]

Finally, traces of the procedural approach can also be found in the jurisprudence of the Supreme Court of Canada. We have already seen that the Court applied some procedural elements in *Irwin Toy*.[80] Furthermore, judges have applied procedural considerations in their dissenting opinions to the decision of *RJR-MacDonald*[81] and *Chaoulli*.[82] In *RJR-MacDonald*, the SCC had found a prohibition of tobacco advertising to be unconstitutional because the legislature had not offered evidence that a total prohibition was necessary for the protection of public health.[83] However, the dissenters argued that the Court should have granted a margin of discretion to the legislature because the legislation was the result of a 20-year process in which all relevant interest groups had been heard and several expert studies had been commissioned.[84]

---

75 *Id.*, at 224–25.

76 *Id.*, at 225.

77 *Id.*, at 239.

78 *Id.*, at 246 (translation by the author).

79 For a similar, procedural interpretation of the *Hartz IV* judgment, see Klaus Ferdinand Gärditz, 'Das verfassungsrechtliche Existenzminimum im "Hartz IV"-Urteil des Bundesverfassungsgerichts', (2010) 3 *Bonner Rechtsjournal* 4, 11; Klaus Meßerschmidt, 'The good Shepherd of Karlsruhe: The Hartz IV decision – A good example of regulatory review by the German Federal Constitutional Court?' in Patricia Popelier, Armen Mazmanyan, & Werner Vandenbruwaene (eds.), *The Role of Constitutional Courts in Multilevel Governance* (Intersentia 2013), 235, 244.

80 See above, n 31 and subsequent citations.

81 *RJR-MacDonald* (n 8).

82 *Chaoulli v. Quebec (Attorney General)*, [2005] 1 S.C.R. 791.

83 *RJR-MacDonald* (n 8), at 345 (per McLachlin J.).

84 *Id.*, at 306–07 (per LaForest J.).

Chaoulli concerned a prohibition of private healthcare in Quebec.[85] The Court argued that the legislation was unconstitutional because the legislature had offered sufficient proof that it was necessary in order to protect the public health insurance system.[86] By contrast, the dissenters argued that the legislature should have been granted deference.[87] The Quebec legislature had commissioned an expert opinion that had recommended a prohibition of private health insurance without limitations.[88] For this reason, the dissenters argued that the legislature had had a sufficient empirical basis for its decision and should have been granted a margin of discretion.

The procedural approach to judicial deference has a lot of normative appeal.[89] On the one hand, it respects the decision-making autonomy of the legislature to a great extent. On the other hand, it tries to discern whether the legislative decision has a rational basis.[90] However, purely procedural review of the legislative margin of discretion is not without problems. In particular, there are no accepted standards for what constitutes a rational decision-making procedure.[91] When did the legislature establish the empirical basis for its decision sufficiently? What are the requirements regarding the experts who are heard? How detailed does the reasoning justifying a decision need to be? Because of these difficulties, courts must apply a rather deferential standard when reviewing the decision-making procedure. The margin of discretion is only limited if the decision-making procedure is clearly deficient. Consequently, a purely procedural standard of review is probably too deferential to guarantee effective review of the legislature.

C. Smoking Out Illicit Motivation

A third approach focuses on legislative motivation. When discussing the conceptual preliminaries, we have seen that the legislature is not always motivated

85 *Chaoulli* (n 82).
86 *Id.*, at 828–831 (per Deschamps J.).
87 *Id.*, at 904 (per Binnie and LeBel JJ.).
88 *Id.*
89 Petersen (n 5), 315.
90 Popelier (n 56), 265.
91 Meßerschmidt (n 79), 242; Petersen (n 5), 315.

to follow scientific advice.[92] It may be captured by powerful interest groups.[93] Furthermore, politics may have reduced incentives to tackle a particular problem because the costs of a mitigation measure are borne by the electorate, while the benefits include positive externalities. Climate change is an illustrative example in both respects. On the one hand, industry lobbying against climate change legislation is intense. On the other hand, the climate is a public good, so that mitigation efforts have positive external effects and politics has incentives to underprovide mitigation.[94] Furthermore, there is a discounting effect because the benefits of mitigation efforts lie in the future.[95]

Consequently, if failures to take into account scientific evidence are due to problematic incentives, one could think of reviewing legislative motivation to determine the extent to which the legislature should be granted discretion.[96] If there is suspicion that the legislature had incentives not to act in the common interest, courts should not defer to the legislative fact-finding procedure, but

---

[92] See *supra*, I. See also Rob van Gestel, & Peter van Lochem, 'Evidence-Based Regulation and the Translation from Empirical Data to Normative Choices: A Proportionality Test', (2018) 12 *Erasmus Law Review* 120 (showing that the Dutch legislature often uses evidence strategically and selectively, not taking into account potential counter-evidence).

[93] For empirical evidence on interest group capture in the US, see Thomas Stratman, 'What Do Campaign Contributions Buy? Deciphering Causal Effects of Money and Votes', (1991) 57 *Southern Economic Journal* 606; Laura I. Langbein, 'Lobbies and Political Conflict: The Case of Gun Control', (1993) 77 *Public Choice* 551; Robert E. Baldwin, & Christopher S. Magee, 'Is trade policy for sale? Congressional voting on recent trade bills', (2000) 105 *Public Choice* 79. See also Geoffrey P. Miller, 'Public Choice at the Dawn of the Special Interest State: The Story of Butter and Margarine', (1989) 77 *California Law Review* 83.

[94] See William Nordhaus, 'Climate Change: The Ultimate Challenge for Economics', (2019) 109 *American Economic Review* 1991.

[95] See Simon Caney, 'Climate change and the future: Discounting for time, wealth, and risk', (2009) 40 *Journal of Social Philosophy* 163.

[96] The review of legislative motivation is discussed, in particular, in the United States. See, e.g., Jerry L. Mashaw, 'Constitutional Deregulation: Notes Toward a Public, Public Law', (1980) 54 *Tulane Law Review* 849, 874–75; Cass R. Sunstein, 'Public Values, Private Interests, and the Equal Protection Clause', (1982) *The Supreme Court Review* 127; Richard A. Epstein, 'Toward a Revitalization of the Contract Clause', (1984) 51 *The University of Chicago Law Review* 703; Cass R. Sunstein, 'Naked Preferences and the Constitution', (1984) 84 *Columbia Law Review* 1689; Cass R. Sunstein, 'Interest Groups in American Public Law', (1985) 38 *Stanford Law Review* 29; Erwin Chemerinsky, 'The Vanishing Constitution', (1989) 103 *Harvard Law Review* 43, 78–81.

second-guess the empirical assumptions of a legislative measure.[97] However, legislative motivation is difficult to observe. Even if legislators take positions in order to satisfy the interests of their donors, they will rarely say so in public. Instead, they will refer to a public interest in order to justify their decision.[98] A US senator blocking climate change legislation will rather cite his fear of inflation than the influence of the coal industry in his home state.[99] Therefore, a review of legislative motivation has to resort to second-order criteria; that is, to find indications that the legislature had a latent illicit motivation.[100]

Two indications have particular importance.[101] The first is the lack of fit between measure and purpose and the second involves inconsistencies in the design of the measure.[102] If the legislature adopts a measure that is not necessary to achieve a certain purpose, this may indicate that the legislature pursued other goals than the ones explicitly stated in the justification of the legislation.[103] Similarly, the lack of consistency of a measure gives an indication that it might have hidden aims.[104] An example from the German Federal Constitutional Court illustrates the point. In the sports betting judgment from 2006, the Court had to decide about the constitutionality of a state monopoly in sports betting in the state of Bavaria.[105] The legislature had argued that the state monopoly served the purpose of fighting gambling addiction. While the

---

97 See Stephen Gardbaum, 'A Democratic Defense of Constitutional Balancing', (2010) 4 *Law & Ethics of Human Rights* 77, 101.

98 Christoph Engel, 'The Constitutional Court – Applying the Proportionality Principle – as a Subsidiary Authority for the Assessment of Political Outcomes' in Christoph Engel, & Adrienne Héritier (eds.), *Linking Politics and Law* (Nomos 2003), 285, 292.

99 See Jonathan Weisman & Lisa Friedman, 'Behind Manchin's Opposition, a Long History of Fighting Climate Measures', *The New York Times* (20 December 2021), https://www.nytimes.com/2021/12/20/us/politics/manchin-climate-change-coal.html?smid=url-share.

100 See Niels Petersen, 'The German Constitutional Court and Legislative Capture', (2014) 12 *International Journal of Constitutional Law* 650, 657–61.

101 *Id.*, 658–61.

102 See Mattias Kumm, 'The Idea of Socratic Contestation and the Right to Justification: The Point of Rights-Based Proportionality Review', (2010) 4 *Law & Ethics of Human Rights* 141, 160–62.

103 Jud Mathews, & Alec Stone Sweet, 'All Things in Proportion? American Rights Review and the Problem of Balancing', (2011) 60 *Emory Law Journal* 102, 124.

104 See Niels Petersen, 'Legislative Inconsistency and the "Smoking Out" of Illicit Motives', (2016) 64 *American Journal of Comparative Law* 121.

105 BVerfGE 115, 276.

Court acknowledged that this was an important aim,[106] it held that the implementation had been inconsistent.[107] In particular, the advertising efforts of the state lottery, presenting sports betting as an innocent leisure activity, were contrary to the stated purpose of the monopoly.[108] Instead, there was suspicion that the monopoly aimed at generating income for the state, which in itself was not a sufficiently legitimate purpose to justify a restriction of the freedom of profession of private sports betting providers.[109]

In judicial practice, there are quite a few cases where the lack of fit or the lack of consistency is considered to be an indication of an illicit motivation of the legislature. In the German case law, the pharmacy case is a paradigmatic example.[110] The case concerned a licensing requirement for establishing new pharmacies which sought to limit the number of pharmacies per inhabitant.[111] The Court indicated that it saw the danger that this licensing requirement served the purpose of restricting competition and protecting incumbent pharmacies quite clearly.[112] However, the Court did not examine the legislative motivation head-on. Instead, its suspicions about the legislature's motivations only served as a justification for its strict level of scrutiny.[113] Ultimately, the Court referred to the lack of fit and consistency of the measure to declare it unconstitutional.[114]

---

106 *Id.*, at 304.

107 *Id.*, at 309–16.

108 *Id.*, at 315.

109 See *id.*, at 307.

110 See Petersen (n 100), 664–66.

111 BVerfGE 7, 377.

112 See *id.*, at 408 ("There is a significant danger of [the legislative decision] being influenced by illicit motives; in particular, it seems likely that the access restriction is supposed to protect those who are already part of the profession against competition—a motive that, according to common opinion, cannot justify an infringement of the freedom of profession") (Translation by the author). See also the analysis of the court files by Fabian Michl, 'Das Sondervotum zum Apothekenurteil', (2020) 68 *Jahrbuch des öffentlichen Rechts* 323, 340–45, highlighting the salience of this issue in the debate among the judges.

113 See Anna-Bettina Kaiser, 'Das Apothekenurteil des BVerfG nach 50 Jahren – Anfang oder Anfang vom Ende der Berufsfreiheit?', (2008) 30 *Juristische Ausbildung* 844, 850; Petersen (n 100), 665. For a parallel development in US Constitutional Law doctrine, see John Hart Ely, 'The Centrality and Limits of Motivation Analysis', (1978) 15 *San Diego Law Review* 1155, 1157; Sunstein, 'Naked Preferences' (n 96), 1700 (arguing that strict scrutiny serves the purpose of smoking out illicit motives).

114 See Petersen (n 100), 664–66.

Consistency considerations and the lack of fit between a measure and its purpose play a prominent role in policing legislative motivations in the context of free-trade agreements. Here, states often cite common purposes, such as environmental or consumer protection, for trade restrictions, while the measure predominantly pursues a protectionist aim. One example from the jurisprudence of the WTO Appellate Body is the *US – Gasoline* case.[115] The case concerned US regulations on the composition of fuel. In certain environmental zones, only fuel with specific, more environmentally friendly characteristics could be sold. To prevent the toxins banned in new fuel from being "disposed of" in regular fuel, regular fuel could not contain more toxins than fuel sold before the regulation was introduced. To do this, manufacturers had to create a baseline of their own fuel based on the characteristics before the regulation was introduced and then adhere to it afterward.

Foreign refineries were not granted the opportunity to create such a reference sample of their own fuel. Rather, their fuel had to meet standard criteria, which often required greater adjustments than the reference samples allowed for US manufacturers. The United States justified this unequal treatment by arguing that the creation of reference samples by foreign manufacturers could not be adequately controlled because the administrative burden was too high. At the same time, the US refineries could not be obliged to comply with the uniform legal requirements in place for foreign manufacturers as this would impose disproportionate costs on them.

The Appellate Body recognized the fundamental need for fuel standards. However, it concluded that the United States had not implemented the measure consistently. If uniform legal standards were too expensive for the domestic industry, then this should also have applied to the foreign refiners. Therefore, if the US wanted to consider the adjustment costs for the fuel industry, it also had to take into account these adjustment costs for foreign manufacturers.[116] The implementation of the measure was, therefore, inconsistent, suggesting that the protection of domestic industry was at least a welcome side effect of the environmental protection measure.

There are also several examples from the case law of the CJEU, where the Luxembourg Court uses inconsistency or the lack of fit as means to weed out protectionist motivations. One example is the judgment on the German Beer Purity Act.[117] The case concerned an absolute marketing ban on beers

---

115 WTO Appellate Body, 29 April 1996, United States – Standards for Reformulated Gasoline, WT/DS2/AB/R.

116 *Id.*, at 28.

117 Case 178/84, *Commission v. Germany*, [1987] ECR 1227. See also the very similar Cases C-13/91 and C-113/91, *Michel Debus*, [1992] ECR I-3636, at paras. 24–25.

containing chemical additives. Germany argued that the ban was justified because it protected public health and that beers brewed according to the German Purity Law would not need to resort to chemical additives.[118] In its decision, the Court of Justice first acknowledged that it is up to each Member State to decide what level of protection it considered necessary for the protection of life and health.[119] However, the Court found it inconsistent to ban chemical additives for beer, while at the same time allowing them for almost all other beverages.[120] The fact that Germany had not generally prohibited chemical additives in food showed that it did not give particular significance to the resulting health dangers. At the very least, Germany should have explained which specific risks would arise from the additives in connection with beer, which it failed to do in the proceedings.[121]

The preceding discussion suggests that scrutinizing legislative motivation for inconsistency and lack of fit is a common judicial practice. Even if courts do not directly refer to legislative motivation, the question is frequently in the background when courts review a legislature's empirical assessments. However, this motive-based review is not without its own problems. On the one hand, there is the problem of potential circularity. Empirical assessments are a central element of the proportionality test or the review of the fit of a measure in constitutional rights review.[122] If the question is whether the legislature should have a margin of discretion in establishing and evaluating these empirical facts, then the lack of fit between measure and purpose cannot be an indication for reducing legislative deference. On the other hand, lack of fit and inconsistency cannot be the only indicators. Just because a measure is consistent, this does not mean that the legislature did not have illicit motives. For this reason, the review of legislative motivation cannot stand on its own, but should only be taken into account in combination with the other factors.[123]

---

118 See *Commission v. Germany*, *supra* note 117, at para. 15.

119 *Id.*, at para. 41.

120 *Id.*, at para. 49.

121 *Id.*, at paras. 38 and 49.

122 See Anne van Aaken, 'Vom Nutzen der ökonomischen Theorie für das öffentliche Recht: Methode und Anwendungsmöglichkeiten' in Marc Bungenberg *et al.* (eds.), *Recht und Ökonomik* (C.H. Beck 2004), 1, 19; David Robertson, *The Judge as Political Theorist: Contemporary Constitutional Review* (Princeton University Press 2010), 80; Moshe Cohen-Eliya, & Iddo Porat, 'Proportionality and the Culture of Justification', (2011) 59 *American Journal of Comparative Law* 463, 469–70.

123 See also Rob van Gestel, & Jurgen de Poorter, 'Putting evidence-based law making to the test: judicial review of legislative rationality', (2016) 4 *The Theory and Practice of Legislation* 155 (arguing that the CJEU should go beyond a mere

CONCLUSION

The discussion in this chapter analyzed different approaches to deal with empirical facts. Courts often avoid assessing empirical facts directly. Instead, the discussion usually revolves around the extent to which the legislative fact-finding procedure can be trusted. The doctrinal instrument of choice is the judicial deference or margin of discretion doctrine. There are several ways in which courts can construct judicial deference. One approach uses substantive criteria. However, this approach faces several problems. In particular, judges still need to evaluate evidence and are often not trained to do so.

For this reason, many courts focus on the procedure establishing the empirical basis of legislative decisions. They grant deference to the legislature if an adequate fact-finding procedure was established. Procedural indicia include whether the legislature adhered to expert advice and took all relevant interests into account in its decision-making procedure. Finally, courts sometimes attempt to smoke out illicit motives. This approach can most often be found in the jurisprudence regarding free-trade agreements. Here, courts second-guess the fact-finding procedure of the legislature by pointing out inconsistencies in the challenged measure or the lack of fit between measure and purpose.

These three approaches are often interwoven with each other. Procedural inefficiencies might be an indication of illicit motivation, and many of the doctrinal indicia of legislative motivation also serve as indicators of a rational fact-finding procedure. Furthermore, none of these approaches to judicial deference is perfect in itself. We have seen that all of them have certain weaknesses. The procedural approach needs to define what a rational procedure entails, which is difficult to do in the abstract. The approach focusing on legislative motivation is insufficient because legislative motivation will often be difficult to prove.

It is, therefore, not surprising that courts in practice apply a combination of these approaches; sometimes, depending on the situation at issue, even in the same decision. Asking courts to strive for theoretical consistency would ask too much of them because such a standard is most likely unachievable in the current system. One can debate whether a stronger focus on social sciences in legal education, the creation of specialized courts or the inclusion of experts in judicial panels would strengthen the judicial capacity to review empirical facts. But without such an institutional reform, the pragmatic and eclectic approach to judicial deference and scientific fact-finding that we observe is probably the best we can achieve.

---

procedural review and directly review the empirical data underlying legislative decisions).

6. Empirical evidence in equality law-making

Alysia Blackham

INTRODUCTION: EQUALITY AND THE PUBLIC INTEREST

There is a clear public interest in advancing equality and addressing inequality. At a societal level, inequality is associated with economic instability and lower economic growth,[1] higher crime rates, lower health outcomes and shorter life expectancy, and lower happiness. Advancing equality therefore has public benefits; equality litigation can and should be seen as a form of public interest litigation.

Equality law is also an area in which judges are commonly asked to make decisions that weigh competing policy choices. Equality law is not unlimited in scope; legislation (and its interpretation and application) often focuses on boundary setting, determining areas and actions that are within and beyond the prohibition of discrimination. Boundary setting particularly occurs through making exceptions to equality law,[2] the granting of exemptions to legislative provisions, or the ability to justify discrimination in certain circumstances.

It is in relation to the justification of discrimination that the weighing of competing policy choices is particularly stark. In the EU and UK, for example, courts are asked to determine whether discrimination is objectively justified as a proportionate means of achieving a legitimate aim. For most protected characteristics, only indirect discrimination can be justified in this way. However, for age discrimination, direct discrimination can be justified as a proportionate

---

1 OECD, *In It Together: Why Less Inequality Benefits All* (OECD 2015) <https://www.oecd-ilibrary.org/employment/in-it-together-why-less-inequality-benefits-all_9789264235120-en> accessed 7 June 2021.

2 Alysia Blackham, 'A Compromised Balance? A Comparative Examination of Exceptions to Age Discrimination Law in Australia and the UK' (2018) 41 *Melbourne University Law Review* 1085.

means of achieving a legitimate aim.[3] This distinguishes age discrimination from all other protected grounds.

The possibility of justifying direct age discrimination means that distinguishing acceptable from unacceptable discrimination is central to age discrimination law.[4] The success of age discrimination law largely hinges on how this justification provision is applied.[5] It requires courts to undertake complex, fact-driven normative judgements regarding when age discrimination might be instrumentally useful, and when this usefulness should yield to the principle of equality.[6]

In practice, most superior case law and scholarship on age discrimination in the UK and EU has related to whether a measure is justified, focusing on three key settings: in relation to mandatory retirement ages,[7] pension provision (and changes to pension provision),[8] and redundancy pay.[9] Courts have struggled to

---

3 See Council Directive 2000/78/EC of 27 November 2000 establishing a general framework for equal treatment in employment and occupation [2000] OJ L303/16, art. 6(1).

4 Sandra Fredman, *Discrimination Law* (2nd edn, Oxford University Press 2011) 101.

5 Mark Butler, 'Marginalising the Objective Justification Defence in Retirement Cases?' (2011) 53 *International Journal of Law and Management* 375, 384–5.

6 Or, if taking individual rights as a starting point, the question might be: when should the principle of equality give way to the instrumental benefits of discrimination? See Malcolm Sargeant, 'The Employment Equality (Age) Regulations 2006: A Legitimisation of Age Discrimination in Employment' (2006) 35 *Industrial Law Journal* 209, 218. On the complexity of this task, see Elaine Dewhurst, 'Proportionality Assessments of Mandatory Retirement Measures: Uncovering Guidance for National Courts in Age Discrimination Cases' (2016) 45 *Industrial Law Journal* 60.

7 See, e.g., Elaine Dewhurst, 'Intergenerational Balance, Mandatory Retirement and Age Discrimination in Europe: How Can the ECJ Better Support National Courts in Finding a Balance between the Generations?' (2013) 50 *Common Market Law Review* 1333; Dewhurst (n 6); Alysia Blackham, *Extending Working Life for Older Workers: Age Discrimination Law, Policy and Practice* (Hart Publishing 2016) ch 3. See *Seldon v Clarkson Wright & Jakes* [2012] 3 All ER 1301.

8 See, e.g., Lydia Seymour, 'The Courts, Non-Discrimination and Systemic Change in UK Public Sector Pension Scheme' in Sinéad Agnew, Paul S. Davies and Charles Mitchell (eds), *Pensions: Law, Policy and Practice* (Hart 2020).

9 See, e.g., Malcolm Sargeant, 'Age Discrimination, Redundancy Payments and Length of Service' (2009) 72 *Modern Law Review* 628; Alysia Blackham, 'Falling on Their Feet: Young Workers, Employment and Age Discrimination' (2015) 44 *Industrial Law Journal* 246.

determine these complex, fact-driven questions of justification. Judicial reasoning in these cases can be opaque, with divergent decisions reached in similar factual scenarios.[10] This risks undermining the certainty and predictability of legal provisions, limiting the practical utility of age discrimination law.

Goosey has therefore argued that distinguishing justified from unjustified discrimination should be seen as a form of moral reasoning, in which competing interests are weighed.[11] For Goosey, a moral reasoning approach helps to make decision-making transparent.[12] Goosey argues that courts should balance five key interests: equality of opportunity (assessed over a complete life), social equality (for participation in social, economic, and political life), respect, autonomy, and efficiency. However, Goosey does not speak to the use of empirical evidence in such reasoning, despite the fact these decisions must be *fact-driven* normative judgements. Indeed, Goosey's approach to equality of opportunity – which sees opportunity as being measured across our complete lives, despite changing governmental and organisational policies and an uncertain future – likely defies empirical operationalisation.

EMPIRICAL EVIDENCE AND JUSTIFICATION

This emphasizes, then, the need for a more structured consideration of how courts apply justification provisions in practice, including how empirical evidence is used and competing considerations weighed. This chapter, then, considers four inter-related questions regarding how courts deploy the justification process:

1. To what extent are courts open about their policy choices?
2. How, if at all, do courts take the potential macro-consequences of their decisions into account?
3. How, if at all, do courts take into account empirical data in their decision-making?
4. How might this affect the legitimacy of judicial decision-making?

These questions are explored via a case study of equality law as a public interest issue. I focus on two joined direct age discrimination cases – *Sargeant v London Fire and Emergency Planning Authority*[13] (*Sargeant*) and *McCloud v*

[10] Blackham, *Extending Working Life* (n 7) ch 3.

[11] Stuart Goosey, *A Pluralist Theory of Age Discrimination* (Bloomsbury Publishing 2021).

[12] Ibid.

[13] [2017] UKET 2202235/2015.

The Lord Chancellor[14] (*McCloud*) – that related solely to the issue of justification. The cases concerned challenges to transitional pension provisions that were based on date of birth.

These decisions represent critical cases for three key reasons. First, they had significant and wide-ranging financial repercussions for the UK government and for individual public sector workers. For the government, estimates put the cost of the decisions at somewhere between £17 billion and £31 billion. Public sector pensions – which are mostly unfunded and must be paid from general taxation and revenue – represent a present and future liability of £2.2 trillion (as of 31 March 2019).[15] For individuals, adequate pensions are key to having a decent standard of living in retirement. The transitional provisions challenged in these cases would have made some affected workers significantly worse off in retirement; these cases therefore are significant at an individual level. Thus, there is a clear public interest in ensuring these pension disputes are adjudicated in a way that appropriately weighs the policy choices being made.

Second, these cases represent one means by which the public service sought to challenge austerity policies in the UK. In the aftermath of the 2008 economic crisis, governments in the UK and EU sought to reduce government spending and increase taxation. Austerity policies have been repeatedly shown to have negative public impacts, including by increasing mental distress for the most marginalized,[16] and negatively affecting health and social outcomes,[17] including mental health.[18] The UK public sector equality duty (PSED) has been repeatedly used to challenge austerity policies.[19] However, the PSED is enforced through judicial review proceedings; remedies are far more limited than those under equality law. In judicial review proceedings relating to the

14 [2017] UKET 2201483/2015.

15 ICAEW, '£31 Billion Charge Shines Spotlight on £2.2tn Pounds Public Sector Pension Liability' (*ICAEW*) <https://martinwheatcroft.com/icaew20200820/> accessed 16 January 2026.

16 Ian Cummins, 'The Impact of Austerity on Mental Health Service Provision: A UK Perspective' (2018) 15 *International Journal of Environmental Research and Public Health* 1145.

17 David Stuckler, Aaron Reeves, Rachel Loopstra, Marina Karanikolos and Martin McKee, 'Austerity and Health: The Impact in the UK and Europe' (2017) 27 *European Journal of Public Health* 18.

18 Laura McGrath, Vanessa Griffin and Ed Mundy, 'The Psychological Impact of Austerity: A Briefing Paper' (2016) 2(2) Educational Psychology Research and Practice 46.

19 Helen Carr, 'The Public Sector Equality Duty – a Mainstay of Justice in an Age of Austerity' (2014) 36 *Journal of Social Welfare and Family Law* 208.

PSED, government decisions are rarely overturned;[20] the remedy may simply be a declaration that the duty has not been complied with.[21] Even requiring reconsideration of a decision might ultimately lead to the same result. Thus, using equality law to challenge austerity – not the PSED – offers significant advantages and opens up creative and important remedial options.

Third, age discrimination law is arguably underutilised as a tool for advancing the public interest. Gosseries invites us to consider how age discrimination law might be applied in creative ways in the public interest[22] including, for example, in environmental litigation to combat environmental degradation and climate inaction.[23] As Gosseries acknowledges, though,

> Whether this can be turned into real, successful cases will depend on the resources of the legal systems at stake. It will also depend on the ability of plaintiffs to transform a vision into conclusive legal argument, maximally exploiting the potential of existing anti-discrimination law while not forcing judges to go beyond what separation of powers allows, or, in the case of the ECJ, leaving enough margin of appreciation to member states.[24]

Thus, success in practice depends on how courts (and advocates) use and apply age discrimination law. These cases therefore help to illuminate how or if age discrimination law might be used for other public interest ends.

PENSIONS AND PROPERTY RIGHTS

While age discrimination law is only one tool that might be used to challenge changes to pension provisions, it has significant advantages over, say, property or contract law. As I have argued elsewhere, pensions could be seen as: a form of *social right* delivered by the government; a form of *deferred wage* (in which individuals might be regarded as having proprietary or contractual rights); or a form of paternalistic *gratuity* or gift (where changes might be limited

---

[20] Simonetta Manfredi, Lucy Vickers and Kate Clayton-Hathway, 'The Public Sector Equality Duty: Enforcing Equality Rights Through Second-Generation Regulation' (2018) 47 *Industrial Law Journal* 365, 386.

[21] See, e.g., *R (on the application of Bapio Action Ltd) v Secretary of State for the Home Department* [2007] EWHC 199 (Admin) (9 February 2007); *R (on the application of Hottak) v Secretary of State for Foreign and Commonwealth Affairs* [2015] EWHC 1953 (Admin); [2015] IRLR 827.

[22] Axel Gosseries, 'Environmental Degradation as Age Discrimination' (2015) 2 *e-Pública* 25, 38.

[23] Gosseries (n 22).

[24] Ibid 39.

by estoppel or detrimental reliance).[25] These different views of pensions will likely apply differently to the three pension "pillars": state or statutory pensions (be they contributory or non-contributory); occupational pensions (again, whether contributory or non-contributory); and individual savings.

Viewing pensions as individual property rights arguably offers the strongest protection against government interference with existing pension schemes. This view of pension rights is supported by the European Convention on Human Rights. Article 1 of Protocol 1 to the Convention says:

> Every natural or legal person is entitled to the peaceful enjoyment of his possessions. No one shall be deprived of his possessions except in the public interest and subject to the conditions provided for by law and by the general principles of international law.
>
> The preceding provisions shall not, however, in any way impair the right of a State to enforce such laws as it deems necessary to control the use of property in accordance with the general interest or to secure the payment of taxes or other contributions or penalties.

This has been held to apply to old-age pensions, even if they are non-contributory. In *Carson v United Kingdom*,[26] the European Court of Human Rights held that while there is:

> no obligation on a State under Article 1 of Protocol No 1 to create a welfare or pension scheme, if a State did decide to enact legislation providing for the payment as of right of a welfare benefit or pension – whether conditional or not on the prior payment of contributions – that legislation had to be regarded as generating a proprietary interest falling within the ambit of Article 1 of Protocol No 1 for persons satisfying its requirements.[27]

Thus, individuals can have a proprietary interest in both contributory and non-contributory pension schemes, so long as they satisfy the legislative requirements. This broad reading of Article 1 is not without its critics: in *R (on the application of Carson) v Secretary of State for Work and Pensions*[28] Lord Hoffmann opined that:

> … my first instinct would not be to regard a social security benefit like a state pension as a possession until it had actually fallen due. But the European Court has developed a somewhat artificial jurisprudence on this question. … In *Müller*

---

25 Alysia Blackham, 'Pensions and the Modern Workforce' in Sinéad Agnew, Paul S. Davies and Charles Mitchell (eds), *Pensions: Law, Policy and Practice* (Hart 2020).

26 *Carson v United Kingdom* 42184/05 [2010] ECHR 338 (16 March 2010).

27 Ibid [64]–[65].

28 [2005] UKHL 37 (26 May 2005); [2005] 2 WLR 1369.

> *v Austria* (1975) 3 DR 25 the Commission said that a claim to contributory benefits was a 'possession' by analogy with the proprietary right of a contributor to a private pension fund. … But the analogy is weak because (at any rate in the United Kingdom) contributions are hardly distinguishable from general taxation, the 'fund' exists purely as a matter of public accounting and no one is entitled to anything beyond that which the legislation may from time to time prescribe. The Strasbourg court has been obliged to accommodate this state of affairs by saying that although a claim to a social security benefit is a possession … it does not entitle one to anything in particular … .[29]

While the Convention may mean that individuals have a right to a statutory old-age pension as a 'possession', this does not equate to any particular quantum of money.[30] This 'right' therefore stands in stark contrast to traditional ideas of property rights at common law. An individual right to a statutory old-age pension – even as a 'possession' – will place few limits on governments changing the quantum of existing state pension schemes.[31]

If States do create a pension scheme, though, they must comply with Article 14 of the Convention.[32] Article 14 says: "The enjoyment of the rights and freedoms set forth in this Convention shall be secured without discrimination on any ground". Any difference of treatment based on an identifiable status or ground will be "discriminatory if it has no objective and reasonable justification; in other words, if it does not pursue a legitimate aim or if there is not a reasonable relationship of proportionality between the means employed and the aim sought to be realised".[33] However, States have "a margin of appreciation in assessing whether and to what extent differences in otherwise similar situations justify a different treatment".[34]

Overall, then, while pension schemes might create some form of property rights, discrimination law arguably offers a more substantive ground for challenging changes to pension schemes. Indeed, under discrimination law it is potentially possible to challenge changes to the *quantum* of statutory pensions.

---

[29] Ibid [11]–[12] (Lord Hoffmann).

[30] See the detailed discussion in *Carson v Secretary of State for Work and Pensions* [2003] EWCA Civ 797 (17 June 2003); [2003] 3 All ER 577, [17]–[23] (Laws LJ). See also *British Gurkha Welfare Society v The United Kingdom* (No 44818/11) [2016] ECHR 755 (15 September 2016), [61].

[31] See, e.g., Andrew Mackley, Djuna Thurley and Roderick McInnes, 'Increases in the State Pension Age for Women Born in the 1950s' (2021) Research Briefing <https://commonslibrary.parliament.uk/research-briefings/cbp-7405/> accessed 11 April 2022.

[32] *British Gurkha Welfare Society v The United Kingdom* (No 44818/11) [2016] ECHR 755 (15 September 2016), [61].

[33] Ibid [62].

[34] Ibid [62].

It is here, then, that discrimination law offers an important legal avenue for challenging government austerity. Further, proprietary rights might attach most strongly to *accrued* pension rights, not those rights that might accrue in the future. This is particularly relevant to the situation in *McCloud* and *Sargeant*.

JUSTIFICATION

Critical to the success of age discrimination law as a tool for challenging pension changes, though, will be how tests of justification are applied in practice.[35] Under the EU Council Directive 2000/78/EC of 27 November 2000 establishing a general framework for equal treatment in employment and occupation ("Framework Directive")[36] Article 6(1),

> Member States may provide that differences of treatment on grounds of age shall not constitute discrimination, if, within the context of national law, they are objectively and reasonably justified by a legitimate aim, including legitimate employment policy, labour market and vocational training objectives, and if the means of achieving that aim are appropriate and necessary.

In the UK, this has been adopted in the Equality Act 2010 (UK) s. 13(2), which provides that less favourable treatment because of age is not direct discrimination "if A can show A's treatment of B to be a proportionate means of achieving a legitimate aim".

In the UK Supreme Court decision of *Seldon v Clarkson Wright and Jakes (A Partnership)*[37] the Court considered whether a retirement age of 65 for law firm partners was objectively justified as a proportionate means of achieving a legitimate aim. Distilling the case law of the CJEU, the Supreme Court identified two legitimate aims that might support a mandatory retirement age: intergenerational fairness,[38] and dignity.[39] While these need to be social policy

---

35 Indeed, as I have argued elsewhere, the ability to justify age-based rules under the European Convention on Human Rights has made it difficult to challenge social security rules using article 14: see *British Gurkha Welfare Society v Ministry of Defence* [2010] EWCA Civ 1098; *British Gurkha Welfare Society v The United Kingdom* (No 44818/11) [2016] ECHR 755 (15 September 2016), [88]; *R (on the application of Smith) v Secretary of State for Defence* [2004] EWHC 1797 (Admin), [2005] 1 FLR 97; Alysia Blackham, 'Age Discrimination beyond Employment' (2019) 52 *Kobe University Law Review* 1.

36 [2000] OJ L303/16–22.

37 [2012] UKSC 16.

38 Ibid [56].

39 Ibid [57].

objectives, of a public interest nature, and beyond the needs of an individual employer, there is flexibility for employers in how they pursue these aims.[40]

Ultimately, the retirement age in *Seldon* was held to be justified;[41] but other retirement ages have not been deemed likewise. Indeed, the Employer-Justified Retirement Age (EJRA) at the University of Oxford (of age 67) has been held to be justified on one set of facts;[42] and not justified on the basis of different evidence.[43] When the two conflicting decisions were appealed to the Employment Appeal Tribunal (EAT),[44] Mrs Justice Eady concluded that neither ET had erred in law; the evidence presented to each ET was different and justified the different findings on proportionality in each case. The EAT concluded:

> the nature of the assessment that has to be undertaken by ETs when determining the question of objective justification is such that it is possible for different ETs to reach different conclusions when considering the same measure adopted by the same employer in respect of the same aims. Although some expressed the view that this was an undesirable outcome in the present cases, none of the parties demurred from the truth of this proposition. …[45]
>
> In some cases, a difference in result may be a consequence of differences in the evidence adduced or in the focus of the evidence, but, even if that is not so, … it is possible that two ETs may reach opposing conclusions on the same facts without either having committed any error of law. In the present appeals, there are, however, two particular issues on which the presentation of the evidence differed in a material respect.[46]

In particular, the latter case heard statistical evidence on the creation of job vacancies that was not available to the earlier ET.[47] Thus, it is critically important to consider how courts use (empirical) evidence to inform their assessment of justification.

MCCLOUD AND *SARGEANT*

To interrogate these issues, this chapter considers a case study of two age discrimination decisions relating to transitional pension provisions. In 2012, the UK government undertook widespread reform of public service pensions, via

---

40 Ibid [50].
41 *Seldon v Clarkson Wright & Jakes*, EAT/0434/13/RN [2014] IRLR 748.
42 *Pitcher v University of Oxford* [2019] ET 3323858/2016.
43 *University of Oxford v Ewart* [2020] ET 3324911/2017.
44 *Pitcher v University of Oxford* [2021] EA-2019-000638-RN (previously UKEAT/0083/20/RN).
45 Ibid [183].
46 Ibid [184].
47 Ibid [185].

the Public Services Pensions Act 2013 (UK) c. 25. From 2015, existing defined benefit pension schemes would close, and new (less generous) schemes would commence. For example, the old pension scheme for judges, under the Judicial Pensions and Retirement Act 1993, provided:

1. An annual pension, accruing at the rate of 1/40th of a judge's final pensionable pay multiplied by the number of years' service up to 20.
2. A lump sum payable on retirement at the rate of 2.25 x the annual rate of pension.
3. A normal pension age of 65.
4. A surviving spouse's or civil partner's pension paid at half the rate of the member's pension.

The new scheme for judges instead offered:

1. An annual pension, accruing at the rate of 1/43rd of pensionable pay on a career average basis (with no upper limit on the length of service).
2. No separate lump sum.
3. Normal pension age at state pension age (65 or, for some younger judges, a higher age).
4. A surviving spouse's or civil partner's pension paid at 3/8ths of the rate of the member's pension.[48]

The new pension scheme was also registered for tax purposes, meaning there was far less advantageous tax treatment of judicial pensions. Some judges were individually estimated to lose several hundred thousand pounds in pension from the change.

For firefighters, the old pension scheme, under the Firefighters Pension Scheme 1992,[49] provided:

1. An annual pension, accruing at the rate of 1/60th of a firefighter's final pensionable pay for the first 20 years, and 2/60th for the next ten years, multiplied by the aggregate length of service in the qualifying role.
2. A lump sum payable on retirement, the lower of one quarter of the value of the pension by HMRC or Scheme rules, or 2.25 x the annual rate of

48 *McCloud* [2017] UKET 2201483/2015, [23]–[24].

49 This scheme closed to new members on 1 April 2006, with new firefighters instead covered by the New Firefighters Pension Scheme 2006. All claimants in *Sargeant* were covered by the old scheme: *Sargeant v London Fire and Emergency Planning Authority* [2017] UKET 2202235/2015, [25].

pension (if retiring between 50 and 55, and without at least 30 years of service).
3. A normal pension age of 55 (but with the ability to retire from age 50 with no penalty with at least 25 years of service).
4. A surviving spouse's or civil partner's pension paid at half the rate of the member's pension.

The new scheme for firefighters instead offered:

1. Pension benefits based on career-average earnings, not final pensionable pay.
2. An annual accrual rate of 1/59.7.
3. A normal pension age of 60.
4. A deferred pension age of 65 or the state pension age.[50]

All existing and new employees would be transferred to the new schemes; however, those within 10 years of retirement age as at April 2012 could remain in the old schemes.[51] All accrued pension rights would be transferred to the new schemes.

These transitional provisions (but not the pension changes themselves) were challenged by firefighters, police, prison officers, and judges as a form of direct age discrimination. The cases relating to firefighters and judges progressed to the Court of Appeal, where it was held that the transitional provisions were not justified as a proportionate means of achieving a legitimate aim,[52] as they were not supported by legitimate aims. Permission to appeal to the Supreme Court was refused.

At first instance, though, the transitional provisions were held to be justified in *Sargeant* (for firefighters); but not justified in *McCloud* (for judges) as they lacked a legitimate aim. The EAT overruled the ET's decision in *Sargeant* on the basis that the ET had failed to appropriately scrutinise whether the transitional provisions were proportionate.[53] The EAT in *McCloud* held that, while there was a legitimate aim, regardless, the provisions were not proportionate.[54] Contrary to the EAT's decision, the Court of Appeal held that the initial ET

---

50 *The Lord Chancellor v McCloud* [2018] EWCA Civ 2844, [104].

51 Seymour (n 8) 293. Tapering protection was offered for those with 10 to 14 years to retirement age: *The Lord Chancellor v McCloud* [2018] UKEAT/0071/17/LA, [41].

52 *The Lord Chancellor v McCloud* [2018] EWCA Civ 2844.

53 *Sargeant v London Fire and Emergency Planning Authority* [2018] UKEAT/0116/17/LA, [84].

54 *The Lord Chancellor v McCloud* [2018] UKEAT/0071/17/LA, [160], [172].

was entitled to find that there was no legitimate aim in *McCloud*.[55] In relation to *Sargeant*, the Court of Appeal held that the ET had failed to adequately consider the legitimacy of the aims underlying the transitional provisions.[56] The *McCloud* and *Sargeant* cases are therefore particularly noteworthy in relation to how we assess the legitimacy of social policy aims, and the evidence required to establish whether an aim is "legitimate".[57]

The aims said to support the transitional provisions for firefighters in *Sargeant* were to protect those closest to pension age and retirement from the effects of pension reform.[58] More particularly, these aims were argued to be:

- to protect those closest to pension age from the effects of pension reform, since they would have the least time to rearrange their affairs before retirement, by making lifestyle changes or alternative financial provision (or by finding alternative employment);
- to take account of the greater legitimate expectation that those closer to retirement would have that their pension entitlements would not change significantly when they were close to retirement;
- to have a tapering arrangement so as to prevent a cliff edge between Fully Protected and Unprotected Groups; and
- in achieving the substantive aims behind the transitional provisions, ensuring that a clear and simple message could be communicated, and that there was consistency across the public sector.[59]

The aims put forward in *McCloud* were less clearly articulated, but were essentially "to protect those closest to pension age from the financial effects of pension reform",[60] as older judges were more likely to have fixed or concrete plans for retirement, which are difficult to change;[61] and to ensure consistency across public sector pension schemes.[62] These aims do not speak to the justification of the pension changes generally; rather, they simply address the need for the transitional provisions themselves.

---

55 Ibid [92], [94]–[95].

56 Ibid [155].

57 Indeed, prior to these decisions, I concluded that establishing a legitimate aim would generally be straightforward, at least in the context of mandatory retirement ages: Blackham, *Extending Working Life* (n 7) ch 3.

58 *Sargeant v London Fire and Emergency Planning Authority* [2017] UKET 2202235/2015, [11.1].

59 Ibid [61].

60 *The Lord Chancellor v McCloud* [2018] EWCA Civ 2844, [41].

61 Ibid [42].

62 Ibid [43].

The aims behind these transitional arrangements, then, focused on distributional aspects (protecting those closest to retirement), protecting legitimate expectations, and achieving consistency. To determine whether these are legitimate aims of a public interest nature, then, we need to consider whether those closest to retirement require additional protection, or have distinct legitimate expectations in relation to pensions that need protection; and whether simple messaging and consistency across the public sector are in the public interest.

MCCLOUD, SARGEANT, AND EMPIRICAL EVIDENCE

At their core, the ET and EAT decisions in *McCloud* and *Sargeant* were fundamentally divided on the degree of evidence required to support a legitimate aim and proportionality. They therefore offer a critical case for examining the role of empirical evidence in judicial decision-making. The decisions – especially at first instance – were also divided regarding the appropriate role of the judiciary in balancing issues of social policy.

These tensions were exacerbated in the cases by the government's failure to produce any empirical evidence in favour of the transitional provisions adopted; as noted in *McCloud*, "there was no analysis or research, whether general or specific, underlying the government's decision to incorporate transitional provisions".[63] Similarly, there was "little independent analysis" of the transitional provisions in *Sargeant*.[64] While government officials understood "the need for cogent, evidence-based arguments" in support of the pension changes, and the need to gather as much evidence as possible,[65] no such evidence was gathered or produced.[66] In *McCloud*, for example, there was no survey of judges and their retirement intentions.[67] These cases, then, offer a warning to governments about the need for evidence-based policy making that moves beyond age-based stereotypes, generalisations, and assumptions.

It is important to recognise, too, that the pension changes in *McCloud* and *Sargeant* raised distinct issues, particular to each profession. In *McCloud*, the new pension scheme was registered for tax purposes; the old scheme was not. This meant being transferred to the new scheme would have a significantly disadvantageous effect on younger judges. In *Sargeant*, the new pension scheme sought to raise the normal pension age for firefighters, from 50–55 to 60–65.

---

63 Ibid [50].

64 *Sargeant v London Fire and Emergency Planning Authority* [2017] UKET 2202235/2015, [44].

65 *McCloud* [2017] UKET 2201483/2015, [50].

66 Ibid [117].

67 Ibid [53].

This raised particular issues around firefighters' fitness and physical capacity into older age.[68]

Disaggregating Age and Proximity to Retirement?

In *Sargeant*, the parties agreed as common ground that the transitional provisions treated younger firefighters less favourably on the grounds of age.[69] The only issue in contention, then, was whether the provisions were objectively justified as a proportionate means of achieving a legitimate aim. Despite this concession, the ET rejected the argument that older firefighters were treated differently due to their age: rather, for the ET, they were treated differently – and more favourably – due to their proximity to retirement: "Whilst retirement is age related, and proximity to retirement is connected with age, there may be good reasons for treating different age groups differently".[70]

This is difficult to reconcile with the prohibition of age discrimination; attempting to disaggregate age from proximity to retirement is clearly an artificial distinction (and could clearly found a claim of indirect discrimination). As Maurice Kay LJ opined in *Chief Constable of West Yorkshire Police v Homer*, "In one sense there is unreality in differentiation between age and retirement. In most cases they are not unrelated".[71] In *McCloud*, then, the ET held that protection under the transitional provisions "depends solely upon a judge's date of birth and therefore his or her age".[72] This was also accepted by the EAT.[73]

Protecting those Closest to Retirement

The transitional provisions in both cases were aimed and drafted to protect those within 10 years of retirement age, by allowing them to remain in the old pension scheme. This was not the approach recommended by the Hutton Commission review of public sector pensions; indeed, the Commission's final

---

68 *Sargeant v London Fire and Emergency Planning Authority* [2017] UKET 2202235/2015, [38].

69 Ibid [10.3]–[10.4], [28]. A similar concession was made in *McCloud*: *The Lord Chancellor v McCloud* [2018] UKEAT/0071/17/LA, [43].

70 *Sargeant v London Fire and Emergency Planning Authority* [2017] UKET 2202235/2015, [70].

71 [2010] EWCA Civ 419 (27 April 2010), [2010] ICR 987, [34]; cited in *Homer v Chief Constable of West Yorkshire Police* [2012] UKSC 15 (25 April 2012), [2012] WLR(D) 122, [17].

72 *McCloud* [2017] UKET 2201483/2015, [22].

73 *The Lord Chancellor v McCloud* [2018] UKEAT/0071/17/LA, [23].

report recommended no transitional arrangements be adopted.[74] All accrued pension rights would be transferred to the new scheme; this meant, then, that those closest to retirement would be the least impacted by the new pension scheme, as they would have the smallest number of years acquiring pension entitlements in the new scheme.[75] This was recognised and acknowledged by the government.[76] Despite this advice, the government decided to adopt transitional measures to protect those within ten years of the normal retirement age as at 1 April 2012.[77] For judges, this meant 85% of serving judicial officers in 2012 would have some transitional protection.[78]

In *Sargeant*, the claimants argued that the government should provide reasons for the more favourable treatment of those closest to retirement. The ET – perhaps surprisingly – disagreed:

> the decisions which are under examination in the present case are decisions for the elected Government. They are social policy choices which may well have a political element.[79] …
>
> This is a situation where a Member State was introducing a measure as a result of having made a social policy decision to protect those within 10 years of retirement. The Government has a wide discretion in social policy matters. The standard of scrutiny involves granting a wide margin of discretion to the Member State. I am satisfied that that is the correct standard in the present case and the stricter test which applies to operational matters of a private sector employer is not the correct test.[80]

Thus, the ET made a distinction between the level of scrutiny that would apply to a private employer, from that applicable to the government in its role as an employer.

For the ET in *Sargeant*, then, it was legitimate for the government to protect those closest to retirement;[81] and, if that was the aim of the provision, then the means adopted were self-evidently proportionate, as they protected those closest to retirement: "there has to be a line drawn at some point. That is a social policy choice and inevitably some individuals will be disadvantaged".[82]

74 *McCloud* [2017] UKET 2201483/2015, [20]; *Sargeant v London Fire and Emergency Planning Authority* [2017] UKET 2202235/2015, [19], [63], [64].
75 *McCloud* [2017] UKET 2201483/2015, [40].
76 Ibid [40], [42].
77 Ibid [21].
78 Ibid [62].
79 *Sargeant v London Fire and Emergency Planning Authority* [2017] UKET 2202235/2015, [75].
80 Ibid [83].
81 Ibid [104].
82 Ibid [115].

Overall, "these are social policy matters for which there is no right or wrong answer and the choice is that of the Government".[83] This circuitous decision-making subjects the government to limited scrutiny in its role as an employer.

Conversely, in *McCloud*, the ET drew a distinction between the pension changes generally – which were a matter of public policy, where government has discretion to define its policy objectives and priorities, and which are not within the ET's "proper purview" – and these specific transitional pension provisions.[84] The ET held that there was "no basis for saying that the government's acknowledged broad discretion in matters of social policy extends beyond that public arena into the arena of private relations between employer and employee".[85]

Unlike in *Sargeant*, then, the ET in *McCloud* rejected the government's assertions regarding the need to protect those closest to retirement:

> There was generalised assertion on behalf of the respondents that older judges would have less time to prepare for the financial effects of pension reform. That is tantamount to saying that older judges are closer to retirement than younger judges and is a truism. Older judges have a shorter time to respond to adverse changes and prepare for their consequences, but that shortness of time is in direct proportion to the adversity of the changes brought about by these pension reforms. In other words, those with the shortest time to retirement have the least adversity to prepare for. Not only was there no evidence that older judges would suffer greater hardship than younger judges, but the evidence was unambiguously and consistently to the contrary.[86]

Protecting those closest to retirement was therefore not in and of itself a legitimate aim:

> To refer to 'those who have ten years or less to their pension age', as the Chief Secretary did, is simply another way of identifying a particular age group. The respondents' objective identifies an age group to be protected, but no wider, 'underlying aim' is identified. Thus far, therefore, the question 'why?' posed above is not answered.[87]

At a minimum, a legitimate aim needs to be identifiable, even if it lacks precision.[88] Further, a legitimate aim must have a rational explanation.[89] In this

---

83 Ibid [97].
84 [2017] UKET 2201483/2015, [78]–[79].
85 Ibid [80].
86 Ibid [51].
87 Ibid [84].
88 Ibid [85].
89 Ibid [87].

case, protecting those closest to retirement was contrary to the actual impact of the pension reforms: the uncontested evidence was that "The older judges are, the less adversely are they affected by the reforms".[90] Even with the margin of discretion to be given to the government, this did not make sense:

> The government has a wide discretion in such matters and its aim does not have to be one with which the tribunal agrees; but its aim may not be, for example, capricious or arbitrary, and it must be capable of being understood. To set out consciously to treat more favourably a group who, as was well known at the time, were the least adversely affected by the reforms appears counter-intuitive and at very least calls for such a rational explanation. In the absence of such explanation it would be difficult to resist [the] categorisation of the result as … bizarre.[91]

The government therefore could not put forward a legitimate aim in support of the provisions:

> Descriptions of a group having 'ten years or less to their pension age', being 'closest to retirement' or having 'less time to adjust' all necessarily define that group by reference to the age of those in the group. In my judgment, an aim which amounts to an intention to treat one group more favourably and another less favourably, solely by reference to the age of those in the groups cannot, without further rational explanation of the reason for it, be legitimate. An aim thus expressed amounts to a declaration of intent to do precisely that which the statute prohibits. The respondents have failed to advance any such rational explanation of their reason. … The respondents have failed to adduce any evidence of disadvantage suffered by the fully protected and the taper-protected groups of judges which called for redress, or any social policy objective which was served by treating those groups more favourably and the claimant group less favourably.[92]

Legitimate Expectations

In *Sargeant*, the government argued that those closer to retirement had a "greater legitimate expectation" that their pension would experience "no sudden changes";[93] those further away from retirement were less focused on their pension, as retirement is a "long way off" and they may experience changes to their careers or "personal circumstances".[94] A similar argument was put forward in *McCloud*:

---

90 Ibid [86].
91 Ibid [87].
92 Ibid [94].
93 Ibid [90].
94 Ibid [90].

> There was further general assertion that older judges would be more likely to have fixed, or concrete retirement plans, the suggested implication being that those plans would be more difficult to change than in the case of a younger judge who had more time.[95]

An assertion of older workers having a "greater legitimate expectation" of a stable pension appears to be a moral or normative statement:[96] that those with a longer period of service, or of a more advanced age, are more likely to have fixed plans or expectations of their retirement, which should not be interfered with. Pension changes may mean people need to "make adjustments to lifestyle and financial arrangements", such as by increasing their personal saving or investment for retirement.[97] Thus, the government saw protecting these older workers as "right"[98] and "fair".[99] This argument was embraced by the government before the EAT in *McCloud*; the legitimate aim was described in government submissions as "couched as a moral judgment allied to a process which was highly political",[100] being "couched in moral terms reflecting the perceived rightness of the decision and fulfilling legitimate expectation [sic]".[101]

This estoppel-style argument sees years of service as being a form of detrimental reliance, in anticipation of a later pension. This makes a number of assumptions about the nature of work and retirement, including that workers can and do plan for retirement; that retirement plans are relatively fixed or concrete; and that it would be unfair or inappropriate for pension changes to interfere with those plans (at least for older workers).

The government put forward no evidence of judges' or firefighters' expectations of retirement.[102] As noted in *McCloud*:

> this Tribunal received no evidence in relation to any judge, or group of judges, concerning their retirement plans or the degree of fixity or concreteness of such plans. Such evidence as I heard consisted of no more than extempore speculation from which I was unable to make any finding of fact consistent with the respondents' assertion.[103]

---

95 *McCloud* [2017] UKET 2201483/2015, [52].

96 *The Lord Chancellor v McCloud* [2018] UKEAT/0071/17/LA, [149], [151].

97 Ibid [39].

98 HM Government, 'Public Service Pensions: Good Pensions that Last' (2011, 6/4855), quoted in *Sargeant v London Fire and Emergency Planning Authority* [2017] UKET 2202235/2015, [22], [67].

99 Hansard, 2 November 2011, (3/1286), quoted in *Sargeant v London Fire and Emergency Planning Authority* [2017] UKET 2202235/2015, [22].

100 *The Lord Chancellor v McCloud* [2018] UKEAT/0071/17/LA, [149].

101 Ibid [151].

102 Ibid [95].

103 *McCloud* [2017] UKET 2201483/2015, [52].

The choice of a 10-year period of protection was derived from the changes to the State Pension Age (SPA).[104] Following an extensive consultation on changes to the SPA, the government gave a 10-year notice period. Evidence in that consultation was that people finalise their retirement plans the closer they get to retirement.[105] More specifically, there was evidence from the National Association of Pension Funds (NAPF) that lifestyle funds move pensions into more conservative investment options 3 to 15 years prior to retirement.[106] A 10-year transition period for changes to the SPA was therefore seen as appropriate by NAPF.[107] Given that public sector pensions are defined benefit pensions, though, there is no need to shift investment strategies in the lead-up to retirement; it is arguable that this evidence from NAPF is less relevant in this context.[108]

Had the government sought empirical evidence to support its argument, it would have found such evidence to be noticeably lacking. First, given the pension changes in both *Sargeant* and *McCloud* respected accrued rights, older judges and firefighters closest to retirement actually experienced the least detriment or impact to their retirement plans with the shift to the new pension arrangements.[109] Thus, the changes could not be said to interfere significantly with retirement plans. For judges close to retirement age, for example, they could accrue the same pension entitlements by delaying their retirement for a few months; or elect to take a very slightly reduced pension.[110] For the ET in *McCloud*, then, the transitional provisions "exacerbate rather than mitigate" the discriminatory impact of the pension changes.[111]

Second, planning for retirement is a privilege reserved for the most well-off workers. Nearly half of people do not financially plan for retirement.[112] Workers who are most likely to plan for retirement are white men of good

---

104 *Sargeant v London Fire and Emergency Planning Authority* [2017] UKET 2202235/2015, [67].

105 Ibid [95]; *The Lord Chancellor v McCloud* [2018] UKEAT/0071/17/LA, [153].

106 *The Lord Chancellor v McCloud* [2018] UKEAT/0071/17/LA, [153].

107 Ibid [153].

108 Though it may be relevant to supplementary, individual savings for retirement, if public sector workers have such additional funds.

109 *McCloud* [2017] UKET 2201483/2015, [40], [42].

110 Ibid [42].

111 Ibid [121].

112 Steve M. Jex and James Grosch, 'Retirement Decision Making' in Mo Wang (ed), *The Oxford Handbook of Retirement* (Oxford University Press 2012) <http://oxfordhandbooks.com/view/10.1093/oxfordhb/9780199746521.001.0001/oxfordhb-9780199746521-e-17> accessed 28 January 2022.

health and high socio-economic status.[113] Thus, relying on planning for retirement and retirement expectations as a justification for preferential treatment will likely exacerbate existing inequalities in the labour market. Further, while not all retirement planning is irrational, Jex and Grosch argue that there is enough irrationality in retirement decision-making to warrant research and academic attention, particularly given cognitive biases may affect decision-making.[114] It is possible, then, that not all retirement plans are sufficiently logical to warrant the same reverent protection.

Third, pension plans are not fixed or unchanging. Individual retirement *intentions* often do not match retirement *behaviours*, though there may be a correlation between retirement intentions and retirement behaviour in a five-year period prior to retirement (not 10 years, as in the transitional provisions).[115] Older workers may retire earlier than they anticipate due to poor working conditions,[116] job loss, low recognition at work,[117] ill health[118] and stress, and caring responsibilities. They may retire later than expected due to financial insecurity.

In the 2018–19 Australian Bureau of Statistics *Retirement and Retirement Intentions Survey*, for example, less than half (46%) of respondents retired

---

113 Martin Hyde, Maria Cheshire-Allen, Marleen Damman, Kene Henkens, Loretta Platts, Katrina Pritchard and Cara Reed, 'The Experience of the Transition to Retirement: Rapid Evidence Review' (2018) <https://www.ageing-better.org.uk/sites/default/files/2018-12/Transition-to-retirement.pdf> accessed 3 May 2021; Phyllis Moen, Stephen Sweet and Raymond Swisher, 'Embedded Career Clocks: The Case of Retirement Planning' (2005) 9 *Advances in Life Course Research* 237.

114 Jex and Grosch (n 112).

115 Per Erik Solem and others, 'To Leave or Not to Leave: Retirement Intentions and Retirement Behaviour' (2016) 36 *Ageing & Society* 259.

116 Petri Böckerman and Pekka Ilmakunnas, 'Do Good Working Conditions Make You Work Longer? Analyzing Retirement Decisions Using Linked Survey and Register Data' (2020) 17 *The Journal of the Economics of Ageing* 100192; cf Chiara Dal Bianco, Elisabetta Trevisan and Guglielmo Weber, '"I Want to Break Free". The Role of Working Conditions on Retirement Expectations and Decisions' (2015) 12 *European Journal of Ageing* 17.

117 Ewan Carr, Gareth Hagger-Johnson, Jenny Head, Nicola Shelton, Mai Stafford, Stephen Stansfeld and Paola Zaninotto, 'Working Conditions as Predictors of Retirement Intentions and Exit from Paid Employment: A 10-Year Follow-up of the English Longitudinal Study of Ageing' (2016) 13 *European Journal of Ageing* 39.

118 Dimitri Mortelmans and Jorre T.A. Vannieuwenhuyze, 'The Age-Dependent Influence of Self-Reported Health and Job Characteristics on Retirement' (2013) 58 *International Journal of Public Health* 13.

Table 6.1 *Reasons why retirees ceased their last job, for those who retired in the last 20 years*

Reason for ceasing last job	**Total persons (%)**	**Average age at retirement (persons)**	**Total males (%)**	**Average age at retirement (males)**	**Total females (%)**	**Average age at retirement (females)**
Retrenched/dismissed/no work available	9.9	58.4	10	59	9.9	57.8
Temporary/seasonal/holiday job	3.8	59.3	3.4	58.6	4.1	59.9
Own business closed down for economic reasons	1.3	59.3	1.9	59.3	0.7	59.4
Own business closed down or sold for other than economic reasons	2.9	58.9	3.1	59.4	2.6	58.2
Unsatisfactory work arrangements/ wanted to work part-time	2.1	55.3	1.2	56.3	2.8	54.7
To coincide with partner's retirement	1.5	62.7	-	-	-	-
Reached retirement age/eligible for superannuation/pension	41.6	63.7	48.1	64.4	34.9	62.6
Own sickness, injury or disability	19.6	54.9	20.5	57.1	18.6	52.4
To have holiday/pursue leisure activities	1.7	60.9	1.5	63.3	1.9	59
To care for children/pregnancy	2.5	46.6	-	-	-	-
To care for ill/disabled/elderly person	4.3	56.3	2.2	57.2	6.5	56

Source: Australian Bureau of Statistics, Retirement and Retirement Intentions Survey, Australia, 2018–2019 and author's own calculations.

because they reached retirement age or were eligible for superannuation; illness, injury, or disability (21%) and being retrenched, dismissed, or having no work available (11%) were also common reasons for retiring.[119] For women, retiring to care for an ill, disabled, or elderly person was also a common experience (8% of women, compared to 2% of men).[120] This is consistent with the reasons why people retired over the last 20 years (Table 6.1). Those who retire due to ill health retire, on average, 8.8 years earlier than those who retire due to reaching retirement age or being eligible for a pension.

The average age at which people expected to retire was 65.5 years; however, the average age of retirement for existing retirees was 55.4.[121] For those who retired five years ago or less, the average age at retirement was 62.7 years. Thus, retirement expectations rarely match retirement realities.

Fourth, this approach ignores the legitimate expectations of a whole range of workers; not only older workers structure their lives around a pension and its availability, and not only the final years of service might be seen as done in reliance on a later pension. Most judges experience a pay cut upon commencing in a judicial role.[122] In *McCloud*, there was evidence that "there had been explicit and strongly worded assurances from the then Lord Chancellor in 2004 to the effect that it was the government's settled view that there should be no change to serving judges' pensions".[123] Past changes to judicial pensions (in 1993) operated prospectively, applying to those who did not yet hold judicial appointment, not retrospectively, to those already in office.[124] Thus, in *McCloud*, the ET opined that

> Judges accept appointment on the understanding that their ability to do other remunerated work either during or following their term of appointment will be severely limited. These claimants did so, in many cases accepting significant reductions in

---

[119] Australian Bureau of Statistics, 'Retirement and Retirement Intentions, Australia, 2018–19 Financial Year' (5–30 August 2020) <https://www.abs.gov.au/statistics/labour/employment-and-unemployment/retirement-and-retirement-intentions-australia/latest-release> accessed 31 January 2022.

[120] Ibid.

[121] This may reflect a lag effect, where older existing retirees intend to (and do) retire at earlier ages, compared with existing workers.

[122] Cheryl A. Thomas, '2020 UK Judicial Attitude Survey: Report of Findings Covering Salaried Judges in England & Wales Courts and UK Tribunals' (2021) 32 <https://www.judiciary.uk/wp-content/uploads/2022/07/JAS-2020-EW-UK-TRIBS-8-Feb-2021-complete.pdf> accessed 31 January 2022.

[123] *McCloud* [2017] UKET 2201483/2015, [36].

[124] Ibid [36].

> earnings, in reliance on assurances that the value of their remuneration package [including pensions] would be maintained.[125]

This was a "fundamental understanding on which judges accept appointment".[126]

In the 2020 Judicial Attitude Survey, judicial pensions were a reason given by 32% of judges for encouraging suitable applicants to apply to join the judiciary.[127] However, a majority of judges (58%) reported that their experience of changes to their pension entitlements meant they would discourage suitable applicants from applying to join the judiciary.[128] The vast majority of judicial respondents – 78% – reported that they closely follow developments around judicial pensions.[129] Arguably, then, judges of all levels of seniority have a keen awareness of their pension entitlements, and strong expectations about pension provision. A majority of judges (59% in 2020, 68% in 2016) report that reductions in pension benefits would encourage them to leave the judiciary early (that is, in the next five years, before reaching the statutory retirement age);[130] conversely, restoration of previous pension entitlements would encourage a majority of judges to remain in post until the statutory retirement age (55% in 2020, 57% in 2016).[131] The nature of judging in the UK, then – as an end of career profession, with comparatively generous pension provision – may mean that the majority of judges, of all ages and levels of seniority, have fairly strong expectations about pension entitlements.

Fifth, for firefighters specifically, one potential area of reliance or expectation may relate to physical fitness. Changes to the NPA for firefighters meant they would need to maintain their physical fitness for longer; for older firefighters, they may have less time to make the dietary, lifestyle, and fitness adjustments to regain or maintain their fitness into older age.[132] The extent to which this is supported by empirical evidence is debatable. Indeed, it depends on the standard of "fitness" imposed on firefighters; if a lower standard (of V02 35 max) is adopted, all firefighters will likely be capable of working until age

125 Ibid [39]. See also *The Lord Chancellor v McCloud* [2018] UKEAT/0071/17/LA, [56]–[58].

126 *McCloud* [2017] UKET 2201483/2015, [38].

127 Thomas (n 122) 76.

128 Ibid.

129 Ibid 44.

130 Ibid 70.

131 Ibid.

132 *Sargeant v London Fire and Emergency Planning Authority* [2017] UKET 2202235/2015, [101].

60.[133] A higher standard (of V02 42 max) may exclude some older firefighters, but the ET heard evidence that most could regain their fitness with appropriate training and support.[134] Thus, "expectations" of retirement can be shaped and supported by workplace policies, training, and support.

Consistency

While achieving consistency across public service pensions could be a legitimate aim,[135] this was not explicitly argued in *McCloud*.[136] Judicial pensions vary substantially from other pensions in the public service; the transitional provisions were one of the few similarities.[137] This undermined any argument on the basis of consistency,[138] and the need for consistency was not explained or justified.[139] Further, judges were in a distinct position to other public servants, which the government acknowledged.[140] For judges, tax changes made the impact of the transitional rules even more disadvantageous, as many younger judges would incur significant additional tax liabilities by being required to join a registered pension scheme.[141] This "[served] to magnify the disparity between the unprotected and the protected judges",[142] and meant the loss to judges was more than that incurred by other public servants subject to pension reform:[143] pension reforms had a "uniquely adverse effect on judges".[144] Further, judging is an end-of-career profession:[145] rules prohibiting return to private practice and mandatory retirement ages mean it is difficult for judges to earn alternative income.[146] Pensions also form a more substantial portion of judicial remuneration compared with other public sector workers.[147] Thus, any argument on the basis of consistency was particularly inappropriate for the judiciary.

133 Ibid [102].
134 Ibid [102].
135 *McCloud* [2017] UKET 2201483/2015, [93].
136 Ibid [91], [94].
137 Ibid [92].
138 Ibid [92].
139 Ibid [93].
140 Ibid [33]–[35].
141 Ibid [30]. Also *The Lord Chancellor v McCloud* [2018] UKEAT/0071/17/LA, [18]–[19].
142 *McCloud* [2017] UKET 2201483/2015, [30].
143 Ibid [31]–[32].
144 Ibid [36].
145 Ibid [37].
146 Ibid [37], [39].
147 Ibid [31].

Despite this, the government adopted uniform transitional provisions across the public service. The rationale for this was unclear; according to government witnesses, transitional provisions were seen as essential for "secur[ing] a deal with the unions".[148] Transitional provisions were "of disproportionate importance to the Unions";[149] the offer needed to be "simple" so members could easily understand what was proposed.[150] That said, the firefighters' union, the FBU, never agreed to the transitional provisions.[151] Regardless, the ET in *Sargeant* emphasised that the unions were involved in negotiations about the change, and that the FBU's representations were taken "seriously".[152] This is arguably not the same as collective consent or agreement to the changes.[153]

On Appeal

The decision in *Sargeant* was overruled in the EAT, on the basis that the ET had failed to appropriately scrutinise whether the transitional provisions were proportionate.[154] The EAT in *McCloud* held that, while there was a legitimate aim, the provisions were not proportionate,[155] meaning the ET's decision was upheld. The Court of Appeal held that the ET in *McCloud* was entitled to find that there was no legitimate aim,[156] and that there was no legitimate aim in *Sargeant*. Thus, the transitional provisions in both cases were found not to be proportionate means of achieving legitimate aims.

In relation to *Sargeant*, the Court of Appeal held that the ET had failed to adequately consider the legitimacy of the aims underlying the transitional provisions.[157] This was, in part, due to the way the government had framed its case:

> In defence of Judge Lewzey's approach, it can fairly be said that the presentation of the Governments' case made it impossible for her to engage in an objective assessment of the legitimacy of the aims. That is because there was no evidence as to the

[148] Ibid [43], [47]; *Sargeant v London Fire and Emergency Planning Authority* [2017] UKET 2202235/2015, [23], [29], [55].

[149] *McCloud* [2017] UKET 2201483/2015, [45].

[150] Ibid [45].

[151] *Sargeant v London Fire and Emergency Planning Authority* [2017] UKET 2202235/2015, [43], [110].

[152] Ibid [71].

[153] On consent, see Blackham, *Extending Working Life* (n 7) 50–51.

[154] *Sargeant v London Fire and Emergency Planning Authority* [2018] UKEAT/0116/17/LA, [84].

[155] *The Lord Chancellor v McCloud* [2018] UKEAT/0071/17/LA, [160], [172].

[156] *The Lord Chancellor v McCloud* [2018] EWCA Civ 2844 [92], [94]–[95].

[157] Ibid [155].

reasons underlying the aims. The Governments' case was advanced to her, as to us, on the basis that the unproved assertions as to the need for, and virtue of, the aims were all she needed in order to rule on their legitimacy. Judge Lewzey was no doubt aware of that; and her view was that their legitimacy did not need to be supported by evidence.[158]

The Court of Appeal disagreed with this: the government's rationale for the transitional provisions needed to be supported by evidence,[159] not just "assertions and generalisations".[160] While governments are afforded a margin of discretion,[161] an objective assessment is critical to ensure the aims put forward are legitimate, and legitimate in the particular circumstances of this employment:[162] "an aim must at least be rational … [A] margin of discretion cannot rescue an aim that is irrational".[163] As the Court of Appeal summarised:

> whilst according the appropriate margin of discretion to the Government in its decision to pursue a particular social policy aim, the tribunal must still be satisfied itself as to the legitimacy of the aim in the particular circumstances of the employment affected by it. If so satisfied, when the tribunal comes to assess the proportionality of the means of achieving such aim, it must again itself be satisfied as to their proportionality, although in making its assessment it must again accord a margin of discretion to the Government in its decision as to means.[164]

Thus, the tribunal should be "objectively satisfied as to [an aim's] legitimacy",[165] whether or not those aims were "political" or "moral" or ones of "social policy".[166] Even "moral" aims require some analysis, assessment or justification.[167] This, then, requires tribunals to ask *why*: *why* were the older firefighters (and judges) so generously protected?[168] It is not enough that it feels "right" or "moral" to protect older workers:[169] as the Court of Appeal noted,

> If the Governments' opinion as to the need to protect the older firefighters was based on something more than visceral instinct, they needed to explain what it was

158 Ibid [156].
159 Ibid [157].
160 Ibid [161].
161 Ibid [143].
162 Ibid [143]. Also [151].
163 Ibid [86].
164 Ibid [144].
165 Ibid [145].
166 Ibid [154].
167 Ibid [160].
168 Ibid [152].
169 Ibid [157].

> so that the tribunal could assess it when considering the legitimacy of the chosen aims.[170]

If it was the government's position that older firefighters close to retirement would face financial difficulties in being placed in the new pension scheme, and that, with extra time, younger firefighters could somehow overcome these financial difficulties, then there needed to be evidence to support that assertion.[171] On the evidence that was available, though, older firefighters appeared to be the most protected by the new pension arrangements, as they were likely to have already accrued the most service and pension rights under the existing (more generous) pension regime.[172] Indeed, the agreed expert evidence was that, for a firefighter who was not protected by the transitional provisions, achieving a similar pension level to those in the transitional scheme would require a full-time firefighter (with a gross basic pay of just under £30,000) to make an annual investment of between £16,000 and £19,000.[173] This was described by the Court of Appeal as "unachievable".[174] Thus, the evidence available directly contradicted the aims put forward.

The Court of Appeal concluded that:

> the burden of proof of the legitimacy of a claimed aim is a high one. So it should be. If the promoter of a policy that is directly discriminatory on age grounds wishes it to be recognised as legitimate, it must prove why it is.[175] …
>
> In our judgment, the absence of supporting evidence as to the claimed legitimacy of the Governments' aims meant that there was no basis upon which Judge Lewzey could properly find that the aims were legitimate. … Her finding to that effect was an error of law on her part.[176] …
>
> The only conclusion to which the tribunal could properly come is that, in the absence of evidence supporting the claimed legitimacy of the aims, the respondents' case as to justification must fail.[177]

There was therefore no need to consider the question of proportionality.[178] Permission to appeal to the Supreme Court was refused.

That the government failed in both *Sargeant* and *McCloud* to show that the provisions were backed by legitimate aims runs counter to previous scholarship,

170 Ibid [157].
171 Ibid [159].
172 Ibid [158].
173 Ibid [122].
174 Ibid.
175 Ibid [161].
176 Ibid [163].
177 Ibid [164].
178 Ibid [165].

which has argued that identifying legitimate aims will generally be reasonably straightforward, at least in relation to mandatory retirement ages.[179] This may mean that legitimate aims will be more closely scrutinised going forward, that legitimate aims are harder to identify for transitional pension provisions than for retirement ages, or just that the government's policy in this case was particularly ill-conceived.

IMPLICATIONS AND CONCLUSIONS

Weighing Policy Choices

First, these cases prompt important reflections regarding how courts see their role in weighing policy choices. In *Sargeant*, the ET rejected the argument that the transitional provisions should be subject to detailed scrutiny; the issues in question were "decisions for the elected Government. They are social policy choices which may well have a political element".[180] Pension reform requires the balancing of competing interests, and this balancing process is "for the Member State … and I must be careful not to substitute my own view for that of the Government".[181] Drawing on CJEU case law, the ET opined that "Member States enjoy a broad discretion in the choice of both aims and means".[182] It was not, then, for the ET specifically or the courts generally to weigh the political, economic, social, demographic, and budgetary factors in play. In social policy matters, particularly where political considerations are involved, "there is no right or wrong answer"; the choice, then, is for government,[183] and not the courts.

In *Sargeant*, then, the ET distinguished the level of scrutiny required to that which would apply to the operational decisions of private employers.[184] While the firefighters were employed by the FRAs (Fire and Rescue Authorities), not the government, it was the government that decided to apply the transitional provisions, having made a social policy decision.[185] The ET therefore afforded this decision a "wide margin of discretion",[186] rejecting a "stricter test" applied

179 Blackham, *Extending Working Life* (n 7) ch 3.
180 *Sargeant v London Fire and Emergency Planning Authority* [2017] UKET 2202235/2015, [75].
181 Ibid [76].
182 Ibid [78].
183 Ibid [97].
184 Ibid [82].
185 Ibid [83].
186 Ibid [83].

to private employers.[187] The ET should not substitute its view for the government's decision on social policy issues.[188] Indeed, the ET appeared to adopt the test used in judicial review cases – of "irrationality" – in scrutinising the transitional provisions.[189]

In *McCloud*, in the EAT, this issue was avoided to some extent by distinguishing the justification of the pension changes generally – which belong "in the realm of public policy and finance" – from the justification of the transitional provisions specifically.[190]

In the joined Court of Appeal decision, the appropriate level of judicial scrutiny to be applied was initially seen as the major legal issue to be addressed:

> When the case was opened to us, [margin of discretion/level of judicial scrutiny] seemed to be the main point of law at issue and, as a point of law, was therefore a proper matter for this court to consider on an appeal from judgments which were otherwise based largely on questions of fact, evidence and judicial evaluation of what are now well recognised concepts of legitimacy of aim and proportionality of means.[191]

Ultimately, though, the Court of Appeal held that it is appropriate for tribunals to scrutinise the "legitimacy" of aims; and, for aims to be legitimate, they must not be irrational. Deferring unquestionably to the decisions of government, even in relation to areas of social policy, is therefore wrong:[192]

> establishing that an aim is capable of being a legitimate aim is only the beginning of the story. It is for the tribunal then, according an appropriate margin of discretion, to decide whether it is legitimate in the circumstances of the case. For this purpose, an aim must at least be rational and, if it is not, the employment tribunal is entitled to say so. Margin of discretion cannot rescue an aim that is irrational.[193]

Arguably, then, the Court of Appeal's approach is not so different from the ET's in *Sargeant* – both approaches consider whether a purported aim is at least not "irrational". For the ET in *Sargeant*, though, any aim put forward by the government must, by its nature, be rational. The Court of Appeal, by contrast, requires courts and tribunals to look beyond a purported aim, to ensure it is backed by some sort of evidence or reason.

---

187 Ibid [83].
188 Ibid [88].
189 Ibid [91], [92].
190 *The Lord Chancellor v McCloud* [2018] UKEAT/0071/17/LA, [73].
191 *The Lord Chancellor v McCloud* [2018] EWCA Civ 2844, [65].
192 Ibid [154]–[155].
193 Ibid [86].

Engaging with Empirical Evidence

Second, then, we can reflect on what these decisions tell us about how courts engage with (a lack of) empirical evidence. As Seymour argues, the government provided minimal evidence regarding why the transitional pension provisions were adopted; the only witnesses called were civil servants, who did not actually make the decision and who could only offer indirect evidence.[194] Over the course of the litigation, the government moved away from trying to put forward specific rationales for the transitional provisions, instead relying on the idea that protecting older workers "felt fair";[195] that is, a moral or normative argument. This litigation strategy spectacularly failed. Thus, the cases imply that courts will demand (empirical) evidence to support assertions, at least in some types of cases.

The cases were fundamentally divided on the extent to which "legitimate aims" should be grounded in evidence. In *Sargeant*, for example, the ET effectively declined to scrutinise the evidentiary basis for the government's purported aims, on the basis that they were "social policy choices" where the ET should not substitute its opinion for that of the government.[196] The EAT in *McCloud*, while more willing to scrutinise the legitimate aims put forward by the government, was mindful of "the particular difficulty of producing evidence where moral or political considerations are to the fore".[197] For the EAT, then, requiring evidence to establish a moral legitimate aim was a misdirection;[198] while moral aims may not be easily established by evidence, they can still be legitimate.

For the Court of Appeal, though, moral aims must be legitimate; that is, they must not be irrational. While the Court of Appeal was reluctant to speak to the relevance of or need for evidence, it is clear that whether an aim is "legitimate" will depend on the evidence presented. For example, in argument in the Court of Appeal, the ET in *McCloud* was criticised for demanding evidence in support of aims that could not readily be supported by evidence. The Court of Appeal rejected these arguments, explaining the ET's approach was *really* about the need for rationality:

> As far as the wish for consistency is concerned while it is true that the judge did hold that the contention was based on generalisation rather than hard evidence, *his*

---

194 Seymour (n 8) 301–2.

195 Ibid 302.

196 *Sargeant v London Fire and Emergency Planning Authority* [2017] UKET 2202235/2015, [75]–[76].

197 *The Lord Chancellor v McCloud* [2018] UKEAT/0071/17/LA, [160].

198 Ibid [160].

> *real point* was that, while consistency requires like cases to be treated alike, the Judges' position was so different from those of other public servants that true comparisons could not be made.[199]

This reluctance to speak to evidence, and the need for evidence, may reflect the nature of the appeal process; the Court of Appeal could engage with errors of law only, not questions of fact or evidence, which are left to the court of first instance. Perhaps due to this reluctance, these cases tell us little about what empirical evidence might be required to establish a "legitimate" aim. Clearly, an aim cannot be irrational, and evidence directly contrary to a purported aim may be determinative. What evidence might be required in more finely balanced cases is still unclear. Most likely, though, the state (and other employers) will be given a significant margin of discretion in determining legitimate aims; evidentiary requirements are unlikely to be onerous. This is an issue that will likely play out repeatedly in later cases.

Age Discrimination as a Public Interest Tool

Third, then, we can consider the broader implications of these cases for the use of age discrimination law to advance the public interest. In these cases, the government's use of "moral" or normative arguments to justify the transitional pension provisions arguably hinges on age-based assumptions and stereotypes. It is likely, then, that age discrimination law is particularly apt for challenging this sort of evidence-absent policy-making. In *Sargeant*, though, the ET adopted an unsympathetic approach to the claimant's arguments, perhaps reflecting the government's argument at first instance that the standard of review in age discrimination cases should be lower than the standard of scrutiny for other grounds of discrimination[200] (this was not accepted by the claimants).[201] By contrast, in *McCloud* no party suggested that the results of the case should depend on which protected characteristic was to be considered, be it race, sex, or age,[202] implying that the standard of scrutiny should be

---

[199] *The Lord Chancellor v McCloud* [2018] EWCA Civ 2844, [93] (emphasis added).

[200] *Sargeant v London Fire and Emergency Planning Authority* [2017] UKET 2202235/2015, [47].

[201] Ibid [62].

[202] "The parties are agreed that the claims for race discrimination, sex discrimination/equal pay also depend on the answer to the same question. In the circumstances of this case no party has suggested that the result should be different depending on which protected characteristic is considered": *McCloud* [2017] UKET 2201483/2015, [10].

the same for all protected grounds. The ability to justify direct age discrimination as a proportionate means of achieving a legitimate aim, though, does mean that age discrimination law provides lesser protection than that relating to other grounds. It may therefore be a lesser tool for advancing public interest ends.

Thus, we must still be attuned to the limits to the use of age discrimination law to advance the public interest, especially in relation to pensions. There are extensive exceptions to age discrimination law, which allow – for example – new employees to be granted less generous pension entitlements, even if this disproportionately affects younger workers.[203] In the firefighters' case, for example, most claimants were members of the (more generous) 1992 Firefighters' Pension Scheme, not the less generous 2006 pension scheme. The "enormous gulf" between the two schemes and their benefits meant, for those in the 2006 scheme, the 2015 changes might have left them better off.[204] Thus, claimants in this case tended to be those born from 1971 to 1988, a very particular demographic "slice".[205] There are therefore clear limits to the practical use and utility of age discrimination law in advancing the public interest.

These cases do illustrate, though, that the government is unable to avoid its obligations as an employer through the idea of a "margin of discretion". Indeed, the Court of Appeal explicitly rejected the idea that it should grant a significant margin of appreciation to the government in determining the issue of justification in social policy cases. This is critical for protecting employment rights across the public sector.[206] However, it may also have implications more broadly for the use of age discrimination law to advance public ends, and speaks to the balance between the executive and the judiciary in public interest matters.[207] These issues – and the level of evidence required to inform these judgments – will continue to evolve in future cases.

Legitimacy and Empirical Evidence

Finally, we can reflect on what these cases mean for the legitimacy of courts as public institutions.[208] As I have argued elsewhere, courts that are seen as disconnected from society and social "truths" are unlikely to cultivate public

203 Equality Act (Age Exemptions for Pension Schemes) Order 2010.

204 Seymour (n 8) 308.

205 Ibid.

206 Ibid 305.

207 Ibid 309.

208 Alysia Blackham, 'Legitimacy and Empirical Evidence in the UK Courts' (2016) 25 *Griffith Law Review* 414.

legitimacy.[209] The skilled use of empirical evidence to inform judicial decision-making can build stronger connections (and reduce disconnections) between courts and society, thereby enhancing the legitimacy of judicial decision-making.[210] In cases such as *Sargeant* and *McCloud*, however, which are characterised by a total absence of empirical evidence, courts and tribunals are essentially being asked to make decisions on public interest questions in an evidential vacuum. While an absence of empirical evidence might be the result of executive errors in advocacy and policy-making, it is potentially the legitimacy of the courts that is affected by such decisions. In these specific instances, the issue was resolved somewhat by the evidential onus being on the government to show that such policy changes were a proportionate means of achieving a legitimate aim. This flags, however, the need to be attuned to issues of legitimacy in court decision-making, and how legitimacy might be undermined by an absence of empirical evidence.

ACKNOWLEDGMENTS

This research was funded by the Australian Government through the Australian Research Council's Discovery Projects funding scheme (project DE170100228). The views expressed herein are those of the author and are not necessarily those of the Australian Government or Australian Research Council.

209 Ibid 414–15.
210 Ibid 415.

7. Unreliable science in the courtroom: shifting the courts' focus from assessing the substance of an expert's analysis to the process by which it was produced

Wendy Wagner

INTRODUCTION

Bad science yields bad legal decisions. Innocent suspects are convicted and sometimes subjected to interminable sentences or even death based on unreliable scientific evidence.[1] Persistent toxic substances seep into water supplies, rivers, and lakes where they decimate native species or cause cancer and a wide range of chronic harms because the initial scientific assessments were biased or incomplete.[2] Urgent crises, like climate change, fester without resolution as policymakers get deadlocked over faux scientific conflicts, fueled by unreliable science.[3]

Yet it is hardly a novel observation to notice that sorting the false and "junky" from the trustworthy science is not easy for nonscientist policymakers.[4] Framing the relevant questions, amassing the relevant research, assessing

[1] See generally NAS Committee, *Strengthening Forensic Science in the United States: A Path Forward* (2009).

[2] See, e.g., Nicole Marie Brennan, Abigail Teresa Evans, Meredith Kate Fritz, Stephanie Allison Peak and Haley Elizabeth von Holst, Trends in the Regulation of Per- and Polyfluoroalkyl Substances (PFAS): A Scoping Review, 18 Int. J. Environ. Res. Public Health 10900 (2021).

[3] See, e.g., Maxine Joselow, Lawsuits target Exxon's social media 'green washing', *E&E Climatewire* (July 22, 2021), at https://www.eenews.net/articles/lawsuits-target-exxons-social-media-green-washing/.

[4] *Kumho Tire Co., Ltd. v. Carmichael*, 526 U.S. 137, 158 (1999) (Scalia, J. concurring).

its veracity, and then synthesizing its implications for a given policy question requires the collaboration of both scientists and policymakers. Value judgments as well as a great deal of rigorous, collective scientific expertise are needed at each stage of the policy-making process.[5] In addition, the difficult work of bringing science to policy requires a formal structure for decision-making that ensures that the scientific information that informs a decision is reliable according to standards and conventions set by the scientific community.[6]

Perhaps nowhere else are these lay decision-maker challenges greater than in the courts. Unlike agencies and even legislators, courts lack a formal infrastructure for accessing and assessing the scientific literature. They rely on litigants for most and generally all of their information, an institutional design that the courts are understandably reluctant to alter.[7] The adversarial nature of court processes not only forces the factfinders to rely on the litigants, but is prone, if not guaranteed, to supply them with "extreme" and often biased information that advances a litigant's position. Given this adversarial design, a well-functioning system for sorting out "bad" or unreliable science is vital to the courts' ability to make sound decisions.[8]

In this chapter, I argue that the institutional structures developed by US courts for evaluating the reliability of scientific evidence are faulty in ways

---

[5] Sheila Jasanoff, Quality control and peer review in advisory science, in *The Politics of Scientific Advice: Institutional Design for Quality Assurance*, ed. Justus Lentsch and Peter Weingart (Cambridge University Press, 2011), 19; Bennett Holman and Torsten Wilholt, The New Demarcation Problem, *Studies in History and Philosophy of Science* Special Issues 91 (2022), 211–220.

[6] See, e.g., Comm. on the Institutional Means for Assessment of Risks to Pub. Health, Comm'n on Life Scis., Nat'l Research Council of the Nat'l Acads., Risk Assessment in the Federal Government: Managing the Process 139–45 (1983) [Red Book].

[7] See, e.g., Edward K. Cheng, The Consensus Rule: A New Approach to Scientific Evidence, Vand. L. Rev. 75 (2022), 407 (discussing the limited use of scientific advisors in courts).

[8] To keep focus on what I view as a significant, yet remediable problem with the current judicial approach to evaluating the reliability of scientific information, I bracket concerns about whether judges and juries—once provided with reliable scientific evidence—actually have the capacity to process and make sense of it. Indeed, some empirical research suggests that lay decision-makers may be surprisingly competent at using scientific information to reach decisions, but this topic is left for another day. See, e.g., Shari Diamond and Jessica Salerno, Empirical Analysis of Juries in Tort Cases in *Research Handbook on the Economics of Torts* ed. Jennifer H. Arlen (Edward Elgar, 2015), 422–23; Neil Vidmar, Expert Evidence, the Adversary System, and the Jury, Am. J. Public Health; Suppl 1 95 (2005), S138–140.

that desperately need attention and reform. When it comes to complex technical information, one of the best ways to distinguish reliable science from unreliable science is to look to the established principles scientists themselves have developed to make such distinctions. But that is not how the courts do it. Comparing the courts' approach to screening the reliability of scientific analyses against the best practices and related processes employed by scientists reveals significant disconnects and sources of errors. Rather than a robust dialogue between courts and scientists, the courts have generally proceeded on their own, focusing on the wrong questions and using tests that have little in common with the methods scientists themselves use to assess the trustworthiness of scientific information.

The analysis unfolds in three sections. The first section provides initial orientation by identifying several distinct types of challenges that arise at the intersection of law and science and then examines one of those challenges in detail—namely, the evaluation of the reliability of scientific analyses. The first section then closes with an exploration of the approaches used within the scientific community to evaluate scientific reliability and argues that the scientists' methods provide a benchmark of sorts from which the courts' approaches should be modeled. The second section describes the courts' current approach to evaluating the reliability of science as set against the processes used by the scientific community for this same purpose. In this section, I consider not only private and criminal litigation, where evidence rules governing admissibility are expected to do some of this important work, but also the courts' review of challenges to the quality of the agency's scientific analyses under the Administrative Procedure Act (APA). Although these two worlds of judicial decision-making tend to be separated in the literature, the key issues are remarkably similar when considering the courts' ability to responsibly evaluate the reliability of the scientific information advanced by advocates. The third section then proposes a reform for the courts' assessment of scientific reliability that comes closer to modeling the practices used by the scientific community.

1. EVALUATION OF THE RELIABILITY OF SCIENTIFIC ANALYSES

A number of important challenges arise at the intersection of science and decision-making. This chapter selects out only one relatively discrete challenge—assessing whether scientific information being used for legal decisions is reliable and trustworthy—and leaves other science-policy problems for another day. After placing the current project in context, this section then reviews the approaches taken by the scientific community in assessing the veracity and integrity of scientific information as a possible guide for courts to follow.

A. Science-Policy Challenges in the Abstract

The literature on science policy is huge and sprawling, but from a high altitude, it appears that most commenters writing on this topic are concerned with one of two complex types of challenges, only the second of which is the topic of this chapter.[9] The first challenge, and again outside the scope of this project, concerns how best to ensure that science is used in ways that are democratically *and* scientifically rigorous. Philosophers, historians, and sociologists of science call this the "new demarcation problem", which involves separating values from science in ways that will ensure that both have their say in public decision-making.[10] Here, the focus is on devising ways that scientific information can be located and successfully integrated into decision-making without giving either "side" (e.g., nonscientists on the one hand and experts on the other) too much control or power.[11] Indeed, this ideal mixing problem of science and values has been so vexing that scholars writing in the area have largely fallen into two camps—those who worry about too much expert power[12] versus those who worry about the dangers of under-utilizing or even ignoring expertise.[13]

Despite these disagreements, considerable progress has been made over the years in designing institutional decision-making processes to maximize the use of the available expertise without allowing it to overshadow value choices. In general, the institutionally preferred solutions break a larger policy inquiry

---

9 See, e.g., Wendy Wagner, No one solution to the "new demarcation problem"?: A view from the trenches, *Studies in History and Philosophy of Science Part A* 92 (2022), 177.

10 See, e.g., Holman and Wilholt, supra note 5; Kevin Elliott, *A Tapestry of Values: An Introduction to Values in Science* (Oxford University Press, 2017).

11 See, e.g., Committee on Risk Assessment of Hazardous Air Pollutants, National Research Council, Science and Judgment in Risk Assessment (1994); Jasanoff, supra note 5; Heather Douglas, Inserting the Public Into Science, in *Democratization of Expertise?: Exploring Novel Forms of Scientific Advice in Political Decision-Making* ed. Sabine Maasen and Peter Weingart (Springer Dordrecht, 2005), 153; Holman and Wilholt, supra note 5, 2022.

12 See, e.g., Richard T. Lackey, Science, Scientists, and Policy Advocacy, 21 *Conservation Biology* 21 (2007), 12.

13 See, e.g., Andrew A. Rosenberg, Fishing for Certainty, *Nature* 449 (2007), 989 (making this argument).

into discrete sub-questions, proceeding sequentially, for scientists.[14] Experts can, for example, summarize the literature informing what scientists understand about fine particulates on asthma. Policymakers can then ask more fine-grained questions about how, within that body of research, vulnerable sub-populations fare at differing exposure levels. Policymakers might also ask scientists to develop computational models to predict adverse effects to diverse, sensitive sub-groups based on a number of default assumptions that comport with policy goals (e.g., weighting studies showing adverse effects at the lowest levels more heavily or relying solely on animal studies when human-based research is not available).[15] These iterative conversations between policymakers and scientists endeavor to retain the "province" of values, set against the "province" of expertise.

This model of "dialogic" approaches to science policy, which begins to break the impasse, is nevertheless plagued by a second worry that has become its own theme and source of writing in the science-policy literature; namely, a concern that some of the research and even some of the researchers informing policy processes are simply not reliable.[16] The research might be contracted out with specific ends already in mind for the results.[17] Or researchers might be affiliated with employers who have a vested interest in the policymaking outcome and who exert some pressure on the researchers. Or the researchers themselves might be associated with less mainstream views that seem to have

---

14 See, e.g., Red Book, supra note 6; National Research Council, Understanding Risk: Informing Decisions in a Democratic Society (1996); see also Wagner, Demarcation, supra note 9 (describing EPA's innovative approach used to set ambient air quality standards).

15 Courts in fact vary among themselves on how they answer these questions (e.g., some courts allow the consideration of testimony based on animal studies and some do not); see, e.g., Carl F. Cranor, *Toxic Torts: Science, Law, and the Possibility of Justice* (2nd ed. 2016), 240–50, but the underlying considerations generally do not include considerations of whether the underlying research is done in a way that is trustworthy, which is the focus here.

16 See, e.g., T. Legg, J. Hatchard and A.B. Gilmore, The Science for Profit Model—How and why corporations influence science and the use of science in policy and practice, *PLoS ONE* 16(6) (2021), e0253272, available at https://doi.org/10.1371/journal.pone.0253272. This topic was the focus of a book I wrote with Tom McGarity, called *Bending Science* (Harvard University Press, 2007). The literature, however, is quite large. See, e.g., David Michaels, *Doubt is Their Product: How Industry's Assault on Science Threatens Your Health* (Oxford University Press, 2008); Naomi Oreskes and Eric M. Conway, *Merchants of Doubt: How a Handful of Scientists Obscured the Truth on Issues from Tobacco Smoke to Global Warming* (Bloomsbury, 2009).

17 See, e.g., McGarity & Wagner, supra note 16, at 60–79.

ideological or normative priors that may compromise their disinterestedness and objectivity.[18]

The second challenge intersects with a more foundational challenge arising within science itself: namely, evaluating whether scientific information is trustworthy.[19] Numerous books and articles document the various ways that research produced to inform high-stakes social issues has been designed by affected parties in ways that are intentionally biased to advance their interests.[20] In these settings, the sponsor or researcher works backwards from the desired result in ends-oriented ways and develops methods or statistical techniques that produce that preferred outcome.[21] The tobacco industry pioneered some of the early techniques, but those methods have grown more elaborate and nuanced and are now used widely across many industries and stakeholder groups.[22] See Figure 7.1 (charting a playbook of these strategies).

Scientists, moreover, are typically one of the targets for these sophisticated deceptions in the hopes that the manipulations will pass through the scientific pipeline undetected.[23] Publishing "bent science" in peer-reviewed journals, writing letters to the editor complaining about the unreliability of adverse findings, and a host of other tactics make advocacy science appear credible to the scientific community. In light of the high stakes for avoiding costly liability and regulation, it is unsurprising that these tactics are sophisticated in ways designed to fool even the best scientists.

In sum, these two distinct types of science-policy challenges—how to incorporate science into policymaking in a democratically robust way and how to ensure that the underlying scientific information is trustworthy—involve some overlap. However, in this chapter, I focus only on the latter challenge and bracket the many problems that arise in locating, translating, and mixing science and values. Although this narrower focus does sidestep important challenges, ensuring the reliability of the scientific information is a first-order problem that largely precedes the second set of science-value challenges. Even the best institutional design that merges expert advice with public values will fail if there is no mechanism for ensuring that the underlying scientific information informing that process is trustworthy.

---

18 See, e.g., id. at 82–87.

19 See, e.g., Wagner, Demarcation, supra note 9 (drawing out the overlap and distinctions between these two types of problems).

20 See supra note 16.

21 See id.

22 See Legg et al., supra note 16.

23 See, e.g., McGarity and Wagner, supra note 16, at 45–48, 52–58.

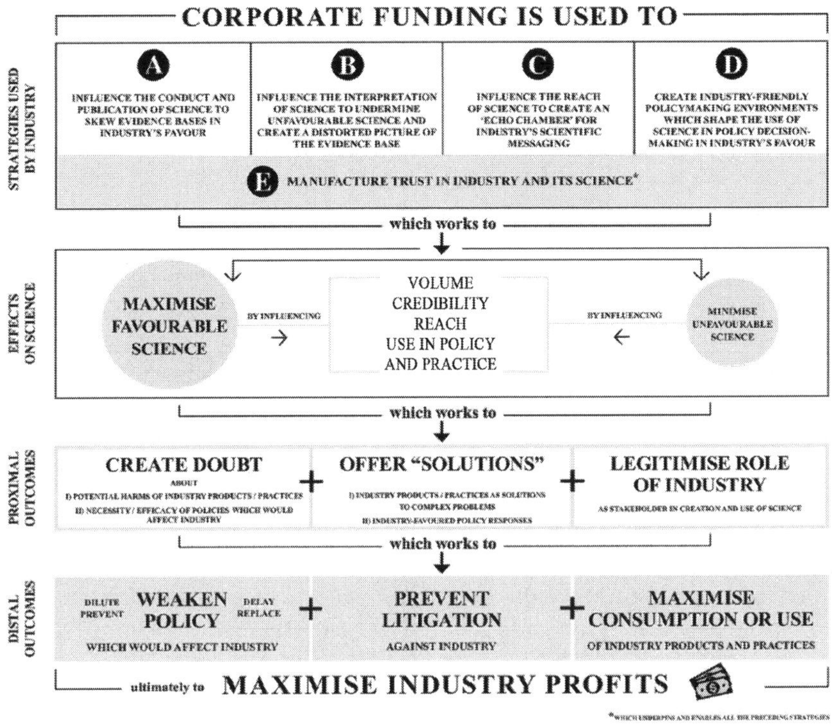

Source: Copied from Legg et al. (2021); see footnote 16.

Figure 7.1 How advocates can impact the production of science

B. Scientists' Approach to Screening Reliable Science

Given this chapter's singular focus on screening the reliability of scientific information informing policy processes, the next question is how to develop an ideal approach to this critical step. How *should* screening be done?

Most authors writing on this issue seem to agree: the best benchmark for assessing scientific reliability is how the scientific community itself assesses the veracity of expert information.[24] Any approach developed by the scientific community will naturally involve some value-laden judgments that overlap with the science-and-value challenges. However, since we are endeavoring to locate scientific information that is reliable, the appropriate source of guidance

24 See, e.g., Bennett Holman and Kevin Elliott, The promise and perils of industry-funded science, *Philosophy Compass* 13 (2018).

should come initially from the experts themselves. Indeed, it is not evident there is a better source of guidance than the scientific community given the esoteric features of complex technical research. Therefore, in this chapter, I conclude that the best source of guidance for the law's own struggles at screening for reliable science should draw from the scientists' own communal standards.[25]

With the deluge of "bent" science arising in policy processes and in scientific journals over the last few decades, the scientific community has not surprisingly dedicated considerable effort to shoring up its own oversight and screening processes to catch this type of ends-oriented evidence.[26] The specifics of these approaches vary, but, in general, reliability is determined by the scientific community by subjecting the research or testimony to at least three process-based scientific conventions: disinterestedness, independence, and rigorous peer scrutiny. While a scientist's ultimate assessment of a study based on these three criteria will fall along a spectrum and be qualitative, the strength and trustworthiness of research are correlated with the rigor with which all three of these key conventions have been followed.

Scientific journals offer an especially helpful illustration of how these process-based conventions have developed and are applied to do this screening work. Scientific journals are highly motivated to not only identify the most impactful research from the reams of submissions but to ensure that that research is reliable and robust.[27] To accomplish this latter inquiry, journals ensure submitted work is thoroughly peer-reviewed. The journals also require that the author certify their independence, specify their unique contribution to the final product in percentage terms, and identify any conflicts of interest or other sources of influence that might bias the research.[28] While the resulting information does not lead to a bright-line test that categorizes the research as "reliable" or "unreliable", the information provides the primary basis by which journal editors assess the trustworthiness of research. No matter how novel, creative, or impactful a study might be, if research is not trustworthy, it will

---

[25] Of course, there are socially constructed concepts of what "reliable" means in different policy settings. Citizen-collected evidence that does not meet scientific standards of reliability might nevertheless be deemed reliable for a number of value-laden and democratic reasons, for example.

[26] See, e.g., McGarity and Wagner, supra note 16, at 90–91, 233–39.

[27] See, e.g., Donald Kennedy, Responding to Fraud, *Science* 314 (2006), 1353; Catherine DeAngelis, The influence of money on medical science, JAMA 296 (2006), 996.

[28] See, e.g., ICJME, Defining the Role of Authors and Contributors, available at https://www.icmje.org/recommendations/browse/roles-and-responsibilities/defining-the-role-of-authors-and-contributors.html.

not be published. To provide more detail on these three conventions, each is discussed in turn.

Peer review. Philosophers and historians of science generally agree that one of the most critical ingredients for rigorous scientific work is subjecting it to critical scrutiny by diverse peers.[29] Scientific analysis, in fact, is not really considered "reliable" or trustworthy *until* it has undergone intensive peer review and vetting—the kind where a skeptic critically picks apart every assumption and unsupported judgment. As such, peer review involves "in its broadest sense, ... the scientific community's effort to police itself and assure a certain minimum level of quality so that scientists and others can rely on the results of reported scientific research".[30] Lawyers might think of this peer review as a process of self-governance that endeavors to introduce checks on research to improve its reliability through a type of internal, deliberative-styled process of expert skepticism.

Additionally, for this peer review to be effective, a representative and diverse set of skeptics—who are independent and disinterested—must be chosen to critique a study.[31] Simply assembling friends or colleagues with a predisposition toward the research undermines the goals of peer review. Reviewers must be primed to give the research as thorough a review as possible.

All scientific journals implement some form of peer review, albeit with varying degrees of rigor and success (as discussed later).[32] But even for the most prestigious journals—whose reputation and market share depend on excellent articles—ensuring adequate peer review is a work-in-progress.[33] Journals are thus constantly striving to improve peer-review processes in light of embarrassing mistakes and surprises, such as when published research is later proved to have involved fraudulent data collection.[34]

---

[29] Naomi Oreskes, *Why Trust Science?* (Princeton University Press, 2020). Oreskes summarizes an extensive line of important work that reaches this conclusion. See also Helen E. Longino, *Science as Social Knowledge: Values and Objectivity in Scientific Inquiry* (Princeton University Press, 1990), 80 (underscoring the role of critical and diverse scrutiny in science).

[30] Lars Noah, Sanctifying Scientific Peer Review: Publications as a Proxy for Regulatory Decisionmaking, U. Pitt. L. Rev. 59 (1998), 677, 693.

[31] Id.

[32] Id. at 696–700 (describing many of these problems).

[33] And, while the nature of this peer review will be different for original research as compared to the review or syntheses of multiple studies, the concept of searching review by diverse peer-skeptics is deployed in effectively the same way. J.B. Ruhl and James Salzman, In Defense of Regulatory Peer Review, Wash. U. L. Rev. 84 (2006), 1, 11 and 38 (discussing these differences and similarities between different forms of peer review).

[34] See, e.g., Kennedy, supra note 27.

Independence and Disinterestedness. A second convention that scientists use to assess reliability is authorship. Ensuring that the creator of scientific information is held accountable for its reliability creates incentives for authors to produce trustworthy research. Accordingly, many journals require that all submissions identify by name and affiliation the primary author(s) of the work, while also itemizing all other contributors and their individualized contributions to the project.[35] Submissions that do not provide this documentation will not be published. These authorship requirements not only place reputational incentives on the listed authors and contributors but help protect against the far too common practice by research sponsors of hiring ghostwriters to craft articles with the named authors simply serving as misleading window dressing for the underlying biased reports.[36]

Researcher Independence. A third and related convention is researcher independence.[37] Researchers should have full control over how they think through problems, design methods, and report their findings. Constraints or influence from funding sponsors or pressures placed on researchers through academic incentive systems can reduce the reliability of this research. For example, the authors may be paid by a sponsor with an interest in the outcome. Even more personal forms of biasing—such as financial conflicts of interest—are considered material and must be disclosed.[38] As a result, some journals ask authors to identify—beyond financial interests—all sources of potential bias. These biasing features may not be disqualifying but they allow editors and peer reviewers to take those influences into account in reviewing the article.

Since this information might not be voluntarily disclosed by most authors, many top journals have instituted formal processes to draw out as much of this

---

[35] See, e.g., PLOS ONE, Authorship Guidelines, available at https://journals.plos.org/plosone/s/authorship.

[36] See, e.g., Drummond Rennie, Veronica Yank and Linda Emanuel, When Authorship Fails: A Proposal to Make Contributors Accountable, JAMA 278 (1997), 579; Anna Wilde Mathews, At Medical Journals, Paid Writers Play Big Role, WSJ, December 12, 2005, at A1, available at https://www.wsj.com/articles/SB113443606745420770.

[37] See, e.g., Sheldon Krimsky, *Science in the Private Interest* (Bloomsbury, 2003), 125–40. For example, the *Journal of the American Medical Association* (JAMA) requires as a condition to publication that "[f]or all reports (regardless of funding source) containing original data, at least 1 named author (e.g., the principal investigator)" must indicate that she or he "had full access to all the data in the study and takes responsibility for the integrity of the data and the accuracy of the data analysis". JAMA Instructions for Authors, Data Access and Responsibility, available at https://jamanetwork.com/journals/jama/pages/instructions-for-authors.

[38] Krimsky, supra note 37.

information as possible using mandatory disclosure forms.[39] The authorship form requires authors to certify that they are the primary author and to identify other contributors and their roles.[40] The conflict-of-interest form requires the disclosure of potential financial conflicts of interest, including an economic stake in the outcome.[41]

At a practical level, journals vary dramatically in how rigorously they deploy these latter two requirements. Some journals require limited only conflict disclosures and/or do not monitor compliance with the disclosures that are required.[42] Other journals are highly committed to collecting these disclosures and certifications. But even the most determined journals experience significant challenges in ensuring full author compliance with their disclosures.[43] If an author lies and withholds conflicts of interest, for example, it is difficult for the editors to learn about the fraud. For example, out of 70 articles published on calcium channel blockers in the scientific literature, 96 percent of the authors who declared them "safe" did not disclose their financial relationship with the manufacturers of the drugs, often despite journal requirements to do so.[44]

Before proceeding, it is important to be clear on the limitations of these screening criteria. While they may be the best methods currently available within the scientific community for assessing the reliability of scientific research, they are certainly not perfect. There are at least several limitations that deserve mention.

First, even when research is free of bias and peer reviewers declare the research to be exemplary, the scientific analyses and research may still end

---

39 See, e.g., Science, "Editorial Policies", available at https://science.org/content/page/science-journals-editorial-policies

40 See, e.g., ICJME, "Defining the Role of Authors and Contributors," available at https://www.icmje.org/recommendations/browse/roles-and-responsibilities/defining-the-role-of-authors-and-contributors.html

41 See, e.g., ICJME, "Disclosure of Interest," available at https://www.icmje.org/disclosure-of-interest/.

42 See, e.g., Kathleen Ruff, Scientific journals and conflict of interest disclosure: what progress has been made?, 14 Environ. Health 45 (2015), available at https://doi.org/10.1186/s12940-015-0035–6.

43 As Catherine DeAngelis, editor-in-chief of JAMA, explained: "I'm not the F.B.I.", and cannot look "in the hearts, minds and souls of authors", much less oversee the completeness of the disclosures accompanying the over 6000 articles submitted annually to her journal. See DeAngelis, supra note 27.

44 See Henry Thomas Stelfox et al., Conflict of Interest in the Debate over Calcium-Channel Antagonists, New Eng. J. Med. 338(1010) (1998), 103–04.

up being wrong.[45] Paradigm shifts in theories, incomplete data, selective data (in ways that nevertheless meet communal standards), and many other factors can undercut the ultimate veracity of scientific evidence that meets these three criteria.[46] Indeed, the "replication crisis", in which published research cannot be replicated, often occurs despite the research satisfying these three conventions.[47] An unfaltering reliance on these three conventions may even unfairly disparage some good research.[48]

Additionally, much of the research of concern in the courts tends to be novel in ways that have not been vetted within the scientific community.[49] Since this work is often developed specifically to answer a particular policy question, rather than test an established theory, the methods used by researchers often proceed in trial-and-error ways.[50] Accordingly, mainstream scientists may lack rigorous ways to conduct peer review over this novel research as a substantive matter, and may even lack interest in conducting or overseeing its quality given its applied nature.[51] Indeed, what makes many of the litigation controversies over applied scientific information so difficult is the fact that there are so few guardrails within the scientific community to rigorously assess its reliability.[52]

Finally, peer review, even in its best incarnations, will be subject to human error at every step in the process. The selection of and number of reviewers,

---

45 Cf. Henry H. Bauder, *Scientific Literacy and the Myth of the Scientific Method* (1992), 48 (citing John Ziman who estimates that 90 percent of the primary literature in physics is wrong).

46 See, e.g., Monya Baker, 1500 Scientists Lift the Lid on the Reproducibility, *Nature* 533 (2016), 452.

47 Another source of unreliable published research can arise from "supplements" to journals that are published as symposia, but often funded by an interested party like industry. See, e.g., Lisa Bero, A. Galbraith and D. Rennie, The Publication of Sponsored Symposiums in Medical Journals, New Eng. J. Med. 327 (1992), 1135, 1137.

48 This is the topic of Thomas Kuhn's famous book, *The Structure of Scientific Revolutions* (University of Chicago, 1962).

49 See, e.g., McGarity and Wagner, supra note 16, at 47–57.

50 See, e.g., Philip Kitcher, Patterns of Scientific Controversies, in *Scientific Controversies: Philosophical and Historical Perspectives* ed. Peter Machamer, Marcello Pera and Aristides Baltas (New York: Oxford University Press, 2000), 31–35.

51 See, e.g., McGarity and Wagner, supra note 16, at 47–57.

52 See William L. Anderson, Barry M. Parsons and Drummond Rennie, Daubert's Backwash: Litigation-Generated Science, U. Mich. J.L. Reform 34 (2001), 619, 630–31 (making this point, observing that "the early lawsuits in any health case are often based on unproven conjecture derived from a limited base of regulatory or other studies").

the limited time and energy they have available to scrutinize the work under review, and their own idiosyncratic biases can all work to compromise assurances of reliability, even for work that survives peer review.[53] As one commentator noted somewhat pessimistically, "[a]t best, … editorial peer review manages to filter out obviously sloppy work".[54] Therefore, it is a significant overstatement to suggest that the scientific community has these reliability issues under control. However, because many of the lapses in scientists' ability to identify unreliable research occur in hindsight, it is not clear there are any better alternatives for assessing scientific reliability outside these process-based conventions. Thus, for the remainder of the chapter, I adopt the communal standards within science as the best option for judging the reliability of scientific evidence.

Accordingly, courts ideally should incorporate these same scientific conventions into their own assessments of scientific reliability. Specifically, they will ask: 1) Does the testimony or research suggest that it has been subjected to critical peer scrutiny of some sort—albeit not necessarily publication—and if so, what did that scrutiny reveal? 2) What do we know about the author's independence? 3) And what do we know about the author's disinterestedness? Even if these questions are asked in ways that yield only qualitative information, the revelations will inform foundational questions that philosophers and scientists seem to agree are vital to ensuring the reliability of scientific evidence.[55] Research that is influenced by interested parties or financial incentives, that is written or conducted by others who are not identified, and that is not subjected to critical peer scrutiny by experts in the field is patently less trustworthy. Even research that might be substantively persuasive will be heavily discounted by fellow scientists and journal editors if it violates one or more of these essential process-oriented conventions.

2. A COMPARISON OF THE ASSESSMENT OF SCIENTIFIC RELIABILITY IN THE US COURTS WITH THAT OF THE METHODS OF THE SCIENTIFIC COMMUNITY

Given this idealized version of how courts *should* evaluate the reliability of scientific evidence and analyses, how in fact *do* they currently engage in this effort? This section describes US courts' current practices and finds

[53] See, e.g., Jonathan P. Tennant and Tony Ross-Hellauer, The limitations to our understanding of peer review, Res. Integr. Peer Rev. 5 (2020), 6, available at https://doi.org/10.1186/s41073-020-00092-1

[54] Noah, supra note 30, at 698.

[55] See, e.g., McGarity and Wagner, supra note 16, at 47.

considerable slippage in the courts' assessment of reliability when compared to the scientific community.[56] Instead of drawing on communal scientific conventions to guide their evaluation of the veracity of scientific testimony, the courts generally assume scientific information is reliable as long as it is "empirical" in nature. More critical courts develop additional screening factors beyond ensuring that evidence is "testable" or empirically based, but there is not much overlap between the substance-based factors that the courts use for this assessment and the process-based conventions used by scientists to assess reliability. The resulting limited oversight by the courts over scientific reliability creates considerable room for manipulative, ends-oriented research and testimony to enter the courts. In fact, this incomplete judicial oversight increases the incentives for stakeholders to develop still more ways to compromise scientific research in ways that pass through the courts' leaky reliability filters.

This section first considers the courts' application of the rules of evidence to screen out unreliable scientific information and then compares the courts' general approach against an ideal version borrowed from scientists which incorporates the conventions of disinterestedness, independence, and rigorous peer review. The second section then conducts the same two-part analysis, focusing on a very different set of reliability issues arising in the courts' review of challenges to the scientific analyses incorporated in agency rulemakings.

A. The Admissibility of Scientific Evidence

The US courts have long struggled to filter out the continuous stream of unreliable science introduced by advocates to gain an edge in litigation. Since factfinders are lay jurors or judges, and are not scientists, they are not well-equipped to evaluate whether scientific testimony or research is trustworthy. This, in turn, creates a cottage industry of sorts for the introduction of commissioned or ends-oriented science.[57] Ends-oriented or "bent" science is especially worrisome in the litigation context since a significant portion of the evidence that arises in these disputes is novel and has not been rigorously pre-screened by the scientific community.[58]

---

[56] Unless otherwise noted, courts include all levels and forms—state and federal, trial and appellate, admissibility of evidence and review of agency rules.

[57] Cf. Peter Huber, *Galileo's Revenge: Junk Science in the Courtroom* (Basic Books, 1991).

[58] Anderson et al., supra note 52, at 621 (observing how reliance on advocates to identify unreliable science "begins to fall apart if lawyers and litigation experts invade the realm of scientific research and manipulate the medical and scientific publication system to achieve their litigation ends").

Judge Kozinski of the Ninth Circuit was particularly concerned by the influx of unreliable science prepared specifically for litigation, dubbing it "litigation science".[59] This "litigation science", he observed, is commissioned with an end result in mind and the applicable scientific methods were then distorted to produce the desired result. As discussed in the first section, "litigation science" is only the tip of the iceberg when it comes to unreliability. Stakeholders are engaged in a much larger universe of "bent science", designed not only to influence specific court cases but also consumers, investors, regulators, legislators, policymakers, and many others well before any litigation commences.[60] The fact that courts will face a deluge of unreliable science at the hands of litigants thus seems both inevitable and a concern that extends well beyond the narrow context of experts hired to testify in a specific case.[61]

In theory, an adversarial process equipped with cross-examination and discovery tools should be well prepared to ferret out the very worst, most unreliable evidence introduced by litigants. But trial processes are expensive, and they run the risk of not succeeding in locating reliability problems. For both judicial economy and judicial competence reasons, then, the courts have long utilized rules of evidence to cull out unreliable evidence and streamline trials. In this section, I first trace how the courts have conducted this task of screening out the unreliable scientific evidence under Federal Rule of Evidence 702. I then compare the courts' screening approach against the way that the scientific community would assess the reliability of this same evidence using the process-based conventions described in section 1.

---

59 Daubert, 43 F.3d 1311, 1318 (9th Cir. 1995).

60 Patterson's article makes this point; he argues the main concern about scientific reliability should be focused on the bent science produced well before the litigation commences, rather than the litigation science (more obvious) problems. Mark R. Patterson, Conflicts of Interest in Scientific Expert Testimony, Wm. & Mary L. Rev. 40 (1999), 1313, 1364. He notes, for example, that the focus on "litigation science" by the Ninth Circuit would admit, without "further scrutiny—research on the safety of the drug that was funded by its manufacturer, if the research predated the litigation". Id. at 1316. The focus on "litigation science" by the Ninth Circuit also caused that court to formulate incomplete screening tests. For example, the court held that as long as research is conducted "independent of the litigation [in the] usual course of business" it is much more likely to provide "important, objective proof that the research comports with the dictates of good science"; Daubert, 43 F.3d 1311, 1317 (9th Cir. 1995). Under the Ninth Circuit's view, the primary sources of bias of concern in litigation were those that arose from experts "biased towards a particular opinion because they were being paid for their litigation work". Id.

61 Anderson et al., supra note 52, at 623–27.

The US courts have followed a long, winding path in developing standards for screening the reliability of scientific evidence. Beginning with *Frye* in the 1940s, the court looked to "general acceptance" of the scientific community to determine reliability, a test that sounds superficially sympathetic to the idea of benchmarking reliability against the conventions of the scientific community.[62] The problem in *Frye* was that there was effectively no inquiry into the basis for the scientific community's judgment—both who was in the relevant scientific community (e.g., all scientists or just vascular neurologists) or why that community "accepted" (or didn't accept) the state of the evidence.[63] The underlying process features that helped explain general acceptance—and would have also helped gain more insight into the veracity of the scientific community's views—were effectively ignored by the courts. This relatively crude test also caused important, novel evidence to sometimes be excluded since it had not yet gained "general acceptance", while at the same time unreliable evidence was sometimes admitted if the relevant (and potentially uniformly biased) "community" (e.g., forensic scientists) agreed it was reliable.[64]

Criticisms of *Frye*, coupled with slight revisions in the Federal Rules of Evidence, led to a re-interpretation of the proper standard for reviewing the reliability of scientific evidence by the Supreme Court in 1993. In *Daubert v. Merrell Dow Pharmaceutical Co.*, the Court instructed the lower courts to screen the reliability of scientific evidence using a more open-ended set of criteria.[65] Foremost among the criteria was ensuring that the scientific testimony was in fact truly "science" and could be empirically tested. But the Court noted that lower courts could also consider where the testimony reflected positions that were "generally accepted in the field", had been "peer reviewed", and reflected a low error rate.[66]

Not surprisingly, these ambiguous instructions for the lower courts led to confusion and inconsistency. The criticisms of *Daubert* are legion.[67] Chief

---

62 *Frye v. United States*, 293 F. 1013, 1014 (1923).

63 See, e.g., Paul C. Giannelli, The Admissibility of Novel Scientific Evidence: Frye v. United States, a Half-Century Later, *Columbia Law Review* 80 (1980), 1197.

64 See, e.g., Giannelli, supra note 63.

65 509 U.S. 579 (1993).

66 Id. at 593–94.

67 See, e.g., David S. Caudill and Lewis H. LaRue, *No Magic Wand: The Idealization of Science in Law* (Bloomsbury, 2006); Cheng, supra note 7, at 19; S. Gatowski, S.A. Dobbin, J.T. Richardson, G.P. Ginsburg, M.L. Merlino, and V. Dahir, Asking the gatekeepers: a national survey of judges on judging expert evidence in a post-Daubert world, Law Hum. Behav. *25* (2001), 433; Margaret A. Berger, What has a decade of Daubert wrought?, Am. J. Public Health 95 (2005),

among them is that the test places "lay decisionmakers in impossible positions, ... [and then] dooms itself to suboptimal decisions".[68]

In the abstract, *Daubert* and even *Frye* seem to gauge the reliability of scientific testimony by deferring to the scientists' collective judgment on controverted testimony.[69] Yet this deference to scientific judgment is based on a "substantive" endorsement that a particular theory or claim is accepted within the scientific community. Courts, in other words, inquire whether an advocate's theory or findings map against what the relevant scientists believe to be substantively true and base reliability on that substantive match. The notion that the courts might instead look to a very different source of wisdom from the scientific community—namely the *process* for determining evidentiary reliability—is effectively ignored. As discussed below, the three scientific conventions (independence and disinterestedness of the author and rigorous peer scrutiny) are rarely if ever considered by the courts in assessing the reliability of scientific testimony.[70]

Disinterestedness, the first of the three conventions, is almost never used by the courts as a basis for assessing the reliability of an expert's testimony. As Patterson notes, "[n]otably absent from [the Daubert list of factors relevant to determining reliability] is any mention of the possible biases or conflicts of interest of the expert".[71] Indeed, bias and sponsor control seem to not only be an endemic feature of adversarial processes, but a feature that therefore must be passed along to the jury without any further inquiry. Of course, cross-examination may play a role in exposing these conflicts for the fact-finder. However, most courts do not use Rule 702 to exclude ends-oriented testimony as unreliable since virtually all experts are hired and paid by litigants.[72] As

---

S59; Eric Helland, The Role of Ideology in Judicial Evaluations of Experts, *The Journal of Law and Economics* 62 (2019), 579.

68 Cheng, supra note 7, at 3, 15. In response to the dismal state of evidence law, a number of scholars have proposed innovative suggestions for reform of the reliability screening standard, including Ed Cheng's inventive "consensus" rule that he proposes should replace the current *Daubert* test. Id.

69 Anderson et al., supra note 52, at 619–20 ("the Supreme Court in Daubert explicitly encouraged federal court litigants to rely on the scientific community, initially and primarily, to protect the courts from unreliable, novel science").

70 In one of the two articles that discuss "bent" science in the evidentiary context, the authors similarly conclude that "litigation science threatens to upset the notions upon which Daubert is built". Anderson et al., supra note 52, at 621.

71 Patterson, supra note 60, at 1319.

72 Patterson, supra note 60, at 1320 (observing that "[c]ourts generally handle biases of expert witnesses in the same way they handle biases of fact witnesses, by permitting cross-examination about the biases and allowing the fact finder to assess the overall credibility of the witnesses").

the 11th Circuit stated in Adams, any “bias in an expert witness’s testimony is usually a credibility issue for the jury”.[73]

There are a few exceptions, including the Ninth Circuit’s (and more particularly Judge Kozinski’s) concern with “litigation science”. A few courts may exclude experts whose opinions were formulated as a result of the litigation or in ways that are directly tied to a continuing role as an expert in litigation.[74] Despite these outliers, however, most courts conclude that cross-examination is the best tool for exposing bias in an expert; bias is not considered in ruling on the admissibility of evidence. Indeed, somewhat perversely, a few courts even hold that “when the expert’s opinion (or the basis for the opinion) is reached before the expert became involved in litigation, the expert’s opinion is *not* biased and is thus reliable”.[75] Given the widespread evidence of corporate sponsorship of research discussed in section 1.B., this approach is wholly oblivious to the fact that sponsors often generate much of their ends-oriented research long before the litigation begins.

The second convention—independence and authorship—is also rarely if ever considered explicitly by the courts in judging the admissibility of evidence. Courts again seem to assume that if testimony was “ghostwritten” or influenced by an attorney or other stakeholder, those features will emerge on cross-examination. The courts thus again delegate the interrogation of scientific reliability almost entirely to the whims of the adversarial system.[76] Such a delegation is misguided not only because of inevitable imbalances in the quality of counsel (particularly with respect to the esoteric area of scientific evidence),[77] but also due to the fact that at least some of the underlying interactions between counsel and the experts they hire, including testifying experts, may be undiscoverable as work product.[78]

“Peer review”, however, is an explicit factor listed by the Supreme Court in *Daubert* as affecting reliability and would appear, at first blush, to be an

73 *Adams v. Lab. Corp. of America*, 760 F.3d 1322, 1331 (11th Cir. 2014); *United States v. McCluskey*, 954 F. Supp. 2d 1224, 1240 (D.N.M. 2013).

74 *National Bank of Commerce v. Dow Chemical Co.*, 965 F. Supp. 1490 (E.D.Ark. 1996); *Black v. Rhone-Poulenc Inc.*, 19 F. Supp. 2d 592, 600 (S.D. W. Va. 1998). See generally Patterson, supra note 60.

75 Anderson et al., supra note 52, at 659 (emphasis added).

76 It is worth noting as well that in some cases litigants may be disinclined to expose these scientific “violations” of reliability for the factfinder since it could be turned against them to expose weaknesses in their own expert testimony.

77 See, e.g., D. Michael Risinger, Navigating Expert Reliability: Are Criminal Standards of Certainty Being Left on the Dock?, Albany L. Rev 64 (2000), 99.

78 See, e.g., Rule 26 of the Federal Rules of Civil Procedure (providing work product protection to draft expert reports).

influential factor informing the courts' admissibility determinations. Yet when it comes to assessing "peer review", most courts simply equate the "peer review" test with publication, rather than with the more process-based idea of ensuring "rigorous and critical scrutiny of the analysis by peers".[79] Accordingly, many (but not all)[80] courts utilize publication as a proxy for satisfying the "peer review" factor.[81] Specifically, if expert testimony or the research upon which it relies has been "published", it automatically meets the peer-review test. Indeed, the Supreme Court itself stated the criteria as "whether the theory or technique has been subjected to peer review *and publication*",[82] although it softened this requirement slightly by acknowledging that publication may not be sufficient and in some cases may not always be possible.[83]

A few courts do at least pay lip service to the underlying idea that publication is useful only because it suggests the research has been subjected to rigorous scrutiny by peers, but even these courts do not seem to undertake any investigation to ensure whether peer review in fact occurred.[84] The Florida

79 Anderson et al., supra note 52, at 622 (discussing in detail how advocates endeavor to get "bent" science publication and view "publication" as "likely the doorway through which lawyers will attempt to legitimize litigation science"); Patterson, supra note 60, at 1387–1389.

80 There is at least one notable exception—one that could be used to reformulate a more useful approach to "peer review". Judge McKenna from the S.D.N.Y. held forensic science testimony inadmissible even though it had been published. "While the literature of forensic document examination may technically satisfy Daubert's publication factor, it fails to meet the expectations of the Daubert court—that a competitive, unbiased community of practitioners and academics would generate increasingly valid science. Given the uncritical nature of the literature, its scrutiny during peer review … is of little significance". *US v. Starzepyzel*, 880 F.Supp. 1027, 1038 (S.D.N.Y. 1995).

81 See generally Noah, supra note 30, at 680, 688–91 (observing that "judges have become enamored with the idea of using the results of the editorial peer review process in biomedical literature as a short-cut for making judgments about important matters of public health" and also noting that this trend was in place before Daubert was decided); *People v. Lehy*, 8 Cal. 4th 587, 611–12 (1994); *Castrichini v. Rivera*, 669 N.Y.S.3d 140, 144 (N.Y. Sup. Ct. 1997); *State v. Wesley*, 633 N.E.2d 451, 456–57 (N.Y.Ct. App. 1994); *Berry v. CSX Transp., Inc.*, 709 So. 2d 552, 569–70 (Fla. Ct. Ap. 1998). For several exceptions to what appears to be a general rule or presumption that equates "peer review" with publication and "editorial peer review", see Noah, supra note 30, at 691.

82 Daubert, 509 U.S. at 593 (emphasis added).

83 Id. at 593.

84 On the remand of Daubert to the 9th Circuit, for example, the panel expressed particular concern about litigation science and indicated that only studies published in "reputable" journals with a "bona fide process of peer review" would

Court of Appeals is illustrative. The court held that "[w]hile the existence of numerous peer-reviewed published, epidemiological studies does not guarantee that the studies are without flaws, such publication here alleviates the necessity of thorough judicial scrutiny of each study at the admissibility stage to sort out the disputes over methodologic errors in studies".[85]

General acceptance has similarly been associated with an expectation that the methods or findings have been published. According to Anderson et al., "[p]ublication and peer review by a scientific journal has long been a hallmark in determining whether expert testimony had gained general acceptance in the relevant community".[86]

Yet if the dispute concerns the reliability of research (or of testimony synthesizing research), this simple proxy of "publication" will sometimes, and perhaps often, yield inaccurate answers since publication can be easily manipulated.[87] As discussed earlier, sponsors can deploy ghostwriting and redundant publications to bolster their positions as appearing "generally accepted" and mainstream.[88] Additionally, there is great variation in the quality of scientific journals,[89] and some are actually dedicated in part to publishing "bent" research.[90] As a result, poor research can generally find a home in one of these scientific journals.[91] Widely varying publication standards among scientific

---

satisfy its test for validity. Daubert, 43 F.3d 1311, at 1318 n.6. (9th Cir. 1995). The Texas Supreme Court somewhat similarly observed that: "Publication and peer review allow an opportunity for the relevant scientific community to comment on findings and conclusions and to attempt to replicate the reported results using different populations and different study designs". *Merrell Dow Pharm., Inc. v. Havner*, 953 S.W.2d 706, 726–27 (Tex. 1997) (noting also that "[p]ublication and other peer review is a significant indicia of the reliability of scientific evidence when the expert's testimony is in any area in which peer review or publication would not be uncommon … Publication is [not] a prerequisite for scientific reliability in every case, but courts must be 'especially skeptical' of scientific evidence that has not been published or subjected to peer review").

85 *Berry v. CSX Transp. Inc.*, 709 So. 2d 552, 569–70 (Fla. Ct. App. 1998).

86 Anderson et al., supra note 52, at 649–50.

87 See, e.g., id. at 635–36 ("Neither courts nor scientists should blithely assume that publication in a purportedly 'peer-reviewed' journal is a seal of approval for a particular methodology or theory").

88 See, e.g., McGarity and Wagner, supra note 16, at 79.

89 Anderson et al., supra note 52, at 639–42 (describing multiple sources of variation and concluding that because of this variation, publication in Daubert is not a "clean, bright-line rule").

90 See, e.g., McGarity and Wagner, supra note 16, at 201–02.

91 See, e.g., Stephen Lock, *A Difficult Balance: Editorial Peer Review in Medicine* (BMJ Books, 1985), 39–41, 85.

journals in fact virtually guarantee that some of the journals will have vastly weaker peer review requirements.[92] As a result, research that has been "published" may not be reliable at all.[93]

To truly understand the rigor and value of the peer review, then, the courts must "investigate the circumstances of the peer review".[94] Publication is sometimes evidence that rigorous scrutiny has actually occurred, but it certainly is not always the case. Indeed, novel theories or inventive syntheses may not yet be published, but testimony or analyses can still be submitted to a diverse set of critical peers to obtain an equal, if not more effective, assessment of the credibility of the methods and theories short of publication. Not only might unreliable work not be published, but excellent, trustworthy work can be rigorously peer-reviewed short of publication.

In sum, although courts try to screen for reliable evidence using crude proxies like publication and general acceptance, they do not apply the actual process standards used by the scientific community to assess reliability.[95] Specifically, the courts do not inquire about the pedigree of an expert's analysis in terms of the authors' independence or disinterestedness. Nor do the courts have a robust way to consider the rigor and integrity of the peer scrutiny applied to that work. Indeed, there appears to be few to no criteria for courts to use in independently evaluating the adequacy of peer review—whether in a journal or occurring pre-publication.[96]

Comparing the courts' approach against scientists' own methods for judging reliability exposes considerable slippage between what the court presumably should be concerned with in screening for reliable expert evidence and what courts are doing in practice.[97] So, for example, the fact that the expert's synthesis is commissioned pre-litigation with a nondisclosure contract that affords the sponsor effective control over the content of the analysis is not factored into the courts' admissibility determinations or methods of formal oversight.[98] Yet this would be a decisive factor in concluding the research is unreliable within the scientific community.

---

92 Noah, supra note 30, at 696 & n.89; Anderson et al., supra note 52, at 646–47.

93 Anderson et al., supra note 52, at 634.

94 Patterson, supra note 60, at 1391.

95 See generally Patterson, supra note 60; Anderson et al., supra note 52.

96 See, e.g., Michael D. Green, Expert Witnesses and Sufficiency of Evidence in Toxic Substances Litigation: The Legacy of Agent Orange and Bendectin Litigation, Nw. U. L. Rev. 86 (1992), 643, 694 n.210.

97 See Patterson, supra note 60, at 1345 (concluding that the courts' approach can deviate from scientific institutions' approach to assessing the reliability of scientific evidence in multiple ways).

98 See generally id.

B. The Courts' Review of the Reliability of Agency Scientific Analyses

Agencies are responsible for setting standards, licensing products, and establishing innumerable other rules and policies that depend heavily on scientific analyses.[99] Indeed, in some of the authorizing statutes, Congress explicitly requires the agency to use the "best available science" in making its decisions.[100] As a result, agency expertise is considered by some to be the "lifeblood" of the administrative state.[101]

To ensure that the agencies' decisions are both democratically accountable and scientifically competent, Congress has directed the courts to serve as neutral arbiters and review challenges to the agency's decisions. This review includes presiding over challenges to the reliability of the agencies' scientific analyses. This section considers the approach the courts take to this more specific, science-intensive responsibility.

However, before delving into the intricacies of judicial review, it is useful to first set the stage by examining why and how the scientific integrity of some agency analyses might be compromised in the US.[102] In terms of independence and disinterestedness, a subset of agency scientific analyses risks being compromised in ends-oriented ways. This occurs because there are rarely "firewalls" between the political officials and the scientific analysts who conduct the foundational work to inform policy.[103] As a result, there are anecdotal accounts of "bullying" by a political official of the scientific staff and demands that an analyst change the parameters of a computational model or analysis

---

[99] See, e.g., Louis J. Virelli III. Science, Politics, and Administrative Legitimacy, Missouri L. Rev. 78 (2013), 511, 515–516 (discussing with rich citations how "[a] gency expertise is a foundational principle of administrative law").

[100] See, e.g., Dennis Murphy and Paul Weiland, Guidance on the Use of Best Available Science under the U.S. Endangered Species Act, Environ. Management 58 (2016), 1, available at doi: 10.1007/s00267-016-0697-z; Safe Drinking Water Act, 42 U.S.C. §300g-1(b)(3).

[101] *Burlington Truck Lines, Inc. v. United States*, 371 U.S. 156, 167 (1962) (Frankfurter, J.).

[102] It is important to note, however, that critical studies of agency science are far fewer in number than the literature documenting ways that private sponsors can "bend" research in ends-oriented ways.

[103] See, e.g., Wendy Wagner, Science-in-Regulation: A Study of Agency Science Decision-making Approaches, Administrative Conference of the U.S. (ACUS) Final Report (2013), at 57–65 (from expert agencies).

to produce a more favorable scientific finding.[104] Even without these direct political interventions, some agencies' decision processes are structured so that political officials work collaboratively with staff scientists.[105] Obviously, this type of institutional structure permits the political biasing of agency scientific analyses, just as nondisclosure contracts allow private sponsors to control the researchers they hire for specific projects. In a recent article, Professor McGarity and I document wide-ranging examples of political interventions in agency expert scientific analyses occurring over the last four decades.[106]

The political control over agency expert analyses can also compromise the rigor of peer review.[107] For example, under the Federal Advisory Committee Act (FACA), political officials determine when or whether a science advisory board will be established to review an agency's scientific work, and can also then select the members for that board.[108] Although conflicts of interest are sometimes frowned upon for individual members in some agency procedures, there are few (if any) hard-and-fast rules governing conflicts of interest and it is not uncommon for panels to be comprised of a significant number of industry members or even overtly "stacked" with politically selected (and biased)

---

104 See, e.g., Office of Inspector General, US Department of the Interior, "The Endangered Species Act and the Conflict between Science and Policy" (2008); see generally Holly Doremus, Scientific and Political Integrity in Environmental Policy, Tex. L. Rev. 86 (2008) 1601; Thomas McGarity and Wendy Wagner, Deregulation Using Stealth Science Strategies, Duke L.J. 68 (2019) 1719.

105 See, e.g., Wagner, ACUS, supra note 103, at 57–65. The first official technical document regarding the listing of an endangered species, for example, is a proposed rule co-authored by both political officials and scientists together. Id. at 57–58.

106 See McGarity and Wagner, supra note 104.

107 Note that some of the older work—particularly Jasanoff's *Fifth Branch* (Harvard University Press, 1990), but see also Louis J. Virelli III, Scientific Peer Review and Administrative Legitimacy, Admin. L. Rev. 61 (2009), 723 and to some extent Ruhl and Salzman, supra note 33—are not privy to the accounts of stacking and ends-oriented bias in the selection of science advisory boards that began appearing more frequently during the George W. Bush presidency. See also Lars Noah, Scientific "Republicanism": Expert Peer Review and the Quest for Regulatory Deliberation, Emory L. J. 49 (2000), 1033, 1066–67 (discussing the stacking worries somewhat prematurely).

108 See, e.g., Robert Steinbrook, *Science, Politics, and Federal Advisory Committees*, New Eng. J. Med. 350 (2004), 1454, 1456 (criticizing the George W. Bush administration for stacking science advisory committees); Noah, supra note 107, at 1054, 1060–61 (describing technical advisory committees at FDA).

members.[109] Empirical evidence confirms that even in aggregate, these panels do tend to have partisan tilts that correlate with the politics of the president at the time they were assembled.[110] The political exploitation of science advisory processes under both Trump Administrations has been particularly notorious.[111]

But even peer review of agency analyses that is not conducted through formal science advisory boards can be compromised in ways that allow for ends-oriented manipulations of the peer review process.[112] For example, despite widely held intergovernmental principles that suggest agencies should commission external peer reviews that are "objective" and "independent",[113] the details of specific agency practices governing peer review are open-ended.[114] And again there are concerns, including within Congress, that these reviewers may be cherry-picked in ways that lead to more favorable peer appraisals.[115] Indeed, whether peer review will actually be used at all in settings in which it might seem warranted is hardly guaranteed.[116] Ruhl and Salzman report, for

---

109 See, e.g., Joe Conley, Conflict of Interest and the EPA's Science Advisory Board, Texas L. Rev. 86 (2007), 165.

110 See, e.g., Brian D. Feinstein and Daniel J. Hemel, Outside Advisers Inside Agencies, Geo. L.J. 108 (2020), 1139 (noting the political valence of advisory boards and arguing, normatively, that it is a positive development because it increases political control over agency decisions).

111 A veritable playbook of strategies for manipulating the use of science advisory boards in ends-oriented ways emerged during Trump's tenure. Among the tactics were: (1) altering the composition of the existing panels to favor industry; (2) creating policies to make future scientific panels more industry-friendly; and (3) reducing scientific advisory board influence when methods 1 and 2 proved ineffective. See McGarity and Wagner, supra note 104, at 1757–67.

112 See, e.g., US General Accounting Office, GAO-03–803. Endangered Species: Fish and Wildlife Service Uses Best Available Science to Make Listing Decisions, But Additional Guidance Needed for Critical Habitat Designations 15–16 (2003) (reporting sloppy peer review practices employed by the FWS, including not publicly disclosing potential conflicts or involvement of peer reviewers and leaving the selection of peer reviewers to those scientists responsible for drafting the analyses). OMB's peer review of its annual cost-benefit report was similarly conducted in this type of slipshod way. See Ruhl and Salzman, supra note 33, at 30.

113 See, e.g., Virelli, supra note 107, at 739, 741; see also Ruhl and Salzman, supra note 33, at 4–5.

114 See, e.g., Wagner, ACUS, supra note 103, at 63–64; see also Wendy Wagner, Expert Agencies: The Good, the Bad, and the Ugly (working draft November 1, 2022).

115 See, e.g., Wagner, ACUS, supra note 103, at 63–64.

116 See, e.g., id. at 46–47 (discussing how in general the risk assessments and analyses prepared by EPA for individual pesticide licensing decisions are not peer

example, that "few regulatory agencies ever subject their regulatory decisions to peer review, and those that do limit the practice principally to standard-setting decisions".[117]

Short of these potential distortions of peer review, there is also a robust body of evidence that suggests a number of other reasons "why agencies might selectively use scientific data in a biased or incomplete manner".[118] Intense mission orientation, personal biases, limited resources, and pockets of agency "capture" by regulated parties can each serve to compromise the scientific integrity of the agency's work.[119] Investigative reporters, for example, have documented systemic industry biases in several EPA science-intensive programs.[120] The possibility that some agency experts themselves might be biased is a real concern in certain regulatory settings.[121]

Against this backdrop of political interference and the risks of biased expert analyses, courts could play a valuable role in overseeing the quality of the agency's work.[122] Insisting that agencies explain how their analysts are free of political interference and bias, as well as insisting that agencies employ rigorous peer scrutiny from independent, critical scientists, could go a long way to

---

reviewed).

117 Ruhl and Salzman, supra note 33, at 14; see also Noah, supra note 107, at 1051.

118 Ruhl and Salzman, supra note 33, at 17.

119 Id. at 17.

120 See, e.g., Sharon Lerner, New Evidence of Corruption at EPA Chemical Division (Sept. 18, 2021), available at https://theintercept.com/2021/09/18/epa-corruption-harmful-chemicals-testing/; Sharon Lerner, The Department of Yes (June 30, 2021), available at https://theintercept.com/2021/06/30/epa-pesticides-exposure-opp/

121 Ruhl and Salzman, supra note 33, conducted a survey of agency officials and practitioners on the reliability of agency science and found that "[o]ver 70 percent of respondents disagreed, 20 percent strongly so, with the statement that agencies generally give appropriate recognition to scientifically reliable data that contradict their preferred decisions, and 56 percent of respondents disagreed with the statement that agencies usually employ adequate scientific analysis when using the data they present as supporting their final decisions". Id. at 20; see also Virelli, supra note 99, at 512, 522 (describing the EPA's reliance on unreliable industry-sponsored studies to conclude an herbicide was not unsafe, despite considerable evidence of bias in the studies and counter-evidence of risk).

122 See Emily Hammond Meazell, Super Deference, the Science Obsession, and Judicial Review as Translation of Agency Science, Mich. L. Rev. 109 (2011), 733, 735, 737 (discussing the courts' important role in reinforcing "administrative law values like participation, transparency, and deliberation" in the course of its review of agency science).

provide a process-based review that disciplines some of the worst abuses. But as we will see, the courts (again) do not rise to this challenge.

The quality of the scientific evidence used by agencies to make national decisions—particularly in rulemakings—is subjected to judicial review under the Administrative Procedure Act (APA). Under the APA, any person may challenge agency rules on multiple grounds, including with respect to the issue of whether the rule is "arbitrary" or "capricious".[123] As a result, challenges engaging the courts in review of the agencies' scientific expertise have been brought with some frequency over the last five decades.[124]

A challenge to an agency's scientific analysis begins with a "notice and comment" process, during which future litigants must first submit comments, including on ways the agency's technical decisions may be in error. The agency is then required to consider these comments and publish its reasons for its ultimate decisions along with the text of the final rule. This process does not simulate external peer review since the stakeholders commenting tend not to be scientists and there is no assurance of independence or disinterestedness by those scientists who do review the agency's work during notice and comment. But the deliberations do provide an opportunity for some experts to weigh in on the quality of the agency's scientific work.

The resulting comments then seed future litigation. Any legal challenges in fact must have been lodged "with specificity" during the comment process first so that the agency is not blindsided.[125] As a result of this necessary upfront investment by a party in the notice and comment process, oversight of the quality of the agency's decision-making can be quite imbalanced, generally favoring those parties with the highest stakes and greatest resources.

In resolving the resulting challenges to an agency's scientific analysis, the courts are equipped with slim statutory guidance; they are directed only to strike down rules that are "arbitrary or capricious".[126] As a result of this ambiguity in the standards governing review, there has been wide variation in the nature of the courts' review of agency science—ranging from complete

---

[123] 5 U.S.C. § 706(2)(A) (requiring reviewing courts to "hold unlawful and set aside agency action, findings, and conclusions found to be arbitrary, capricious, an abuse of discretion, or otherwise not in accordance with law").

[124] See generally Meazell, supra note 122.

[125] See, e.g., Gabriel H. Markoff, The Invisible Barrier: Issue Exhaustion as a Threat to Pluralism in Administrative Rulemaking, Tex. L. Rev. 90 (2012), 1065, 1078.

[126] 5 U.S.C. § 706

deference to micromanaging agency expert decisions.[127] This variability by itself presents cause for concern.[128]

To make judicial review more consistent and predictable, the courts have developed a series of doctrinal guidelines or "canons" that operate as general rules of thumb.[129] Yet here again, the canons developed by the courts are limited in scope and also tend to direct the courts' attention away from overseeing the process features of the agency's scientific work and toward evaluating the substance of the scientific disputes.

The first and most widely cited canon provides great deference to agency decisions lying at the "frontiers of scientific knowledge".[130] The underlying logic for this test is that decisions involving novel science are so imbued with policy considerations, as well as cutting-edge expertise, that courts are better off staying out of an intensive review of the merits. In applying this deference test, courts do not inquire about the integrity of the agencies' analytical processes: for example, whether political officials reserved the right to manipulate the technical findings, whether the agency considered only input and research

127 Meazell, supra note 122, at 736–37 & n.15 (citing literature); Wendy Wagner, The Science Charade in Toxic Risk Regulation, Columbia Law Review 95 (1995), 1613, 1666–67 (describing how courts review the technical features of agency rules in ways that resemble a lottery due to the unpredictability and inconsistency). Just as there is considerable variation in how courts review challenges to the reliability of agency scientific findings and analyses, there is even more variation—not considered here—in the nature of the types of challenges that can be brought implicating the agency's science. Meazell, supra note 122, at 744. Not under consideration here are arguments that an agency's decision contradicted its own [underlying and reliable] scientific analysis, thus putting science and politics in direct conflict. See, e.g., Virelli, supra note 99. Also not considered here are arguments that the agency's judgments regarding uncertainties violate the statutory instructions. See, e.g., Meazell, supra note 122, at 744–46 (calling these other forms of disputes over the use of science "metapolicy" and "mesopolicy" choices). These relatively common sets of arguments stray from the focus here on the underlying reliability of the agency's scientific analysis.

128 See, e.g., Wagner, supra note 127, at 1666.

129 For an illuminating discussion of the different role for courts in reviewing science in the administrative law context—as compared to the Daubert evidence context—see Meazell, supra note 122, at 755. None of these differences, however, justify a complete neglect of ensuring the scientific integrity of the underlying scientific information in either type of judicial decision-making.

130 *Baltimore Gas & Electric Co. v. Natural Resources Defense Council, Inc.*, 462 U.S. 87, 103 (1983). Emily Hammond (Meazell) dubs this the "super deference" test. See Meazell, supra note 122, at 734.

from industry, and whether the analyses were subject to skeptical peer scrutiny to ensure their veracity.

Precisely because the "frontiers of scientific knowledge" test is so deferential, many courts over the last several decades have begun to supplement it with a second, complementary canon requiring "reason giving".[131] Under the reason-giving doctrine, courts defer to the agency's scientific analyses only if the agency supplies sensible reasons for its contested choices.[132] However, sensible reasons in this context only reach into the *substance* of the challenged science and not the *process* by which the science was produced. To illustrate, the court will consider whether the agency adequately explained why it dismissed a particular study or weighted a different study more heavily in its model.[133] But the court's inquiry generally stops short of looking to features of the agency's decision process, such as whether the staff was firewalled from political officials or sought out and engaged with critical, skeptical experts who were disinterested.[134]

A third, widely used "canon" by the courts defers to the agencies' scientific analyses in settings in which there is a battle of the experts. Simply put, "[w]hen specialists express conflicting views, an agency must have discretion to rely on the reasonable opinions of its own qualified experts even if, as an original matter, a court might find contrary views more persuasive".[135] Again, however, this deference does not require the agency to first justify the integrity of its decision process following the three basic scientific conventions. Instead, the agency enjoys this deference even if it turns out that a political official was working behind the scenes to manipulate the scientific analyses being challenged.

Finally, at least a few courts place some weight on evidence that an agency's decision was consistent with—or departed from—its own expert peer reviewers.[136] These same courts, however, rarely consider whether some peer review

---

[131] See Meazell, supra note 122, at 772 (describing this trend).

[132] Meazell explains that in these cases, "the court describe[s] the science at issue, the particular contentions of the parties, and the basis in the record for concluding the agency engaged in reasoned decision making". Id. at 776.

[133] See, e.g., Thomas O. McGarity and Wendy E. Wagner, Legal Aspects of the Regulatory Use of Environmental Modeling, Environmental Law Reporter 10 (2003), 10751.

[134] Id.

[135] *Marsh v. Oregon Natural Resources Council*, 490 U.S. 360, 378 (1989); see also *Carstens v. NRC*, 742 F.2d 1546, 1550–51 (D.C. Cir. 1984) (same).

[136] See, e.g., *Am. Farm Bureau Fed'n v. EPA*, 559 F.3d 512, 520 (D.C. Cir. 2009) (per curiam) (finding the EPA's explanation of the choice of standard insufficient in view of risks flagged by CASAC).

should have occurred for the challenged agency analysis. However, if the agency did assemble an expert peer-review panel to review its work, the courts sometimes benchmark the agency's decision against it.

Given this elevated level of deference running through all of the courts' canons, an agency's scientific analysis is often struck down as unreliable when the agency's findings were contradicted by mainstream evidence or expert opinions, and, in response, the agency supplied no good reasons to justify the divergence. In the most dramatic cases, the agency's analyses appear flat-out wrong. For example, maybe the agency presumed that a substance was a gas when it actually was a liquid.[137] More commonly, however, a challenged agency's analysis is found to be arbitrary because the agency supplied few to no reasons in support of it.[138]

How well do these canons map against the methods the scientific community would use to judge the reliability of contested scientific analyses? Again, like the courts' review of scientific evidence, the three conventions that provide critical insights for the scientists' evaluation of scientific reliability—independence, disinterestedness, and rigorous peer scrutiny—are ignored or badly neglected by the courts in reviewing challenges to the reliability of agency science.

Much of this neglect arises not only from the courts' tendency toward affording agencies great deference, but also from the courts' failure to review the integrity of the agency's scientific *processes* underlying its record and findings. In their review, courts instead focus on presiding over the substance of the scientific disagreements: in other words, which position is "correct".

More specifically, and with respect to ensuring the "independence" and "disinterestedness" of the agency scientists conducting the work, the courts seem to assume these qualities are satisfied and do not inquire further, even when the government's scientists are not listed by name.[139] In the courts' review, then, anonymously-authored government scientific assessments (sometimes

137 See, e.g., McGarity and Wagner, supra note 133, at 10762.

138 See, e.g., Meazell, supra note 122 (listing these cases).

139 This naivety may be well-placed prior to 2000. In the first twenty years, there are fewer anecdotes of political meddling in agency scientific work, and all of them occurred during the early Reagan Administration. See, e.g., McGarity and Wagner, supra note 104, at 758–59. Moreover, the scores of agency handbooks and interagency requirements for peer review and scientific integrity certainly give the impression that somewhere in those guidelines there are assurances for independence and disinterestedness at all levels of the analysis. See, e.g., Wagner, supra note 103. But this turns out not to be so! Id. It is almost as if the agencies amass these guidelines to combat political encroachment, but lacking the power ultimately fail; yet at the same time, the encroachers enjoy using this aura of regularity as cover.

appearing for the first time in the *Federal Register*) are afforded the same deference as government reports that provide meticulous attribution for each contributor and even for peer reviewers.[140] Thus, despite a few early opinions in which a judge advocated that the court should focus its review on evaluating the integrity of the underlying agency processes—rather than on the contested substantive findings—there are virtually no decisions critically examining the integrity of the agency's scientific processes, including such simple measures as listing out the individual agency contributors by name.[141] And, as discussed, we know that this inattention by the courts is not because agency scientific analysis processes are above reproach. Rather, there is evidence of sometimes significant, unaccounted-for political interference in an agency's technical analyses.

The courts' obliviousness to the integrity of the agency's process might instead be blamed primarily on the fact that most litigants do not appear to raise these process features—like political interference or "bias"—as a basis for finding the agency's work "arbitrary". This neglect, in turn, may occur because the litigants themselves generally cannot learn of this political interference in the agency's scientific analyses due to "deliberative process" protections that shield all internal political discussions from public view.[142] Since internal governmental deliberations are "confidential" and exempt from FOIA, outsiders are unlikely to be able to determine the extent to which an agency analysis—like a literature review or initial scientific assessment—has been corrupted by political pressures.

However, even when a litigant is able to piece together ways that an agency's scientific analysis (like the initial literature search) was heavily influenced, if not controlled, by political officials, the one court that was presented with this evidence refused to credit this fact as material in its review. In *Mississippi v. EPA*, for example, the appellant produced evidence that the White House

---

140 See, e.g., Wagner, ACUS Report, supra note 103, 129–32.

141 Judge Bazelon essentially advocated for this kind of process-based approach in the courts' review of agency science when this area of judicial review was first getting started. See *International Harvester Co. v. Ruckelshaus*, 478 F.2d 615, 652 (D.C. Cir. 1973) (concurring); *NRDC v. NRC*, 547 F.2d 633, 653 (D.C. Cir. 1976).

142 Although it was initially a common-law creation, the deliberative-process privilege is most commonly invoked as an exemption to the Freedom of Information Act, allowing an agency to withhold "inter-agency or intra-agency memorandums or letters which would not be available by law to a party other than an agency in litigation with the agency". See 5 U.S.C. § 552(b)(5) (2012); see also Shilpa Narayan, Proper Assertion of the Deliberative Process Privilege: The Agency Head Requirement, Fordham L. Rev. 77 (2008), 1183, 1187–1193 (describing the history and development of the deliberative-process privilege).

actually selected the final number for an air standard and agency experts were directed to work backwards with their scientific analyses to justify it. The court simply ignored this argument and struck down the rule because the agency had not provided sufficient substantive scientific reasons in support of its decision.[143]

By contrast, the third scientific convention—rigorous scrutiny by independent peers (or peer review)—occasionally does influence some courts' review, albeit in only a limited set of cases where that peer review has been voluntarily solicited by the agency. Specifically, *if* the agency has sought out peer review and that peer review is either favorable or adverse, then that fact weighs into the courts' substantive review of the challenged analysis.[144] However, in considering the results of the peer review, the courts seem to assume that the peer review was conducted in a rigorous way. They do not question the possibility that the panel might have been stacked in an ends-oriented way to support an agency's analysis.[145]

Indeed, courts appear to defer completely to the agency's judgment not only in *how* to deploy peer review (e.g., were the reviewers disinterested and representative of the larger scientific community), but *whether* to use it at all. I could not find any cases in which a court finds that the absence of peer review provides a supplemental basis for an arbitrary and capricious challenge brought against the reliability of an agency's scientific analysis.[146]

In sum, the courts reviewing challenges to agency science—much like their approach to applying the evidence rule—focus on substance (e.g., scientific agreement with the findings) rather than process (e.g., independence,

---

143 744 F.3d 1334, 1362 (D.C. Cir. 2013); see Wendy Wagner, A Place for Expertise, Columbia L. Rev. 115 (2015), 2019, 2055–56 (describing this case and others like it). At least one theory for this refusal to consider White House interference is that the courts do not wish to insert themselves into the political process; yet this preference is in direct conflict with the courts' responsibility for reviewing challenged scientific analyses. See id.

144 See generally Elizabeth Fisher, Pasky Pascual and Wendy Wagner, Rethinking Judicial Review of Expert Agencies, Texas L. Rev. 93 (2015), 1681.

145 Id.

146 See, e.g., McGarity and Wagner, supra note 133, at 10769 (observing how courts remain completely deferential to EPA's decisions of whether to employ peer review of computational models). This lapse in oversight might ultimately be traced back to the possibility that no litigant has ever thought to argue, for example, that "at the very least the agency should have assembled some independent peer review of this contestable analysis to provide public assurances of its veracity". Whatever the reasons, there is no indication that the courts will wade into disputes over whether the agency followed minimal scientific best practices to ensure the reliability of its analysis.

disinterestedness, and peer scrutiny) in assessing scientific reliability. This misplaced focus not only creates more room for errors in attempting to determine what the scientific community might believe on a contested fact, but it misses the core tests the scientific community uses itself to assess reliability. Moreover, as long as judicial review remains blind to these process features, agencies face few consequences for: producing scientific analyses that provide no indicia of authorship, much less independence for its staff experts; structuring decisions in ways that allow for secretive political control over in-house scientific analyses; and cherry-picking peer reviewers.

3. REFORM

The courts' current approach to evaluating the reliability of scientific evidence in the United States offers considerable room for improvement. This final section suggests a proposal for reform.

The reform proposed here makes two changes to the status quo. The first and most radical change relies less on casting the courts as "adjudicators" over the substance of each piece of challenged evidence and more on their ability as authoritative overseers who can demand from the parties documentation of the integrity of the process underlying their expert testimony and reports. Seen from this vantage point, a far better way to enhance the reliability of scientific evidence used in the courtroom is to conceive of courts as gatekeepers with judicial powers to insist on heightened transparency of the underlying processes used to produce the scientific evidence, rather than as toll-bridge styled gatekeepers (e.g., presiding over whether evidence is "in" or "out"). Such a reconceptualization also draws on the courts' strengths in overseeing process while recognizing their well-documented limitations in accurately judging the substantive accuracy of contested scientific information.[147]

Second, to accomplish this new role, the courts would borrow from the scientific community's approach and institute standardized, qualitative disclosures that require scientists to document the processes by which their expert analyses were produced.[148] Specifically, the disclosures would require information on

---

147 See, e.g., Cheng, supra note 7 (discussing competency issues in the courts' review of science).

148 The approach taken here is in accord with, although it expands, the disclosure emphasis in Patterson, supra note 60, at 1386. See also Anderson et al., supra note 52, at 622–23 (and later) (advocating more rigid disclosure and oversight as a condition to admissibility). Anderson et al., supra, which provide by far the most thorough review of some of the problems arising in evidence law, also focus explicitly on "litigation science" (arising from litigation or serial litigation) and generally refer to this problem as occurring primarily with plaintiff's evidence.

the "disinterestedness" and "independence" of the expert-author and require the expert to provide details on how vigorously she sought out, and responded to, rigorous peer scrutiny. This would be required both of experts testifying at trial as well as for the scientific staff preparing the analyses that inform agency rules. Some of this information is currently inaccessible to courts and litigants, either as a practical or a legal matter. The disclosures would thus provide a centralized dossier for judges and litigants to better understand the integrity of the processes by which an expert produced an analysis that informs a dispute.[149]

Even with new disclosures in place under this proposal, the courts could still exclude or strike down as "arbitrary" patently unreliable expert evidence and analyses—as they do now. However, when the courts serve in this more adjudicatory role, the existence of the disclosures will hopefully shift or at least broaden the courts' considerations to include a consideration of the process by which the scientific analyses are produced. Disclosures that reveal worrisome influence over an expert in ways that lead to "significant bias", for example, might provide a new basis for excluding testimony or finding it arbitrary.

This alternate focus also plays on the courts' strengths. Rather than attempting to gauge the reliability of expert analyses based on its substantive fit with the larger expert community, the courts instead will evaluate scientific reliability based on process features. As Lars Noah recommends in a related context, "Instead of struggling to evaluate critically the substantive merits of a rule, reviewing courts may focus on questions of procedural adequacy".[150]

Since some litigants and agencies will strenuously oppose a disclosure requirement, the ultimate decision to submit these disclosures should be made voluntary.[151] Courts can find ways to strongly encourage the use of disclosures

---

Their exclusionary tests thus apply only to "litigation science" and not to bent science that may have been published for decades before litigation began in earnest, like for example the tobacco litigation. See id. at 666–76. Indeed, Anderson et al. suggest that regulatory agency findings should be used to determine the reliability of scientific positions taken in litigation, see, e.g., id. at 666–76, which as noted below is a problematic screening test. Patterson, by contrast, focusses almost exclusively on industry-commissioned research occurring well before litigation and thus adopts a more defendant-oriented focus. Patterson, supra note 60, at 1350.

149 Thus, if an agency does not utilize peer review, it is not a basis for striking down its findings under this test. Peer review—both its form and extent—is left to the agency's judgment and reviewed at most in a "reason-giving" framework deployed by the courts.

150 See also Noah, supra note 107, at 1076.

151 By requesting voluntary disclosures from agencies, moreover, courts will not be creating new "requirements" or "processes" (in contravention of Vermont Yankee in the administrative law context). See *Vermont Yankee*, 435 US 519, 524–25 (1978) (rejecting the courts' ability to impose extra procedures—beyond those

by, for example, recommending that factfinders draw adverse inferences from an expert's choice not to disclose some or all of this information.[152] However it is done, the courts can introduce the option of disclosures but establish the supporting decision processes in ways that strongly encourage their use.

In terms of the content of the standardized disclosures, ideally a committee of the National Academies of Sciences—or perhaps a team of experts from the Federal Judicial Center—could formulate the requirements, borrowing heavily from the disclosures and related practices of the top biomedical journals.[153] More specifically, one disclosure could require the expert to document her independence and authorship in preparing the testimony and supporting analysis (or ask the agency staff-authors to vouch for this information on the scientific analyses incorporated in or referenced in a final rule). A second disclosure would solicit all information on potential conflicts of interest or other biasing influences on the expert analysis. A final disclosure would then require the expert-author to explain and document any peer scrutiny, including who and how the peers were selected and the authors' response to this input.[154] Appendix A provides a preliminary, illustrative sketch of these disclosures.

Once disclosures are in place and hopefully used by at least some litigants, much of the courts' work in overseeing the reliability of science entering the courtroom should be done. Litigants in trial settings can use the disclosures (or their absence) to convince juries that certain testimony is unreliable. Courts relying on court-appointed experts may even find the disclosures useful as a way to enhance the reliability and transparency of their own expert's recommendations.[155] In administrative settings, the disclosures will likely be even

---

designed by Congress—on the agencies). Rather, the courts are simply considering the litigants' own explanations for how their evidence was produced with respect to the scientific integrity of these processes.

152 Agencies would ideally document some or all of these disclosures as part of their final rule or even as the rule moves through the notice and comment process, again with the ability of challengers to identify in their challenges curious gaps in or the complete absence of these disclosures for key scientific analyses that inform an agency decision as partly suggestive of an "arbitrary" decision process.

153 The top biomedical journals have been using and refining process-based oversight mechanisms for decades and understand best how to draw out the key information regarding the process underlying an analysis. See supra section 1.A.2.

154 See, e.g., Patterson, supra note 60, at 1382 (similarly suggesting that experts in litigation be expected to obtain a peer review by "some other, practicing scientist").

155 These types of disclosures might have been useful in the use of science advisors in the breast implant litigation, for example. See, e.g., Laural L. Hooper, Joe S. Cecil and Thomas E. Willging Assessing Causation in Breast Implant Litigation: The Role of Science Panels, Law and Contemp. Probs. 64 (2001), 139, 140–41.

more beneficial; not only can the challengers utilize the agency disclosures in this similar adversarial way, but the general public and political branches would be put on notice of institutional features that might compromise the trustworthiness of agency analyses. These added transparency-enhancing benefits are particularly useful for the politicization of science occurring in some agencies, a problem that the political system has thus far been incapable of addressing.[156]

To make the proposed recommendations here more concrete, consider this illustration of how the reform might apply in practice. In the evidence context, a plaintiff may seek to admit expert testimony of a reputable scientist who has studied the patient's record and concludes that the plaintiff's latent disease was caused by a negligent prescription of an overdose of a particular drug.[157] This testimony would be accompanied by three forms. In the first, the authorship form, the expert would explain the extent to which she prepared and wrote her testimony as the sole author. On the second, the conflicts form, she would be expected to explain who funded the analysis and the role of that sponsor, including all contracts and other written documentation governing the commissioned testimony, as well as other biasing influences. Ideally, she would also identify the extent to which the research upon which she relies in her analysis also involves conflicts of interest. Finally, on the third form, the expert would explain whether or the extent to which she sought peer scrutiny of her testimony, who she solicited for this critical review, and their reaction(s).[158] Perhaps peers were consulted informally or asked to review her deposition or written testimony. How much or what an expert provides on these forms is completely open-ended. But whatever the case, the expert would be encouraged to disclose these key facts about the process by which the testimony was prepared or else risk adverse inferences from the refusal to provide the information.

In the case of agencies, when promulgating a final rule, the agency would ideally provide the three disclosures for each discrete scientific report or

156 See, e.g., Brennan Center Report, at https://www.brennancenter.org/our-work/policy-solutions/proposals-reform-volume-ii-national-task-force-rule-law-democracy.

157 The facts are modeled on *Zuchowicz v. United States*, 140 F.3d 381 (2d Cir. 1998)

158 As one court of appeals panel noted, in reviewing novel science, "independent peer review [that follows best practices] may be extraordinarily helpful to the court. … Precisely because the data has not been scrutinized, however, the court has particular interest in having access to both favorable and unfavorable peer reviews". Asbestos Information Ass'n/North Am. v. OSHA, 727 F.2d 415, 421 n.15 (5th Cir. 1984).

analysis that informs that rule. To be effective, moreover, agencies would need to separate out the foundational scientific analyses or even literature reviews and make them publicly available, independent of and prior to the subsequent policy discussions. This separation of the scientific report, standing alone, would be a beneficial change from many agencies' practice of merging scientific analyses with policy discussions.[159] But the disclosure provides still more additional needed transparency since agencies would then (voluntarily) document how or whether the staff scientists preparing the report were the sole authors; whether those authors were influenced by political officials or others; and how external peer review was employed to improve the quality of the scientific analysis. Each of these disclosures would mark a significant improvement both on current institutional approaches and the transparency surrounding those approaches.[160]

A. The Benefits of the Disclosure Proposal

If these three disclosures are used by at least some portion of the litigants (or agencies), they will enhance the reliability of the courts' oversight of scientific reliability in several important ways.

First, the disclosures will provide new, valuable information to assess scientific reliability, much of which is not currently available to adversaries, or at least not in ways that make that information easily accessible. The most striking transparency benefits will occur when agencies use disclosures to document the scientific integrity of their decision processes. As noted *supra* in section 2.B, internal government deliberations are currently protected from the Freedom of Information Act as deliberative process. Whether or how an agency's scientific analysis has been influenced by political officials or even the legal team cannot be determined by outsiders. The nature of the contributions made by various staff experts and political officials within the government, and even the identity of the staff themselves, is often not voluntarily disclosed and can again be kept secret.[161] Even internal government decisions about whether and how to employ external peer review and which reviewers to solicit for that review can sometimes be kept confidential. The proposed disclosures—which again are voluntary (but federal agencies might feel compelled to publicly document the integrity of their scientific analyses)—would share this vital process-based information publicly. And in disclosing it, the

---

159 See Brennan Center, supra note 156 (advocating for this separation); McGarity and Wagner, supra note 104 (same).

160 See, e.g., Wagner, ACUS, supra note 103 (making a similar recommendation).

161 See, e.g., Wagner, ACUS, supra note 103, at 57–58, 130–32.

agencies might even alter their internal processes in beneficial ways to anticipate and avoid criticism.

In evidence disputes, discovery typically provides litigants with more opportunity for investigating these process-related issues.[162] But discovery on these hostile lines of investigation is expensive and time-consuming. Similarly, determining whether, how, and the extent of peer scrutiny that has been applied to an expert's analysis requires a considerable investment of time and resources by litigants. Whether a litigant will perceive the added effort to be worth the payoff—particularly if it is not clear what they will find—may again tip the scales in favor of foregoing producing this additional process-based information. By contrast, if the critical information is provided automatically and at no cost to the opposition through disclosures, it should significantly bolster the ability of the advocates to zero in on foundational problems with the reliability of some expert analyses.

A second benefit to the proposed disclosures is that they will help correct power asymmetries between litigants that often become aggravated when scientific reliability is at issue.[163] Courts depend heavily on counsel to locate the issues and develop supporting facts and arguments regarding unreliable scientific evidence. By providing more transparency on these issues, disclosures could institute a more level adversarial playing field by limiting the resources litigants need to track down critical information about the foundational processes underlying their opponents' expert testimony. Disclosures might even spark an intermediary market of "certified" peer reviewers or independent analysts to review testimony or research with respect to these criteria.[164]

Third, disclosures allow courts to better adjust to the natural dynamism of science. Rather than select the "best" substantive scientific theory or answer arising in a case, the courts will focus instead on the integrity of the underlying scientific processes. Thus, when theories or conventional wisdom change within science, the courts do not need to adjust their reliability determinations

---

162 Rule 23 and informal agreements between counsel, however, can sometimes be used to obscure the role that the lawyers play in priming and prepping expert analysis.

163 See, e.g., Margaret A. Berger, What Has a Decade of Daubert Wrought? *American Journal of Public Health* 95 (2005), S59, https://doi.org/10.2105/AJPH.2004.044701 (discussing this inconsistent application of Daubert).

164 Rather than the "market for lemon experts" generated by the loose scientific standards used by the courts, a market for excellence experts and reviewers could emerge. Anderson et al., supra note 52, in fact suggest a nonprofit expert body that could provide, among other things, targeted independent review of particularly controversial litigation science and other novel evidence. See id. at 679–81.

since they remain interested only in *how* the science was produced, rather than *what* it found.[165]

A final benefit of disclosures is the disciplining effect they will have on the parties and experts themselves. One of the widely recognized benefits of disclosures more generally is to spark positive behavioral changes by those producing the disclosures simply due to the threat of having one's internal dirty secrets made public.[166] As already noted, with respect to agencies, this enhanced transparency might cause some agencies to reinvent their decision processes. Walling off political influences and providing more rigorous approaches to utilizing external peer review could take higher priority if the agencies feel they must go on the record with how their decision processes actually work.

In civil and criminal trials, repeat litigants may also find this new scrutiny of the process underlying expert analyses to be disciplining in positive ways. On the plaintiff side, plaintiffs may find themselves significantly more constrained in their selection of experts and the conditions under which those experts testify. On the defendants' side, the disciplining effect of disclosures may be even more extensive. Most of the "bent" science is produced by large corporate defendants long before litigation begins, although with an eye to the possibility of this downstream litigation.[167] Drawing out the problematic, ends-oriented features of this research will spotlight the underlying nature of industry sponsorship more publicly and comprehensively.[168] While the ends-oriented studies themselves will likely not be under review, the experts' own synthesis will need to come to terms with these underlying conflicts in each study, particularly when the experts' own credentials are on the line.

---

165 This is almost the opposite of how the current evidence tests work in the US courts. For an illustration of the problematic consequences for courts when they must adjust to changes in scientific theories and general acceptance using the *Daubert* or *Frye* tests, see Deborah Tuerkheimer, *Flawed Convictions: Shaken Baby Syndrome and the Inertia of Injustice* (Oxford University Press, 2015), 202–05.

166 See, e.g., William M. Sage, Regulating Through Information: Disclosure Laws and American Healthcare, Colum. L. Rev. 99 (1999), 1701, 1778 (arguing that information disclosures can exert a powerful influence on internal decision making and can reveal valuable information that changes these internal decisions); see also Bradley C. Karkkainen, Information as Environmental Regulation: TRI and Performance Benchmarking, Precursor to a New Paradigm?, Geo. L.J. 89 (2001), 257, 346 (same).

167 See supra section 1.A.

168 Currently much of this work of tracing the ends-oriented nature of industry science is reserved primarily for the academic literature. See, e.g., Legg et al., supra note 16 (review the reference list supporting their synthesis of this literature).

Even the behavior of the experts themselves—whether testifying in a trial or working in agencies—may be changed for the better. The disclosures will undoubtedly bring some reputational stigma and reduce the fees for experts who are compromised with respect to their disinterestedness or independence. However, the opposite would also seem true for experts who submit squeaky clean disclosures; they may emerge as "heroes" and find themselves in high demand. Indeed, if the disclosures do succeed in rewarding neutrality and quality of experts, this reward may draw more reputable experts into the judicial system (as well as the agencies).

B. Troubleshooting Concerns

There are a number of potential drawbacks and challenges in the implementation of the disclosure proposal that might undermine its effectiveness. In this section, I consider and attempt to troubleshoot at least a few of these worries.

First, since lay competence is always a challenge at the intersection of science and the law, it is important to imagine the ways that our lay factfinders, particularly judges, may find this alternative focus for assessing reliability to be just as difficult to implement as substantive scientific review (the status quo). Experts might present testimony that has been peer-reviewed, for example, but in the event that the reviewers identify flaws in the analyses that are not corrected and are defended as appropriate by the live expert, what then? The judge or jury will be forced to assess the severity of criticisms in the cold record against the experts' responses. This sort of battle of the experts takes us full circle back to judging the reliability of the substance of the testimony, the very fate that we hoped our process test would avoid.

However, even in this situation, the disclosures should provide a more structured and comprehensive set of issues that both narrow and sharpen the inquiry. First, the very existence of disclosures as noted is expected to discourage some fringe experts, just as these processes help cull untrustworthy research in journals. Within the remaining set of higher-quality experts, moreover, it is expected that the courts' screening role will not only occur less often but will be more concerned with process. Issues of bias and independence will now be more accessible and visible to the courts, as compared to the substantive challenges that occupy the courts currently. Even the cross-examinations should be more streamlined, likely zeroing in on issues of process (if applicable) and important, material issues raised by peer reviewers. This use of peer review, when it is available, should also help focus the areas of concern, as opposed to simply stabbing in the dark in attempting to discredit an expert.

The *Sandoz* case provides a potential illustration of these streamlining benefits for the courts.[169] In *Sandoz*, the court excluded the plaintiffs' experts under *Daubert*, holding that their inferences were too unreliable for extrapolating evidence that a drug that caused one type of (embolic) stroke also caused a different type of stroke (hemorrhagic) suffered by plaintiffs.[170] The court's exclusion of this expert testimony is harshly criticized by some commentators as overstepping the court's gatekeeping role and ignoring the scientists' own methods of inference and induction in making these types of extrapolatory judgments.[171] If disclosures had been used in this case, they may have alerted the court to first consider whether any of the experts were patently unreliable because of significant bias or the lack of peer scrutiny over their analyses. If the experts' testimony appeared to meet the process standards set by the scientific community, then deciding the plausibility of their testimony and inferences would then probably be left to the adversarial process.

Second, in *Sandoz*, and many other cases as well, the expert analysis that informs the courts consist not only of scientific information but also involve expert extrapolations of that information to the pressing policy questions. For example, there may be no scientific consensus on whether doubling a drug's prescription level will cause a rare and fatal disease because there is no data or research testing humans on this question.[172] Experts must necessarily extrapolate from what is known to better understand these questions, and they will disagree about how to do this untested work.

At first blush, these inferences and judgments that are routine for expert testimony would seem to present a new challenge for implementing the disclosures. But on closer reflection, there is no reason this more value-laden feature of expert testimony couldn't (and shouldn't) continue unimpeded. As long as the experts appear to be able to produce reliable scientific analyses, then their analyses will be considered and judged against scientists who similarly use reliable research but reach different results with different inferential methods. These extrapolations are precisely the kinds of value-laden judgments the factfinders should be presiding over.

---

169 See, e.g., *Rider v. Sandoz Pharm.* Corp., 295 F.3d 1194, 1201–02 (11th Cir. 2002) (rejecting plaintiffs' evidence as speculative where it extrapolated from studies of similar drugs and animal studies).

170 Id.

171 See, e.g., Joe S. Cecil, Ten Years of Judicial Gatekeeping Under Daubert, *American Journal of Public Health* 95 (2005), S74 (arguing that the courts' troubling exclusion of the experts in Sandoz was based on a conclusion that their "broadly approved professional practices are scientifically unsound and, therefore, do not meet the standards for admissibility").

172 See, e.g., Zuchowicz, supra note 157.

Finally, some savvy litigants will undoubtedly find ways to game the disclosures. They may invest added effort to locate the most biased experts whose biases are ideological rather than financially based. Litigants can also dangle the prospect of future employment for these experts in ways that might escape standardized disclosures and can only be inferred circumstantially.[173] Certainly gaming could also occur in the selection and utilization of peer review, as well as in preparing responses to those comments that are either designed to obscure problems or simply overwhelm the factfinder with technicalities.[174]

Moreover, even if disclosures do reveal irregularities in an expert's analysis—for example, peer review of the testimony was limited or an expert was hired by the same class of litigants in the past—this information is not necessarily disqualifying. Multiple compromised features of the experts' analysis may cumulatively cause the testimony to be inherently unreliable, but that testimony might still squeak through the process precisely because of the qualitative nature of the disclosures. Factfinders will then be responsible for taking these process-related concerns into consideration in weighing the evidence.

In some settings, litigants may even contract around the disclosures—each side agreeing not to use them because they feel they have more advantages in presenting their case without these strictures. Presumably, the advantages of using summary judgment and other dispositive motions against an opposition's unsavory experts will lead one party to believe that they should not agree to waive disclosures, but this is difficult to predict in advance.

Litigants' creative compliance with the disclosures—presenting experts who appear credible but in fact are badly biased—is a critical concern; opponents will need to invest considerable resources to do the detective work to root out these hidden sources of bias. Thus, the best response to this worry is that even though this creative compliance will likely occur, the net effect of disclosures will still be beneficial in gaining leverage, however limited, over the problems of unreliable science in the courtroom. For example, the information in disclosures should help litigants expose problems with expert analyses that previously were invisible or too costly to root out. Presumably, the system will begin to discourage some of the worst, ends-oriented forensic experts from making a steady living testifying in a line of cases; this occupational bias will show up quickly in their disclosures. Hence, the scientists themselves may have less to

---

173 See, e.g., Patterson, supra note 60, at 1339 (discussing these risks); David E. Bernstein, Expert Witnesses, Adversarial Bias, and the (Partial) Failure of the Daubert Revolution, 93 Iowa L. Rev. 93 (2008), 451, 454.

174 See, e.g., Patterson, supra note 60, at 1333–36 (discussing this problem). And Patterson assumes, too, that the submissions are honest; in cases of fraudulent disclosures, sanctions should be exceedingly high.

gain from covert biases since fees from one case may be insufficient to cause them to stick their necks out in presenting biased testimony in the next case.

Indeed, if the disclosures have their intended effect, they should produce more positive incentives for the scientific community's engagement in providing analyses destined for the judicial system. Currently, some respected scientists are apparently reluctant to testify, in part because of the embarrassment of potentially being excluded under *Daubert* and in part because of the courts' tolerance for "hired gun" experts, which stigmatizes all experts more generally.[175] A disclosure system for expert testimony that resembles journal practices might be viewed by reputable scientists as a way to advertise their integrity to peers and others. Thus, in contrast to the status quo, experts might perceive that engaging in judicial decisions provides a way to maintain or even enhance their professional reputations.

In sum, this proposal for disclosures is not a panacea that will eliminate all difficulties courts face in assessing the reliability of expert analyses. However, the proposal does seem capable of making progress in improving the courts' use of scientific evidence, as well as disciplining the litigants' and agencies' own problematic incentives. At the same time, the courts can adjust their own screening standards in ways that are more in line with the scientific community, which would seem to move reliability determinations in the right direction.

CONCLUSION

Ensuring that the expert analyses that inform judicial processes are trustworthy is of vital importance to ensuring the accuracy of court decisions as well as the integrity of the judicial branch more generally. Judges have long struggled with the challenge of evaluating the scientific reliability of expert testimony. The analysis here suggests that some of these challenges may be alleviated by changing the courts' focus from assessing the "substantive" accuracy of scientific testimony to assessing instead its procedural integrity. Equally convenient, making this shift may not require a new infrastructure of doctrinal rules but could be accomplished by crafting a voluntary, standardized set of disclosures that parties should (but need not) submit as part of the litigation process. While these disclosures will not eliminate all the challenges that courts face at the intersection of science and law, the proposed disclosures have the potential to make some potentially significant improvements over the status quo with limited downsides.

---

175 See, e.g., David Ozonoff, Epistemology in the courtroom: a little "knowledge" is a dangerous thing, Am. J. Public Health 95 (2005), S13.

APPENDIX: DRAFT SAMPLE DISCLOSURES

Disclosure 1

Who are the main authors and contributors to the study or report? Provide the names and affiliations of these authors and describe their respective contributions. Also identify all other contributors, with information on both the nature and percentage of each of their contributions.

Disclosure 2

In what ways might the source of the research funding have affected the design, conduct, or reporting of the research or testimony?[176] Be sure to include in this disclosure:

- Any role (reserved or used) by the sponsor or other party external to the research in influencing any feature of the research.
- Any legal contracts that reserved publication decisions for non-authors of the study.
- Any past or anticipated future employer or personal investments potentially impacted by the outcome of the study or testimony.

To the extent you are not aware of potential conflicts or sources of influence on one or more studies, please provide that information as well.

You must also identify any sources of bias or conflicts in the research and data you synthesize as part of your analysis. Identify for each dataset or study cited the disclosed conflicts or other sources of bias. When that information is not provided, identify that fact as well. This list of potential conflicts in the underlying research should be prepared as a separate sheet to accompany your reference list.

Disclosure 3

In what ways was your analysis, testimony, and pertinent underlying research scrutinized by expert peers? In answering this question, please provide answers to the following questions:

- How extensive was this peer scrutiny?
- How were the experts selected and by whom? How did you ensure they represented a diverse cross-section of the scientific community on this topic?

---

[176] Patterson, supra note 60, at 1357 citing PHS.

- Did any of the peer reviewers hold a financial or employment interest that would be impacted by the outcome of your testimony/research?
- What were the reviewers' reactions/suggestions?
- What changes were made as a result?

With respect to all these questions, you must certify that when you are not able to provide a complete answer, you acted with due diligence to obtain the information but were unable to do so. In making this certification, provide the reason(s) you were unable to obtain the requested information.[177]

[177] See Patterson, supra note 60, at 1375 (providing the draft text for this final paragraph).

8. The misuse of AI in US sentencing

Jed S. Rakoff

INTRODUCTION

While many of the chapters in this volume have focused on the theoretical difficulties of utilizing scientific evidence in judicial decision-making, this piece will center on an actual example of these problems; namely, the use – and misuse – of artificial intelligence in sentencing in United States courts. The underlying question raised by these cases is whether it is fair to increase the amount of prison time a judge imposes on a defendant on the basis of an algorithmic score that indicates the likelihood that the defendant will commit future crimes. Many states in the US now say yes, even when the algorithms they use for this purpose have a high error rate, a secret design, and a racial bias.[1]

One might think that the very notion of a defendant having his prison time increased, not on the basis of the crime of which he was convicted, but also on the basis of a prediction about the likelihood that he will commit other crimes in the future, is troubling on its face.[2] Such so-called "incapacitation" – depriving the defendant of the capacity to commit future crimes – is usually defended on the ground that it protects the public against the likelihood of future crimes and that the defendant cannot be heard to complain since the sentence is still within the upper limits set by the legislature for the defendant's underlying

[1] Usage by states changes from year to year, of course. At present, predictive instruments for sentencing or parole (or both) are used by at least California, Colorado, Connecticut, Florida, Massachusetts, Michigan, Montana, Nebraska, Nevada, Oklahoma, Oregon, South Dakota, Texas, West Virginia, and Wisconsin, plus some parts of New Mexico and New York.

[2] This issue was dramatically raised in popular entertainment when a short story by a well-known science fiction author was made into a major motion picture (Philip K. Dick, The Minority Report, 4 *Fantastic Universe* 4 (Jan. 1956); see also Philip K. Dick, *The Minority Report and Other Classic Stories* (2002), 103; Steven Spielberg, dir., *Minority Report* (20th Century Fox 2002)).

crime.[3] But the reality is that the defendant is receiving punishment for crimes he never committed, and that seems wrong.[4]

Nonetheless, Congress and the state legislatures have long treated incapacitation as an approved goal of sentencing. For example, the primary federal statute setting forth the "factors to be considered in imposing a sentence"[5] provides, among other things, that "the court in determining the particular sentence to be imposed, shall consider ... the need for the sentence imposed ... to protect the public from further crimes of the defendant".

And how is the likelihood of "further crimes of the defendant" to be determined? Until recently, most judges simply looked at a defendant's age and criminal history. If the defendant had committed numerous crimes in the past, the presumption was that he was likely to commit further crimes in the future. In theory, this could mean locking him up for the statutory maximum term

---

3 See, e.g., Franklin Zimring & Gordon Hawkins, *Incapacitation: Penal Confinement and the Restraint of Crime* (Oxford University Press, 1995); William Spelman, *Criminal Incapacitation* (Springer, 1994). A particular version, or theory of this rationale for punishment is selective incapacitation, premised on the idea that a small number of individuals commit a large proportion of crimes because they recidivate, i.e., they are "career criminals". See Peter W. Greenwood & Allan Abrahamse, Selective Incapacitation (1982) (Rand Study); Peter W. Greenwood, C. Peter Rydell, Allan Abrahamse, Jonathan P. Caulkins, James Chiesa, Karyn Model, & Stephen P. Klein, Three Strikes and You're Out: Estimated Benefits of California's New Mandatory Sentencing Law (1994) (U.S. Dep't of Justice, Office of Justice Programs Report (1994); Ben Vollaard, Preventing Crime Through Selective Incapacitation, 123 Econ. J. 262 (2012). Empirical studies tend to refute this theory. See, e.g., Rudy Haapenen, *Selective Incapacitation and the Serious Offender: A Longitudinal Study of Criminal Career Patterns* (Springer, 1990); Kathleen Auerhahn, Selective Incapacitation and the Problem of Prediction, 37 *Criminology* 703 (1999); Stephen D. Gottfredson & Don M. Gottfredson, Behavioral Prediction and the Problem of Incapacitation, 32 *Criminology* 441 (1994); Christina Stahlkopf, Mike Males, & Daniel Macallair, Testing Incapacitation Theory: Youth Crime and Incarceration in California, 56 Crime & Delinq. 263 (2010).

4 For a discussion of the constitutional concerns raised by predictive instruments, see Michael Brenner, Jeannie Suk Gersen, Michael Haley, Matthew Lin, Amil Merchant, Richard Jagdishwar Millett, Suproteem K. Sarkar, & Drew Wagner, Constitutional Dimensions of Predictive Algorithms in Criminal Justice, 55 Harv. Civ. Rights-Civ. Liberties L. Rev. 267 (2020). The authors conclude that "many risk-assessment tools in use today raise serious constitutional concerns. With fundamental liberties at stake, properly balancing the value of the technology with the constitutional questions is an urgent and critical matter for the criminal justice system". Id. at 309.

5 18 U.S.C. sec. 3553 (enacted in 1984).

of imprisonment permitted for the underlying crime. In my experience, however, few judges felt comfortable following this theory of incapacitation to its logical conclusion of maximum imprisonment – especially if the defendant's present and prior crimes were nonviolent, or if there was a realistic possibility of rehabilitation, or if the defendant had simply aged out (there being studies indicating that most repeat felons stop committing crimes after the age of 35 or so).[6] But in any individual case, all of this was educated guesswork at best.

In a recently published book, former federal judge Katherine Forrest reports that during her years on the bench, she felt obligated by the existing legal requirements to base her sentences in part on what she describes as "my personal assessment of the individual's ... likelihood of recidivating, and the extent to which any recidivism would harm the community or those around him".[7] She freely admits that she does not know, even today, whether those assessments were accurate. She therefore concludes that if the law requires the prediction of future risk, good artificial intelligence (AI) could theoretically help a judge make such predictions. But, she argues, the current algorithms used for this purpose are so deficient that they provide only the illusion of accuracy and fairness. One might therefore conclude that, if the law thus requires the prediction of future risk, good artificial intelligence (AI) could theoretically help a judge make such predictions.[8] But the current algorithms used for this purpose are so deficient as to provide only the illusion of accuracy and fairness, not the reality.

---

[6] One of the most robust correlations in social science is between crime and youth. See, e.g., David P. Farrington, Alex R. Piquero, David P. Farrington, Wesley G. Jennings, & Darrick Joliffe, *Offending from Childhood to Late Middle Age: Recent Results in the Cambridge Study in Delinquent Development* (2nd ed. Springer, 2023); Michael R. Gottfredson & Travis Hirschi, *A General Theory of Crime* (Stanford University Press, 1990); Gary Sweeten, Alex R. Piquero, & Laurence Steinberg, Age and the Explanation of Crime, Revisited, 42 Empirical Res. 921 (2013). Even studies arguing that the correlation should be reconsidered support the finding that crime decreases beyond the age of 40. See David P. Farrington, Age and Crime, in Michael Tonry & Norval Morris, eds., 7 *Crime & Justice* 189 (1986).

[7] Katherine B. Forrest, *When Machines Can Be Judge, Jury, and Executioner: Justice in the Age of Artificial Intelligence* (World Scientific, 2021).

[8] See Christopher R. Slobogin, *Just Algorithms: Using Science to Reduce Incarceration and Inform a Jurisprudence of Risk* (Cambridge University Press, 2021), 86–98.

ARTIFICIAL INTELLIGENCE

While the term "artificial intelligence" covers a wide spectrum of software,[9] we are concerned here with computer programs that not only scrutinize vast quantities of data but also adjust how they proceed on the basis of the data they analyze. What they "learn" from the data, and how they react to it, are dictated by a pre-programmed set of instructions called "algorithms".[10] The classic analogy to a simple algorithm is a cooking recipe. The recipe tells you what ingredients to use, in what order, how to cook them, and how to adjust the cooking depending on how the dish is turning out. The "designer" of this algorithm is the author of the recipe, the recipe itself is the equivalent of software, and you, your food, and your oven are the hardware.[11]

Most computer algorithms are, of course, far more complex than in this example. But the use of the terms "AI" and "algorithm" tends to conceal the huge role that the human designer of the program plays. It is the designer who determines what kinds of data will be input into the system and from what sources it will be drawn. It is the designer who determines what weights will be given to different inputs and how the program will adjust to them. And it is the designer who determines how all this will be applied to whatever the algorithm is meant to analyze.

In some fields, there are well-established standards governing the designer's choices, frequently based on scientific studies. But in the case of programs designed to predict recidivism, no such standards exist, and so there is a large element of subjectivity in the choices the designer makes. And unless the designer's choices are transparent, what is already highly subjective becomes utterly mysterious, a so-called "black box".[12]

---

9 See generally Stuart Russell & Peter Norvig, *Artificial Intelligence: A Modern Approach* (4th ed. Pearson, 2022).

10 See generally Thomas H. Cormen, *Algorithms Unlocked* (The MIT Press, 2013); Panos Louridas, *Algorithms* (The MIT Press, 2020).

11 See Sebastian Pauli, MAT 112 Integers and Modern Applications for the Uninitiated, https://mathstats.uncg.edu/sites/pauli/112/HTML/secalgdef.html; Johannes Zeller, Algorithms are Like Recipes (Sarah Smithson-Compton, trans. Goethe Inst., 2020), https://www.goethe.de/ins/be/en/kul/prj/21877729.html

12 See Brenner et al., supra note 4, at 272, 279; Cynthia Rudin, Caroline Wang, & Beau Coker, The Age of Secrecy and Unfairness in Recidivism Prediction, Harv. Data Sci. Rev. 2.1 (Mar. 31, 2020). The authors conclude that this potentially violates the Constitution. They state: "Processing information by means of a proprietary algorithm may thus violate due process because the defendant cannot effectively challenge the accuracy of the process by which the algorithm reaches its conclusions". Id. at 279–80.

COMPAS

The most commonly used algorithm for predicting recidivism is a privately produced product called "COMPAS" (Correctional Offender Management Profiling for Alternative Sanctions), made by a company called Northpointe (doing business under the name "Equivant").[13] For competitive reasons, COMPAS's design is mostly kept secret, and several courts have upheld the maintaining of such secrecy even from a criminal defendant who wants to challenge the design.[14]

Perhaps the use of a mysterious "black box" algorithm might be justified if it somehow produced accurate and fair results. But the computer programs used to predict recidivism provide neither. Regarding accuracy, studies suggest they have an error rate of between 30% and 40%, mostly in the form of false positives (i.e., wrong predictions that the defendants will commit more crimes in the future).[15] In other words, out of every 10 defendants who these algorithms predict will recidivate, 3–4 will not. To be sure, no one knows if judges who don't use such programs are any better at predicting recidivism (though one study, mentioned below, finds that even a random sample of laypeople is as good as the most frequently used algorithm in predicting recidivism). But the use of such programs supplies a "scientific" facade to such assessments that the large error rate belies.[16]

---

13 The company's headquarters are in Traverse City, Michigan. It rebranded itself as Equivant in 2017. The mission statement that appears on the company's website states: "We build decision support into everything we do because it just makes sense. Our tools are used nationwide for evidence-based decision making, helping to remove biases by equipping justice professionals with the research and rationale they need for making informed, defensible decisions." https://www.equivant.com/ (homepage).

14 See Alyssa M. Carlson, The Need for Transparency in the Age of Predictive Sentencing Algorithms, 103 Iowa L. Rev. 303 (2017).

15 Jennifer L. Skeem & Jennifer Eno Louden, Assessment of Evidence on the Quality of the Correctional Offender Management Profiling for Alternative Sanctions (COMPAS) (2007) https://perma.cc/PYQ6-WD4V.

16 The user's guide for the COMPAS algorithm provides the following explanation for the basis of its predictions:

> Think about the different steps taken in the medical field to find a solution to an illness or a problem. When you don't feel well and you go to the doctor, what is the first thing that the doctor does – Asks about symptoms, when did they start, how severe are they? She asks about your medical history, are you taking any medications, have you had this or a similar problem before? And, she runs tests, takes your temperature, takes your

Furthermore, these programs are materially worse at predicting recidivism and violence for Black defendants than for white ones.[17] Exactly why this is so is the subject of debate, made considerably more difficult to resolve because so much of the design of these programs is kept secret. But their increased unreliability in the case of defendants of color is not in dispute, and thus their use is likely to enhance the already racially discriminatory tendencies of the US criminal justice system. Perhaps the leading case addressing the use of these algorithms in sentencing is *State v. Loomis*, a 2016 decision of the Supreme Court of Wisconsin.[18] Eric Loomis, who had a prior criminal record, was originally charged with being the driver in a drive-by shooting, a charge he consistently denied. The state allowed him to enter into a plea bargain in which he pleaded guilty to two much less severe charges: operating a vehicle without the owner's consent and attempting to flee a traffic officer.[19] However, the state

---

> blood pressure, blood tests, MRIs, etc. What does she do with all of this information? She makes a diagnosis and prescribes an effective treatment.

https://s3.documentcloud.org/documents/2840784/Practitioner-s-Guide-to-COMPAS-Core.pdf at 4 [hereinafter cited as COMPAS Users Guide]. What is obviously problematic about this analogy is that medical care is sought voluntarily by the patient and designed to be beneficial to that patient. More generally, and just as obviously, there is no sense of social condemnation, no damage to one's moral reputation, in being the subject of medical care.

17 See Julia Angwin, Jeff Larson, Surya Mattu, & Lauren Kirchner, Machine Bias: There's Software Used Across the Country to Predict Future Criminals. And It's Biased Against Blacks, 23 *ProPublica* 77 (2016); Jeff Larson, Surya Mattu, Lauren Kirchner, & Julia Angwin, How We Analyzed the COMPAS Recidivism Algorithm, *ProPublica* (2016), https://www.propublica.org/article/how-we-analyzed-the-compas-recidivism-algorithm.

The study compiled data on 11,757 criminal defendants in Broward County, Florida, comparing actual recidivism rates two years after release with the COMPAS scoring at the time of arrest. Some of its conclusions were as follows:

- Black defendants were often predicted to be at a higher risk of recidivism than they actually were. Our analysis found that Black defendants who did not recidivate over a two-year period were nearly twice as likely to be misclassified as higher risk compared to their white counterparts (45% vs. 23%).
- White defendants were often predicted to be less risky than they were. Our analysis found that white defendants who re-offended within the next two years were mistakenly labeled low risk almost twice as often as black re-offenders (48% vs. 28%).
- The analysis also showed that even when controlling for prior crimes, future recidivism, age, and gender, Black defendants were 45% more likely to be assigned higher risk scores than white defendants.

18 371 Wisc. 2d 235, 881 N.W.2d 749 (Wis. 2016).

19 371 Wisc. 2d at 244; 881 N.W.2d at 754.

reserved the right to apprise the sentencing judge of the evidence it believed showed that Loomis had been the driver in a drive-by shooting.[20] And the judge was also provided with a presentence investigation report prepared by the court's probation office that, using the COMPAS algorithm, scored Loomis as a high risk for future violent crimes.[21]

At sentencing, the judge stated to Loomis: "You're identified, through the COMPAS assessment, as an individual who is at high risk to the community. In terms of weighing the various factors … the risk assessment tools that have been utilized suggest that you're extremely high risk to re-offend".[22] The judge then sentenced Loomis to a combined six years of imprisonment on the two modest crimes to which he had pled guilty.[23]

On appeal, first to an intermediary court and then to the Wisconsin Supreme Court, Loomis focused much of his attack on the refusal of the state, the probation office, and the sentencing court to provide him with even the most basic information about how COMPAS computed his recidivism score.[24] In response, the Wisconsin Supreme Court said this:

---

[20] The plea agreement provided: "The other counts will be dismissed and read in for sentencing, although the defendant denies he had any role in the shooting and only drove the car after the shooting occurred. The State believes he was the driver of the car when the shooting happened. The State will leave any appropriate sentence to the Court's discretion but will argue aggravating and mitigating factors"; 371 Wisc. 2d at 244; 881 N.W.2d at 754. The prosecutor drove a hard bargain here in providing that the judge could consider actions by Loomis that he denied and had not been proven in trial. This seems to be one example of the general problem that prosecutors wield overwhelming power, particularly in this era of sentence enhancement. See John Pfaff, *Locked In: The True Causes of Mass Incarceration –And How to Achieve Real Reform* (Basic Books, 2017); Jed S. Rakoff, *Why the Innocent Plead Guilty and the Guilty Go Free: And Other Paradoxes of Our Broken Legal System* (Farrar, Straus and Giroux, 2021), 22–31.

[21] 371 Wisc. 2d at 245; 881 N.W.2d at 754. The Court stated:

> As the [presentence investigation report] explains, risk scores are intended to predict the general likelihood that those with a similar history of offending are either less likely or more likely to commit another crime following release from custody. However, the COMPAS risk assessment does not predict the specific likelihood that an individual offender will reoffend. Instead, it provides a prediction based on a comparison of information about the individual to a similar data group.

[22] 371 Wisc. 2d at 247; 881 N.W.2d at 755.

[23] 371 Wisc. 2d at 248; 881 N.W.2d at 756.

[24] Id.

> Northponte, Inc., the developer of COMPAS, considers COMPAS a proprietary instrument and a trade secret. Accordingly, it does not disclose how the risk scores are determined or how the factors are weighed. Loomis asserts that because COMPAS does not disclose this information, he has been denied information which the [sentencing] court considered at sentencing. [However], [a]lthough Loomis cannot review and challenge how the COMPAS algorithm calculates risk, he can at least review and challenge the resulting risk scores set forth in the [report to the judge].[25]

For the Court, that was good enough to deny Loomis's appeal;[26] but to me it seems like a complete non sequitur. Without knowing how the algorithm is designed, what inputs it receives, and how they are weighed, how can one possibly challenge the resulting risk scores in any given case?

COMPAS provides a multi-page user's guide, titled *Practitioner's Guide to Compass Core*.[27] The Guide "does not disclose what machine learning it is based on, or its algorithm, precise inputs, weightings, or data sets used".[28] And as the *Loomis* case illustrates, the manufacturer of COMPAS has for the most part successfully resisted disclosing such specifics on the ground that they are legally protected trade secrets. As a result, we know very little about COMPAS's designers, what choices they made, what tests were undertaken to establish COMPAS's reliability, to what extent its methodology was independently scrutinized, what its error rate is, whether it employs consistent standards and methods, and whether it is generally accepted in the scientific community.

What this means is that if it were sought to be presented at a trial, its admissibility would be doubtful under either of the standards used in US courts

---

[25] 371 Wisc. 2d at 258; 881 N.W.2d at 761.

[26] The Court added: Ultimately, we disagree with Loomis because consideration of a COMPAS risk assessment at sentencing along with other supporting factors is helpful in providing the sentencing court with as much information as possible in order to arrive at an individualized sentence. 371 Wisc. 2d at 266; 881 N.W.2d at 765. But the helpfulness of the assessment depends on the quality of the information – that was the basis of Loomis's challenge.

[27] COMPAS Users Guide, supra note 16. The document describes its products as follows:

> COMPAS is a fourth generation risk and needs assessment instrument. Criminal justice agencies across the nation use COMPAS to inform decisions regarding the placement, supervision, and case management of offenders. COMPAS was developed empirically with a focus on predictors known to affect recidivism. It includes dynamic risk factors, and it provides information on a variety of well-validated risk and needs factors designed to aid in correctional intervention to decrease the likelihood that offenders will reoffend.

[28] Forrest, supra note 7.

for determining the admissibility of expert testimony at trial (known as the "*Daubert*"[29] standard and the "*Frye*"[30] standard). But COMPAS is not used at a trial. It is used for purposes like setting bail and determining sentences, where no such rigor is mandated by current law.[31]

---

29 *Daubert v. Merrell Dow Pharmaceuticals, Inc*, 509 U.S. 579 (1993). *Daubert*, one of the most widely cited cases in American law, established the standards for the admissibility of scientific evidence in American federal courts. It overruled an earlier decision, *Frye v. United States*, 293 F. 1013 (D.C. Cir. 1923), which held, as a matter of federal common law, that scientific evidence was only admissible if it was generated by a method that was "generally accepted" in the applicable scientific community, id. at 1129–30. The *Daubert* Court held that the adoption of the Federal Rules of Evidence (drafted by the Supreme Court but adopted as revised by Congress, Pub. L. 93–595, 88 Stat. 1926 (1975)), superseded federal common law. Rule 402 of the Federal Rules provides that if scientific knowledge "will assist the trier of fact to understand the evidence or to determine a fact in issue, a witness qualified as an expert by knowledge, skill, experience, training, or education, may testify thereto in the form of an opinion or otherwise". To implement this standard, the Court held that the presiding judge should make an expert testimony regarding scientific knowledge admissible if it meets the methodological standard that it can be tested for its truth or falsity, whether it has been subject to peer review, its error rate, the standards that control its operation and its degree of acceptance in the scientific community. 509 U.S. at 593–94.

In other words, the Court interpreted the enacted Federal Rules of Evidence to establish a more permissive, multi-factored test for the admissibility of scientific evidence. But even under this standard, the COMPAS algorithm could not be used at trial (that is, to determine guilt or innocence). It may indeed be testable, but it has not been subject to peer review, its error rate appears to be high, it is not subject to standard scientific controls, and it is far from generally accepted.

30 *Frye v. United States*, 293 F. 1013 (D.C. Cir. 1923). While the Supreme Court held that the *Frye* standard has been displaced by the Federal Rules, and while the concept of general common law on which it is based has been rejected, its standard is still applied in some American jurisdictions and its rationale has not been rejected (and is in fact incorporated as one factor in the *Daubert* standard). Clearly, the COMPAS algorithm would be inadmissible according to this more demanding test – far from being generally accepted, it is highly controversial.

31 According to the *New York Times*, predictive algorithms are also used to identify crime "hot spots". Mitch Smith, In Wisconsin, A Backlash Against Using Data to Foretell Defendants' Futures (*New York Times*, June 22, 2016). This is significant because preventive, "microgeographic" policing is being adopted by a number of important jurisdictions, including New York City. See Anthony A. Braga, Brandon C. Welsh, & Cory Schnell, Can Policing Disorder Reduce Crime? A Systematic Review and Meta-Analysis, 52 J. Crime & Delinq. 569 (2015); Lawrence W. Sherman, Policing for Crime Prevention, in *Evidence-Based Crime Prevention* ed. David P. Farrington, Doris Layton MacKenzie, Lawrence

RELIABILITY OF COMPAS

What we do know about COMPAS's design, moreover, is far from reassuring. According to Northpointe, COMPAS ultimately rests on certain sociological theories of recidivism – the "Social Learning Theory", the "Sub-Culture Theory", the "Control/Restraint Theory", the "Cultural Opportunity Theory", and the "Social Strain Theory".[32] Even a brief review of the sociological literature discloses that many of these theories are controversial, most have been only modestly tested and with mixed results, several are inconsistent with each other, and all partake of the "softness" that is typical of many sociological theories.[33] Indeed, as several of the peer reviews of these theories note, the theories are constantly being "revised" to account for unexpected results: a

---

W. Sherman, & Brandon C. Welsh (Routledge, 2002); David Weisburd, From Criminals to Criminal Contexts: Reorienting Criminal Justice Research and Policy, 10 *Advances Criminological Theory* 197 (2002); David Weisburd & John E. Eck, What Can Police Do to Reduce Crime, Disorder and Fear?, 593 Annals Am. Acad. Pol. & Soc. Sci. 42 (2004). Preventive policing does not raise the same constitutional or moral problems that the use of algorithms for sentencing does, but if the information that it is based on is inaccurate, the police will be going to the wrong places at the wrong times, which leaves truly high crime areas unprotected and creates a sense of threat, and possibly a pattern of unnecessary arrests, in others.

[32] COMPAS Guide, supra note 16, at 5–6. For an explication of these theories, see generally Robert Agnew & Joanne M. Kaufman, *Anomie, Strain and Subculture Theories of Crime* (Routledge, 2010); J. Robert Lilly, Francis T. Cullen & Richard A. Ball, Criminological Theory: Context and Consequences (7th ed. SAGE Publications, 2018); Eugene McLaughlin & Tim Newburn, eds., *The SAGE Handbook of Criminological Theories* (SAGE Publications, 2010).

[33] See, e.g., Shane Blackman, Youth Subcultural Theory: A Critical Engagement with the Concept, its Origins and Politics, from the Chicago School to Postmodernism, 8 J. Youth Stud. 1 (2005) (theoretically outdated and conceptually confused); Velmer S. Burton & Francis Cullen, The Empirical Status of Strain Theory, 15 J. Crime & Justice 1 (1992); Matt DeLisi, Kevin M. Beaver, Michael G. Vaughn, Chad R. Trulson, Anna E. Kosloski, Alan J. Drury, & John Paul Wright, Personality, Gender, and Self-Control Theory Revisited: Results from a Sample of Institutionalized Juvenile Delinquents, 6 Applied Psych. In Crim. Justice 32 (2010) (only partially predictive, and only for males); Keith Hayward, Situational Crime Prevention and its Discontents: Rational Choice Theory Versus "The Culture of Now", 41 Soc. Pol. & Admin 232 (2007) (applicable to limited types of crime and over-reliant on rational choice theory); Travis C. Pratt, Francis T. Cullen, Christine S. Sellers, L. Thomas Winfree Jr., Tamara D. Madensen, Leah E. Daigle, Noelle E. Fearn, & Jacinta M. Gau, The Empirical Status of Social Learning Theory: A Meta-Analysis, 27 Justice Q. 765 (2010) (mixed empirical results).

classic indication that they are not sufficiently reliable to meet the legal standards for admissibility of scientific evidence.

Nor are we given any clue as to which of these theories the designers of COMPAS applied with respect to their choices of data sets, algorithmic responses to those data sets, etc. But what we do know is that even the validation studies that COMPAS itself has chosen to disclose show an error rate of between 29% and 37% in predicting future violent behavior and an error rate of between 27% and 31% in predicting future non-violent recidivism. In other words, on COMPAS's own disclosures (which might well be biased in COMPAS's favor), COMPAS gets it wrong about one-third of the time.[34]

Worse still, COMPAS gets it wrong more often with Black defendants than with white defendants.[35] Even the *Loomis* court felt obliged to note that:

> A recent analysis of COMPAS's recidivism scores based upon data from 10,000 criminal defendants in Broward County, Florida, concluded that Black defendants "were far more likely than white defendants to be incorrectly judged to be at a higher risk of recidivism". Likewise, white defendants were more likely than Black defendants to be incorrectly flagged as low risk.

Why this is so is, of course, indeterminable as long as COMPAS largely keeps secret how its algorithm is designed. Such secrecy has not prevented Northpointe from challenging the results of the independent (and transparent) studies confirming such racial bias.[36] Forrest, who devotes an entire chapter of her book to analyzing this debate in detail, concludes in the end that there is "no longer any real debate that COMPAS and other AI assessment tools

---

[34] See COMPAS Users Guide, supra note 16, at 12–15.

[35] See Angwin, Larson, Mattu, Kirchner, & Angwin, supra note 17; Larson, Mattu, Kirchner, & Angwin, supra note 17; Cecelia Klingele, The Promises and Perils of Evidence-Based Corrections, 91 Notre Dame L. Rev. 537, 577 (2015); Sonja B. Starr, Evidence-Based Sentencing and the Scientific Rationalization of Discrimination, 66 Stan. L. Rev. 803, 806 (2014). The ProPublica study, supra note 17, which is probably the most widely discussed, is challenged in Anthony W. Flores, Kristin Bechtel, & Christopher T. Lowenkamp, False Positives, False Negatives and False Analyses: A Rejoinder to "Machine Bias: There's Software Used Across the Country to Predict Future Criminals. And It's Biased Against Blacks", 80 Fed. Probation 28 (2016). This response is in turn questioned in Dressel & Farid, note 39. For a balanced assessment of the issue, see Slobogin, supra note 8, at 86–98.

[36] William Dieterich, Christina Mendoza, & Tim Brennan, COMPAS Risk Scales: Demonstrating Accuracy, Equity and Predictive Parity (Technical Report, Northpointe, Inc. 2016).

produce different results for Black versus white offenders".[37] But this did not stop the Wisconsin Supreme Court, and other courts since, from allowing COMPAS scores to be used by judges as a factor in sentencing.

To be sure, the court in *Loomis* tried to have it both ways by saying that even though "COMPAS can be helpful to assess an offender's risk to public safety", it "may not be used … to determine the severity of the sentence".[38] The best I can make out of this Janus-like formulation is that a sentencing judge in Wisconsin, confronted with a COMPAS score indicating a high risk of recidivism, can treat this (dubious) information as part of its sentencing mix but cannot expressly make it the factor that "determines" the length of the sentence. This may satisfy the Wisconsin Supreme Court, but to this trial judge it appears to be nothing but camouflage. If a sentencing judge, unaware of how problematic COMPAS really is, is told that this "evidence-based" instrument has scored the defendant as a high recidivism risk, it seems unlikely to suppose that the judge will not give substantial weight to this score in determining how much of the defendant's sentence should be weighted toward incapacitation.

Of course, one might argue that there is still a role for COMPAS if judges assessing recidivism without COMPAS get it wrong even more often than COMPAS does. But while there is no real way to study this with certainty, a well-received study published in 2018 by Julie Dressel and Hany Farid (then both professors of computer science at Dartmouth) strongly suggests otherwise. The study showed that a random sample of everyday people from a popular online website "are as accurate and fair as COMPAS at predicting recidivism".[39] The study also found that "although COMPAS may use up to 137 features to make a prediction, the same predictive accuracy can be achieved with only two features", namely, age and prior criminal history – the same two features that judges have traditionally used to predict recidivism.[40]

---

37 Forrest, supra note 7.

38 371 Wisc. 2d at 273; 881 N.W. 2d at 768.

39 Julia Dressel & Hany Farid, The Accuracy, Fairness and Limits of Predicting Recidivism, 4 Sci. Advances EEAO 5580 (2018). The authors state: "commercial software that is widely used to predict recidivism is no more accurate or fair than the predictions of people with little to no criminal justice expertise who responded to an online survey".

40 Id. "Although Northpointe does not reveal the details of their COMPAS software, we have shown that their prediction algorithm is equivalent to a simple linear classifier. In addition, despite the impressive collection of 137 features, it would appear that a linear classifier based on only 2 features—age and total number of previous convictions—is all that is required to yield the same prediction accuracy as COMPAS".

CONCLUSION

COMPAS and other such recidivism-predicting algorithms are used mostly in state (as opposed to federal) courts. This is partly because the National Center for State Courts has, since 2015, encouraged such use in order to make bail and sentencing terminations more "data-driven"[41] – a mantra that entirely begs the question of whether these tools are accurate, unbiased, and reliable. But even the federal government has dipped its toes in this water, using a federally-developed algorithm called Post Conviction Risk Assessment ("PCRA") for such limited purposes as determining which defendants should be subject to special scrutiny while on probation. Nonetheless, studies of PCRA demonstrate that its predictive accuracy is higher for white than Black offenders. So, why are we still using it, even for such limited purposes?

More broadly, the fundamental question remains: even if these algorithms could be made much more accurate and less biased than they currently are, should they still be used in the criminal justice system in determining whom to lock up and for how long? My own view is that increasing a defendant's sentence of imprisonment on the basis of hypothesized future crimes is fundamentally unfair. But even if "incapacitation" has a role to play, I worry that even much better algorithms than we currently have will perversely cause judges to place undue emphasis on incapacitation, at the expense of alternatives to prison that might actually serve to make defendants better citizens and less likely to commit future crimes.

41 National Center for State Courts, The Racial Justice Organizational Assessment Tool for Courts, Appendix A-1 Data-Driven Decision Making for Courts (2023). This is the final report for an initiative announced by the Obama Administration to ameliorate the problem of mass incarceration through "a bipartisan coalition of 67 city, county, and state governments who have committed to using data-driven strategies". The White House Office of the Press Secretary, Fact Sheet: Launching the Data-Driven Justice Initiative: Disrupting the Cycle of Incarceration (Jul. 14, 2015).

PART III

Balancing the promise and the problems

9. Macro effects in climate change mitigation cases: four empirical challenges

Elbert de Jong

In climate change mitigation litigation, macro effects play a central role. Macro effects are effects of litigation that are felt by non-litigants (i.e., third parties). This chapter focuses on the macro effects of litigation seeking a court order for corporate greenhouse gas emissions reductions. It discusses three levels of macro effects that can be created by mitigation litigation. They can be 1) implied in a reduction obligation; 2) related to the implementation of a reduction obligation, and thus to norm-compliant behavior; and 3) related to the broader social, political, and economic conditions that shape climate policies. Further, the chapter discusses four empirical challenges that courts face when they want to take the potential macro effects of their (intended) ruling into account. These challenges relate to 1) the lack of available knowledge about the effects of climate change litigation on (corporate) climate change governance; 2) methodological issues that arise when obtaining insights into the relationship between the occurrence of macro effects and litigation; 3) the fact that civil courts are to a great extent dependent on the parties for providing reliable and adequate empirical knowledge; and 4) challenges related to assessing and understanding the relevance of empirical information about macro effects. On the basis of Dutch climate change mitigation litigation, including the *Urgenda* case and the *Shell* case, this chapter will illustrate how the distinctive macro effects can be present in climate change cases and how the four challenges can arise.

1. INTRODUCTION

The tide of tort law-based climate change litigation against corporations is rising: worldwide litigation is pending or expected against, among others, aviation companies, oil and gas companies, energy companies, financial institutions, pension funds, and insurers. In these cases, corporations are often being sued under national tort law for their allegedly unlawful greenhouse gas emissions and their failure to reduce those emissions. Most of the cases focus on injunctive relief (seeking a court order to reduce emissions instead of compensation). In addition to the Dutch Shell climate case,[1] one could think of litigation in Switzerland, New Zealand, France, the United States, Australia, and Germany.[2] These cases are often brought to court not only to assess the need for legal protection between the litigating parties, as is usually the case in civil law proceedings, but also to bring about changes in (global) corporate climate change governance and corporate greenhouse gas emissions. Often, the goal of climate change litigation is to regulate and change corporate climate change policies. In other words, these cases are a clear example of public interest litigation: winning the case at hand on the legal merits is important, but for the litigating interest groups, the broader impact of litigation is equally or even more important.

The use of tort law as a regulatory tool to mitigate emissions is having a mixed reception. A central point of critique concerns the effects and (in) effectiveness of using tort law to reduce greenhouse emissions. This criticism, which is related to the effects and (in)effectiveness of mitigation cases, can be raised in various ways. First, there is the argument that tort law is an inherently ineffective tool because in litigation "only" a few polluters can be forced to reduce emissions, whereas an effective approach to the climate crisis requires that all (major) polluters, ideally at the global level, are obliged and forced to reduce emissions.[3] Closely related to this is the argument that the use of national tort law leads to a fragmented and inconsistent framework of national reduction obligations, causing legal inequality and uncertainty which also complicates global corporate emissions reductions.[4] Finally, there is the

---

1 District court of The Hague 26 May 2021, ECLI:NL:HR:2019:1278 (*Milieudefensie v. Shell*) and Court of appeal of The Hague 12 November 2024, ECLI:NL:GHDHA:2024:2099 (*Milieudefensie v. Shell*).

2 See for an overview of the pending cases in these, and other, jurisdictions: https://climatecasechart.com/.

3 See for this line of reasoning for instance *Smith v. Fonterra Co-operative Group Limited and others* [2020] NZHC 419; [2020] 2 NZLR 394. See about this case M. Hook, C. Warnock, B. Allan & M. Pirini, 'Tort to the Environment: A Stretch Too Far or a Simple Step Forward? Smith v Fonterra Co-operative Group Ltd and Others [2020] NZHC 419' (2021) 33 *Journal of Environmental Law* 195.

4 See, however, also M. Hinteregger, 'Civil Liability and the Challenges of Climate Change: A Functional Analysis' (2017) 2 *Journal of European Tort Law* 238, 246–247, who argues that "unlike administrative or tax law, the functioning of civil liability is not constrained to the territory of one country. Claims for damages can be directly asserted abroad or brought against foreign parties before domestic courts and subsequently enforced abroad. Consequently, civil liability

argument that tort law creates negative side effects that undermine its effectiveness, such as substitution effects that might occur when other actors fill the gap created by greenhouse reductions by an actor that is legally ordered to reduce emissions. Sometimes, the argument is made that intervention through tort law works counterproductively and leads to an increase in emissions: think of a climate case against an oil company that results in the export of certain carbon-intensive activities to a country with more lenient reduction standards or to a facility that produces more emissions.[5]

Ultimately, the underlying point of criticism is that when courts intervene, they may settle the legal dispute between the litigating parties, but they do not solve the underlying societal issue (i.e., a lack of global corporate emissions reductions) and could even make it worse. For instance, in the context of the first instance judgment in the climate case of Milieudefensie against Shell, where the court ordered Shell to reduce its scope 1, 2, and 3 emissions, several authors argued that the actual contribution of the Dutch ruling to global greenhouse gas emissions reductions is a relevant factor in assessing the legitimacy of the ruling.[6] The first instance ruling was overturned on appeal and the

---

claims, or even the pending threat of such claims, may induce emitters of greenhouse gases to reduce their emissions regardless of the climate protection policy of their state". Hinteregger, however, also identifies drawbacks since much would depend on whether emitting corporations are actually held (fully) responsible.

5 See in general the discussion between Mayer and Burger: B. Mayer, 'The Duty of Care of Fossil-Fuel Producers for Climate Change Mitigation: Milieudefensie v. Royal Dutch Shell' (2022a) 11 *Transnational Environmental Law*, 407; L. Burgers, 'An Apology Leading to Dystopia: Or, Why Fueling Climate Change Is Tortious' (2022) 11 *Transnational Environmental Law* 419; B. Mayer, 'Judicial Interpretation of Tort Law in Milieudefensie v. Shell: A Rejoinder' (2022b) 11 *Transnational Environmental Law* 433. See also the reasoning of the court of appeal in the *Shell* climate case, Court of appeal of The Hague 12 November 2024, ECLI:NL:GHDHA:2024:2099.

6 In English: B. Mayer, 'Judicial Interpretation of Tort Law in Milieudefensie v. Shell: A Rejoinder' (2022b) 11 *Transnational Environmental Law* 433. In Dutch: L. Smeehuijzen, 'De veroordeling van Shell tot 45% CO2-reductie in 2030. Over legitimiteit en effectiviteit' (2022) *NJB* 458. See also about the implications of the effects of the Shell ruling: J. Spier, 'Milieudefensie v Shell: een sirenenzang? Suggesties voor een beter alternatief' in: W. J. M. van Veen, A. Hammerstein, J. L. Smeehuijzen, A. F. Verdam & J. Spier (eds), *De klimaatzaak tegen Shell (ZIFO-reeks nr. 35)*, Deventer: Wolters Kluwer 2022; J. Spier, 'SDGs: tussen droom en daad: een processie van Echternach: Het Shell-vonnis: stormram of eendagsvlieg', *Tijdschrift voor Vennootschapsrecht, Rechtspersonenrecht en Ondernemingsbestuur*, 2021 afl. 6, p. 176. See for a skeptical outlook on tort law as a regulatory device in relation to climate change: G. Dwyer, 'Climate Litigation:

reduction order was dismissed. Nonetheless, the discussion in the context of the *Shell* case about the meaning of its potential macro effects is illustrative of the topic central to this chapter. Therefore, both the first instance ruling and the court of appeal ruling will be used as illustrations.

According to some scholars, a court reduction order is only legitimate if it contributes, or at least does not impede, emissions reductions at the global level. Accepting this line of reasoning would ultimately imply that civil courts, when faced with a request for a reduction order, should consider the effects and (in)effectiveness of their rulings. In addition, defendants in specific climate change cases might bring forward defenses that relate to the effects and (in) effectiveness of tort law-based climate change litigation, thereby also raising the question as to whether – and if so, how – courts could take these effects into account.

This chapter discusses the empirical challenges that courts face when they want to take the potential macro effects of their (intended) ruling into account. The focus is on cases seeking to force corporations to reduce their greenhouse gas emissions and the effects thereof on third-party greenhouse gas emissions. Dutch climate change litigation-seeking court-based reduction orders and Dutch civil law are central to the analysis. In the context of this chapter, the concept of macro effects refers to the extent to which litigation about a reduction obligation of one specific actor influences emissions reductions (or efforts thereto) of non-litigants (i.e., third parties, such as governments, businesses, or citizens). First, I will define the term macro effects and identify three types of macro effects that are relevant in the context of (tort law-based) mitigation cases (section 2). Based on this definition, I will then discuss the empirical challenges courts face when trying to take such macro effects into account (section 3). These challenges create a serious risk that civil courts lack adequate and comprehensive insights into the potential macro effects of their rulings. That begs the question of how courts can deal with the risk of having to rule in cases that might have far-reaching effects without adequate knowledge about the specific macro effects of their decisions.

2. MACRO EFFECTS OF TORT LAW-BASED REDUCTION ORDERS

Court rulings can produce (non-legal) effects that are felt both by the litigants and by non-litigants, i.e., third parties. When a ruling also influences the interests, behavior, or policies of third parties, one speaks of macro effects.

A Red Herring among Climate Mitigation Tools' in B. Mayer & A. Zahar (eds), *Debating Climate Law* (Cambridge University Press 2021).

The type of macro effects that may arise can be diverse. In the context of climate change litigation, one could think of effects on the availability of energy products and the prices thereof, the economic competitiveness of (national) economies and companies, the availability of jobs, the shift towards renewable energy sources, and others. Typical examples of such macro effects are carbon leakage effects, substitution effects[7] (e.g., if one actor is obliged to reduce emissions, others will fill the gap) or effects related to the behavior of customers (e.g., if an oil company's obligation to reduce its scope 3 emissions leads to a price increase, customers will get their fuel somewhere else). Macro effects are effects whose (non)occurrence is not always a necessary condition for norm compliant behavior. They are not necessarily prescribed by a legal obligation and also are not necessarily conditional on a court ruling enforcing that obligation. Nonetheless, they are related to norm compliant behavior: they are side effects of corporate and societal responses to court rulings.[8] Although macro effects are present in various types of procedures, they are particularly pronounced in the context of climate change litigation. This is because 1) NGOs litigate specifically to bring about these effects; 2) climate change is caused by numerous (and diverse) actors; and related to this, 3) climate change is a polycentric problem – addressing climate change involves many different and competing interests, all of which can be impacted by a single case.

In at least three interrelated ways climate change litigation can induce effects on (global) greenhouse gas emissions reductions by third parties.[9] They can be 1) inherent to a reduction order; 2) related to the implementation of a reduction obligation, and thus to norm-compliant behavior; or 3) related to the broader social, political and economic conditions that shape climate policies.

---

7 On substitution effects in the context of climate change litigation see G. Dwyer, 'Market Substitution' in the Context of Climate Litigation' (2022) 12 *Climate Law* 1.

8 See on this topic in general N. MacCormick, 'On Legal Decisions and Their Consequences: From Dewey to Dworkin' (1983) 58 NYU L. Rev. 239.

9 See for a different distinction, namely that between direct and indirect effects, J. Lin, 'Climate Change and the Court' (2012) 32 Legal Stud. 35; H. M. Osofsky, 'The Continuing Importance of Climate Change Litigation' (2010) 1 *Climate Law* 3. See J. Peel & H. M. Osofky, *Climate Change Litigation: Regulatory Pathways to Cleaner Energy* (Cambridge University Press 2015), who build further on this distinction. They distinguish direct and indirect regulatory effects of climate change litigation. Direct regulatory effects occur when litigation results in a formal change in climate change laws and policies. Indirect effects occur when litigation triggers behavioral changes. See also their work on p. 36 for a model to interpret the impact of climate change litigation.

Firstly, the occurrence of macro effects may be inherent in a court ruling ordering a party to reduce its emissions. An example is provided by *Urgenda*.[10] The court order required the Dutch government to achieve a 25% reduction in greenhouse gas emissions by the end of 2020 compared to the 1990 level. That this tightening would also affect the interests of third parties is undeniable. The same applies to the first-instance *Shell* ruling: in particular, with regard to the adopted scope 2 and 3 reduction obligation, it is clear that it will have an effect on third parties, since inherent in these reduction obligations is that Shell has to reduce the emissions of their chain partners and end users. As mentioned, the first-instance ruling was overturned on appeal. However, in line with the first-instance ruling, the court of appeal reasoned that corporations can have a duty to reduce their greenhouse gas emissions, including their scope 3 emissions. Nevertheless, regarding Shell's scope 1 and 2 emissions, the court ruled that Shell is not in breach of its reduction obligation. For scope 3 emissions, the court reasoned that it could not establish a concrete reduction target and pathways that Shell should adhere to. To that end, it reasoned that:

1. There is no applicable legislation containing reduction target and pathways for companies or sectors.
2. The global average reduction standard of 45% by 2030 cannot be applied to a specific sector.
3. There is too much scientific uncertainty regarding the reduction target and pathways that specifically apply to the oil and gas sector.

As a result, the type of macro effects that can logically be triggered by the recent ruling in the *Shell* climate case falls into the third category of macro effects.

Secondly, macro effects can be connected to the *implementation* of a reduction obligation by an actor who is legally ordered to reduce emissions.[11] Examples can be found in both *Urgenda*[12] and the *Shell* case. Urgenda and the first instance ruling in the *Shell* case prescribe that a certain reduction target must be achieved or that there is a significant best effort obligation to meet a specific reduction target, but they do not specify *how* that reduction target must be achieved. To comply with the reduction obligation, policy choices

10 Dutch Supreme Court, 20 December 2019, ECLI:NL:HR:2019:2006, *NJ* 2020/41, comm. J. Spier (*Urgenda*).

11 Or anticipates the adoption of such a possible reduction obligation.

12 I discuss Urgenda only for the purpose of illustrating the concept of macro effects. Urgenda is not about corporate responsibility and liability for climate change. Nonetheless, it provides a good example of macro effects in the context of climate change litigation.

have to be made, but what these choices should be is not prescribed in these cases. Of course, the type of policy choices to be made and the legal framework that governs these choices differ (i.e., governmental policy choices in *Urgenda* versus corporate policy choices in *Shell*). Nonetheless, in both cases the specific choices made when implementing the court order may influence the speed and amount of greenhouse gas emissions reductions by third parties. These possible macro effects might not always contribute positively to reducing the overall emissions. In relation to *Urgenda,* it was for instance argued that in certain sectors the policies that were implemented to meet the reduction order have led to a slight increase in emissions elsewhere in the world.[13] The *Urgenda* standard has been achieved and Dutch emissions reduced, but global emissions have not, the argument goes. With respect to the first instance ruling in the *Shell* case, Mayer noted that the order "might end up hindering mitigation action, for instance, if a reduced supply of gas hinders the phasing down of coal or forces energy consumers to rely on more carbon-intensive sources of oil and gas".[14] The possibility of Shell selling oil fields to third parties that are not making sufficient efforts to reduce their emissions, or might even emit more than Shell, has also been raised by some scholars as a critical point of the first instance judgment.

The crucial issue with this type of macro effects is that while the Dutch government and Shell might act in accordance with their legal obligation(s), the reductions achieved by them might not lead to an overall reduction. Moreover, the worldwide greenhouse gas emissions reduction target might even get more out of reach because the reductions by the State or Shell will be outweighed by an emission increase elsewhere. On appeal in the *Shell* case, the court was sensitive to this argument. Although the court accepted that Shell may have an obligation to reduce its scope 3 emissions, it also concluded that Milieudefensie has no legal interest in securing a judicial order requiring Shell to reduce its emissions. The court reasoned that granting such an order would not protect the interests Milieudefensie represents (the interest of inter alia Dutch citizens of being protected against the effects of dangerous climate change), particularly because the effects of the reduction order on worldwide greenhouse gas emissions reductions could be undone by substitution effects.[15]

Remarkably, a procedural aspect seems to be influential for this part of the judgment. Under the first instance ruling, Shell was granted freedom in

---

13 B. Mayer, 'The Contribution of Urgenda to the Mitigation of Climate Change' (2023) 33 *Journal of Environmental Law* 167.

14 B. Mayer, 'Judicial Interpretation of Tort Law in Milieudefensie v. Shell: A Rejoinder' (2022b) 11 *Transnational Environmental Law* 433, 436.

15 Court of appeal of The Hague 12 November 2024, ECLI:NL:GHDHA:2024:2099, paras 7.97–7.110.

choosing the measures to meet its scope 3 reduction obligation, without being required to consider market substitution effects.[16] The court of appeal noted that Milieudefensie did not challenge this aspect of the first instance court's decision.[17] Under Dutch appellate procedural law, this means that on appeal this part of the first instance ruling remains intact. In its reasoning, the court therefore had to assume that Shell has freedom in determining how to implement the reduction order. The court suggested that its reasoning might have been different if Milieudefensie had challenged this part of the judgment and requested the appeal court to impose specific requirements on the implementation measures to be taken. In other words, the outcome *might* have been different if Milieudefensie had provided arguments on how substitution effects should be avoided by Shell.

This line of reasoning is not without critique. For one, the effectiveness assessment empirically appears limited in scope as it only considers substitution effects. While the court acknowledges the potential "signaling function" of legal proceedings for other corporations, it concludes that the link between such an effect and the assumed unlawful acts of Shell is too remote.[18] This reasoning raises the question whether the court should have addressed other potential effects that could contribute to the effectiveness of litigation.[19] Moreover, the reasoning appears somewhat cynical: the court first acknowledges that corporations may have a mitigation obligation, but concludes that enforcing such an obligation via an injunctive relief procedure would be ineffective. The court thereby seems to assume that (other) corporations will not comply with their mitigation obligations. While this might be true in a (descriptive) *factual* sense, it prompts the question of whether non-compliance of non-litigants with their responsibility should be taken as a starting point for a (prescriptive) *legal* assessment of the effectiveness of a court order.

Thirdly, litigation and the threat thereof can create behavioral effects and policy changes by corporate actors and governments that influence the social, political, and economic conditions that are relevant for the adoption and enforcement of climate change governance and regulation. To put it briefly, one could also say that these types of effects influence the "flow" of regulatory,

---

16 See on how to further specify a scope 3 emissions reduction obligation E. Brans & M. Peters, 'Liability of non-state actors for scope 3 emissions', in E. R. de Jong et al. (eds.), *Corporate accountability and liability for climate change* (Edward Elgar 2024) 252–270.

17 Court of appeal of The Hague 12 November 2024, ECLI:NL:GHDHA:2024:2099, para 7.101.

18 Court of appeal of The Hague 12 November 2024, ECLI:NL:GHDHA:2024:2099, para 7.109.

19 Provided that they have been brought forward by the litigants.

political, economic, and societal EDJ events that are relevant for corporate climate change governance and reduction policies.[20] The occurrence of these types of macro effects does not necessarily depend on norm-compliant behavior of actors that have been legally obliged to reduce emissions. Likewise, their occurrence does not necessarily depend on the legal outcome in a specific case. While it is obvious that litigation with a climate-favorable outcome is more impactful than unsuccessful litigation, success of the claimant is not a necessary condition for these types of macro effects to occur.

Unsuccessful litigation might also have an impact on corporate reduction efforts.[21] The list of these *potential* macro effects that *could* occur due to litigation is long. By way of example, one can think of agenda-setting effects, such as the impact of litigation on political attention[22] and media coverage of climate change.[23] One could also think of the fact that litigation can shape narratives about climate change facts and legitimize – or delegitimize – the climate science behind those facts.[24] Partly because of this, litigation can also influence public concern about climate change.[25] Litigation can also make information available about corporate internal knowledge concerning climate change risks and policies, and create narratives about the corporate culture of dealing with climate change risks. Among other things, this can affect corporate reputation,[26] which is an important driver behind corporate policy making.

---

20 See Peel & Osofsky 2015, p. 23, with reference to C. Parker & J. Braithwaite, 'Regulation' in P. Cane & M. Tushnet (eds), *The Oxford Handbook of Legal Studies* (Oxford University Press 2003) 119.

21 B. J. Preston, 'The Influence of Climate Change Litigation on Governments and the Private Sector' (2011) 2 *Climate Law* 485.

22 Interestingly, in an experimental study, Kovács et al. found no direct link between strategic climate litigation and changes in policy attitudes. See A. Kovács, K. Luckner, A. Sekuła, & J. Kantorowicz, 'Beyond courts: Does strategic litigation affect climate change policy support?' (2024) 79 *International Review of Law and Economics* 106213.

23 A. Wonneberger & R. Vliegenthart, 'Agenda-Setting Effects of Climate Change Litigation: Interrelations Across Issue Levels, Media, and Politics in the Case of Urgenda against the Dutch Government', (2021) 15 *Environmental Communication: A Journal of Nature and Culture* 699.

24 H. M. Osofsky, 'The Continuing Importance of Climate Change Litigation' (2010) 1 *Climate Law* 3, 5; M. Lee, 'The Sources and Challenges of Norm Generation in Tort Law' (2018) 1 *European Journal of Risk Regulation* 34.

25 R. J. Brulle, J. Carmichael and J. Craig Jenkins, 'Shifting public opinion on climate change: an empirical assessment of factors influencing concern over climate change in the US, 2002–2010' (2012) 114 *Climate Change* 169.

26 See in general on this topic R. Shapira, '*Reputation Through Litigation: How the Legal System Shapes Behavior by Producing Information*' (2016) 91

In addition, one could think of regulatory action taken by the legislature in response to legal proceedings or in anticipation of it;[27] for example, because the business community is lobbying for a clear legal framework to counteract any legal uncertainty associated with the threat of litigation. *Urgenda* provides an example of this kind of effect: when the Dutch Climate Act was created, *Urgenda* was discussed as a signal from society and seen as a push for actual implementation of the Act.[28] Also, the reasoning in successful cases can provide a blueprint or inspiration for other cases, which is clearly illustrated by the relevance of *Urgenda* for several human rights-based climate change cases, such as the judgment of the European Court of Human Rights in the *KlimaSeniorinnen* case.[29] In addition to this point, court rulings can be promotive for the initiation of new litigation.[30] Illustrative of this dynamic is that in January 2024, Milieudefensie, stimulated by the first instance ruling in the *Shell* case, announced a new mitigation case against ING, a Dutch bank. Among other things, it demands that ING substantially reduces its emissions, requires climate change transition plans from major clients and, under certain circumstances, stops cooperating with polluting companies. According to Milieudefensie, the court of appeal's ruling in the *Shell* case also provides

Wash. L. Rev. 119; R. Shapira, *Law and Reputation: How the Legal System Shapes Behavior by Producing Information* (Cambridge University Press 2020).

27 See also B. J. Preston, 'The Influence of Climate Change Litigation on Governments and the Private Sector' (2011) 2 *Climate Law* 485.

28 Kamerstukken II, 2015/16, 34534, nr. 3, pp. 4 & 16.

29 European Court of Human Rights, 9 April 2024, ECLI:CE:ECHR:2024:0409JUD005360020 (*Verein klimaseniorinnen Schweiz and* others/Switzerland).

30 In 2021, Setzer and Higham identified 37 cases that have likely been inspired by or built on the approach taken in the *Urgenda* case. See J. Setzer & C. Higham, 'Global trends in climate change litigation: 2021 snapshot' (Londen: Grantham Research Institute on Climate Change and the Environment and Centre for Climate Change Economics and Policy, London School of Economics and Political Science 2022) 23; J. Peel & R. Markey-Towler, 'Recipe for Success?: Lessons for Strategic Climate Litigation from the *Sharma*, *Neubauer* and *Shell* cases' (2021) 22 *German Law Journal* 1484. On the basis of an analysis of three cases, *Sarma* (Australia), *Neubauer* (Germany), and *Shell* (The Netherlands), they analyze how the three cases combine careful, strategic planning with legal imagination and innovation to generate outcomes that heighten their capacity for broader impact. According to the authors, evaluating the success of these types of prominent climate cases provides important guidance for future case design. See also about the fact that litigation can inspire other claimants: J. Peel & H. M. Osofsky, 'Litigation as a Climate Regulatory Tool' in C. Voigt (ed), *International Judicial Practice on the Environment: Questions of Legitimacy* (Studies on International Courts and Tribunals, Cambridge University Press 2019) 325.

opportunities for a new successful mitigation case; after the ruling on appeal, it announced that it will proceed with the case against ING.[31] It also announced a second case against Shell, dealing with its investments in new oil and gas fields. This illustrates that even cases where the claims are dismissed can be promotive for new litigation.

Also, the related perception of liability risks may lead companies to adjust their policies, possibly following legal advice on their liability risks. Finally, one could think of financial impacts of climate change litigation, for example on the share value of companies that are or may be exposed to litigation,[32] which can in turn also trigger shareholders' action or actions by public supervisors.

3. EMPIRICAL COMPLICATIONS

In order to take macro effects into account when determining the role of tort law, one should have adequate and comprehensive empirical knowledge about the likelihood of their occurrence in the future (ex ante) and their actual occurrence in the past (ex post). Here we face four challenges, at least, which relate to the lack of available knowledge about the effects of climate change litigation on (corporate) climate change governance, methodological issues that arise when obtaining insights into the relationship between the occurrence of macro effects and litigation, the fact that civil courts are to a great extent dependent on the parties to provide reliable and adequate empirical knowledge, and challenges related to assessing and understanding the relevance of empirical knowledge about macro effects.

In 2022, the IPCC signaled that litigation can have an impact on meeting climate goals. The mere fact that the IPCC pays attention to the significance of climate change litigation and considers it as part of a broader governance and regulatory structure for achieving climate goals is an indication of the (increasing) importance of litigation as a regulatory mechanism.[33] In addition, it stated that "climate-related litigation is increasing, with a large number of cases in some developed countries and a smaller number in some developing countries. In some cases, litigation has influenced the outcome and ambition of climate governance (medium confidence)".[34] The IPCC, however, also notes that it is "still unclear the extent to which climate litigation actually results

[31] See https://milieudefensie.nl/actueel/waarom-we-doorgaan-met-de-klimaat-zaak-tegen-ing-3-redenen, last accessed 15 January 2025.

[32] M. Sat and others, 'Impacts of Climate Litigation on firm value' (Grantham Research Institute on Climate Change and the Environment 2023).

[33] Of course, the analysis of the IPCC is not limited to climate change litigation against corporations.

[34] IPCC, *Climate Change 2023. Mitigation of Climate Change* (Working group III for the 6th IPCC Assessment Report, 2022) 110.

in new climate rules and policies and to what degree this holds true for all cases".[35] Setzer and Vanhala arrive at a similar insight when they stress "the limits of existing work and the need for future research – not limited to legal scholarship – to evaluate the impact of both regulatory and antiregulatory climate-related lawsuits".[36] This is particularly true for the impact of litigation against oil and gas companies. This is not to say, however, that there have been no studies at all on the effects of climate litigation. It is widely recognized in the (mainly legal) literature that climate change litigation, and in particular litigation that is successful for the claimant, can lead to new climate cases elsewhere, which in turn can also achieve reduction effects.[37] Information about the legal success ratio of climate litigation is also relevant in this context.[38] In addition, there are empirically embedded studies that do zoom in on some specific non-legal effects of litigation on climate change governance.[39]

To summarize, there is no question that litigation can have macro effects on, among other things, greenhouse gas emissions and their reduction.[40] The

---

[35] IPCC, *Climate Change 2022. Mitigation of Climate Change* (Working group III for the 6th IPCC Assessment Report, 2022) 31. See also J. Setzer & L. C. Vanhala, 'Climate Change Litigation: A Review of Research on Courts and Litigants in Climate Governance' (2019) 10 *Wiley Interdisciplinary Reviews: Climate Change* e580; S. McCormick, R. L. Glicksman, S. J. Simmens, L. Paddock, D. Kim & B. Whited, 'Strategies in and Outcomes of Climate Change Litigation in the United States' (2018) 8 *Nature Climate Change* 829. See also K. Bouwer & J. Setzer, 'New Trends in Climate Litigation: What Works?' (Working paper presented at the New Trends in International Climate and Environmental Advocacy Workshop, Johns Hopkins University SAIS Europe and European University Institute 2020).

[36] J. Setzer, 'The Impacts of High-Profile Litigation against Major Fossil Fuel Companies' in C. Rodríguez-Garavito (ed), *Litigating the Climate Emergency: How Human Rights, Courts and Legal Mobilization Can Bolster Climate Action (Globalization and Human Rights)* (Cambridge University Press 2022) 218.

[37] See section 2.

[38] See, e.g., J. Setzer & C. Higham, 'Global trends in climate change litigation: 2024 snapshot' (London: Grantham Research Institute on Climate Change and the Environment and Centre for Climate Change Economics and Policy, London School of Economics and Political Science 2024).

[39] See the examples mentioned in section 2.

[40] In addition to studies on the impact of climate litigation, there are examples of litigation in other areas that did produce significant macro effects. See, among many others: W. K. Viscusi (ed), *Regulation through litigation* (American Enterprise Institute-Brookings Institution 2002); A. P. Morris, B. Yandle & A. Dorchak, *Regulation by Litigation* (Yale University Press 2008); P. Luff, 'Regulating Tobacco through Litigation' (2015) 47 *Arizona State Law Journal* 126; W. Wagner, 'When All Else Fails: Regulating Risky Products Through Tort

problem, however, is that, as things stand now, the picture about the macro effects possibly resulting from climate change litigation is not complete. Nor is there knowledge that convincingly predicts what specific effects may occur as a result of (possible) future rulings in pending cases. In 2022, a review was carried out of 280 publications addressing the impacts of climate change litigation (note: not restricted to corporate climate change litigation).[41] Aside from concluding that much of the literature addresses high-profile cases (according to the authors, these are cases at the highest courts, attracting a lot of media attention or presenting novel legal arguments), the authors conclude that the discussion about the effects of litigation is "typically brief and speculative[,] written close in time to case developments and therefore limited in assessment of longer-term impacts".[42] A telling conclusion of the report is that "existing literature on the impacts of climate change litigation has significant limitations and gaps. There is a pressing need for more in-depth, systematic, and longitudinal studies to provide reliable insights into the types of impacts that may flow from climate change litigation and the circumstances in which such impacts may arise".[43]

It goes without saying that comprehensive and specified (ex ante and ex post) knowledge is crucial for, inter alia, scientists, lawyers, policymakers, and courts to adequately assess and address the possible macro effects of litigation. More specifically for courts, a lack of unequivocal knowledge creates the risk that when they want to consider macro effects of their decision, they do so on the basis of an incomplete factual picture or even on speculation. This

Litigation' (2007) 95 *The Georgetown Law Review* 693, fn 81 with further references; T. D. Lytton, *Using Tort Litigation to Enhance Regulatory Policy Making: Evaluating Climate-Change Litigation in Light of Lessons from Gun-Industry and Clergy-Sexual-Abuse Lawsuits*, (2008) 86 *Texas Law Review* 1837.

41 J. Peel, A. Palmer & R. Markey-Towler, 'Review of Literature on Impacts of Climate Litigation: Report' (London and Melbourne: Children's Investment Fund Foundation and University of Melbourne) <https://www.unimelb.edu.au/__data/assets/pdf_file/0008/4238450/Impact-lit-review-report_CIFF_Final_27052022.pdf>.

42 Peel, Palmer & Markey-Towler, 'Review of Literature on Impacts of Climate Litigation: Report' (London and Melbourne: Children's Investment Fund Foundation and University of Melbourne) <https://www.unimelb.edu.au/__data/assets/pdf_file/0008/4238450/Impact-lit-review-report_CIFF_Final_27052022.pdf> 18.

43 Peel, Palmer & Markey-Towler, 'Review of Literature on Impacts of Climate Litigation: Report' (London and Melbourne: Children's Investment Fund Foundation and University of Melbourne) <https://www.unimelb.edu.au/__data/assets/pdf_file/0008/4238450/Impact-lit-review-report_CIFF_Final_27052022.pdf> 28.

issue may have also played a role in the *Shell* case on appeal, where the court reasoned that even a possible signaling function of a judicial decision does not alter its conclusion that a court order is not effective.[44] Consequently, the court's assessment of whether an injunction is effective is primarily grounded in the potential occurrence of substitution effects. From an empirical perspective, this approach is problematic because it overlooks other possible effects that could be relevant to the effectiveness of the reduction order. By focusing narrowly on substitution effects, other effects that might enhance the efficacy of litigation in addressing climate change are not considered.

In response to the first challenge, one could argue that more knowledge is needed to enable the judge to make an adequate assessment. This brings me to the second challenge. There are important methodological constraints in understanding the relationship between macro effects and court rulings. Generally speaking, it is notoriously difficult to identify links between (the threat of) litigation and governmental or corporate behavior, if only because the behavior of actors is determined by a "complex interplay of causal factors and feedback effects that can prompt and shape policy-making activity".[45] Probably, the best we can do is predict why certain effects are highly likely or unlikely based on extrapolation of existing empirical data in combination with certain policy and empirical theories about corporate behavior. In addition, there is as yet no widely accepted method for assessing the link between (corporate and governmental) climate change governance, specific macro effects, and a particular climate change case or set of cases. This is not to say that it is impossible to get a picture of specific macro effects of judicial decisions: after all, there are studies available that do adequately address the relationship between litigation and specific effects.[46] Moreover, qualitative research can also provide insights into the perceptions of actors, such as corporate decision makers, of the impact of litigation on corporate climate change governance.[47]

---

[44] See section 2.

[45] Unfortunately, there is only thin empirical evidence available about the real behavioral effects of tort law in general and, particularly, in relation to specific behavior. This is partly due to the challenges empirical researchers face in establishing clear causal links between tort law and behavior, and to filter out other relevant behavior-modifying factors (such as the availability of insurance and heuristics and biases). See W. J. Cardi, R. D. Penfield & A. H. Yoon, 'Does Tort Law Deter Individuals?' (2013) 9 *Journal of Empirical Legal Studies* 567.

[46] See section 2.

[47] For further reflection, see J. Peel & H. M. Osofsky, 'Litigation as a Climate Regulatory Tool' in C. Voigt (ed), *International Judicial Practice on the Environment: Questions of Legitimacy* (Studies on International Courts and Tribunals, Cambridge University Press 2019) 328. See also Peel, Palmer &

However, it remains methodologically difficult, maybe even impossible, to get a *comprehensive* overview of macro effects of climate change litigation.[48] This creates the risk of cherry picking when assessing the potential macro effects of a court ruling, largely because empirical research into the effects of (tort law) litigation is ex post in nature: it often looks at the effects of completed litigation. If the court is asked to consider possible macro effects during the adjudication of a case, and hence during the decision-making process, it will also need to get a prospective picture of possible future macro effects prior to its ruling. In doing so, the court will be required to work with scenarios that address the relationship between various changing societal, economic, and regulatory conditions and the possible outcomes in the case before the court. Partly due to a lack of an adequate methodology, it is questionable whether this will provide reliable and adequate insights.[49] In addition, there are also procedural and practical objections: the research will probably impose an unacceptable burden on the proceedings and may lead to unacceptable delays. Consider debates about who draws up, oversees, and carries out the research, as well as about the substantive scenarios to be used. Finally, there is the fundamental objection that to meaningfully shape the various scenarios, the court must provide insight into its views on the legal issues before it and the possible ways of assessing these issues.

The third challenge relates to the principle of party autonomy, a central element of civil procedure in Dutch law and many other jurisdictions. It arises from the fact that litigants determine the scope of the legal dispute as well as which facts are considered in assessing their legal dispute. As a consequence, the input of information about macro effects is primarily the litigants' responsibility. Thus, to estimate the macro effects, the court depends on macro information provided by the litigants and has, generally speaking, limited possibilities to collect its own empirical data or scientific evidence.

The problem is that the litigants might not have an incentive or interest to fully bring forward the information about macro effects that is available to

---

Markey-Towler, 'Review of Literature on Impacts of Climate Litigation: Report' (London and Melbourne: Children's Investment Fund Foundation and University of Melbourne) <https://www.unimelb.edu.au/__data/assets/pdf_file/0008/4238450/Impact-lit-review-report_CIFF_Final_27052022.pdf> 28.

[48] See for a possible methodological model: T. D. Lytton, 'Using Tort Litigation to Enhance Regulatory Policy Making: Evaluating Climate-Change Litigation in Light of Lessons from Gun-Industry and Clergy-Sexual-Abuse Lawsuits' (2008) 86 *Texas Law Review* 1837.

[49] In the first instance ruling in the *Shell* case, for example, the court could not have foreseen the outbreak of the war in Ukraine and the following energy crisis, an external circumstance that undoubtedly affects climate governance.

them. This danger arises with macro information that the parties do not consider directly relevant for deciding the legal issues at hand or that does not support their legal argumentation. For example, an oil company that is a defendant in a mitigation case has an interest in bringing forward the argument that tort law intervention might create substitution effects, but not that it might also create other incentives that are beneficial for global emission reductions. As a consequence, the question is whether – even when the macro information is generally available – the litigants will provide all the relevant information needed to gain a comprehensive understanding of the macro effects of possible court decisions.[50] Also, there is a risk that the litigants generally point out the potential macro effects of a (proposed) decision or only summarily provide the necessary information, thereby leaving it unclear how the general macro information relates to the specific issues in the case at hand. All this raises questions about the reliability and comprehensiveness of the macro information that has been submitted to the court. This challenge can, of course, be addressed by appointing experts or exploring the possibilities of amicus curiae.[51] To a certain extent, these options might be helpful. However, in this case, the lack of general knowledge about the actual and potential macro consequences discussed in section 3 cannot be fully overcome by the experts or amici and hence might still pose a problem.

4. ASSESSING IMPACT INFORMATION: THE UNCERTAINTY AND EXPERT PARADOX

The last challenge relates to estimating and assessing, among other things, the completeness, reliability, and substantive implications of the information concerning macro effects of judicial decisions. A study on the use of climate science insights in climate litigation comes to the telling conclusion that "evidence submitted and referred to in climate change litigation lags considerably behind the state of the art in climate science".[52] In part, this is because the

[50] See already P. Cane, 'Tort Law as Regulation' (2002) 31 *Common Law World Review* 305, 313.

[51] Under Dutch law the possibilities for amicus curiae are limited to preliminary question proceedings before the Supreme Court (Article 393 section 2 Code of Civil Procedure) and cassation proceedings in the interest of the law.

[52] R. F. Stuart-Smith, F. E. L. Otto, A. I. Saad, G. Lisi, P. Minnerop, K. C. Lauta, K. van Zwieten & T. Wetzer, 'Filling the Evidentiary Gap in Climate Litigation' (2021) 11 *Nature Climate Change* 651. On the further implications of this, and possible solutions, see F. E. L. Otto, P. Minnerop, E. Raju, L. J. Harrington, R. F. Stuart-Smith, E. Boyd, R. James, R. Jones & K. C. Lauta, 'Causality and the Fate

parties (see above in section 3) submit incomplete information or present the information scientifically incorrectly, either consciously or unconsciously. In part, according to this study, courts would also make incorrect assumptions about the relevance and reliability of climate science insights. The study does not deal specifically with the use of macro information, but it nevertheless indicates problems that are relevant in that context.

A recurrent challenge is that both the parties and the court must assess complex and uncertain information for which they often lack the required subject matter expertise. Partly because of this lack of subject matter expertise, the judge faces uncertainty and expert paradoxes when understanding and assessing macro information.[53] To adequately take the possible macro effects into account, a judge needs clear and understandable information as well as sufficient certainty about the potential effects involved. However, that information is only available to a limited extent and, moreover, difficult to obtain (see section 3). In that case, the impact information that is available could also lead to the conclusion that, given the current knowledge gaps, there is much uncertainty about the potential macro effects of a particular court ruling.

In finding a solution to this uncertainty paradox, an expertise paradox may arise. When courts consult scientific literature or experts to obtain the desired clarity and certainty, that consultation would also point towards the relevant uncertainties or ambiguities, because scientists and the scientific literature will stress the lack of knowledge and the uncertainties and ambiguities that are inherent to the scientific state of the art (see again section 3). In addition, conclusions about the potential impact of the case at hand will not arise directly from the available macro information. After all, it is unlikely that specific studies have already been carried out on the impact of pending or completed litigation (see section 3). Therefore, there will always be "knowledge gaps" between the available impact information and the specific inferences drawn as to the significance of that knowledge for the case at hand. Drawing conclusions about the potential impact in that situation therefore requires an inference to the best explanation. This means that distinct causal pathways and explanations about the relationship between climate change litigation in general and particular remedies in the case at issue before the court must be made. Subsequently,

of Climate Litigation: The Role of the Social Superstructure Narrative' (2022) 13 *Global Policy* 736.

53 The notion of the uncertainty paradox has been derived from E. Vos, 'The European Court of Justice in the face of scientific uncertainty and complexity' in M. Dawson, B. De Witte & E. Muir (eds), *Judicial Activism at the European Court of Justice* (Edward Elgar 2013). For a discussion of the uncertainty paradox in the context of European law, see M. B. A. van Asselt & E. Vos, 'The Precautionary Principle and the Uncertainty Paradox' (2006) 9 *Journal of Risk Research* 313.

these causal pathways and explanations need to be ranked in terms of validity, likelihood, and probability. Because of the existence of knowledge gaps, this ranking always involves a degree of *expert judgment*. The challenge for a judge, who is not an expert, is to avoid entering this inference to the best explanation on improper or even non-scientific grounds.

The aforementioned issue may pose significant lawmaking challenges, possibly leading to judicial restraint in amplifying norms. This is partly the case because the issue of assessing scientific uncertainty is a relatively new phenomenon and there is no clarity yet on the legal framework that is relevant in this context. The discussion in the *Shell* case on the reduction target and pathway that applies to Shell is illustrative of this problem.[54] As discussed in section 2, there is no applicable legislation containing reduction targets and pathways for specific corporations or sectors. Also, the court concluded that the global average reduction target of 45% reduction by 2030 cannot be applied to a specific sector. Therefore, the court examined, on the basis of expert evidence presented to it, whether scientific consensus exists regarding the reduction target applicable to the oil and gas sector. Uncertainties and disagreements among scientists about the appropriate reduction pathways and targets are inherent to climate science, which raises the question whether the degree of consensus among scientists is indeed the right criterion (aside from the question of how consensus is determined). A follow-up question is to what exactly the consensus should pertain: should it concern the most cost-effective reduction pathway at sectoral and societal levels, the minimum required reduction, the pathway that is most economically viable for the corporation, or the pathway most aligned with the precautionary principle?[55] In my view, the answer to that question remains open.

---

[54] Although determining a reduction target and pathway is a different issue than assessing macro effects, the underlying challenge of dealing with scientific uncertainties is the same.

[55] In para. 7.95, the court considers that the precautionary principle applies to situations where the effects of certain actions are uncertain, but not to situations where the applicable standard is unclear. For this reason, the court does not take the precautionary principle into account when determining the reduction target. However, the precautionary principle provides a framework for standard setting in cases of scientific uncertainty related to risks. The relevant uncertainties may pertain to various aspects of a risk, such as the potential effects, the causes of those effects, the timeframe within which they may occur, and the measures needed to prevent them. Particularly in the context of climate change, uncertainty and ambiguity about the measures to be taken are always present, while it is unequivocally clear that severe and irreversible damage is imminent (and already occurring).

5. CONCLUSION

In climate change litigation, macro effects play a central role. First of all, a characteristic of these cases is that courts are used as vehicles for societal change, and hence for creating all kinds of macro effects. Secondly, due to the nature of the causes of climate change (i.e., activities that are an integral part of our societal and economic infrastructure), cases dealing with mitigation responsibilities undeniably create effects that transcend the litigants. As stated at the beginning of this chapter, some argue that the role of tort law and civil courts in the context of climate change mitigation should be limited because of such effects, in particular because the use of tort law might create negative side effects or even be counterproductive. However, when looking into the current knowledge available about the effects of mitigation litigation, the question is whether the plea for judicial restraint is empirically justified. In general, litigation can have both positive and negative effects on meeting reduction goals. Yet we lack a comprehensive picture of the specific effects that occurred and could occur due to specific climate change litigation. In any event, there is no conclusive empirical argument for restricting tort law on the grounds that it creates unintended side effects, is ineffective, or counterproductive. Nonetheless, in specific cases, courts might need to take possible macro effects into account; for example, because one of the parties brings forward arguments related to such effects. Thus, courts cannot simply close their eyes to potential macro effects. However, courts face several challenges in gaining sufficient and adequate insight into specific macro effects, challenges that undermine the empirical soundness of their assessment. These challenges and, more importantly, how to address them are underexplored. Given the fact that climate change mitigation litigation is there to stay, identifying both procedural and substantive law strategies for courts to address the lack of macro information and the uncertainties surrounding it is paramount.

The precautionary principle is largely based on the recognition 1) that uncertainty about, among other things, the necessary measures is often falsely used as a reason for the postponement of taking (sufficient and timely) action; 2) there is a need to counter this dynamic; because 3) experience shows that in cases of health and environmental risks, precautionary measures are usually taken too late and are often insufficient; with 4) severe and irreversible damage as a result. It is therefore arguable that the court should have examined whether Shell is using scientific uncertainty about the reduction pathways as an unacceptable justification for failing to reduce emissions to a level necessary to prevent or minimize severe and irreversible climate damage. In this light, it is also notable that the court does not establish a minimum reduction target for Shell. For further discussion of the precautionary principle in relation to various uncertainties, see E. R. de Jong, *Voorzorgverplichtingen* (diss. UU), The Hague: Boom Juridisch 2016.

10. Climate science and the courts—science takers or science makers?

J.B. Ruhl

INTRODUCTION

What role have courts played in the production of climate science to support climate change mitigation and adaptation? What role should they play? Litigation regarding the causes and consequences of climate change has exploded in courts around the world.[1] This trend necessarily inserts questions of science into the judicial decision-making process. For example, in a study of over 600 US court decisions involving climate change issues decided from 1990 through 2016, McCormick et al. found an increasing trend of science generally being a central factor in shaping a court's decision.[2] Climate science, specifically, was a presence (partial or central) in 40 percent of those decisions.

The upward trend in climate change litigation is likely to continue as litigants turn to the courts either to press for more actions by political and regulatory institutions to regulate greenhouse gas (GHG) emissions, or to push back against such actions. In addition, a building wave of litigation in many nations attempts to attach tort and other forms of liability for the consequences of climate change to sources of GHG emissions, such as large fossil fuel and energy production companies.[3] Hence, we can expect a steady and building diet of climate science for courts thrust into the climate litigation fray.

---

[1] The Sabin Center for Climate Change Law at Columbia University Law School maintains and regularly updates a database of ongoing and concluded climate change litigation matters including, as of this writing, over 1,400 US judicial litigation matters and 560 judicial litigation matters in other nations. See http://climatecasechart.com/about/ [hereinafter Sabin Center Database].

[2] Sabrina McCormick et al., *Science in Litigation, the Third Branch of U.S. Climate Policy*, 357 SCIENCE 979 (2017).

[3] *See* Karen C. Sokol, *Seeking (Some) Climate Justice in State Tort Law*, 95 WASH. L. REV. 1383 (2020) (providing a history and overview through 2020); Jacqueline Peel, Hari Osofsky & Anita Foerster, *Shaping the "Next Generation"*

The relevant science, however, presents difficult issues for courts. Some aspects of climate science enjoy high degrees of certainty, but in some contexts that certainty can confound judicial decision making. Other aspects of climate science have high degrees of uncertainty, which also is problematic for courts asked to weigh in on questions of agency action or corporate liability.

This chapter explores how courts have grappled with permutations of climate science certainty and uncertainty and how courts could use mechanisms, such as precautionary principles and statutory interpretations, to better navigate through them when the science is contested in litigation. The analysis focuses on US federal court cases, particularly those decided during the first Trump Administration, which downplayed climate change and was openly hostile to regulation of GHG emission sources. McCormick et al. ended their study in 2016, immediately before the first Trump Administration took office, but predicted that a "spate of litigation is likely if federal agencies ignore or give short shrift to climate effects" and that "litigants in such cases will need to muster scientific support for their claims that agencies arbitrarily ignored climate issues".[4] Indeed, a 2021 study found over 375 climate change litigation matters filed or resolved during the first Trump Administration's four-year term, many of which involved questions of how regulatory agencies used climate change science.[5] And with the political branches backing out of taking action on climate change during the period of the first Trump Administration, one could also expect to find intensified litigation efforts to force government action and to impose tort liability on private actors as well, such as the growing number of cases US municipalities and environmental non-governmental organizations (ENGOs) have brought against energy companies.[6] Although by no means has climate science dropped out of the judicial arena, the Trump era thus appears to have especially put climate science in the judicial spotlight.

The discussion proceeds in four sections. The first section generally discusses the role of courts in managing the production of science. I distinguish between judicial neutrality regarding how substantive and procedural rules

---

of Climate Change Litigation in Australia, 41 MELBOURNE U. L. REV. 793 (2017). *See also* Sabin Center Database, *supra*, Common Law Claims, http://climatecasechart.com/case-category/common-law-claims/. For a review of the role of science in these cases, see Rupert F. Stuart-Smith, *Filling the Evidence Gap in Climate Litigation*, 11 NATURE CLIMATE CHANGE 651 (2021).

4 McCormick et al., *supra*, at 980.

5 Korey Silverman-Roati, Sabin Center for Climate Change Law, U.S. Climate Litigation in the Age of Trump: Full Term (2021).

6 This appears to have been the trend. *See* Sabin Center Database, *supra*, Common Law Claims, http://climatecasechart.com/case-category/common-law-claims/.

courts design influence the production and advancement of science, which I will call "science taking", versus a practice of designing such rules based at least in part on how they influence science, which I will call "science making". The second section uses a case study of a proposed port facility to match climate science with practical regulatory and liability contexts, showing where certainty and uncertainty are found in the science and their effects on regulatory and judicial decision making, and using representative examples of cases decided under the US National Environmental Policy Act (NEPA) and Endangered Species Act (ESA), both of which require federal agencies to assess the impacts of their actions (including actions of entities receiving federal permits) on environmental resources. The third section then describes how courts have managed issues of certainty and uncertainty in climate science in regulatory contexts. This analysis then extends beyond the NEPA and ESA regulatory statutes to the constitutional and tort liability litigation contexts. Following that case law discussion, the last section outlines some methods courts could employ to take more active roles in the making of climate science. The conclusion provides a normative assessment of how courts should choose between science taking and science making in the context of climate change litigation.

COURTS AS SCIENCE TAKERS OR MAKERS

Courts are voracious consumers of science. To be sure, by no means are courts simply consumers, passively accepting and using whatever science comes into the courtroom. Rather, legal scholars routinely describe courts as "gatekeepers" of science, deciding first what science to allow into evidence through a variety of mechanisms, and only then managing the admitted science as part of the body of factual evidence fed into the applicable legal doctrine. But Sheila Jasanoff has suggested that courts do more, describing courts as "sites of translation" at which science is transformed into evidence relevant to legal decision making.[7] But what happens on the court translation side of the gate necessarily influences what happens on the science production side. For example, as Jasanoff explains, judges decide whether legal issues demand expert testimony and, if so, whether a particular expert's science is entitled to consideration. These decisions ratify and privilege some scientific methods and practices over others, which surely will not go unnoticed by scientists and the litigants seeking their expert testimony. Going even further, Ziaja and Fullerton argue that in contexts where science plays a large role in explaining

---

[7] Sheila Jasanoff, *Science, Common Sense, & Judicial Powers in U.S. Courts*, 147 Daedalus 15 (2018).

complexity and uncertainty, as it does pervasively in fields such as environmental law, this two-way effect puts courts in the position of a boundary organization mediating between science and policy.[8] As "major arenas for science-informed decision-making", courts "can become deeply emmeshed in the scientific complexities ... to the point where they guide and inform the process of socially relevant science production".[9] Ziaja and Fullerton identify three roles courts take on in this process. First, by making policy, such as through statutory interpretation, courts shape the production of science necessary for effectuating that policy.[10] Second, they point to the familiar gatekeeper role discussed previously.[11] Third, they argue that courts manage science production through procedural decisions, such as placing timelines on agency decision making, and substantive decisions, such as how to treat uncertainty under applicable legal doctrine.[12]

Here, I unpack these boundary roles into two broad modes of practice, *taker* and *maker*. Courts act as science takers when they make science management and other decisions within their authority without considering the influence those decisions have on science production. Courts in this mode are focused entirely on the court side of the "gate", designing and applying doctrines such as deference to agencies and burdens of proof to decide which party prevails when the science is contested. Those design decisions manage how and what science is used in litigation, but a science *taker* court does not also consider their direct or incidental effects on science production when making those design decisions.

By contrast, a court acts as a science maker when it reaches across the gate boundary by taking science production effects into account when making those design decisions, with the objective of advancing and improving the science available to its decision making. To be clear, science making by courts, as I frame it, remains focused on the court side of the gate, with the self-interested goal of improving the science available to courts in resolving issues riddled with complexity and uncertainty. The difference is that a science making court takes an active and intentional role in improving the science, albeit through management of practices and doctrines operating on the court side of the gate.

Science making is not the same as courts practicing and producing science, a role usually seen as outside their legitimate domain, but rather one of courts

---

8 Sonya Ziaja & Christopher Fullerton, *Judging Science: The Rewards and Perils of Courts as Boundary Organizations*, 21 HASTINGS WEST NORTHWEST JOURNAL OF ENVIRONMENTAL LAW & POLICY 217 (2015).

9 *Id.* at 223–34.

10 *Id.* at 225–27.

11 *Id.* at 228–36.

12 *Id.* at 236–40.

intentionally prodding the production of science by others—agencies, companies, advocacy organizations, cities—who are involved in science-driven litigation. Nor does science making presume choosing sides in the design decisions—plaintiffs versus defendants—but rather focuses solely on the benefit to courts in their role as adjudicators of science-laden litigation disputes. Science making also must be practiced within the constraints of judicial practice and applicable law. Even with those caveats, however, courts adopting a science making posture could have a profound influence on climate science production. The question is whether they should. To build out this framework, one can envision courts taking different roles along a spectrum of science taking and making, as follows:

Avoider: Courts can altogether avoid the taking or making of science through mechanisms that block access to the judicial forum. In the US climate change litigation context, for example, some courts have dismissed liability claims based on a finding of nonjusticiability, such as applying the political question doctrine on the basis that regulating GHG emissions is a matter for legislatures, not courts.[13]

Observer: Judges do not necessarily need or desire to erect a gate to exercise any control over what science enters the judicial forum. They could, for example, allow parties to present whatever science they want and let juries sift through and evaluate as they see fit. To a large extent, courts act initially as observers in litigation involving judicial review of administrative agency action—they typically do not constrain the scientific evidence parties entered into the administrative record and advance into the judicial review stage. But ultimately, the judicial review court must make determinations regarding whether the science supports the agency decision within the applicable standard of review (e.g., substantial evidence), which involves more than observer status.

Gatekeeper: Gatekeeping involves the traditional "boundary" concept of filtering what science is allowed into the judicial process based on qualitative factors, such as through the *Daubert* rule applied in US federal courts.[14] In its classic sense, the gatekeeper court is focused solely on the judicial side of the gate, notwithstanding that it could incidentally influence how science is conducted and packaged on the science production side to satisfy the gatekeeping standards.[15]

Translator: This function captures Jasanoff's conception of courts as "sites of translation" at which science is transformed into evidence relevant to legal

---

[13] *See, e.g.*, *Juliana v. United States*, 947 F.3d 1159 (9th Cir. 2020).

[14] *See* Stephen Breyer, *Science in the Courtroom*, XVI (4) Issues in Science and Technology (2000).

[15] As suggested by Ziaja & Fullerton, *supra*, at 228–36.

decision making.[16] Examples include jury instructions that explain what science the jury should take into account, and written opinions in liability and regulatory litigation matters summarizing the scientific evidence. Even without intention, the ways and language through which a court translates science could influence science production.

Evaluator: In many contexts, courts must evaluate the science that has been accepted into the judicial forum. For example, some US regulatory statutes expressly require agencies to base decisions on the "best available science", requiring a reviewing court to explicitly evaluate whether the science the agency used meets that standard. When those statutory regimes involve "repeat player" dynamics, under which the agency action type is frequently subject to judicial review litigation, those evaluations over time can substantially influence how the agency produces and packages its scientific evidence.[17]

Publisher: When courts publish decisions in litigation with substantial scientific content, they could limit their discussion of the science to a translation function, providing only as much discussion as needed to explain the court's evaluation and decision reasoning. But a court could make intentional decisions, reflected in the translation and the evaluation of the science involved, to influence science production. For example, a court finding an agency decision unsupported by the science the agency used could devote considerable attention to the reasons why the science was insufficient with the intention of sending a message to the agency about its future science production methods for similar actions, such as issuing regulatory permits that must comply with environmental quality standards.

Influencer: Many legal questions inherently are scientific questions, such as whether an area is a "wetland" or other type of habitat subject to regulatory jurisdiction under environmental statutes. As Jamison Colburn puts it, "laws make some facts relevant and thus can exert a kind of demand-pull on scientists".[18] Courts play an important role in this effect. Courts often describe the kind of scientific information they need in order to apply legal tests. For example, the US Supreme Court recently articulated the factors determining whether a discharge of a pollutant into groundwater in subject to regulation if the pollutant eventually seeps into a nearby surface water body, with many of those factors requiring production of scientific data.[19] Similarly, through statutory interpretation that alters legal standards, broadening or narrowing

---

16 Jasanoff, *supra*, at 15.

17 *See* Elizabeth Fisher, Pasky Pascual & Wendy Wagner, *Rethinking Judicial Review of Expert Agencies*, 93 TEX. L. REV 1681 (2015).

18 Jamison E. Colburn, *To Limit Air Pollution's Risks: A Law/Science Success Story*, 41 VIRGINIA ENVT'L L. REV. 114, 115 (2023).

19 *County of Maui v. Hawaii Wildlife Fund*, 140 S. Ct. 1462 (2020).

their scope, courts can influence which facts are relevant. In both instances, the judicial action influences the production of science designed to respond to the legal requirements.

Producer: Although it would be unusual for a court to conduct scientific research itself to assist in the resolution of a dispute—i.e., to directly produce science—it is not necessarily universally prohibited. Court-appointed experts, who generally are employed to assist a court in translating or evaluating science, might engage in literature reviews like those often published in scientific journals.[20] Still, that falls short of conducting scientific experiments and other forms of science production. We can include production in the spectrum, therefore, as more of a bookend, with *avoider* defining the opposite extreme.

CERTAINTY AND UNCERTAINTY IN CLIMATE SCIENCE

The modes of science taking and making described in the first part are most relevant when science over a domain is evolving and uncertainties dominate—that is when the role of courts in the production of science to reduce uncertainty is put into play, if it is at all. Climate change is revealing both what we know about climate science and what we did not know—it is fraught with certainties and uncertainties. Courts administering litigation involving climate science thus face the challenge of how to manage a broad span of scientific certainty.[21]

To unpack the complications this presents in a practical context, consider a company that wishes to build a coastal port shipping facility that will require government permit approvals. In many nations the agency administering the permit program must conduct an environmental impact assessment (EIA), such as under the US National Environmental Policy Act, and litigants establishing standing to sue can challenge the merits of the EIA in a judicial forum. Although the port facility will use renewable energy sources for some of its activities, it will be the source of some GHG emissions (e.g., ships docking; heavy vehicles using diesel fuel) and fossil fuels such as coal and liquefied natural gas will be shipped through the port on the way to their final use and burning. The facility location is also near a marine reserve and coastal residential developments.

Now consider the permit-issuing agency's EIA for the facility. On the one hand, it is certain that GHG emissions contribute to climate change—that is a scientific fact. If the agency failed to acknowledge this in its EIA, therefore,

---

20 *See* Daniel L. Rubinfeld & Joe S. Cecil, *Scientists as Experts Serving the Court*, 147(4) DAEDALUS 152 (2018).

21 For a summary see Jamison, supra, at 118.

a court could find that the EIA was defective. On the other hand, it is also certain that the GHG emissions directly attributable to the facility's operations will have a minuscule effect on climate change in the grand scheme of things. Beyond requiring that the EIA acknowledge that the facility will emit greenhouse gases, and perhaps requiring those emissions to be quantified, this scientific certainty confounds efforts to require that an EIA attribute the precise impact of its *particular* emissions on the climate. On the other hand, fossil fuels being shipped through the facility will eventually be burned and will then generate GHG emissions, likely many times more than the facility's direct emissions. How should the EIA for the port facility take those indirect emissions into account?

Consider also how assessments like these would play out in private liability claims that the facility's GHG emissions will cause specific climate-related harms, such as degradation of the marine preserve or flooding in the residential areas. It is a scientific certainty that climate change can have those effects, but it is also a scientific certainty that a ton of GHG emissions from the facility has the same causal effect in that local context as a ton of GHG emissions from a facility on another continent. Attributing tort or other forms of liability to the port facility for those local impacts thus would be difficult to justify—all emissions sources around the globe share in the causation, and every molecule of carbon dioxide is equally to blame. The same would be true of the GHG emissions from the fossil fuels shipped through the facility and later consumed.

This double-edged sword of certainty helps explain the finding McCormick et al. made that the role of science in climate change litigation exhibits context-specific variation.[22] The macro-level certainty that GHG emissions influence climate can support standing for litigants claiming injury and supports large-scale findings such as that climate change is affecting an endangered species, but the micro-level certainty that all GHGs contribute equally to climate change regardless of location of emission or impact has been an obstacle to going much further with respect to agency EIAs and tort liability claims. We can add to that the problems associated with scientific *un*certainty. In the case of the port facility, for example, the types of impacts to which GHG emissions will contribute generally may be well established—such as sea-level rise and rising temperatures—but the extent at any location may not be. It is scientifically certain that climate change is causing some degree of sea-level rise, posing potential risks to the coastal community as well as to the facility itself. The agency's EIA thus should acknowledge that sea-level rise could present flooding and other problems for the area around the port over the long term, and that the port could be designed to minimize impacts from those issues, perhaps by

22 McCormick et al., *supra*, at 980.

incorporating a seawall. But how high and where should the seawall be? That depends on how high the sea rises, which depends on how far global warming advances and many other factors for which scientific certainty is lacking to some or a significant degree. To summarize, climate science is a broad field in which varying degrees of certainty define different features of the mechanisms and impacts of climate change:

Higher Certainty Features:

- Burning fossil fuels emits GHGs.
- GHGs disperse globally through the atmosphere.
- Increasing concentrations of GHGs contribute to increasing temperatures over land surfaces and water bodies.
- Increasing temperatures disrupt global climate patterns.
- All molecules of GHGs contribute equally to those disruptions regardless of place of emission.

Lower Certainty Features:

- The sensitivity of temperature changes to increasing GHG concentrations.
- The degree and intensity of climate disruption impacts at local scales at different increases in temperature.
- Potential nonlinear tipping points in biophysical processes as temperatures rise.

SCIENCE TAKING AND MAKING IN CLIMATE CHANGE LITIGATION

Climate change litigation takes many forms.[23] For purposes of this chapter on climate science and the courts, that universe can be simplified into three buckets—(1) regulatory decision litigation; (2) governance failure litigation; and (3) harms liability litigation. Regulatory decision litigation involves claims that an administrative agency has improperly implemented its authority in some regulatory context, such as a rulemaking or issuance of a permit. The other two forms of climate litigation arose and have been fueled by dissatisfaction with the progress of regulatory initiatives and implementation, which

---

[23] The Sabin Center Database, *supra*, includes numerous categories. *See also* Dave Markell & J.B. Ruhl, *An Empirical Survey of Climate Change in the Courts: A New Jurisprudence or Business as Usual*, 64 FLORIDA LAW REVIEW 15, 30–38 (2012) (describing a typology of litigation claim types).

in the US became acutely apparent during the first Trump Administration. Governance failure litigation involves claims that political governance institutions (e.g., Congress in the US) have failed to take sufficient action to arrest climate change in violation of some constitutive duty (e.g., public trust doctrine) or protected right (e.g., right to a clean environment). Harms liability litigation involves claims that a public or private actor responsible for GHG emissions has caused harm (e.g., damage from sea-level rise) for which the plaintiff can seek some form of injunctive or damages remedy. The following sections provide a brief survey of the most substantial contexts in which climate science is playing or unquestionably will play an increasingly important role in these three litigation realms.

A. Regulatory Decision Litigation

In its landmark 2007 majority opinion in *Massachusetts v. EPA*,[24] the US Supreme Court pointed to the work of "respected scientists" to conclude that the rise in global temperatures has coincided with, and is related to, a significant increase in the concentration of carbon dioxide in the atmosphere. The Court traced the history of federal scientific research on climate change to support its ruling that the EPA has statutory authority under the Clean Air Act to regulate carbon dioxide as a pollutant. Although this was not the first instance of a US court turning to climate science to guide its judicial review of agency action—regulatory decision litigation had been underway in the US since the mid-1990s—it legitimized, if not implicitly required, the courts' careful use of climate science. By no means, however, has climate science been as straightforward in application as it was in *Massachusetts v. EPA*, where all that mattered was whether increased GHG emissions are contributing to climate change, which they are with a high degree of certainty. The certainty/uncertainty factor has particularly driven judicial decision making under NEPA and the ESA in two contexts—defining GHG emission footprints and evaluating climate change impacts.

An important component of climate science for regulatory purposes focuses on the science of GHG emissions. The more that is known about GHG emissions, the better climate scientists can model climate trends and the better policy makers can design regulatory tools. This has both qualitative and quantitative dimensions. The qualitative aspect involves defining what emissions to attribute to a particular source. For example, in NEPA cases involving federal agency permitting of fossil fuel production and transportation facilities, courts increasingly required the permitting agency to include in their environmental

24 *Massachusetts v. EPA*, 549 U.S. 497 (2007).

assessment so-called "downstream" indirect emissions from the users of the fuel, such as coal and gas-fired power generation facilities.[25] Requiring this kind of analysis improves understanding of how and how much carbon and methane move through production and supply chains to ultimate use (burning) and transformation into GHGs. Courts also increasingly required NEPA analyses to quantify direct and indirect GHG emissions where doing so is data-based and not speculative.[26] As one court put it, once the volume of fuel to be burned is known, estimating GHG emissions is fairly straightforward.[27] Courts have been less demanding regarding estimation of cumulative emissions—emissions from other sources that aggregate with the source under NEPA impact assessment—given difficulties of reliably identifying and assessing them, especially at global scales.[28]

The clear trend under NEPA, therefore, was for courts to demand robust qualitative and quantitative assessment of a facility's direct and indirect "emissions footprint". This interpretation of NEPA's requirements, which the US Supreme Court recently narrowed,[29] was an example of a design decision having science production effects, although in none of the judicial opinions has any court described that as an objective of the statutory interpretation. As more sophisticated techniques are developed for estimating cumulative impacts—which is a key input in climate modeling—courts reviewing EIAs likely would demand the same. In this sense, the degree of certainty regarding the emissions footprint of actions reviewed under NEPA led US courts to calibrate how strictly to apply their review of the agency's assessment. In other words, courts used scientific certainty to push more robust scientific analysis by agencies.

Describing the movement of carbon through supply chains and estimating GHG emissions from known volumes of fuel enjoy high degrees of certainty.

---

25 *Ctr. for Biological Diversity v. Bernhardt*, 982 F.3d 723 (9th Cir. 2020); *WildEarth Guardians v. Zinke*, 368 F.Supp.3d 41 (D.D.C. 2019); *Western Organization of Resource Councils v. U.S. Bureau of Land Mgmt.*, 2018 WL 1475470 (D. Mont. 2018); *Sierra Club v. Fed. Energy Regul. Comm'n*, 867 F.3d 1357 (D.C. 2017).

26 *Ctr. for Biological Diversity v. Bernhardt*, 982 F.3d 723 (9th Cir. 2020); *WildEarth Guardians v. Zinke*, 368 F.Supp.3d 41 (D.D.C. 2019); *Wilderness Workshop v. U.S. Bureau of Land Mgmt.*, 342 F.Supp.3d 1145 (D. Colo. 2018).

27 *Sierra Club v. Fed. Energy Regul. Comm'n*, 867 F.3d 1357 (D.C. 2017).

28 *Compare Wilderness Workshop v. U.S. Bureau of Land Mgmt.*, 342 F.Supp.3d 1145 (D. Colo. 2018) (cumulative emissions are less foreseeable), with *WildEarth Guardians v. Bernhardt*, 502 F.Supp.3d 237 (D.C. 2020) (agency must do more to quantify regional and cumulative emissions).

29 *Seven County Infrastructure Coalition v. Eagle County*, 605 U.S. 168 (2025).

Requiring that agencies include that information in EIAs thus is an appropriate judicial intervention. By contrast, courts have thus far been much less inclined to demand more than generalized assessments of the impacts of those emissions. It has usually proven sufficient for agencies to draw from existing impact models performed by other governmental and academic institutions, rather than preparing their own specific prediction of impacts caused by the source under EIA assessment.[30] Similarly, courts have usually been deferential to agency predictions of biophysical impacts of climate change on species protected under the ESA, siding more often than not with agencies' arguments that available data is insufficient to reach detailed conclusions and not meddling with expert agency science.[31] And courts also have deferred to agency decisions not to use the Social Cost of Carbon methodology in assessing the socio-economic impacts of a facility's emissions.[32]

Although courts usually do not expressly delve into the certainty/uncertainty dilemma of climate science, it likely explains the courts' approach on impact assessment. As noted, it is a certainty that burning fossil fuels emits GHGs and that all GHG molecules have an equal impact on climate, but it is much more uncertain what that impact is at any location. Courts thus have shown little patience with agencies that attempt to evade the task of describing and quantifying emissions footprints by hiding behind the uncertainty of impacts. But courts also have shown little patience for plaintiffs' demands that being able to quantify emissions with precision means agencies must identify impacts with precision.

There are exceptions to this general trend of deference to agency decisions regarding climate change impacts. A research team recently conducted an extensive study of NEPA and ESA cases involving claims that agencies

---

30 *WildEarth Guardians v. Bernhardt*, 501 F.Supp.3d 1192 (D.N.M. 2020) (general local and regional impact assessments were adequate and global cumulative impact assessment is not required); *Sierra Club v. Fed. Energy Regul. Comm'n*, 867 F.3d 1357 (D.C. 2017) (agency is not required to draw connections between the emissions and specific climate impacts).

31 *Turtle Island Restoration Network v. U.S. Dep't of Com*, 878 F.3d 725 (9th Cir. 2017); *Oceana, Inc. v. Ross*, No. 12-0041, 2020 WL 5834832 (D.D.C. 2020); *WildEarth Guardians v. U.S. Fish & Wildlife Serv.*, 416 F.Supp.3d 909 (D. Ariz. 2019); *Alaska Oil and Gas Ass'n v. Ross*, 722 Fed.Appx 666 (9th Cir. 2018).

32 *Sierra Club v. Fed. Energy Regul. Comm'n*, 867 F.3d 1357 (D.C. Cir. 2017); *Utah Physicians for a Healthy Env't v. BLM*, 2021 WL 1140247 1 (D. Utah March 24, 2021); *WildEarth Guardians v. Bernhardt*, 501 F.Supp.3d 1192 (D.N.M. 2020); *Wilderness Workshop v. U.S. Bureau of Land Mgmt.*, 342 F.Supp.3d 1145 (D. Colo. 2018); *Western Organization of Resource Councils v. U.S. Bureau of Land Mgmt.*, 2018 WL 1475470 (D. Mont. 2018).

reached unsupported decisions in an environment of scientific uncertainty.[33] Such claims face stiff barriers given the standard of review federal courts apply to such decisions and the degree of deference courts give to expert agencies on matters of science within their scope of authority. Nevertheless, the study found courts intervening to reverse agency decisions in four contexts: (1) when an agency fails to make a rational connection between the scientific uncertainty and the action it took; (2) when an agency fails to consider an important aspect of the problem before it when conducting its analysis; (3) when the agency decision runs counter to what scientific evidence is available; and (4) when an agency selectively chooses from available scientific evidence to "reverse engineer" a justification for its decision. These categories, however, define flaws in agency decision making, not flaws in the agency science. When agencies reliably outline the available science, cogently describe how uncertainty bears on the decision at hand, and clearly explain how that uncertainty led to the decision made, the study finds courts affording deference to the agency far more often than not. On the other hand, by calling out agency decision making flaws, courts push agencies to engage in that kind of best practices approach to managing scientific uncertainty in regulatory decisions.

B. Governance Failure Litigation

Even before the first Trump Administration reversed course on regulatory initiatives, fueling the regulatory litigation backlash, the boldest form of climate litigation was underway in the form of governance failure claims. The most prominent and successful of these claims is from the Netherlands. In 2013, the Urgenda Foundation sued the Dutch government, arguing it did not meet a minimum carbon dioxide emission-reduction goal established by scientists to avert harmful climate change and was endangering the human rights of Dutch citizens as set by national and European Union laws.[34] The District Court's 2015 opinion upholding the claim included an extensive review of climate science, none of which the government contested.[35] Rather, the government's position was that it has no duty to regulate GHG emissions to any prescribed level and that the controversy was in any event nonjusticiable as

---

33 Daniel Kim, Robert L. Glicksman & Keziah Groth-Tuft, *Judicial Review of Scientific Uncertainty in Climate Change Lawsuits: Deferential and Nondeferential Evaluation of Agency Factual and Policy Determinations*, 46 Harvard Environmental Law Review 367 (2022).

34 *State of the Netherlands v. Urgenda Foundation*, ECLI:NL:HR:2019:2007, Judgment (Sup. Ct. Neth. Dec. 20, 2019) (Neth.).

35 *Id.*

such regulatory decisions are a political question outside the judiciary's competence.[36] The protracted and contentious litigation resulted in a 2019 decision by the Supreme Court ruling that the matter is by law justiciable and that the Dutch government is obligated to take actions to reduce the nation's GHG emissions.[37]

The most prominent US version of governance failure litigation is *Juliana v. United States*,[38] in which a group of children brought suit against the United States government in 2015, alleging that the government's failure to adequately regulate GHG emissions violated its constitutional duties and the children's constitutional rights. Like the *Urgenda* litigation, their presentation of core climate science regarding the mechanics of climate change was uncontested—the primary dispute was over the extent of US contribution to global emissions—and their legal claims met with success at the federal district court level. At the appellate level, however, the government's nonjusticiability arguments derailed the litigation. Governance failure litigation against US state governments has so far met the same fate.

Urgenda and *Juliana* suggest that the certainty of climate science on the mechanisms of global warming is critical to the plaintiffs' argument that the increased pace and rate of GHG emissions reduction is necessary and that government action is not keeping up.[39] Indeed, the certainty behind that science makes it uncontestable in the governance failure litigation—neither the Dutch nor the United States governments refuted the science. Rather, they used the science to build the case for nonjusticiability, arguing that the certainty that climate change is a complex global causal phenomenon makes it inherently a matter exclusively for the legislative domain. Indeed, more and better science will only make those features of climate change more certain. From there, courts must decide whether, as a question of judicial constraint, that global complexity makes the governance failure nonjusticiable. *Urgenda* and *Juliana* represent opposite conclusions on this question, the consequence in the Netherlands being that the courts are likely to be asked to engage in governance failure litigation many more times as litigants like the Urgenda Foundation continue to claim the government has not done enough. In the United States, judicial reluctance to adjudicate the governance failure claims is likely to fuel more regulatory decision litigation as plaintiffs must contest government decisions piecemeal.

---

36 *Id.*

37 *Id.*

38 *Juliana v. United States*, 947 F.3d 1159 (9th Cir. 2020).

39 Quirin Schiermeier, *The Science that Supports Climate Lawsuits*, 597 Nature 169 (2021).

C. Harms Liability Litigation

As the federal government pulled back from GHG emissions regulation during the first Trump Administration, and with the impacts of climate change beginning to manifest through rising seas, heat waves, and extreme weather events, litigants began creatively using private law tort and other private and public law liability regimes to claim that fossil fuel producers and sources of substantial GHG emissions are liable for the damaging impacts of climate change. An initial litigation effort at the federal court level, asserting a federal common law remedy, failed when the Supreme Court ruled any such federal remedy had been displaced by the federal Clean Air Act statutory regime.[40] Plaintiffs regrouped and initiated litigation in state courts asserting state tort claims, in most cases with a public entity as lead plaintiff to boost the case for standing.[41] Defendants in many of the cases characterized the state claims as proxies for federal remedies and sought to transfer the cases to federal courts under what is known as "removal" procedure. Those transfer actions have largely failed—the federal courts have been unwilling to reframe state law claims as federal for purposes of removal—and the litigants are back in state courts where the proceedings are at the time of this writing only beginning to move towards the substantive merits.

As this wave of litigation draws closer to judicial consideration of the substantive merits, climate science will play an even more important role than it has in the regulatory decision and governance failure contexts.[42] Unlike the governance failure context, the defendants are likely to contest the plaintiffs' science as it moves from general descriptions of climate change causes and effects to specific attribution of an alleged impact to a defendant's actions. Unlike the regulatory decision context, courts are unlikely to accord any deference to the plaintiffs' science, particularly regarding specific attribution. Yet, an analysis of over 70 judicial decisions from around the world (most from the US) found that "the evidence submitted and referenced in these cases lags considerably behind the state of the art in climate science, impeding causation claims".[43] There clearly is room for some science making in this realm.

---

[40] *American Electric Power v. Connecticut*, 564 U.S. 410, 423 (2011).

[41] The cases are collected at the Sabin Center Database, *supra*. For a contemporaneous discussion of the shift in forum and its potential, see Tracey D. Hester, *A New Front Blowing in: State Law and the Future of Climate Change Public Nuisance Litigation*, 31 Stanford Environmental Law Journal 49 (2012).

[42] Quirin Schiermeier, *The Science that Supports Climate Lawsuits*, 597 Nature 169 (2021).

[43] Rupert F. Stuart-Smith, *Filling the Evidence Gap in Climate Litigation*, 11 Nature Climate Change 651 (2021).

In their recent comprehensive study of this attribution challenge, Burger et al. identify its many problematic certainty/uncertainty facets for plaintiffs.[44] One is the uncertainty over how to identify impacts attributable to climate change when the causal event, such as a storm or wildfire, is a common and frequently occurring event. Climate science is grappling with the problem of how to isolate climate change as a causal factor in, for example, an unusually intense storm event. Did climate change make the storm more likely or more intense, and if so, by how much? Which impacts and harms are attributable to that climate change component? Even where that can be determined, the certainty that every GHG molecule in the atmosphere, including those emitted at a far distance and back in time, has contributed equally to any harm complicates claims that a specific impact is attributable to a specific defendant. Unless attribution science makes great strides, the plaintiff's causal claims must rely on generalities—i.e., GHG emissions cause climate change; climate change causes harmful impacts; the defendant emitted GHGs and therefore is liable. Without more specificity, that argument is unlikely to get far.

Burger et al. identify three main categories of attribution challenges—extreme events, impacts, and source—and provide detailed analyses and case discussions addressing the three categories used in this chapter. They focus largely on harm liability litigation because it presents the largest gap between scientific certainty and the demands of applicable legal doctrine. They also suggest a number of ways courts can influence the development and use of attribution science, which leads to the next section.

METHODS OF JUDICIAL SCIENCE MAKING IN CLIMATE LITIGATION

Most of the judicial action in the climate change science space has taken place in the regulatory decision litigation category and has mostly centered on emission footprints and impact assessments. There, courts have acted mostly as science takers—they factor certainty or uncertainty into existing legal doctrine and decide accordingly. The important caveat is that courts will demand, through their translation and publication functions, that agencies be transparent and use best practices regarding how uncertainty has factored into their decisions, which can have the effect of improving agency use of science. In the government failure litigation context, courts have not had to choose between taking or making—the plaintiffs' science has been robustly certain

---

[44] Michael Burger, Jessica Wentz, & Radley Horton, *The Law and Science of Climate Change Attribution*, 45 Columbia Journal of Environmental Law 57 (2020).

and uncontested. But that is largely because the litigation is over the global state of climate change and the respective nation's progress in reducing GHG emissions. By contrast, harm liability litigation, which is just beginning to reach substantive merits in the US, will necessarily run into the uncertainties present in the current state of attribution science at more granular scales. It is yet to be seen how courts manage those uncertainties and whether they will engage in science making, particularly through the influencer mode.

Courts could do more to act as science makers in the sense used herein—i.e., not as the producers of science, but as providing incentives for its production through translation, publication, and influencing modes. Moreover, doing so would not require courts to act radically, appearing to engage in "judicial legislating". Rather, courts could use a number of conventional judicial mechanisms to promote climate change science making.

In the regulatory decision litigation context, judicial statutory interpretation can lean in favor of incentivizing science making. Indeed, the US Supreme Court did exactly that in *Massachusetts v. EPA* by construing the term "pollutant" broadly to include carbon dioxide. The cases in which courts construed NEPA impact assessment to require consideration of downstream GHG emissions, and to require data-based emission quantification, provide another example. Of course, US courts follow particular approaches to statutory interpretation and canons of construction, but one factor courts of other nations could consider, within their appropriate bounds of practice, is the effect of their statutory interpretations on the production of science relevant to their judicial review of agency regulatory decisions.

Some regulatory statutes, such as the ESA, expressly require agencies to base decisions on the "best available science". But even in the absence of an express statutory provision, demanding that agencies use the best available science is defensible as a core tenet of administrative law.[45] In the climate change science context, doing so will have the effect of requiring agencies to continuously update the science on which they rely to reflect the most current and reliable scientific results and findings. Whether an agency itself produces the science or relies on science produced by other agencies or by academic researchers, requiring best available science as the benchmark for agency science used to support decisions either directly or indirectly influences science production.

As explained above, when regulatory agencies exercise authority in an environment of scientific uncertainty, US courts have generally deferred to the agency decision when it has used best practices for managing uncertainty. Under some statutes, however, courts have included as a best practice erring

---

45 Kim et al., *supra*.

on the side of precaution. Under the ESA, for example, courts have pointed to uncertainty in climate science as a basis for rejecting agency decisions not to extend protection to a species, on the basis that the ESA demands a "cautious approach".[46] To the extent this precautionary approach could result in, for example, extensive regulation of land development to comply with ESA requirements, it would influence land development interests to produce science that convincingly reduces that uncertainty.

Harms come in many forms, one of which is increased risk. Recently, for example, scientists concluded that climate change has made heatwaves in India 30 times more likely to occur.[47] Burger et al. suggest that increased risk from climate change could provide the basis for establishing requisite injury to support standing to sue,[48] and by that logic it could also be used in harm liability litigation as a form of compensable injury. While that might not support a claim for damages, it could provide the basis for establishing standing or for a harm monitoring remedy analogous to medical monitoring remedies for exposure to toxic substances.[49] A climate harm monitoring remedy, for example, could require the periodic assessment of sea-level rise and its potential impacts, which necessarily would influence science production over time. Of course, it would still require that the harm of increased risk somehow be attributed to particular defendants.

Attribution is the ultimate puzzle in the harm liability litigation context, but it is not insurmountable. For example, Burger et al. suggest that courts could borrow from market share liability doctrines to fashion attribution for climate harms based on a defendant's share of GHG emissions.[50] This approach would likely only be viable when the defendants in a case are cumulatively major contributors of GHG emissions, which is the case in many of the municipal plaintiff tort liability suits described above. Once the prospect of emissions share liability were made salient, it likely would incentivize more refinement of both attribution science and impact assessment science, as parties would engage in contested science battles to deem total harms and the allocation of liability. To be sure, that could result in defendants prevailing, but the point of

---

46 *Crow Indian Tribe v United States*, 343 F. Supp. 3d 999, 1021 (D. Mont. 2018), aff'd 965 F.3d 662 (9th Cir. 2020).

47 *See* Mariam Zachariah et al., Climate Change Made Devastating Early Heat in India and Pakistan 30 Times More Likely (May 2022), https://www.worldweatherattribution.org/wp-content/uploads/India_Pak-Heatwave-scientific-report.pdf.

48 Burger, *supra*, at 227–28.

49 *Id.* at 239.

50 Quirin Schiermeier, *The Science that Supports Climate Lawsuits*, 597 NATURE 169 (2021).

science making by courts is not to choose sides but rather to incentivize the production of science relevant to the adjudication of disputes.

CONCLUSION—THE CASE FOR JUDICIAL SCIENCE MAKING IN CLIMATE CHANGE LITIGATION

The foregoing establishes two propositions: First, that climate change litigation is permeated by a range of scientific certainty and uncertainty regarding different features of the causes and impacts of climate change relevant to judicial determinations in the regulatory decision, governance failure, and harm liability litigation contexts. Second, that courts could take steps—steps well within the province of conventional judicial doctrine (at least in the US)—to incentivize production of science that will help them more effectively manage science relevant to those adjudications. Figure 10.1 summarizes examples drawn from the discussion above.

Clearly, there is opportunity for courts to engage in more science making than has been exhibited thus far in US climate change litigation. A survey of litigation in other nations may reveal more or less judicial appetite. The ultimate question, however, is whether courts should take those steps to act as science makers.

It would be difficult to identify a more compelling case than climate change for courts to engage as science makers. Humanity faces potentially hundreds of years of unprecedented and novel risks and harms, producing a "no-analog" future that will challenge science with complexities and uncertainties. To be sure, climate science will advance, but courts occupy a role unlike other government institutions in mediating a broad variety of contexts where science plays an important role—regulatory decisions, governance, and harm liability—giving them influence over how government agencies, corporate actors, and other interest groups practice and produce relevant climate science. In particular, harm liability litigation zeros in on granular impact assessment requiring qualities of attribution science that might not be as important to other institutions, such as legislatures, focused on "bigger" issues.

Importantly, none of the proposed science making modes and mechanisms are out of bounds with judicial practice. Indeed, the modes (e.g., translator, publisher, evaluator) are core judicial functions, and the methods all borrow from standard practice (e.g., statutory interpretation) or previous innovations in other science-driven contexts (e.g., risk as harm). Given the threat of climate change and its deep certainty/uncertainty complexities, courts might be inclined to adopt them regardless of their science production effects. But the possibility that they could promote advancement of science relevant to the judicial challenges ahead offers yet another justification for courts moving in the direction of science makers influencing the production of climate science.

	Mode	Example
Avoiding	Avoider	As many have already, courts avoid climate science by erecting obstacles to harms liability and governance failure litigation through nonjusticiability doctrines
	Gatekeeper	Courts impose qualitative standards for climate attribution science in harms liability litigation
	Translator	Courts summarize and describe climate science in jury instructions and written opinions
Taking	Publisher	Courts extensively discuss their evaluation of climate science in written opinions
	Influencer	Courts specify the type and quality of climate science needed to satisfy legal standards and determinations, such as the level of detail needed in EIA emissions footprints or the factors that go into making jurisdictional determinations
Making	Producer	Courts appoint experts to synthesize and summarize climate science relevant to attribution in harms liability litigation

Source: Author's own.

Figure 10.1 *Modes and examples of judicial treatment of science*

To be sure, courts should be careful in this practice, cognizant of concerns that may arise regarding the possible unintended consequences of overt science making and of public perception of them overstepping their judicial imprimatur. Yet, with waves of climate litigation of all variety underway and more on the horizon, it will be impossible for courts to extract themselves from science making through incidental effects of their methods and decisions. Better that they are at least aware of those effects, and arguably better still that they assume some intentionality given the catastrophic disruptions that will follow unchecked climate change.

11. Courts and expertise in environment dispute resolution – a tale of two models

Sharngan Aravindakshan and Dewy Pistora

1. INTRODUCTION

It is generally accepted that judicial review in cases involving environmental law and policy requires a certain level of technical or scientific expertise.[1] The challenges generalist judges frequently face in such cases include scientific uncertainty, filtering out junk science, and weighing competing scientific or technical considerations or evidence. The existence of these challenges has strengthened the perception that judges need expertise – either judges themselves might be trained to become more knowledgeable in scrutinizing scientific evidence, or third parties could provide technical and scientific input for judicial decision-making.[2] This led to the development of different models that aimed to incorporate expertise in environmental dispute resolution.[3] Some jurisdictions established specialized environmental courts and tribunals (ECT) with technical experts assisting the judges or as co-adjudicators.[4] In other countries, general courts continue to deal with these cases, but with the power to receive input from court-appointed (external) experts.[5] The objective

[1] Tiina Paloniitty & Mariolina Eliantiano, 'Scientific Knowledge in Environmental Judicial Review: Safeguarding Effective Judicial Protection in the EU Member States?' (2018) 27 (4) *European Energy and Environmental Law Review* 108 <https://kluwerlawonline.com/journalarticle/European+Energy+and+Environmental+Law+Review/27.4/EELR2018013> accessed on 20 June 2023.

[2] ibid.

[3] United Nations Environment Programme (Law Division), 'Environment Courts and Tribunals - 2021: A Guide for Policy Makers' (2022) 5 <https://wedocs.unep.org/handle/20.500.11822/40309> accessed on 20 June 2023.

[4] ibid.

[5] ibid.

in all these models is to enable courts to gather and employ scientific knowledge from independent non-party sources for decision-making.

ECT models vary, but the hybrid ECT model combining judges who are legally trained with lay arbiters with scientific expertise has proved popular.[6] The non-lawyers in this model typically take the form of professionals who are trained in specializations that are highly relevant for environmental decision-making including environmental economics, biodiversity management, forest management and conservation, natural resource management, pollution, air quality, water quality, and soil quality, among others.[7] Their specialized knowledge is then applied to complex disputes, whereby "decision-making quality, effectiveness, and efficiency can be enhanced".[8] Having both legal and technical experts is believed to create a synergy, and the expertise the technical members bring to the table may help in the final determination of the dispute.[9] The National Green Tribunal in India (hereafter "NGT") is a specialized hybrid tribunal, with both judicial and expert members adjudicating environment cases together. That its hybrid expertise is central to its functioning is clear – the NGT's website declares it as a "specialized body equipped with the necessary expertise to handle environmental disputes involving multidisciplinary issues".[10] However, although the NGT was initially lauded for advancing environmental protection in India through innovative and practical orders,[11] more recently it has come increasingly under attack. Critics have noted its "rise

---

6 ibid.

7 ibid.

8 Brian Preston, 'Characteristics of Successful Environmental Courts and Tribunals' (2014) 26 *Journal of Environmental Law* 365, 377 <https://www.jstor.org/stable/26168843> accessed on 20 June 2023.

9 See Gitanjali Nain Gill, 'Environmental Justice in India: The National Green Tribunal and Expert Members' (2015) 5 (1) *Transnational Environmental Law* 175.

10 National Green Tribunal, 'About Us' <https://www.greentribunal.gov.in/about-us> accessed on 20 June 2023.

11 George Pring & Catherine Pring, 'Environmental Courts & Tribunals: A Guide for Policymakers' (2016) United Nations Environment Programme 35 <https://wedocs.unep.org/handle/20.500.11822/10001> accessed on 20 June 2023.

and fall",[12] declaring that it has swung from "ascendancy to crisis"[13] and that it is "losing its bite".[14]

Another innovative model in this regard, however, exists in the form of the Dutch system of designating a specific institute, the Stichting Advisering Bestuursrechtspraak voor Milieu en Ruimtelijke Ordening (STAB) [the Foundation of Independent Court Experts in Environmental and Planning Law], to provide technical and scientific knowledge to general administrative courts in environmental and planning cases. This model is considered "atypical" since there is no equivalent anywhere in the EU and its use came to be through unique circumstances.[15] It is meant to serve as an "external panel of scientific experts" that can be consulted by the court if necessary.[16] The assumption here appears to be that as long as expertise is supplied from an independent, reliable source, the generalist judge is fully capable of properly assimilating it into judicial decisions, and the challenges of lack of or competing evidence are resolved. The Dutch system has been evaluated positively, with the STAB adequately serving judicial needs. However, some concerns exist with respect to its functioning as well. We will explore these more in detail hereafter.

We compare these two judicial decision-making models with interesting and different approaches toward assessing scientific evidence in environmental disputes between government bodies and private parties. The specific question we are concerned with is what particular (dis)advantages are perceived to be held by each model with respect to optimizing judicial decision-making in environmental cases and what is known about how these hold in actual practice. Are these advantages realized and, if not, what could be the possible reasons?

---

12 See Gill, 'Mapping the Power Struggles of the National Green Tribunal of India: The Rise and Fall?' (2020) 7 (1) *Asian Journal of Law and Society* 85 <https://tinyurl.com/yeze6tmn> accessed on 20 June 2023.

13 Geetanjoy Sahu & Ritwick Dutta, 'The Green Tribunal in India After 10 Years: From Ascendancy to Crisis' (*Economic and Political Weekly*, 2021).

14 Maya Ramesh, 'Nearly a Decade Old, Is the National Green Tribunal Losing its Bite?' (*The Wire*, 11 May 2019) <https://thewire.in/environment/nearly-a-decade-old-is-the-national-green-tribunal-losing-its-bite> accessed on 20 June 2023.

15 Chris Backes, 'Organizing Technical Knowledge in Environmental and Planning Law Disputes in the Netherlands – the Foundation of Independent Court Experts in Environmental and Planning Law' (2018) 27 *European Energy and Environmental Law Review* 143, 143–144; Luc Lavrysen and Farah Bouquelle, 'Waarom Zijn Milieurechters Noodzakelijk?' (2022) *Ars Aequi* 556.

16 Pring & Pring (n 11), p. 5.

Both models have substantial access to expertise and both deal with environmental cases. The presumed strength of the NGT is its in-house expertise in the form of Expert Members in the panel of judges whose scientific knowledge and experience can directly feed into decision-making, while the presumed strength of the STAB model is that Dutch judges can directly consult external expertise in the form of the STAB, whose employees possess scientific knowledge and experience in a wide range of technical areas. Although the STAB can be accessed by district courts as well, our focus in this chapter is its use by the Administrative Jurisdiction Division of the Dutch Council of State, which is the highest administrative court in the Netherlands (hereafter; the Council). Both the NGT and the Council have wide powers of inquiry and ready access to scientific and technical data. Neither is bound by strict rules of procedure, and both have original and appellate (final, in the case of the Council) jurisdiction with respect to environmental cases.

Essentially, both models attempt to address the same issue – the need to incorporate independent expertise into the judicial decision-making in environmental cases. However, the means through which they attempt to do so are radically different. This chapter explores these methods and their differences.

The second part of the chapter describes the Indian model of environmental dispute resolution in the form of the NGT. It details the procedures followed as well as how expertise is reflected in the NGT and used by it to resolve competing claims concerning scientific facts and knowledge. The third part explains how the Dutch model works with respect to environmental disputes. We describe the role of the Council, judicial procedures followed, and the Council's use of the STAB as a source of expertise for informing its decision-making. In the final part, we note the different challenges faced by both models with respect to synthesizing law and science, and contextualize these different challenges in terms of the institutional or legal-cultural settings within which the models operate. We conclude that both models have strengths and weaknesses and that, besides model design, additional factors such as institutional or legal-cultural settings are also important considerations for optimizing decision-making.

2. THE INDIAN MODEL

The NGT's historical background is relevant to understanding its functioning and role. Its establishment was heavily driven by the Indian Supreme Court, which in the immediate aftermath of the development of public interest litigation, was faced with a rising number of cases concerning environmental justice.[17] This forced the court to repeatedly deal with issues of technical and scientific complexity. In several decisions including *MC Mehta v. Union of India*,[18] *Indian Council for Enviro-Legal Action v. Union of India*,[19] and *AP Pollution Control Board v. MP Nayadu*,[20] the court urged the government to consider setting up specialized tribunals with the capacity to evaluate, assess, and incorporate scientific knowledge into judicial decision-making. On the Court's urging, the Law Commission of India undertook a detailed comparative study of different models of environmental dispute resolution including the Land and Environment Court in New South Wales and the Environment Court in New Zealand.[21] It proposed the establishment of specialized environmental courts that included technical experts who could provide the requisite scientific and technical input for decisions.[22]

The NGT was thus established under the National Green Tribunal Act, 2010, with panels or "benches" in five major cities. Benches consist of judicial and expert members who decide cases as co-equals. The NGT has a broad mandate to advance environmental protection and exercises original and appellate jurisdiction. It has original jurisdiction over all civil cases where a "substantial question pertaining to the environment" is involved and such question concerns the implementation of legislations specified in Schedule I of the NGT Act 2010.[23] These laws include the Environment (Protection) Act, 1986, the Water (Prevention and Control of Pollution) Act, 1974, the Air (Prevention and Control of Pollution) Act, 1981, the Forest (Conservation) Act, 1980, and the Biological Diversity Act, 2002.[24] The NGT can also grant monetary and other forms of relief to victims of environmental damage and pollution.[25] It exercises appellate jurisdiction over appeals from decisions by various appellate authorities constituted under legislations including the Water (Prevention

---

17 Geetanjoy Sahu, 'Implications of Indian Supreme Court's Innovations for Environmental Jurisprudence' (2008) 4 (1) *Law, Environment and Development Journal* 3 <https://lead-journal.org/content/08001.pdf> accessed 19 June 2023.

18 *MC Mehta v. Union of India*, 1987 SCR (1) 819.

19 *Indian Council for Enviro-Legal Action v. Union of India*, 1996 AIR 1446.

20 *AP Pollution Control Board v. MP Nayadu,* 1999 (2) SCC 718.

21 The Law Commission of India, 186th Report (2003), p. 82 <https://cdnbbsr.s3waas.gov.in/s3ca0daec69b5adc880fb464895726dbdf/uploads/2022/08/2022081021-1.pdf> accessed on 19 June 2023.

22 ibid 165.

23 Section 14, National Green Tribunal Act 2010. It also includes the Water (Prevention and Control of Pollution) Cess Act, 1977 and the Public Liability Insurance Act, 1991.

24 Schedule I, National Green Tribunal Act 2010.

25 Section 15, National Green Tribunal Act 2010.

and Control of Pollution) Act, 1974, the Forest (Conservation) Act, 1980, and the Environment Protection Act, 1986.[26]

The NGT consists of the chairperson, judicial members (between 10 and 20 full-time members) and expert members (between 10 and 20 full-time members).[27] The chairperson and judicial members are required to be serving or retired judges of the Supreme Court or the High Courts, while expert members are required to have advanced degrees in the sciences, engineering or technology with a minimum of 15 years' experience in the relevant field, including five years' practical experience in the field of environment and forests in a reputed national-level institution.[28] Alternatively, the expert member may have "administrative experience" of 15 years, including five years' experience in environmental matters in the Central or in a State Government or in a reputed national or state-level institution.[29] While the chairperson is appointed by the Central Government in consultation with the Chief Justice of India, the judicial and expert members are appointed by a selection committee constituted under the relevant rules.[30]

The NGT has wide access to both internal and external sources of expertise. Besides the in-house expert members, it can access external experts and constitute committees for various purposes, including receiving technical and scientific inputs to assist its decision-making, as well as monitoring the implementation of its orders.[31] The NGT is free to regulate its own procedure and rules of evidence, and as an inquisitorial court, has wide powers of discovery including the power to summon individuals, require document production, and receive evidence on affidavits.[32] Expert members can also conduct site visits to verify technical facts.[33] Not bound by any particular standard of review, the NGT as a specialist tribunal is required to address and resolve all aspects of a dispute.

The NGT model is designed to gather and deploy expertise in service of its decision-making. The technical knowledge and expertise brought in by the in-house expert members play an important role in the NGT's decision-making.[34]

---

[26] Schedule I, National Green Tribunal Act 2010.
[27] Section 4, National Green Tribunal Act 2010.
[28] Section 5, National Green Tribunal Act 2010.
[29] ibid.
[30] Section 6, National Green Tribunal Act 2010.
[31] Rule 24, National Green Tribunal (Practices and Procedures) Rules, 2011; *The State of Meghalaya v. All Dimasa Students Union*, (2019) 8 SCC 177.
[32] Section 19, National Green Tribunal Act 2010.
[33] *Ministry of Environment and Forests v. Nirma*, Civil Appeal No. 8783 of 2013, Order dated 4 August 2014.
[34] Gitanjali Nain Gill (n 9) 3.

This is evident when the NGT is required to conduct a "merit review", i.e., a *de novo* assessment of the primary decision-maker's decisions.[35] For instance, a large number of cases in the NGT concern challenges to the grant of environmental clearances (ECs) for various projects that impact the environment. These ECs are typically granted by the federal or state government (depending on the project) after taking into account expert input on a variety of factors, including potential impacts on the environment and social benefits or harms.[36] In such cases, the NGT conducts a merit review, i.e., it verifies the correctness of highly technical factual information, reviews for deficiencies in environmental impact assessment (EIA) reports, and examines if all relevant material including any sectoral standards or guidelines were considered.[37] For example, in *Save Mon Federation v. Union of India,* an NGO challenged the grant of an EC for the construction of a dam in north-east India for generating hydroelectricity on the ground that it would adversely affect wintering sites for the Black-necked Crane, an endangered bird species.[38] The NGT reviewed the documents filed by the project applicant and referred to studies on the presence of migratory bird species such as the Black-necked Crane.[39] It then ruled that a study examining the "environmental flow requirements" for protecting the bird species was required.[40] It suspended the EC until such study was conducted.[41]

The technical and expert nature of the review conducted by the NGT is also exemplified by another case, *T Murugan v. Union of India*, in which the grant of an EC for setting up a coal-based thermal power plant in a coastal town was challenged.[42] The NGT initially determined that the EIA report did

35 *Hanuman Laxman Arloskar v. Union of India*, Civil Appeal No 12251 of 2018, para 120.

36 Under the current regulations, projects classified under "Category A" have to be granted an environmental clearance. Expert Appraisal Committees or EACs at the federal level are constituted by the Ministry of Environment, Forests and Climate Change and play an important role in evaluating applications for the grant of environmental clearances for various projects. See Shibani Ghosh, 'Demystifying the Environmental Clearance Process in India', (2013) 4(3) NUJS Law Review <http://nujslawreview.org/2016/12/05/demystifying-the-environmental-clearance-process-in-india/> accessed on 19 June 2023.

37 *Hanuman Laxman Arloskar* (n 35).

38 *Save Mon Region Federation v. Union of India and Others,* Appeal No. 39 of 2012.

39 ibid, paras 15–16.

40 ibid, para 22.

41 ibid.

42 *T. Murugan and Others v. Ministry of Environment and Forests and Others*, Appeal No. 50 of 2012.

not evaluate the impact of the project in combination with other industries or activities in the vicinity and stressed the importance of conducting a cumulative environmental impact assessment report (CEIA).[43] On receipt and review of the CEIA along with other project documents, it noted that the project applicant had failed to collect relevant data such as the combined impact of effluent discharge on the marine environment or the combined impact of emissions from the industries on air quality.[44] It therefore quashed the EC and directed a fresh CEIA to be conducted.[45] Heavy with scientific language, the text of the judgment reflects the technical nature of the NGT's review.

Expert members have also been noted to utilize their expertise to help develop or advance legal regulation concerning the environment. In *Asim Sarode and Anr. v. Madhya Pradesh Pollution Control Board*, the NGT had to deal with a petition that raised the issue of unauthorized burning of tyres.[46] On questioning the State Pollution Control Board, it became clear that their practices for managing used tires were not entirely scientific.[47] The expert member in this case highlighted the need to consider the management and disposal of used tyres through a "life cycle approach", taking into account the pollution potential, techno-economic viability, tyre generation data, etc., and the NGT panel directed the State Pollution Control Board to conduct a scientific study in this regard, based on which long-term strategy could be prepared.[48] The subsequently notified state regulations acknowledge the NGT order on the issue and the life cycle assessment method it recommended.[49]

When disputes raise complex and multidisciplinary issues that may be beyond an expert member's competence, the NGT often addresses them by appointing ad hoc committees of external experts from different fields. The NGT's power to constitute such committees has also been affirmed by the Supreme Court.[50] These committees provide technical input to inform their decision-making, conduct site visits to verify facts and monitor compliance with their orders. The expert reports have to be submitted within specified timelines, after which they are released to the parties for comment and objections. The reports are

---

43 ibid, para 26.

44 ibid, para 46.

45 ibid para 64(1).

46 *Asim Sarode and Anr. v. Madhya Pradesh Pollution Control Board*, Application No. 43/2013 (WZ).

47 ibid, paras 7–8.

48 Gill (n 9), p. 21.

49 Maharashtra Pollution Control Board, Notification No. Bo/P & L. Divn./B-2144, <https://mpcb.gov.in/sites/default/files/standing_orders/notification_guidelines_tyre_retreading_05072016_0.pdf> accessed on 19 June 2023.

50 *All Dimasa Students Union* (n 31), para 161.

then used to inform the NGT decisions. For instance, in *Manoj Kumar Mishra & Anr. v. Union of India & Ors.*, the NGT had to decide a challenge to the construction of a dam on the grounds that it would have adverse seismological effects, that it would impact drinking water supply, and that it would harm the flora and fauna in the region.[51] The NGT acknowledged that it "needed the opinion of domain experts to facilitate [an] informed decision" and constituted an expert committee consisting of representatives from the Ministry of Water Resources, the Directorate of Cold Water Fisheries Research, the Geological Survey of India, Indian Institute of Technology (Rourkee), Ministry of Social Justice and Empowerment, the Wildlife Institute of India and the Institute of Seismological Research.[52] The expert committee had to undertake a feasibility study of the project within four months and submit the report to the NGT, as well as upload it on a government website for stakeholder access.[53] Parties were given leave to file objections within one month after receipt of the report.[54] Based on the expert committee's report that the project was viable[55] and the fact that none of the parties had filed any objections to the report, the NGT upheld the grant of EC for the dam.[56]

Employing external expertise in this manner can also be useful when parties put forth conflicting scientific claims. In *Navroz Mody v. Union of India & Ors.*, the case concerned the remediation standard used by a company to remedy mercury contamination in a particular area.[57] The company was employing 20 mg/kg as the standard, whereas the applicant claimed the standard was 6.6 mg/kg.[58] The NGT called for an expert opinion from a committee of experts from various technical and research institutes in India.[59] The experts considered relevant materials including a government-issued guidance document titled "Development of Methodologies for National Programme for Rehabilitation of Polluted Sites in India", and concluded that 6.6 mg/kg could

51 *Manoj Kumar Mishra & Anr. v. Union of India & Ors.*, Appeal No. 35 of 2021, Order dated 20 January 2022.

52 ibid, para 6.

53 ibid, para 7.

54 ibid, paras 7–8.

55 *Manoj Kumar Mishra* (n 51), Order dated 19 September 2022, para 8.

56 ibid, para 8. Although the expert committee found the project viable from an environmental standpoint, it nevertheless recommended certain additional safeguards which the NGT made binding in its order.

57 *Navroz Mody v. Union of India & Others,* Original Application No. 211/2018.

58 ibid, paras 3–4.

59 ibid, para 5.

not be used as the remediation standard for the case at hand.[60] Based on their report, the NGT dismissed the case.[61]

Similarly, expert committees have been used to determine modalities for the safe transport of coal[62] and assess whether erosion of coastlines was caused by port construction.[63]

3. THE DUTCH MODEL

In the Netherlands, the government is responsible for land habitability and environmental protection.[64] The protection of the environment is mainly regulated via administrative law. However, regulation is currently very fragmented: there are many specific laws that deal with different aspects of the environment, such as the Air Pollution Act and the Environmental Management Act.[65] Ensuring compliance and enforcement of these laws is a matter for the government – in particular the lower tiers of government. When the government makes a decision concerning the environment, natural persons and legal entities (including non-governmental organizations) with a specific interest in the decision have access to administrative courts that will review the decision.[66] Disputes in environmental matters will, therefore, primarily be brought against the government in general administrative courts – there are no specific environmental courts in the Netherlands. Access to administrative courts is, however, limited. Administrative action in a court is only possible if there is an "order", like the issuing of a permit for activities that affect the environment,[67] in terms of the General Administrative Law Act (Algemene wet bestuursrecht, GALA). Some types of administrative decisions are specifically excluded, such as generally binding regulations and policy rules.[68] Moreover, not everyone

---

60 ibid, para 6.

61 ibid, para 9.

62 *All Dimasa Students Union v. State of Meghalaya,* Original Application No. 13 of 2014.

63 *Wilfred and Another v. Ministry of Environment and Forest*s, Original Application No. 74 of 2014.

64 This is laid down in the Dutch Constitution, in particular in article 21. The Netherlands has no such thing as an Environmental Protection Agency.

65 De Wet inzake de luchtverontreiniging en de Wet Milieubeheer. At the moment, the government is working on a bill to incorporate all more specific laws into an overarching law: the Environment Act (de Omgevingswet).

66 Article 1:2 of the General Administrative Law Act (GALA).

67 For example, permits for combustion plants or intensive cattle farming or land use plans allowing industrial parks.

68 Article 1:3 GALA.

can bring a case before the administrative courts – only those stakeholders with a relevant legal interest. There are additional requirements for public interest organizations.[69] In general, however, it can be argued that there is wide access to Dutch administrative courts as far as environmental issues are concerned. If the administrative route is not available, civil litigation via a tort action against the government might be initiated.[70]

Judicial review of decisions that concern the environment is adjudicated in the first instance by the administrative law division of a district court. Appeals from these decisions lie with the Council.[71] The Council also hears some types of environmental cases as a court of first and only instance.[72] The Council generally adjudicates cases with three judges, although sometimes a simple case is heard by a single judge. The Council consists of three chambers: a General Chamber (Algemene kamer), a Migration Chamber (Vreemdelingenkamer), and, since 2019, a Spatial Planning Chamber (Omgevingskamer).[73] The environmental chamber deals with both environmental and planning law disputes. It is divided into four units, and cases are divided within the units by geography and by specialty. Each unit has unit-bound legal staff, but the Council judges work for the entire chamber and, therefore, need to have broad knowledge about environmental and spatial planning law. The Council judges are not

69 Article 1:2 (3). See about these requirements, for example, Berthy van den Broek and Liesbeth Enneking, 'Public Interest Litigation in the Netherlands – A Multidimensional Take on the Promotion of Environmental Interests by Private Parties through the Courts' (2014) 10 *Utrecht Law Review* 77.

70 Ibid. See also Tom Barkhuysen & Michiel van Emmerik, 'Judicial Review in Dutch Environmental Law: General Observations', in: Jurgen de Poorter et al. (eds.), *Judicial Review of Administrative Discretion in the Administrative State* (TMC Asser Press 2019), pp. 106–108.

71 The Council is not the only highest administrative court. There also exists the highest courts regarding specific issues, like the Central Appeals Tribunal (in Dutch: Centrale Raad van Beroep) for cases involving civil servants and social security issues, the Court of Appeal for appeals against tax assessments, and the Trade and Industry Appeals Tribunal (in Dutch: College van Beroep voor het Bedrijfsleven) for disputes in the area of socio-economic administrative law and for appeals for specific laws, such as the Competition Act.

72 The Council used to be the court at first and only instance in most environmental disputes. This changed, however, in 2010, when first instance at administrative district court was introduced. See e.g. Lex Michiels, 'Veertig jaar milieurecht: enkele algemene thema's' (2013) 65 *Milieu en Recht* 285 and Maarten Verhoeven, 'Drie jaar milieurechtspraak in eerste aanleg' (2014) 18 *Tijdschrift voor Milieu en Recht* 81.

73 See https://www.raadvanstate.nl/overrvs/organisatie/afdeling

bound to any chamber and generally work in more than one chamber.[74] When allocating the cases to the judges, several factors are taken into account, such as the degree of expertise, experience, and previous involvement in a case.[75]

Facts matter at the Council's level as well.[76] With regard to fact finding, there are no written rules of substantive law on evidence in administrative procedural law. This means that there are no written rules regarding the scope of proof, the distribution of the burden of proof, the evaluation of evidence, and rules concerning the means of evidence. In this regard, a "free evidence doctrine" applies: the administrative law judge has much freedom in the distribution of the burden of proof, the choice of means of proof, and in the valuation of evidence.[77] At the same time, there are some limitations in the form of the margin of appreciation and discretion extended to administrative bodies and the Council's own case law.[78] The administrative law system does contain some written rules of evidence concerning the procedures for taking evidence in trials, such as provisions that regulate the summoning of witnesses and the appointment of expert(s) by the court.[79] As the focus of administrative adjudication is on "finding the material truth", the Council is supposed to be proactive and has broad investigatory powers. However, in practice, the Council does not make full use of these powers and requires the litigating parties to provide the necessary factual information.[80]

---

74 Roos-Marie van der Hoeve & Lex Michiels, Het handwerk in de Omgevingskamer, in: Louise Verboeket et al. (eds.), *Bestuursrecht in het echt. Vriendenbundel voor prof. mr. drs. Willemien den Ouden* (Wolters Kluwer 2021).

75 *Regeling toedeling zaken Afdeling bestuursrechtspraak van de Raad van State 2020* (Stcrt. 2019, 65197).

76 This is different when compared to the Dutch Supreme Court, which is a court of cassation in civil, criminal, and tax matters and, therefore, mainly focuses on legal uniformity, the development of law, and safeguarding legal protection. These three functions are, however, relevant as well. See Jurgen de Poorter and Kars de Graaf, *Doel en functie van de bestuursrechtspraak: een blik op de toekomst* (Raad van State 2011), pp. 232, 251.

77 See e.g. Tom Barkhuysen & Ymre Schuurmans, 'Waarheidsvinding in het bestuursrecht' (2012) 87 *Nederlands Juristenblad* 1515 and Marc Loth et al., *Waarheids en waarheidsvinding in het recht (Handelingen Nederlandse Juristen-Vereniging 2012–1)* (Wolters Kluwer 2012), pp. 171–173.

78 Loth (n 77), pp. 171–173.

79 See e.g. article 8:33 and following GALA.

80 See e.g. Raymond Schlössels, Roel Schutgens & Sjoerd Zijlstra, *Bestuursrecht in de sociale rechtsstaat. 2. Rechtsbescherming, Overheidsaansprakelijkheid (Handboeken staats- en bestuursrecht),* (Wolters Kluwer 2019), pp. 99–101. See also Backes (n 15), p. 145.

The Dutch model for judicial access to expertise in environmental and spatial planning cases is unique and requires some explanation about the historical context. Until 1988, appeals against administrative decisions in environmental disputes were heard by the Crown (the Government and the King through the Minister responsible for planning and environmental issues), whose decisions were final. In this procedure, the Minister was supported by the Administrative Litigation Division of the Council of State (a predecessor of the current judicial wing of the Council), which provided recommendations.[81] Its recommendations were based on relevant technical data or information provided by an expert unit within the Ministry of Housing, Planning and the Environment. This unit was the predecessor of the current STAB and exclusively provided advice on technical questions to the Council in planning and environmental cases. These reports included mostly information about the determination or the (technical) valuation of facts that concerned both the disputed claims as well as the environmental policy. At the time, the appeals were decided on the merits since they were heard by administrative agencies themselves. The Council almost always followed the conclusions from the expert advice.[82]

In 1988, after the European Court of Human Rights ruled that the appeal procedure to the Crown (read: the central government) violated the right to a fair trial as stipulated in article 6 of the European Convention on Human Rights (ECHR), it was abrogated and appeal before an independent general administrative court was introduced – which included most members of the former Council.[83] The legislature wanted to preserve several aspects of the Crown appeals, such as the full review used by the Crown (both legality and expediency review) and the expert opinion through reports.[84] The Council continued to rely on the expert body, resulting in strong calls for the creation of an independent expert institution, as it was considered undesirable for a non-independent institution to have such a big influence on the outcome of cases.[85] Consequently, it was given a statutory basis and insulated from the government through placement in an independent foundation. Its task is now legally

[81] These were not legally binding, but in practice always followed by the minister. See Backes (n 15), p. 146.

[82] In 90% of the cases. For more elaboration on the history of the Council and the STAB, see Taco Coen Leemans, *De Toetsing Door de Bestuursrechter in Milieugeschillen: Over Rechterlijke Toetsingsintensiteit, Bestuurlijke Beslissingsruimte en Deskundigenadvisering* (Boom Juridische uitgevers 2008), pp. 7–17.

[83] Also known as the *Benthem* case. See ECtHR 23 October 1985, ECLI:NL:ECGR:1985:1023-JUD000884880.

[84] Leemans (n 82), p. 9.

[85] Ibid, pp. 10–17.

described as providing impartial and independent advice to the administrative law judge at his or her request.[86]

In 1994, the Council in its current shape was created, together with a new administrative law system (the General Administrative Law Act (GALA)). In the beginning, the Council of State maintained full review of administrative decisions. The Council considered that the nature of the environmental regulations which regulated the granting of permits left little to no discretion to the competent administrative body.[87] Consequently, it assessed, for example, whether a permit had been rightly granted or refused and/or whether the regulations attached to the permit were necessary, often resolving the dispute itself by rejecting the permit or adding additional conditions to it.[88] The Council continued to use the reports of the STAB as standard practice. After 1998, the Council adopted a more deferential stance towards the executive agencies' decision-making, granting them a wide margin of discretion.[89] Consequently, the Council looks more into the procedural aspects of the authorities' decision-making process, instead of substantive ones. The Council continued to use the STAB's expert reports, but the frequency and way of using them changed over the years.[90]

The STAB is an independent and impartial institution which is financed by the government and has a legal basis in the main acts dealing with environmental and spatial planning law.[91] To ensure its independence and impartiality, it is stipulated by law that employees are not allowed to hold positions outside the STAB that would compromise their impartiality and independence.[92] The STAB is the permanent expert of the Council, and the Council makes use of only the STAB, despite the legal possibility to appoint other experts. This has to do with the STAB's long history and tradition as an expert body that was

---

86 Article 20:14 of The Environmental Management Act (Wet milieubeheer), article 8:5 of the Planning Act (Wet ruimtelijke ordening) and article 6.6b of the General Provisions of Environmental and Planning Law At (Wet algemene bepalingen omgevingsrecht). See also the original law of 1995 Stb. 1995, 270.

87 Leemans (n 82), pp. 9–10.

88 Ibid (n 82), p. 12.

89 This margin of discretion was limited to what the most recent generally accepted environmental insights are. See more elaborately about this development Leemans (n 82), pp. 13–17 and Barkhuysen & Van Emmerik (n 70), pp. 112–113.

90 See more elaborately in section 4.

91 Environmental Management Act, Planning Act and General Provisions of Environmental and Planning Law Act.

92 There is also a code of conduct applicable. See article 20.16 Environmental Management Act and article 8.5 and 8.7 Planning Act. See also Backes (n 15), p. 148 and Leemans (n 82), pp. 16–17.

consulted by the government. There are practical considerations involved as well. There are no additional costs involved in requesting the STAB for expert advice, as it is paid by the government. In other types of disputes, it is not common to have a permanent expert body.[93]

The STAB has around 40 advisors that are all specialized in specific disciplines, but who also (together) have broad training to be employed in all cases in the field of environmental law.[94] The STAB deals with a great variety of environmental issues, from noise or odor nuisance to the effects of certain projects on air pollution or the level of nitrogen emissions.[95] The STAB conducts an investigation on the basis of the questions put forward by the Council. The experts can provide general information about the case, such as the facts and the circumstances of the case, the relevant legal framework and explanations of technical(-legal) issues, but also more case-specific information. The experts work in teams and provide integrated reports – when it lacks expertise, the experts often have connections to get access to relevant expertise. The STAB usually delivers its advice within three months. After the STAB has delivered its advice, the report is sent to the parties and the parties are able to respond to the report within four weeks.

The reports of the STAB function as a "third opinion" – mainly in addition to the information parties provided on disputed aspects of the case. The STAB can conduct its own research into the issue at hand and with that aim, for example, visit and inspect sites and installations and interview all parties involved.[96] The STAB can also analyze the reports that the administrative agency based its decision on. One example is a recent case concerning nitrogen deposition in the Netherlands.[97] This case concerned a dispute about a decision by the Minister regarding a specific calculation method to measure the impact of nitrogen depositions resulting from construction work on highways. The government's calculation method set a limit of up to 25 kilometers radius for calculating nitrogen deposition for a project requiring a permit – if the deposition is too high within this range, then getting a permit is complicated. All nitrogen deposition outside the 25 kilometers range will not be attributed to the project. This calculation method was disputed: appellants argued that this calculation method is not suitable as the 25 kilometers range is too limited to appropriately protect the natural areas that fall outside this range, since

93 Leemans (n 82), pp. 198–199.

94 Backes (n 15), p. 144. See also stab.nl/over-stab/medewerkers/.

95 See e.g. Backes (n 15), pp. 148–149. See also the website of the STAB: stab.nl/expertise-en-producten/vakgebieden/.

96 See Backes (n 15), pp. 143–150 and more elaborately Leemans (n 82), pp. 198–218.

97 ABRvS 5 April 2023, ECLI:NL:RVS:2023:1299.

they would still absorb deposited nitrogen. The Council involved the STAB in this case and requested information about the (un)suitability of the measures. The STAB analyzed the reports from expert organizations such as the Rijksinstituut voor Volksgezondheid en Milieu (RIVM) and the Nederlandse Organisatie voor Toegepast Natuurwetenschappelijk Onderzoek (TNO),[98] which have been used for the decision by the Minister. In short, the STAB concluded, among other things, that the method used had incorporated the best available scientific insights with regard to nitrogen disposition. The Council concluded that the Minister could use this calculation method.

There are no procedural legal rules on the functioning of the STAB or on the use of the expertise of the STAB. The Council decides whether to involve the STAB or not – the parties can suggest that advice should be sought, but it is at the discretion of the Court to request the STAB's advice and also to determine what questions should be put forward. Historically, the STAB's expert opinions were sought as a standard practice. Now, the Council appears to seek an opinion only if it believes that its knowledge is inadequate, which means that over the course of years there has been a decrease in the use of the expert opinions of the STAB by the Council.[99] The Council generally follows the advice of the STAB – when the Council does not follow its expert advice, it has to explicitly state its reasons for deviation.[100]

4. ANALYSIS

The NGT and the Council-STAB models for environmental dispute resolution represent innovative approaches. In this section, we will briefly highlight some challenges with the functioning of both models. The NGT, which was

98 The first is an independent research agency of the Ministry of Health, Welfare and Sport – the National Institute for Public Health and the Environment. The second is an independent research organization – the Netherlands Organisation for Applied Scientific Research.

99 Leemans (n 82), pp. 188–198. See also Isabelle Ouwehand & Ymre Schuurmans, 'Deskundige toetsing door de bestuursrechter', in: Rutger Schutgens et al. (eds.), *Toetsingsintensiteit. Een vergelijkende studie naar het variëren van de toetsingsintensiteit door de rechter* (Wolters Kluwer 2021). Retrieved from https://hdl.handle.net/1887/3494109.

100 The Council has, as an administrative court, the legal obligation to state reasons for its decisions, which can be found in article 8:77 Awb. Moreover, according to case law it is a guiding principle that the administrative law judge can follow the opinion of an independent expert if the reasoning of this expert seems convincing to him. See e.g. CRvB 23 May 2018, ECLI:NL:CRVB:2018:1615. See more about this Leemans (n 82), pp. 188–198 and Ouwehand & Schuurmans (n 99).

specifically designed for injecting specialist expertise in judicial decision-making, seems to face challenges concerning such expertise. This is different in the case of the STAB, which seems to be serving judicial needs well enough by functioning as an advisory body, although improvements could be made here as well. We trace these challenges to certain institutional and legal-cultural settings within which both models operate (explained below).

The NGT model is meant to reflect and foster environmental expertise as an expert adjudicatory body. As Gill has argued, the model's key strength lies in the use of the technical experts who are directly involved in decision-making. Based on fieldwork, she reports that expert members are involved in pre-hearing, post-hearing, and pre-judgment writing conferences where judicial members explain legal positions and expert members provide technical input relevant for the case.[101] Members agree on the final output, i.e., the judgment.[102] According to Gill, this process produces a sense of "collegiality" that fosters shared, mutual growth and training – the expert members become trained in the law and the judicial members become more familiar with technical concepts, which in turn enhances the quality of decision-making over time.[103] This synergy is supposed to enable the NGT to effectively promote environmental decision-making in India. It is evident, therefore, that expert members were expected to play a crucial role in ensuring the effectiveness of decision-making.

However, it is clear the NGT faces some serious limitations with respect to its expertise. Reports have recently emerged alleging an "excessive delegation or outsourcing of expert investigations to committees" and that the NGT's decision-making is being taken over by a "committee-raj".[104] On several occasions, the Supreme Court has also rapped the NGT for failing in its duty as an expert body to conduct proper merit reviews. For instance, in *Hanuman Arloskar v. Union of India*, the Supreme Court reprimanded the NGT for not conducting a merit review and deferring to the decision to grant an EC for the construction of a major international airport.[105] In another case concerning the expansion of a petrochemical complex, the NGT had again deferred to the granting of EC and did not consider the petitioner's contentions concerning

---

101 Gill (n 9), p. 193.
102 ibid.
103 ibid, p. 192.
104 Ramesh (n 14); Hazarika, 'Supreme Court pulls up NGT; says tribunals passing orders based on committee reports without hearing parties' (*BarandBench*, 14 February 2023) <https://tinyurl.com/5xrervm6> accessed on 20 June 2023.
105 *Hanuman Laxman Arloskar* (n 34), para 121.

environmental harm.[106] The decision was subsequently overturned by the Supreme Court for the NGT's failure to rule on whether or not the expansion would cause environmental harm.[107]

These criticisms raise questions pertaining to the NGT's claims to expertise. On a closer look, we notice (a) challenges with expert member appointments; and (b) challenges with the hybrid model design, compounded by the NGT's own practice.

With respect to the first challenge, expert member appointments have to be approved by the central government. Sahu and Dutta have argued that most of the expert member positions in the NGT lie vacant for reasons including the relevant ministry "not taking an active interest", and financial and budgetary constraints.[108] In 2017, the number of vacancies was so high that a High Court asked the counsel for the Central government if it "planned to wind up the NGT".[109] Even when expert members are appointed, more than 50% of them tend to be career bureaucrats from the Indian Forest Service or the Indian Administrative Service who are unable to provide technical input in (other) environmental disputes.[110] This particular problem can be traced to Section 5(2)(b) of the NGT Act 2010 which allows the appointment of persons with "administrative experience" in the field of environment as expert members.[111] The dominance of bureaucrats as expert members has also been criticized as limiting relevant technical input needed for environment decision-making.[112] Hence, the NGT is seriously under-staffed with respect to its expert members, which in turn can affect the quality of its decision-making. In this regard, it is noteworthy that although expert members were previously appointed on the recommendations of a committee comprising representatives from the judiciary, the executive, and members from the scientific

106 *Sangher Zuber Ismail v. Ministry of Environment, Forests and Climate Change and Ors.*, Civil Appeal No. 4543 of 2021, paras 6–8.

107 ibid, para 9.

108 Sahu & Dutta (n 13), p. 9.

109 Harish V. Nair, 'Supreme Court Seeks Explanation from Centre on Acute Shortage of Judges in the NGT' (*India Today*, 3 December 2017), <https://www.indiatoday.in/mail-today/story/ngt-judges-vacancy-supreme-court-centre-appoint-judges-1099148-2017-12-03> accessed on 20 June 2023.

110 Debayan Roy, 'NGT working with just 6 members instead of at least 21, zonal benches vacant for 2 yrs now' (*The Print*, 4 November 2019) <https://theprint.in/environment/ngt-working-with-6-members-instead-of-at-least-21-zonal-benches-vacant-for-2-yrs-now/314616/> accessed on 20 June 2023.

111 Section 5(2)(b), National Green Tribunal Act 2010.

112 Sahu & Dutta (n 13), p. 9.

community,[113] the central government in 2017 introduced rules that sought to exclude the judicial role in expert member appointments to the NGT.[114] In a case challenging the constitutionality of the new rules, the Supreme Court struck down the rules holding that attempts to "keep the judiciary away from … appointment and selection of members" in tribunals were unconstitutional since they encroached upon the judiciary's independence.[115] With respect to the NGT, the court issued an interim order directing that the "terms and conditions of service of members of the National Green Tribunal shall be governed by the provisions of the National Green Tribunal Act, 2010".[116] This tussle between the executive and the judiciary reflects how important the proper appointment of expert members is to the NGT model of adjudication.

With respect to the second challenge, an inherent limitation with the model is that even when an expert member is appointed with appropriate qualifications, their expertise is necessarily restricted to particular specializations. NGT panels often consist of one judicial member and one expert member hearing cases together. Given the NGT's wide jurisdiction over disputes that cover a range of areas including water pollution, air pollution, biodiversity protection, sanitation, and waste disposal, etc., it is not uncommon for an expert member who has degrees in biodiversity protection to hear cases concerning air pollution. In such cases, the NGT is likely to resort to ad hoc committees for the technical input needed to resolve the dispute. No clear rules or regulations govern the NGT's appointment of these committees either. The NGT does not appear to maintain a list or panel of certified experts from which professionals can be selected for such committees, raising questions of transparency. The NGT, an expert body meant for resolving technical environment disputes in a scientific manner, evidently lacks the requisite expertise and draws in external input as a matter of regular practice.

---

113 Rule 3, National Green Tribunal (Manner of Appointment of Judicial and Expert Members, Salaries, Allowances and Other Terms and Conditions of Service of Chairperson and other Members and Procedure for Inquiry) Rules 2010 <https://drive.google.com/file/d/1qUiinuFeZf1xpQ60k7tO72ipLWoS1zaw/view> accessed on 20 June 2023.

114 Tribunal, Appellate Tribunal and other Authorities (Qualifications, Experience and other Conditions of Service of Members) Rules, 2017 <https://tinyurl.com/ycy5nvh5> accessed on 20 June 2023.

115 *Roger Mathews v. South Indian Bank Ltd. and Others*, Civil Appeal No. 8588 of 2019, para 157.

116 Jayanta Basu, 'SC Breather for green tribunals' (*The Telegraph*, 20 June 2023) <https://www.telegraphindia.com/india/sc-breather-for-green-tribunals/cid/1335461> accessed on 20 June 2023.

The *institutional* settings within which the NGT operates, i.e., its interactions with other institutions such as the Central Government, are therefore clearly important for effective decision-making. Since the NGT is dependent on the Central Government for expert member appointment, inter-institutional support between the executive and the judiciary is crucial and (the lack of it) impacts NGT functioning. This challenge, compounded by the challenge of the expert members' restricted specializations, hinders optimal synthesis of law and science in the NGT's decision-making.

The externally sourced expertise model presented by the Dutch STAB appears to be a promising approach in this regard. Unlike the NGT's expert members, the STAB as an institution has experts in a broad range of specializations who can assist the court in all manners of environmental cases without the need to consult any other body. Further, although funded by the government, it is an independent body and according to Backes, it enjoys a high level of trust both among the judges and litigants.[117] The objectivity, impartiality, and independence of the STAB are legally guaranteed. Additionally, a permanent institutional source of scientific and technical knowledge like the STAB would likely avoid the challenges faced in the appointment of ad hoc committees that the NGT appoints in cases where the expert members may not be able to adequately contribute to decision-making. Moreover, the STAB does not face a lack of support from the government. On the contrary, the government is facilitating the STAB by providing funding and, therefore, making it accessible for the Council to use.

Evaluations of the STAB have mostly been positive.[118] These evaluations have highlighted beneficial aspects of the system, which include saving time and costs in obtaining reliable expert reports and the long-standing working

---

[117] Backes (n 15), pp. 147–149. See also one of the evaluation reports, only available in Dutch: Lenny van Klink et al., 'eindrapportage subisidie-evaluatie STAB 2007-2013' (RebelGroup Executives 2013).

[118] See Backes (n 15), pp. 147–149 and Leemans (n 82), pp. 198–201. These evaluations are conducted by (legal) scholars and by consultancy organizations. See Annelies Freriks and Jan Robbe, *Vijf jaar STAB: een onderzoek naar de kwaliteit van de deskundigenadvisering door de Stichting Advisering Bestuursrechtspraak voor Milieu en Ruimtelijke Ordening gedurende de eerste vijf jaar van haar bestaan* (Boom Juridische Uitgevers 2001); Berthy van den Broek, Toon de Gier & Aster Veldkamp, *Tien jaar STAB. Een onderzoek naar het functioneren van de Stichting Advisering Bestuursrechtspraak in het recente verleden en haar rol in de recente toekomst* (Boom Juridisch Uitgevers 2006); van Klink et al. (n 117). Katja Crooijmans & Enno Gerdes, 'STAB: Meerwaarde door Verbinding 2016' (Rebelgroep 2016), retrieved from: https://stab.nl/wp-content/uploads/2020/01/Rebelgroup.pdf.

relationship between the STAB and the judges of the Council. While different from the "collegiality" between the NGT's judicial and expert members, the latter has enabled mutual and shared learnings between the judges and the STAB experts. The experts are familiar with the kind of information courts need for legal application, how to translate difficult technical insights into language that judges understand, what the fundamental procedural rules are, and what is expected from them. This also results in a more consistent determination of facts and circumstances.[119] Considering these positive evaluations, it appears to be serving judicial needs for expertise well enough.

However, there are some concerns with regard to the STAB's position and use as a permanent expert of the Council as well.[120] These concerns or challenges include the lack of procedural clarity concerning the use of expertise and evidence and a deferential culture of judicial review which could be said to hinder optimal decision-making in the Dutch model.

With respect to the first challenge, the relationship between the STAB and the Council is largely dependent on, and determined by, judicial practice – there are no legal rules governing its use by the Council, nor has the Council chosen to clarify this through case law. The Council retains complete discretion on whether or not to involve the STAB in a given case, regardless of whether parties request it. The STAB used to be involved on a standard basis, as it had an important function to structure and clarify the (rather technical) facts of the case. However, this practice changed over the years. It is no longer standard practice for the Council to involve the STAB in its decision-making. According to Backes, the Council has only requested the STAB's reports in 3% of its environment and planning caseload.[121]

The STAB's reduced use by the Council may be the result of changes in procedural law and practice. For instance, a change in procedural law in 2010 led to lower administrative district courts becoming courts of first instance and the Council becoming a court of appeal with respect to certain types of environment. Since the facts in such cases are established at first instance at administrative district courts, there is less emphasis on the facts at the appellate level in the Council. Simultaneously, there is an increase in use of the STAB within the district courts.[122] The practice of the Council also changed in the sense that it increasingly relied on the parties to provide the facts, as opposed to

[119] This follows from previous research involving interviews with the judiciary and litigants. See Backes (n 15), p. 149, Leemans (n 82), pp. 199–200 and the research to which they refer.
[120] See more elaborately about concerns or points of discussion Backes (n 15), pp. 149–150 and Leemans (n 82), pp. 200–202.
[121] Backes (n 15), p. 145.
[122] Ibid.

investigating them on its own. Only in cases where there is uncertainty does the Council take a more proactive role in investigating the facts. This has to do with an increased focus on the *recours subjectif* of the judicial administrative review process and with the prevailing culture of judicial deference to the government.[123] The standard of judicial review employed is deferential, with a broad margin of appreciation extended to the decision-making authorities.[124]

Although the above suggests why the Council involves the STAB to a lesser extent now than before, the STAB's underutilization by the Council can be considered problematic. This is because even at the Council level, it is still the appellant that bears the burden of proof that the executive decision is flawed, which can be a heavy burden. This burden of proof can be hard to meet, especially in highly technical cases that require specific expertise, which is often the case in environmental disputes. At the same time, the Council generally assumes a broad level of discretion for the administrative body; unlike the NGT, the standard of review is only a marginal one.[125] This can seriously affect the legal protection of the appellants. It may therefore be desirable, in line with recent general calls for a more active protective role of the Council,[126] if the Council would take a more proactive role and involve the STAB more often.

---

123 With the adoption of the GALA it seems that more emphasis has been placed on the *recours subjectif.* In a *recours subjectif* the legal position and interests of the litigant are important, and therefore, the parties are at the center, rather than the enforcement of objective law, as is the case in a *recours objectif.* This places more responsibility on the litigants. The practice of the Council changed according to this renewed focus. See Backes (n 15), p. 145 and B. Assink, *Het recours objectif, een herwaardering (Staat en Recht nr. 56)* (Wolters Kluwer 2022), para 1.3 and R.M. van Male, 'Recours objectif revisited' (2013) *Nederlands Tijdschrift voor Bestuursrecht*, pp. 71–73.

124 See about this standard more elaborately Dirk Sanderink, 'Toetsingsintensiteit en deskundigenadviezen in milieugeschillen', in: Rutger Schutgens et al. (eds.), *Toetsingsintensiteit. Een vergelijkende studie naar het variëren van de toetsingsintensiteit door de rechter* (Wolters Kluwer 2021); Bart Jan van Ettekoven, 'Judicial Review in Dutch Environmental Law: a judge perspective', in: Jurgen de Poorter et al. (eds.), *Judicial Review of Administrative Discretion in the Administrative State* (TMC Asser Press 2019) and Barkhuysen & Emmerik (n 70).

125 Sanderink (n 124).

126 Since the childcare benefit scandal in the Netherlands, there are serious calls for a more active protecting role of the administrative judges with regard to governmental decisions. It might be expected that the Council will accept a more active role, also in environmental disputes. See e.g. the reflection report from the Council of 2021, available at raadvanstate.nl/lessen-uit-de-kinderopvangtoeslagz aken/.

Simultaneously, even if the STAB is involved, there are other important procedural limitations as well. The parties to the dispute do not necessarily have an opportunity to provide input on the questions to the STAB, even though the way the question is framed is of course important for the outcome of the dispute.[127] Moreover, there is no opportunity for the parties to comment on the draft report of the STAB before it is delivered to the court – comments are only possible within four weeks after the Council receives the report. Expert reports are in principle not public and are not made available by the STAB.[128] Hence, it is also difficult to assess the STAB's work, raising transparency issues. Another concern is that perceptions of the STAB's (lack of) "independence" as the permanent advisory body of the Council of State can make the Council less critical towards the expert reports, creating a "monoculture in consulting".[129] This refers to a culture in which the expert is not motivated to be self-critical and to address "knowledge gaps", while the judge is generally uncritical of the expert. This is compounded by the fact that it is very costly and time-consuming for parties to call the STAB's report into question, as this involves the need to bring in specialized contra-expertise. This somewhat defeats the STAB's purpose as a neutral expert meant to balance the evidence brought into courtrooms by parties with deep pockets, such as the government.

Put together, the issues identified above point to the relevance of the *legal-cultural* settings within which the Council-STAB partnership operates in the Netherlands and how they can impact decision-making. The Council-STAB's challenges as a model for environmental decision-making relate to (a) the *legal* settings within which it operates, i.e., the lack of clarity of legal rules regulating its use by the Council as well as the lack of opportunity for parties to play a meaningful role in assisting or challenging the STAB's expertise when it is in fact used; and (b) the *cultural* settings within which it operates – the shift to emphasis on the *recours subjectif* and the pervading culture of judicial deference causing the Council to employ a relatively marginal standard of review and utilize the STAB on a relatively lesser scale.

---

127 Backes (n 15), pp. 149–150.

128 Interested parties in an appeal procedure can request the report through court. Since May 2022 the Open Government Act (WOO) has been in force. This act provides for more possibilities to request documents from governmental (and other public) bodies. Hence, on request public bodies have to disclose information. However, there are exceptions as not every document falls under this Act. It seems that the reports of the STAB fall under one of these exceptions, as they have been considered court documents. See rijksoverheid.nl/documenten/woo-besluiten/2023/06/06/besluit-op-woo-verzoek-over-stab-rapport-bij-uitspraak-raad-van-state.

129 Leemans (n 82), pp. 200–201.

It is difficult to say that the NGT model is a better alternative with respect to these challenges, but we may note there are similarities and variations between the functioning of the NGT and the Council-STAB here as well. Concerning legal rules, it has already been highlighted that the NGT's own procedures such as its appointment and use of ad hoc expert committees also suffer from lack of clarity and transparency. However, with respect to judicial deference, what can be said is that the NGT's status as an expert tribunal was intended to enable it to resist governmental assertions of superior expertise.[130] Further, the NGT's chairperson is statutorily required to be a former judge of the Supreme Court or a Chief Justice of a High Court, both constitutional courts with extensive powers of judicial review.[131] The judicial members are also statutorily former Chief Justices or judges of High Courts.[132] Given the significant role of the higher judiciary in developing law and policy in India, together with the privileged status of the NGT chairperson, it may be fair to say that the NGT's decision-making is not necessarily pervaded by a deferential culture. The tyre-burning case in *Asim Sarode* provides one example of how expertise, whether in-house or external, is sometimes deployed to question the government's policy choices concerning the environment and innovative solutions are devised. Although empirical research is required for any definitive statement, judicial deference therefore might matter to a lesser extent for the NGT's problems with expertise than the STAB, as opposed to the other institutional settings identified above.

5. CONCLUSION

With the rise in complex environmental disputes, the question has shifted from whether to how court decisions should be properly informed by credible and reliable scientific knowledge. This led to the development of different models to involve external expertise in environmental dispute resolutions, such as ECTs and general courts with court-appointed (external) experts. We attempted to take a closer look at two different judicial decision-making models with varying approaches towards incorporating scientific knowledge with the aim of understanding the specific advantages that are perceived to be held in each model and to see whether they hold in practice.

130 *AP Pollution Control Board* (n 20), para 42. The Court stated, "Of paramount importance in the establishment of environmental courts, authorities and tribunals is the need for providing adequate judicial and scientific inputs rather than leave complicated disputes regarding environmental pollution only to officers drawn from the executive".

131 Section 5(1), National Green Tribunal Act 2010.

132 ibid.

In light of the "explosion" in adoption of ECTs, we looked into the assumptions and perceived strengths of hybrid ECTs taking the NGT as an example of a hybrid ECT. At the time of inception, the NGT model was lauded as achieving the perfect harmonization of science and law. In reality, however, the NGT's expertise is questionable, suffering from institutional handicaps caused by government chokeholds over the appointment of the Expert Members and the limited range of specializations in the Expert Members. This has resulted in a hybrid expert tribunal heavily relying on external sources of expertise such as ad hoc committees. Further problems of transparency and procedural clarity are identified with the use of such committees for generating the expertise needed for environmental cases.

This is contrasted with a general administrative court with a permanent, institutional source of expertise in the form of the STAB, a remnant from an earlier legacy of the Crown hearing appeals in environment and planning cases. On the face of it, the STAB appears to be a credible alternative to the in-house expertise that ECTs have made popular. It has been generally evaluated positively by both judges and litigants as being a reliable expert body that provides good quality reports on a broad range of technical expertise in a timely manner. We note some challenges that can be improved upon. As explained, legal rules surrounding the Council's use of the STAB are unclear raising issues of transparency. Further, and crucially, the STAB is potentially underutilized at the Council level, with possible reasons being a culture of judicial deference in combination with recent procedural changes giving lower administrative courts a greater role in environmental cases. Since the burden for parties to bring in their own expertise remains high, this development at the Council level can raise concerns. However, as we explained, even if the STAB is involved, it can be difficult to call the STAB's reports into question.

We have pointed to certain advantages in each model vis-à-vis the other. That is, the STAB's broad range of institutional expertise may better enable scientific decision-making than the NGT's ad hoc approach of appointing committees. At the same time, unlike the NGT, the STAB's use is limited by the deferential approach of the Dutch courts towards agency expertise. However, more research is required to determine which model could better enable a sound scientific basis for judicial decisions in environmental cases. That question is not what we attempted to answer here. Indeed, our research highlights the equal importance of factors besides model design, such as the institutional or legal-cultural settings within which the models operate, for effective decision-making. Our analysis shows that for a holistic understanding of the relative merits and disadvantages of judicial models to involve external expertise in environmental dispute resolution, accounting for such institutional and legal-cultural settings is crucial.

Conclusion

Rob van Gestel, Jurgen de Poorter and Edward L. Rubin

RELYING ON TRADITION …?

Let us board the aircraft of Lofty Perspective and fly over the City of Modern Government. What do we see? There is the executive district, a vast area with many clusters of buildings. The buildings in each cluster are multi-storied concrete structures with wide windows through which massive data processing computers can be seen as we pass by. Their flat roofs bristle with communications equipment. The buildings in each cluster, and between the clusters, are connected by broad motorways filled with a constant flow of cars and trucks. Proceeding past all this construction and activity, we reach the legislative district. It is much smaller, consisting of a single group of buildings, often of pre-modern design. Many of the windows have been widened, in some cases sufficiently for us to see a limited number of processing computers inside. Communications equipment appears on their roofs, often wedged between the gables and turrets dating from the era when these buildings were constructed. The motorways that connect them are not as wide as those in the executive district, but they are also filled with traffic, and most extend past the boundaries of the legislative district and into the executive.

Now we reach the judicial district, but we must watch closely or we will miss it. There is a moderately sized building of medieval design, and a number of diminutive structures scattered around it. The building's windows are covered in stained glass, so that nothing inside it can be seen. A single antenna is awkwardly attached to the sloping roof amid a profusion of turrets and gargoyles, and connected to the interior of the building by a hanging wire. Between the main building and its surrounding structures are narrow, unpaved paths, and similar paths connect these to the other districts. These paths cannot carry motor traffic, but as we fly by, we catch sight of some messengers running along them holding pieces of paper in their hands.

As many commentators have argued, there is a strong argument for the judiciary to adopt a policy making role in modern government. Democracy has been a great success in the two centuries during which it has taken hold and expanded in the Western world, but, by its own definition, it is subject to many serious defects, from the tyranny of the majority or the distortions of the electoral and administrative process by affluent minorities, to transnational problems such as climate change that cannot be dealt with effectively by national democracies in isolation. As De Tocqueville noted in the first sociological account of democratic government, it is both ideologically naive and naively ideological to assume that all our goals – liberty, equality and governmental effectiveness – can be achieved on the basis of the single principle that "the people" should rule.[1] So they should, we believe, but there needs to be some control to counteract their prejudices and restrain their tendency to reach decisions that they will later regret. That is the role that has befallen to modern judiciaries. One of the great triumphs of our current government design has been to take an institution developed to resolve disputes and adapt it to serve this control function through its interpretation of statutory and constitutional law. The result has been a triangular relationship between fundamental rights, democracy and the rule of law in the Western world, instantiated by the dialogue among the legislature, the executive, administrative agencies and the judiciary,[2]

It might be argued that it would have been preferable to begin anew, after the Industrial Revolution and the advent of democracy at the end of the eighteenth century, to design a control institution from the ground up, with a structure specific to its purpose, staffed by officials whose training and experience was similarly specific. But that is not the way that institutional change typically occurs, even in revolutionary times. While Britain's transition to democracy was so gradual as to be difficult to ascribe to any particular event,[3] the United States and France achieved that transition by violent revolutions that no one, either at that time or subsequently, could possibly ignore or dismiss. Yet the

1 Alexis de Tocqueville, *Democracy in America* (Harvey C. Mansfield & Delba Winthrop, trans.) (Chicago: University of Chicago Press 2002).

2 See Alexander Bickel, *The Least Dangerous Branch: The Supreme Court at the Bar of Politics* (Indianapolis: Bobbs-Merrill, 1961); Louis Fisher, *Constitutional Dialogues: Interpretation as Political Process* (Princeton, N.J.: Princeton University Press 2016); Rob van Gestel & Jurgen de Poorter, *In the Court We Trust: Cooperation, Coordination and Collaboration between the ECJ and Supreme Administrative Courts* (Cambridge University Press 2020).

3 But it clearly occurred sometime during the last quarter of the eighteenth century. For an account of the political events that produced the transition, see William Hague, *William Pitt the Younger* (New York: Knopf, 2005); Andrew Roberts, *The Last King of America: The Misunderstood Reign of George III* (New York: Viking, 2021).

basic democratic institutions that those revolutions produced were adapted from pre-existing models. Most European nations had some sort of legislative body in the Middle Ages, typically exercising the power to approve or reject special taxation (that is, taxation beyond accepted feudal dues). In Britain, the commoners who were members of that body, and soon formed a separate division of it, had been elected by a segment of the populace since the mid-thirteenth century.[4] Administrative agencies had emerged in the Middle Ages as well. One of the most notable was the English Exchequer that managed the king's finances, a hierarchically organized and professionally run institution that had been the subject of an administrative law treatise written in the twelfth century.[5] The revolutionary regimes of France and the United States adapted both these institutions, creating democratic governments based on representative legislatures and rationalized agencies. In fact, even their chief executives, although elected, exercised powers that resembled those of the non-absolutist English monarchs of the Early Modern period, specifically the appointment of leading officials and command of the armed forces.

This adaptation process is not simply a failure of imagination or a concession to the forces of resistance. It can also be seen as the most effective way to implement institutional change. The problem with creating entirely new institutions is that no one in society would know how to operate them. It is one thing for a visionary leader to conceive of novel and idealized innovations that would lead society into a better future, but quite another to implement such visions in the grimy real world. How, for example, can entirely new institutions be staffed with people who can carry out their daily functions? At the time of the American and French revolutions, people in these nations had a reasonable amount of cultural experience with elected legislatures and quasi-bureaucratic agencies. This is also true of nations such as Sweden, Denmark and the Netherlands that instituted democratic government in the succeeding decades. The political agonies experienced by Russia and by many current nations in the Global South when they have attempted to follow this path indicate the crucial importance of cultural experience.

The same is true for courts. By the time of the democratic revolutions in America and France, and of Britain's gradual transition to full democracy, all three nations had extensive experience with the use of courts as their institutional means for resolving disputes between private parties, or between private

---

4 See David Carpenter, *The Struggle for Mastery* (New York: Penguin 2005); J.R. Maddicott, *The Origins of the English Parliament, 924–1327* (Oxford, UK: Oxford University Press 2010).

5 Richard FitzNeal, *Dialogus de Scaccario* (date uncertain). For the English translation, see Emilie Amt, *Dialogus de Scaccario: The Dialogue of the Exchequer* (Oxford, UK.: Oxford University Press 2007).

parties and the government. The adaptation of this institution for the purpose of exercising control over executive and legislative policy making was thus not only an inspired idea, but a practical means of implementation. Ever since, however, there has been a tendency in democratic nations toward self-congratulation and complacency. Judicial review of governmental action on both constitutional and statutory grounds has been celebrated as securing the rule of law, as protecting human rights, and as demonstrating the ability of democratic governments to criticize and discipline themselves.

INSTITUTIONAL JUDICIAL DISABILITIES

All this may be true, but it does not exempt modern democracies from the charge that they are implementing this admittedly essential mode of control through an institution that was developed during the Middle Ages and has not changed very much since then. When confronting the complexities of modern government, courts suffer from a range of institutional disabilities. They cannot initiate investigations or develop their own programs but can only act by adjudicating disputes brought to them by other parties. When doing so, they are generally restricted to considering the issues raised by those parties. They cannot assess the results of their decisions, nor can they rescind or revise their decision if the results prove unsatisfactory. Courts are seriously understaffed, depending on judges, individual decision makers who generally lack any significant amount of institutional support. These decision makers are usually trained only in law, and their primary expertise is the interpretation of legal documents. That is certainly an important capability, but its value is limited when exercising control over the public policy analysts, economists, scientists, social scientists, engineers, physicians, chemists and so many others who staff governmental agencies.

The restrictions on their communication with other government officials and with private parties, while developed for the laudable purpose of ensuring judicial independence, also mean that judges can obtain information only from intensely self-interested litigants. Their ability to gather information is further limited by rules of evidence, rules that serve important purposes but also impose significant restrictions. These rules, as Frederick Schauer observes, exclude many relevant facts as well as irrelevant ones, rely on witnesses who often lack firsthand knowledge, demand a closed record that limits inquiry into matters not presented to the court, and limit investigation into related situations that may be more representative of the issue being litigated.[6] The result, Schauer concludes, is that judges are "informationally disabled".

Many of these issues manifest themselves in limitations on the courts' ability to obtain and apply empirical data. Changing that will not transform or modernize the institution in its entirety; it will not enable courts to initiate cases, for example, or to frame remedies that extend beyond the limits of the issue presented to them. But it represents a significant means of detaching the courts from their medieval origins and equipping them to function effectively in modern government. It may well be the most significant and beneficial change that can be effectuated within the existing institutional structure of the courts; that is, the structure that Western society has developed over the course of a millennium and that is now so securely ensconced in both our institutional system and our conceptual framework. In other words, it is far-reaching but pragmatically achievable.

WHAT DO THE CHAPTERS IN THIS VOLUME RECOMMEND?

The chapters in this volume point toward specific steps that can be taken to enable courts to use empirical data, and to specific pitfalls that they should avoid in doing so. In Part I, the Promise of Empirical Data in Judicial Policy Making, both Rubin and de Augustinis and van Gestel urge courts to rely more on statistical analysis. This can be achieved relatively easily by adding specialists in statistics to the judiciary's existing staff. It requires a certain amount of funding, but the economic consequences of even a single major discrimination case are significantly larger. Of course, the mere availability of statistical expertise would not necessarily persuade judges to make use of it, but the addition of such staff members would probably increase the judges' sense that statistical analysis is both legitimate and beneficial. Dissenting opinions would be likely to amplify this effect. If the majority opinion was statistically illiterate, the dissenters would be motivated to use this as one basis for their criticism, particularly if they had ready access to staff members who would carry out the analysis at their direction.

Another means of inducing judges to rely on statistical analysis would be to add it to the law school curriculum. This could be readily accomplished by signaling the relevance of statistics in first-year courses (a week or so of material may be sufficient) and then adding an advanced course ("Statistical

[6] Frederick Schauer, *Our Informationally Disabled Courts* (Dædalus 2014), p. 111 (https://www.amacad.org/sites/default/files/daedalus/downloads/Su2014_Invention-of-Courts.pdf).

Analysis for Lawyers"). In nations with career judiciaries, a similar course could be included in the judicial training programs. These reforms would be essentially equivalent to the introduction of economics into legal education, perhaps the largest curricular change of the last several decades. That change was accomplished without any structural alteration in legal education or any major allocation of resources. As a result of this fairly modest curricular reform, many judges are capable of carrying out at least a rudimentary economic analysis, and most are at least aware of economic issues when those issues are relevant to the decision. An equally modest reform would be likely to provide judges with at least a rudimentary level of statistical literacy.

The field experimentation recommended by Dyevre would involve a similar type of reform. Here again, courts would need to add staff members with specialized training, in this case for judges to rely on in framing their remedies but also to implement the experimental program. Again, judges might be encouraged to rely more on the use of empirical data, statistics and small-scale experiments if training in certain social science methods was added to the law school and judicial educational program, but this would also not be impossible. Judges would mostly need to know how to assess and make use of the data gathered by, for example, field experiments and not necessarily be trained to set up such experiments themselves. The experimentation itself might be carried out by specialized staff, just as judges currently use special masters for operational tasks like restructuring an institution or surveying political boundaries.

Unlike statistical analysis, field experimentation would also require some alteration of existing legal procedure and legal doctrine regarding the remedies that courts are permitted to impose. This change of law regarding remedies, though, could itself be guided by experimental legislation allowing courts to test these new procedural rules and evaluate the procedural innovation before turning it into more permanent legislation. Implicit in Dyevre's proposal is that each of the alternative remedies would be one that the court in question could impose. Instead of simply choosing one alternative, which is the present approach, the court would order a number of alternatives, with each to be imposed on a subset of the subject population, of course.

The major doctrinal change would be to hold the court's jurisdiction open until the alternatives were implemented and evaluated, rather than terminating jurisdiction at the time the initial remedy is imposed. This is hardly revolutionary; a number of courts have already done so in structural reform cases where a special master is appointed, such as the American cases of the 1970s and 80s that effectively reformed American prisons.[7] We can observe a rise of similar structural remedies in other jurisdictions, such as India, South Africa and Colombia, where courts sometimes appoint scientific committees, organize public hearings to discuss empirical data or scientific evidence, and use writs of continuing mandamus to keep a case open so that they can monitor the consequences of their rulings that may have third party effects. In some cases, they ask the executive branch to develop a remedial plan, subject to court approval, rather than crafting the plan themselves. This can lead to a constitutional dialogue that generates interbranch cooperation without impairing the independence of the judiciary.

To be sure, Dyevre's recommendation would also involve some additional resources, but the costs imposed on society by a single judicial remedy that produces an undesired result could be substantially greater. Consider the *Test Achats* case of the Court of Justice of the European Union (CJEU) discussed by de Augustinis and van Gestel, which forbids auto insurance companies from charging different premiums for men and women, despite the fact that there are statistically relevant differences between their accident rates (i.e., women are, on average, more careful drivers than men). If the CJEU had conducted an experiment regarding the economic consequences of unisex premiums, it would likely have concluded that the premiums for both men and women would have increased if it had followed through with its decision. While this is certainly not a social catastrophe in the order of global warming, the economic impact of this one rather technical-sounding case, which would be an increase in auto insurance premiums for all of Europe, would probably dwarf the entire budgetary allocation needed to implement Dyevre's proposal.

The chapters in Part II, The Problems of Empirical Data in Judicial Policy Making, counsel caution in implementing reforms, but none of them conclude that the effort to use such evidence should be abandoned. Instead, they point to other amplifications and improvements for this effort, many of which are even more delimited and practical than the recommendations implied by the chapters in Part I. Petersen's chapter approaches the problem in general terms. He argues that courts adopt a general stance of deference when reviewing legislative and executive decisions. But courts should not abandon their essential role as guardians of the national constitution and its implicit norms, even when confronted with complex technical questions and extensive empirical data. Instead, he argues that they should employ a mixture of substantive, procedural and motive-based review, and concludes with the same recommendation

[7] See Malcolm M. Feeley & Edward L. Rubin, *Judicial Policy Making and the Modern State: How the Courts Reformed America's Prisons* (New York: Cambridge University Press 2000).

that Rubin and de Augustinis and van Gestel advance: judges should receive more training in empirical methods and obtain more staff to assist them in this effort.

These recommended changes are obviously necessary in order to engage in the substantive review of government decisions. But they are also necessary for procedural review, so that the court can identify the procedural lapses that are likely to produce ineffective or counterproductive legislation, as opposed to merely technical errors that should fall within the area where courts defer to legislative action. Finally, they are necessary for the more generalized review of legislative motivation; to overcome the strong presumption that a popularly elected legislature has acted properly, and instead conclude that it has hidden an illicit motive behind a screen of presumptive legitimacy, a court must be able to discern a serious gap between what the legislature has declared and what it has accomplished. This once again requires access to an analysis of empirical information.

The other three chapters in Part II lead to more specific recommendations, all of which could be readily implemented within the ambit of current institutional structures. Blackham's chapter shows that making decisions that affect the public interest in an evidential vacuum will negatively affect the legitimacy of judicial decision making. This means that courts cannot simply pretend that there is no need for the skilled use of empirical evidence to fill gaps in the government's decision making process. But their institutional role astride the path between the decision and its implementation provides them with the resources that can remedy the problem and thus preserve the legitimacy of their own decisions. Courts can either demand that the government provide sufficient empirical evidence to support its decision or, more aggressively, strike down the government's action for lack of such support. In the final analysis, of course, this is no different from the power that the courts possess to decide a case that is presented to them one way or another. Blackham's recommendation, however, is that they do so with specific reference to the empirical evidence that the government has provided. Although this provides a way for the court to preserve its legitimacy, it need not be based on the questionable Bickelian basis that the court is trying to protect its institutional status,[8] but rather on the more justifiable goal of reaching a decision that is valid and effective on public policy grounds.

[8] See Alexander Bickel, *The Least Dangerous Branch: The Supreme Court at the Bar of Politic*s (New Haven: Yale University Press, 1986). For questions about this approach, see Gerald Gunther, The Subtle Vices of the Passive Virtues: A Comment on Principle and Expediency in Judicial Review, 64 Colum. L. Rev. 1 (1964).

Wendy Wagner's chapter speaks to the way empirical evidence should be evaluated by the court once it is presented. Some of the best academic legal research questions stem from wonderment. Wagner wonders why courts have so far paid so little attention to the methods scientists use to filter out flawed empirical research or scientific evidence, although the adversarial system, particularly in public interest cases, tends to lean on biased evidence brought by the litigants. Wagner expresses further surprise that courts have tried to reinvent the wheel when it comes to the scrutiny of scientific evidence. She believes that they could learn from the methodology that scientists themselves employ, which features critical peer review, independence of those who collected the evidence, and disinterestedness from those who produced it.

Not only does this proposal fit comfortably within the existing structure of American and European courts, but it in fact fits better than the standards that it would replace, such as the Daubert standard in American federal courts.[9] The sorts of determinations Wagner recommends are ones that courts are qualified to make, being procedural rather than substantive. Courts regularly determine whether one institution has adequately reviewed another (e.g., did an agency's appeals tribunal correctly supervise the hearing officers) and whether a particular decision maker was independent and unbiased (should a lower court judge have recused herself, was the agency's hearing officer independent of its prosecutorial or policy staff). Wagner insists that courts learn the procedural norms that scientists use to assess the validity of research, but she does not require them to learn any science.

Rakoff's proposal can be implemented with similar facility. It is perhaps too disparaging to attribute the practice of American judges when dealing with proprietary AI sentencing programs to outright laziness. More likely, they are simply too willing to defer to an entity that claims expertise in an area where they feel they have none. While this might seem to indicate a certain receptiveness to empirical data, it is in fact the opposite – a failure to understand, apply and evaluate such data that leads to the extremes of either instinctive rejection or blind acceptance. Rakoff's solution, closely allied to the recommendations of Rubin, van Gestel and de Augustinis, Dyevre, Petersen, Blackham and Wagner, is that judges obtain the training and staff support necessary to recognize the need for empirical data and to determine the reliability of the data that is provided to them.

Judges do not need the ability to construct predictive algorithms any more than they need the ability to titrate DNA samples or apply censored regression

---

9 *Daubert v. Merrell Dow Pharmaceuticals, Inc*, 509 U.S. 579 (1993) (requiring a court to determine, inter alia, that scientific evidence must be generated by the "scientific method").

models. What they need is sufficient familiarity with empirical data, sufficient staff support to implement their data-related decisions, and sufficient commitment to the use and value of such data so that they can function as effective decision makers in the post-medieval world. In the particular case of AI sentencing algorithms, Rakoff argues that they should never accept a proprietary program that does not disclose its data sources and its methodology. American and European intellectual property law is well developed and should provide as much protection for a private firm as it requires to protect its products. If the firm refuses to disclose the necessary information, then judges should rely on two other well-developed features of American and European society, the first being competitive capitalism that will generate other firms willing to comply with judicial demands, and the second being administrative government that can provide public services in areas where private firms are either unable or unwilling to compete. What judges should not do, Rakoff insists, even or particularly in the face of the modern world's complexities, is to abdicate their basic responsibilities. The need for and availability of empirical data that the modern world creates should empower judges, not disable them.

The chapters in Part III, Balancing the Promise and the Problems, point toward more comprehensive changes in the existing institutional structure. While many of the advantages can be obtained, and many of the defects avoided, within the current capabilities of European and American judicial institutions, resolving interplays between the two will often call upon a wider range of institutional resources, and thus require more extensive innovations. Nonetheless, the recommendations implicit in the final set of chapters also fall within the ambit of incremental change, rather than demanding radical transformations.

In the first chapter of Part III, Elbert de Jong focuses on the macro consequences of judicial policy making, that is the effect of the ruling on those who are not parties to the litigation. For example, some have argued that the *Urgenda* decision led to increased emissions in sectors outside energy production, such as waste disposal, and in nations outside the Netherlands. When courts act as policy makers, they are not required to conduct an explicit ex ante evaluation or impact assessment of their rulings, a requirement often imposed on executive policy makers. But how then should courts assess the macro consequences of their decisions? It seems quite clear that courts do not currently possess the knowledge needed to make such assessments. Predictions of this sort are a notoriously difficult task for any government decision maker, if only because the behavior of actors is determined by a complex interplay of causal relations and feedback effects.

These epistemological considerations point toward more comprehensive institutional reform than the chapters in Parts I and II recommend. It is not simply a matter of developing the capacity for statistical or other empirical analysis (Rubin, de Augustinis and van Gestel, Petersen), or for testing remedies (Dyevre), nor can it be achieved by demanding that the government provide empirical support for its conclusions (Blackham, Rakoff) or that its experts conform to professional norms (Wagner). Rather, both conceptual and institutional changes are needed. Conceptually, courts need to redefine what is meant by a "case". Where the issue significantly and predictably involves macro effects, the parties who introduce evidence and advance arguments should not be limited to the plaintiff and defendant, but rather must extend to others who will be affected, or whose cooperation needs to be obtained. This means, in essence, that the judge must shift from a dispute resolution to a more policy planning mode. The question that must be answered – and it is a legal question, although one that depends on modern notions of legality – is not who wins the case but what benefits can be achieved or what harms can be avoided for society in general.

Institutionally, courts can rely on traditional mechanisms such as amicus briefs or settlement conferences to implement this shift, but new mechanisms should be developed as well. Through voluntary and involuntary joinder and intervention, the judges must be able to obtain information and listen to the voices of all the parties in the path of the case's macro effects. They must be able to call on the necessary staff resources, not only a magistrate with training and outlook similar to their own but also technically trained researchers and investigators. Judges must also be able to assert continuing jurisdiction so that they can develop or revise their decisions over time. Thus, the courts would be engaging in a legal dialogue, constitutional or statutory, with other branches of government and other actors in society beyond the litigants. Taken together, these conceptual and institutional shifts might sound like radical and unmanageable change, but it must be kept in mind that it applies only to the small minority of cases that truly exercise macro effects or, in Petersen's terms, that escape the judiciary's general stance of deference. In other words, the recommendation that can be derived from de Jong's discussion is that the courts must adopt new conceptual and institutional approaches, but only on the relatively rare occasions when they are dealing with wide-ranging policy determinations.

Ruhl's chapter can be regarded as an amplification of this view. As a science taker, courts are functioning within their traditional framework, although they are using the methodologies recommended in Parts I and II. Science making, as suggested by Ruhl, might be limited to the sorts of demands for empirical evidence that Blackham recommends. The court might demand that the government, or a plaintiff, develop some specified scientific evidence and either strike down a program or deny relief to a private party until such evidence is provided. But the court might also adopt a more active role. This would involve both the conceptual and institutional changes implied by de Jong. The court would conceive of itself, in policy cases requiring scientific evidence, as a proactive problem solver rather than a reactive adjudicator. Instead of deciding the case after evidence and arguments were presented by the parties, it might retain jurisdiction and order the production of scientific evidence that it deems necessary for a final resolution.

There are several institutional mechanisms that might be employed for the production of such evidence. One, already discussed in many of the preceding chapters, is an amplification of the judiciary's professional staff. Given that policy-making cases are only occasional, it might not be feasible to maintain a permanent staff of scientists in a range of specialties, but a smaller staff with the authority and funding to hire academic or private sector researchers on a project-by-project basis would not be prohibitively expensive. Again, the economic impact of many policy-based judicial decisions, such as *Urgenda*, is certainly sufficient to justify this expenditure. Second, courts could order the executive, as either plaintiff or defendant, and private parties, in their role as plaintiffs, to carry out specified research projects. The courts' traditional reluctance to retain jurisdiction for the necessary length of time should be overcome. Judges, after all, tend to have much longer tenures than administrators, whether they are appointed for a fixed term or for life. Moreover, concerns about continuity can be mitigated by organizing groups of judges in a particular jurisdiction to participate in the remedy phase of an important policy decision. The independence and quasi-isolation of the judge or panel could be retained for reaching the legal conclusions that determine liability, but remedies, even in traditional cases, are often governed by pragmatic considerations rather than doctrine, and can readily be implemented by a larger or rotating group of judges acting for extensive periods.

The final chapter, by Pistora and Aravindakshan, discusses the most far-reaching institutional, and possibly conceptual change that might be adopted to enable the judiciary to deal with empirical data. This is the creation of specialized courts, with judges who are specially trained and procedures that are specially designed to facilitate the acquisition and analysis of data. Despite the extensive nature of this change, it has already been instituted by at least two democratic nations, as Pistora and Aravindakshan describe – the National Green Tribunal of India and the STAB of the Netherlands. These courts move toward fully modernizing the judicial process – replacing the medieval architecture, stained glass windows, turrets and gargoyles with a truly contemporary design. But comprehensive change is difficult, and the performance of both institutions reveals that one should not have unrealistic expectations.

At the time of inception, the NGT model was lauded as achieving the perfect harmonization of science and law. In reality, however, its expertise is questionable, suffering from institutional handicaps caused by political control over the appointment of the expert members and the limited range of specializations these members possess. This has resulted in a hybrid tribunal too heavily reliant on external sources of expertise such as ad hoc committees. In other words, what looks good on paper does not necessarily function well in practice. A specialized environmental court with limited resources and expert arbiters with one-sided knowledge or partiality towards government agencies may simply replace one set of problems with another.

According to Pistora and Aravindakshan, STAB has more effectively maintained both its expertise and its independence. But it has done so under the protective wing of the Dutch Council of State, for which it serves as a largely advisory body, rather than a separate decision maker. The Council of State decides when STAB offers its opinions and how much impact those opinions will have. Moreover, once the Council of State has done so, the resulting decision is its judicial responsibility, and STAB is insulated from any questions or challenges that are raised.

These two examples present us with the quandary of choosing between incremental and comprehensive reform efforts. Comprehensive reform, such as the reconceived judicial institutions that Pistora and Aravindakshan describe, promises to free us from a past that is perhaps irrational or path dependent and is in any case outmoded, but their account demonstrates that the unfamiliarity of such institutions often leads them to be undermined or marginalized. Incremental change, of the sort that the other chapters in this volume recommend or imply, will often be more palatable, but it will be encumbered by the very notions that the reform is intended to replace. Perhaps the answer lies in a hermeneutic relationship between the two. Imagining new institutions can inspire incremental change, and that change, if sustained, may ultimately lead to changes that transform the institution that they were only intended to improve.

SUMMING UP

As with all academic work, this research project certainly did not answer every question regarding how courts could or should deal with empirical data and scientific evidence. The chapters in this volume certainly suggest possible avenues of reform, but they also raise new questions and concerns that require further study and debate. In summing up these chapters, three important issues concerning the use of empirical data and scientific evidence are worth noting: *When and why (not) to use empirical data and scientific evidence in court?*

We can fairly say that empirical data and scientific evidence do not directly determine the outcome of legal decisions, which necessarily have a normative component. At the same time, such data may be able to clarify factual questions that are relevant for policy judgments. While the use of empirical data and scientific evidence in public interest cases is certainly not a panacea for complex judicial problems, it is important, and will become increasingly important, in enabling courts to fulfill their responsibilities.

What must be kept in mind, however, is that the purpose of empirical evidence in judicial decisions is not the same as its purpose in technology or academic inquiry. Judicial decision making is a combination of different rationalities. Truth seeking is, for instance, not the only goal in civil procedure. Judicial decisions also need to be reasonable, persuasive, justifiable and in line with legal principles. Judicial law making is not primarily focused on producing new reliable knowledge, as is the case in scientific research, but to end a dispute in a justifiable and hopefully socially acceptable manner. This implies that judges need room to weigh different types of arguments, both empirical and normative.

This point can be clarified by considering the frequency with which courts need to apply a proportionality test. The proportionality principle is a mechanism to scrutinize administrative or legislative measures. It can be seen as a trade-off device that helps resolve conflicts between different norms, principles and values. Stone Sweet and Mathews have operationalized the principle by identifying three analytical steps to balance factual and normative considerations.[10] Namely, (1) is a certain measure suitable to achieve the goals set out by the legislature; (2) is it necessary in the sense that there are no less intrusive alternatives available to reach the policy goals; and (3) are the costs not excessive in comparison with the benefits of the selected measure. Empirical data and scientific evidence play a role in each of these determinations, but they are not the only relevant considerations. In the Dutch *Alcohol Lock* case,[11] for example, the administrative authority responsible for driver safety required drivers with multiple drunk driving arrests to install an alcohol lock that prevents the car from starting unless the driver passes a breathalyzer test. Although a significant amount of evidence was presented about the effectiveness of this device, the court declared it unlawful because it violated the proportionality principle by failing to take sufficient account of the personal situation of different drivers and their dependence on a driving license.[12]

Given these complexities, one value of using empirical data may be to falsify certain claims by the litigating parties, as opposed to using this same information to predict future consequences and establish causal relationships

---

10 A. Stone Sweet and J. Mathews, 'Proportionality Balancing and Global Constitutionalism', 47 *Columbia Journal of Transnational Law* 73–164 (2008).

11 See more in-depth about this example: R.A.J. van Gestel and P.J.P.M. van Lochem, 'Evidence-Based Regulation and the Translation from Empirical Data to Normative Choices: A Proportionality Test', 2 *Erasmus Law Review* 120–133 (2018).

12 ABRvS 4 March 2015; ECLI:NL:RVS (2015), 622.

between judicial decisions and macro consequences of such decisions. It might be interesting to select a number of cases where courts have successfully used empirical evidence to falsify factual claims brought by the litigants in order to study whether one could find patterns in the methods and techniques that courts have adopted in these cases and to what extent they differ from approaches in judicial decisions that were considered flawed with hindsight. This could also be a learning experience with regard to what kind of methods courts may use to falsify claims made by the litigants regarding facts, empirical data or (contested) scientific evidence as one, for example, frequently finds in climate change cases.

A second issue concerns the judicial evaluation of the relevance and reliability of empirical data and scientific evidence. When scientific evidence is available, courts need to assess the relevance of this evidence for the legal question that is the basis of the dispute between the litigating parties. If the validity of the evidence is challenged, the court will need to make a decision about the quality of the evidence. One possible response would be to conduct an experiment in which two groups of judges are instructed to decide a mock case: one group according to the existing rules and practices and another group according to some specific reform proposal. A third group of judges could perhaps be given the opportunity to collect their own data and scientific evidence.

As Grunwald has argued, most judges and legal scholars would support the use of natural and social science data in particular judicial decisions if it were certain that the research findings are valid, replicated, consistent across studies, and directly applicable to the legal question at hand.[13] The problem, though, is that most of the available science is suboptimal, which raises the question of how to give courts more guidance in dealing with this situation. At the same time, the alternative approach, where judges follow their intuition, unguided by systematic data, seems likely to lead to more severe mistakes. While problems of bias or incompleteness may be impossible to eliminate, scientific findings can offer at least some degree of insight beyond what appears to be commonsensical, but is in fact hypothetical, untested and suppositional.

The third issue concerns the process of information gathering. How do courts collect and select relevant scientific evidence and other empirical data? A major problem in both civil law and common law legal systems, as noted in basically all the chapters in this volume, is that courts rely heavily on the evidence that the litigating parties bring to the court instead of carrying out their own research.

---

13 Ben K. Grunwald, 'Suboptimal Social Science and Judicial Precedent', 161 *University of Pennsylvania Law Review* 1409–1443 (2013), p. 1411.

In *Mitchell et al. v. JCG Industries,* Judge Richard Posner, always alert to opportunities for publicity, had his law clerks re-enact a task that the plaintiffs were required to perform in order to test the validity of their claims about the length of time the task required.[14] While most of his colleagues were willing to accept the results of this in-house experiment, one predictably dissented on the grounds that it lay outside the proper boundaries of appellate review. But how much do we really know about less intentionally conspicuous modes of judicial information gathering?[15] What do we know about judges "googling" scientific information? And what instruments do judges have at their disposal to help them find the right scientific evidence and empirical data? What about the use of expert committees like the Indian Supreme Court frequently appoints to get informed about legislative facts? Scholars in the US and the UK point to the unsystematic and unprincipled treatment of scientific evidence and empirical data concerning legislative facts and a lack of procedures establishing how and under what conditions courts can admit empirical data and scientific studies.[16] A good way to gather more systematic information about this would be to conduct a comparative analysis of nations that grant courts different amounts of authority and resources to collect empirical data and scientific evidence. The goal would be to assess the relative accuracy of the conclusions that these different courts had reached and the relative effectiveness of the remedies that they imposed.

Although we will proceed with efforts to address these questions, we would conclude that it is time to renovate, if not replace, the fussy old judicial building in the City of Modern Government. Judicial policy making will play an increasingly important role in that city, especially in situations where legislatures are unwilling or unable to act. In most Western countries, legislators and executive policy makers have failed to take action to protect people against the long-term effects of climate change because the short-term economic costs to do what is necessary are high and the electoral gains are low. Their failure has been even greater in dealing with threats and dangers that are not presently announcing their imminence by frying our crops and suffocating our city dwellers. Outer space, once the setting for science fiction movies and an occasional exploratory flight, is now a valuable military and economic resource.

---

14 *Mitchell et al. v. JCG Industries*, 745 F. 3d 837 (7th Cir. 2014).

15 See A.O. Larsen, 'Confronting Supreme Court Fact Finding', 98 *Virginia Law Review* 1262 (2012).

16 See for example A. Blackham, 'Legitimacy and empirical evidence in the UK courts', 25(3) *Griffith Law Review*, 414–440 (2016); D.L. Faigman, *Constitutional fictions: A unified theory of constitutional facts* (Oxford University Press 2008) and S. Kolitch, 'Constitutional fact finding and the appropriate use of empirical data in constitutional law', 10(3) Lewis & Clark L. Rev. 673 (2006).

If we do not find some mechanism for governments to regulate it, space may soon become an arena for exotic weapons that fight soundless battles with each other and rain indiscriminate destruction on the people below, while our planet becomes surrounded by a Saturn-like ring of garbage. Many computer scientists believe that artificial intelligence will replace somewhere between half to four-fifths of the current labor force. Others disagree, but there is at least a possibility that, in addition to two hundred million climate refugees, the future will present us with two billion people who have no means of supporting themselves. In addition, advances in bioengineering and genome mapping suggest that society may soon be dealing with technologies that can transform the human body. Current economic inequalities, severe though they may be, will seem trivial if the wealthy can buy procedures that make their children stronger and smarter than the rest of humanity. Meanwhile, the less fortunate, in desperation, may buy low-cost bioengineering alternatives that promise improvements and produce monstrosities. The amount of attention that current policy makers devote to these impending crises is, to the nearest approximation, zero. If that continues, the one certainty about all the uncertainties that these possibilities present is that they will end up on judicial dockets.

In Europe, supranational human rights law provides courts with tools to address a violation of rights by legislatures and executive agencies that fail to protect the public interest. This is why concerned citizens and NGOs pin their hopes on courts to act as the grown-ups in the room and trigger the political branches of government to act. In the US, the Constitution provides less guidance but similar opportunities; at least when the Supreme Court is not controlled by justices determined to ensure that the government is unable to deal with pressing problems such as climate change, gun violence and a healthcare system that falls below acceptable standards.

When they act to remedy the failures of political institutions, courts have received increasing criticism. They are accused of judicial activism, engaging with what are basically political questions and thereby violating the separation of powers doctrine. Judges, on the other hand, have largely remained silent. They usually take the position that courts speak through their decisions and do not engage with scholarly or political debates. Simultaneously, however, most judges seem to uphold the myth that all they are doing is "simply interpreting the law". They regularly hide behind textualism in an attempt to escape the criticisms that are leveled at their efforts to deal with the complex policy questions that are presented to them by the failures and lapses of the political branches. The question is to what extent this approach is sustainable in the long run. More and more people are becoming aware of the fact that judicial lawmaking implies making policy choices. A refusal to acknowledge this may make judicial lawmaking less credible over time.

One approach to this crisis of judicial legitimacy is to focus more on the methodology of judicial lawmaking. As soon as courts start to admit that we have moved beyond Montesquieu's ideas of judges as the mouthpiece of the legislature, the emphasis shifts to the question of how exactly courts create law. This is particularly relevant for policy making cases because these cases, by definition, have broad consequences that go beyond the interests of individual litigating parties. So far, the debate on the legitimacy of judicial lawmaking by highest courts has mainly focused on the role that courts have to protect fundamental rights, which may sometimes be seen as a precondition for democratic decision making. A less explored avenue so far is the methodology for rationalizing judicial lawmaking through the use of empirical and scientific data. The contributions in this volume aimed to do exactly this. They deal with a wide range of questions concerning when empirical data and scientific evidence may – or may not – be used to fill in open norms or assist in proportionality assessments; how to scrutinize the relevance and reliability of this type of evidence by the courts; and to what extent courts should be allowed to collect their own empirical data and scientific evidence in the event that the litigating parties fail to provide it. We hope to have given a new impulse to the debate, but we also realize the work is far from done.

Index